THE MASTER MUSICIANS

BIZET

SERIES EDITED BY R. LARRY TODD
FORMER SERIES EDITOR, THE LATE STANLEY SADIE

THE MASTER MUSICIANS

Titles Available in Paperback

Bach • *Malcolm Boyd*
Beethoven • *Barry Cooper*
Berlioz • *Hugh Macdonald*
Handel • *Donald Burrows*
Liszt • *Derek Watson*
Mahler • *Michael Kennedy*

Monteverdi • *Denis Arnold*
Mozart • *Julian Rushton*
Musorgsky • *David Brown*
Puccini • *Julian Budden*
Schumann • *Eric Frederick Jensen*
Vivaldi • *Michael Talbot*

Titles Available in Hardcover

MacDowell • *E. Douglas Bomberger*
Rossini • *Richard Osborne*
Schoenberg • *Malcolm MacDonald*

Byrd • *Kerry McCarthy*
Tchaikovsky • *Roland John Wiley*
Verdi • *Julian Budden*

THE MASTER MUSICIANS

BIZET

HUGH MACDONALD

OXFORD
UNIVERSITY PRESS

OXFORD
UNIVERSITY PRESS

Oxford University Press is a department of the
University of Oxford. It furthers the University's objective
of excellence in research, scholarship, and education
by publishing worldwide.

Oxford   New York
Auckland   Cape Town   Dar es Salaam   Hong Kong   Karachi
Kuala Lumpur   Madrid   Melbourne   Mexico City   Nairobi
New Delhi   Shanghai   Taipei   Toronto

With offices in
Argentina   Austria   Brazil   Chile   Czech Republic   France   Greece
Guatemala   Hungary   Italy   Japan   Poland   Portugal   Singapore
South Korea   Switzerland   Thailand   Turkey   Ukraine   Vietnam

Oxford is a registered trade mark of Oxford University Press
in the UK and certain other countries.

Published in the United States of America by
Oxford University Press
198 Madison Avenue, New York, NY 10016

© Oxford University Press 2014

All rights reserved. No part of this publication may be reproduced,
stored in a retrieval system, or transmitted, in any form or by any means,
without the prior permission in writing of Oxford University Press,
or as expressly permitted by law, by license, or under terms agreed with
the appropriate reproduction rights organization. Inquiries concerning
reproduction outside the scope of the above should be sent to the
Rights Department, Oxford University Press, at the address above.

You must not circulate this work in any other form
and you must impose this same condition on any acquirer.

Library of Congress Cataloging-in-Publication Data
Macdonald, Hugh, 1940-, author.
Bizet / Hugh Macdonald.
pages cm.—(The master musicians)
Includes bibliographical references and index.
ISBN 978-0-19-978156-0 (hardback : alk. paper)   1. Bizet, Georges, 1838-1875.
2. Composers—France—Biography.   I. Title.
ML410.B62M12   2014
780.92—dc23
[B]   2013041576

Winton Dean (1916–2013)
IN MEMORIAM

Contents

Preface ix
List of Illustrations xi

1   1838–1857: *Le Docteur Miracle* 3

2   1858–1860: *Don Procopio* 35

3   1860–1863: *Les Pêcheurs de perles* 56

4   1864–1865: *Ivan IV* 84

5   1866–1867: *La Jolie Fille de Perth* 103

6   1868–1870: *La Coupe du Roi de Thulé* 137

7   1870–1872: *Djamileh* 167

8   1872–1873: *Don Rodrigue* 190

9   1873–1875: *Carmen* 209

10 1875–2014: *Life after Death* 234

Appendices

A. Calendar 251

B. List of Works 255

C. Personalia 270

Select Bibliography 277
Works Index 285
Index 289

Preface

ENGLISH-SPEAKING READERS HAVE BEEN WELL SERVED FOR MANY YEARS BY THE books on Bizet by Winton Dean and Mina Curtiss in addition to the continuing stream of articles, reviews and popular glosses on *Carmen*. As one of the most frequently performed operas in the repertoire, *Carmen* offers a permanent challenge to stage directors whose concept of the femme fatale or of the place of gypsies in society or of the otherness (to the French) of Spanish music may be represented, it seems, in an infinite variety of ways. Conductors and singers continue to find the allure of the opera *Carmen* as irresistible as the gypsy Carmen was to Don José himself.

My own inclination to offer a new study of Bizet in English is prompted less by a desire to add anything new to the discussion of *Carmen*, and more by curiosity about the rest of his œuvre and by a desire to set the composer in the context of French music of the Second Empire in which he displayed, as far as his contemporaries could tell while he was still alive, great talent but not actual genius. For Bizet himself *Carmen* was a part of his consciousness only during the last two years of his life. It is easy to judge his earlier music with the hindsight that *Carmen* provides, but it is historically unfair to do so since each work had to contend with the librettists, the performers, the managements, the public and the press that circumstances offered, not with some distant goal of which not even an embryonic outline can be traced. I have attempted therefore to judge each work on its merits and on what it meant to Bizet himself and his public. I have avoided the concern with Verdi and Wagner that has obsessed critics from his own time up to the present, since although he may have occasionally adopted gestures or musical language from those composers, consciously or not, they were of little significance in his own development as a composer. I also discuss Bizet's operas and songs in the form in which he wrote them, not in any of the spurious versions that have become ingrained in tradition and habit.

Winton Dean's book in this series of *Master Musicians* appeared in 1948, and despite his harsh criticism of certain works he has always been seen as a champion of Bizet in the face of the casual dismissal that works other than *Carmen* continue to attract. He was also severe on the French for their failure to treat Bizet as a great national figure. There is still no critical edition of his works and no collected correspondence, important tools for the study of his life and works whose absence would be unthinkable if Bizet had been German.

When Mina Curtiss's book on Bizet appeared in 1958, our knowledge of his life and character was enormously enlarged since she had access to a vast collection of documents passed down in the Halévy family through Bizet's widow. Dean accordingly expanded his book for a second edition in 1965. In the present book I do not claim to provide any deeper insights into those aspects of Bizet's life, especially since Bizet's more recent French biographers Rémy Stricker and Hervé Lacombe have both used the Halévy documents sensitively and comprehensively in their depictions of the composer.

My first aim was to establish a comprehensive catalogue of his works, a task which had not been attempted before, it being deemed impossible so long as the archives of the publisher Choudens remained inaccessible to scholars. In recent years, however, these materials have become more accessible, yet the catalogue remains provisional, as all such catalogues must be. My *Bizet Catalogue* is to be published online through Washington University Libraries (digital.wustl.edu/bizet) or in book form in due course.

In assembling the *Catalogue* it became clear to me that the story of Bizet's life needed to be rewritten since new works and new details about the composition, performance and publication of the known works were coming to light. I have divided the main part of the book into chronological sections, each one of which encompasses one of his nine main operatic adventures. The vast extent of Bizet's work as a transcriber of other composers' works, furthermore, has never been grasped before, shedding light on his relationships with his older contemporaries, especially Gounod and Reyer, and on his sometimes competitive, sometimes fraternal relationships with musicians of his own age. The work of the two French biographers just mentioned, Stricker and Lacombe, has provided much that needs to be incorporated in the story, as well as the invaluable work done by Lesley A. Wright over a period of thirty years. I am happy to acknowledge a profound debt to all three scholars and to dedicate the book to the memory of Winton Dean, whose encouragement over forty years ago (when my concern was Berlioz, not Bizet) has stood me in good stead ever since.

Hugh Macdonald
St Louis, 2014

List of Illustrations

1. Jules Didier, *Watering Place in the Mountains, Italy.* Musée des Beaux-Arts, Pau.
2. Gaston Planté, drawing of Bizet, September 1860. Bibliothèque Hachette.
3. Caricature by H. Meter. *Diogène,* 28 September 1863. Braam Collection, Munich.
4. Bizet in the Garde Nationale, 1870. Photograph. *La Revue musicale,* 20 (1939), p. 66.
5. Célestine Galli-Marié in May 1875, photograph by Liébert. Institut de France, Paris.
6. Photograph of Bizet by Carjat. John Knowles Paine, Theodore Thomas, and Karl Klauser, *Famous Composers and their Works* (Boston: J. B. Millet Co., 1891), vol. 3, opposite p. 697.
7. Letter to Ambroise Thomas. Stiftelsen Musikkulturens Främjande, Stockholm, MMS0393.
8. The *Boléro* in *Vasco de Gama,* autograph full score. Private collection.

THE MASTER MUSICIANS

BIZET

CHAPTER ONE

1838–1857: Le Docteur Miracle

GEORGES BIZET WAS A PARISIAN ALL HIS LIFE. APART FROM THE TWO YEARS SPENT IN Italy as the winner of the Prix de Rome and short trips to Baden-Baden, Brussels, Beauvais, and Bordeaux, he barely ever ventured out of the capital, only to the outlying suburbs, and he showed no perceptible interest in provincial cities or foreign parts. French musicians and men of letters have always regarded Paris as the only possible place to live and work, many of them, like Berlioz and Balzac, definitively turning their backs on provincial life. The baby Bizet was delivered in 1838 into the heart of Paris's music, amid the greatest concentration of musicians in Europe and there he remained. This was the Ninth Arrondissement, the area north of the Boulevard des Italiens and the Boulevard Montmartre, which housed both the Opéra and the Conservatoire, twin magnets that drew into their ambit composers, pianists, singers and the whole cavalcade of aspiring musicians who swarmed to Paris during the July Monarchy. The area was to be violently disrupted in the 1860s by Haussmann's grandiose boulevardisation of Paris, but during Bizet's childhood and student years it had a homogeneity and community feeling that bred a unique concentration of cultural life, feeding the spectacular expansion in the output and consumption of music in Paris between the Revolutions of 1830 and 1848.[1] Parisian musical life at that time attained a level of prestige never equalled before or since.

The city's population expanded beyond one million in this period in the wake of industrial and commercial enterprises of many kinds and the prosperity they brought. At the west of the city a grand new avenue, named after the Elysian Fields of mythology, led up to Napoleon's immense Arc de Triomphe, completed in 1836 at the same time that a tall Egyptian obelisk was erected at the eastern end of the

---

1. See Macdonald (2008).

avenue in the Place de la Concorde. The church of the Madeleine, consecrated in 1842, faced it from the north. The sprawling palaces of the Tuileries and the Louvre occupied the right bank of the Seine, while elsewhere the core of the city retained its maze of mediaeval streets. The ring of six large railway termini was added during the boom of the 1840s.

In the rapid advance of music at this time an institution and a machine led the charge. The institution was the Paris Opéra, already boasting a proud tradition from the time of Louis XIV and now housed in a large theatre built in 1821 on the Rue Le Peletier. It was heavily subsidised and closely regulated by the government, but its director enjoyed a franchise that allowed him to win or lose money on a grand scale. The Opéra presented the best French singers in a series of spectacular productions that emphasised large-scale, realistic décor and took advantage of the latest in lighting technology. Regular attendance at the Opéra was universal among Paris's educated classes, whether they were musical or not. Discussion and criticism being such an essential element of French social exchange, no one with any claim to intelligence could afford not to see the latest productions, and foreign visitors reported on the Opéra as a matter of course.

The genre we now call French Grand Opera flourished in these years. Its principal practitioners were the composers Giacomo Meyerbeer and Fromental Halévy and the librettist Eugène Scribe, together with some notable designers. It was not truly a French product since it grew out of the works of the Italian Spontini, played in the Napoleonic period, and was greatly indebted to the newer Italian style embodied by Rossini, who himself contributed to its repertoire. (Meyerbeer, born in Berlin and trained in Italy, never regarded himself as a Parisian.) These operas normally ran to five acts; they filled a long evening, featured virtuoso singing, a large chorus and corps de ballet, and the latest in instrumental novelty in the pit. They kept the audience riveted to a story in which private passion is thwarted by religious or tribal conflicts and ends (usually) with the deaths of both tenor and soprano. The genre is more familiar to us today from the works of Verdi, whose operas, at least in his early and middle years, leaned heavily on the French model. French composers prominent in this field are little heard today, notably Auber and Halévy, and even Meyerbeer's music is far from familiar. The most successful works of the repertoire at the time of Bizet's birth were Auber's *La Muette de Portici*, Rossini's *Guillaume Tell*, Meyerbeer's *Robert le diable* and *Les Huguenots*, and Halévy's *La Juive*.

The machine that boosted the status of Paris was the piano. After its emergence in the late eighteenth century, the pianoforte expanded in range and volume and rapidly became the domestic instrument of choice, supplanting the harpsichord, guitar and harp. In its upright formulation the piano was cheap and popular; as a concert instrument it was now able to sustain an entire concert, in the form of a recital, and produce sounds brilliant and shrill enough to beget a generation of great virtuosi, travelling from city to city and enthralling crowds with their dazzling fingerwork. Beethoven's preferred pianos had been Austrian and English, but supremacy was soon captured by French pianos. No less than 102 piano makers are listed in the 1836 Paris directory,[2] chief among them the Erard and Pleyel families of bold innovators and enterprising businessmen. To be heard and applauded in Paris and to be taken up by Parisian hostesses was the ambition of all young pianists everywhere. Liszt came from Hungary, Chopin from Poland, and both stayed for many years. Many others came, from all corners of Europe. The emergence of female piano virtuosi was a special feature of Parisian music too.

The list of foreign musicians drawn to Paris in these years includes almost anyone of any standing in the wider world. The Italians Rossini, Bellini, Donizetti and Verdi all spent long periods in Paris. Cherubini had settled and risen to the position of Director of the Conservatoire. Paganini and Ernst were the visiting violin stars. Mendelssohn came in 1831, Wagner spent two years there, and that trio of foreign musicians, Halle, Hiller and Heller—all with great careers ahead of them—spent important portions of their lives there. Hiller reminisced about sitting at a *terrasse* on the Boulevard des Italiens with Chopin, Mendelssohn and Liszt as if it were perfectly normal company to be keeping, none of them French. Karl Halle eventually became celebrated in England as Sir Charles Hallé, and Stephen Heller adopted Paris as his home. French was the international language spoken by educated people everywhere, and French fashions and literature were exported all over the globe.

The French themselves displayed no resentment whatever at the intrusion of foreigners in their midst; they were proud of the prestige of their culture. After the fervent passions of the Revolution and the Napoleonic wars Paris cultivated a generous cosmopolitanism that welcomed foreign visitors and foreign artists, as it still does. Berlioz, whose compositions in the 1830s were the most strikingly modern by any Frenchman, had a circle of friends largely made up of foreign musicians, and he married an Irish actress.

An institution only marginally less prestigious than the Opéra was the Conservatoire. To read the reminiscences of Berlioz or Debussy about their studies there is to form an impression of hopeless stagnation and reaction, but in fact the influence and the teaching of the Conservatoire, founded soon after the Revolution, had a profound and positive effect on French music. We will look more closely at its teaching when Bizet enrols there as a student, but it fulfilled its function of providing opportunities for talented musicians of all classes for little or no fee. It oversaw the publication of widely used teaching manuals and it turned out operatic, orchestral and military musicians with a thorough background in the techniques

---

2. *Agenda* (1836), pp. 75–79.

of music. As far as the public was concerned, its most visible activities were the concerts given by the Société des Concerts du Conservatoire, an orchestra founded by Habeneck in 1828 to promote symphonic music and to give regular seasons of concerts for its subscribers. Both this organisation and its mother institution served as a model for many other conservatoires abroad founded on similar principles.

The Conservatoire's location in the Rue de la Cité-Bergère, five minutes' walk from the Opéra, ensured the concentration of musicians' residences in that same *quartier*, while the *haute-bourgeoisie* remained in the Faubourgs St-Honoré and St-Germain. Even closer to the Opéra was the Opéra-Comique, housed just across the Boulevard des Italiens in the Salle Favart. Its new theatre opened there a few months after Bizet was born, replacing an earlier theatre occupied by the Théâtre-Italien, which moved a little further away to the Salle Ventadour. These three companies, the Opéra, the Opéra-Comique and the Théâtre-Italien, enjoyed a triple monopoly set up by Napoleon, who laid down specific distinctions between them: the Opéra's repertoire was to be the grand, all-sung, serious opera; the Opéra-Comique had to play lighter fare with songs interspersed with dialogue; and the Théâtre-Italien had to play Italian opera sung in Italian. Bizet's career in opera was shaped by the Conservatoire and geared to this administrative hierarchy, with the addition of the Théâtre-Lyrique, which emerged in the 1850s and contributed to the evolution of the new framework of Parisian opera within which he was to work.

Sacred music and chamber music were not invisible, but they were the domain of their own circles of practitioners and adherents. Every concert with an orchestra would have involved a chorus and vocal soloists too, although choral singing in large groups did not take off as a popular activity until the middle of the century. During Bizet's childhood and student years opera was supreme, it was accessible to all comers, whether musically literate or not, and it was *fashionable*, a word the French eagerly adopted from English. Reviews in the press of new operas always preceded reports of concerts, even in the three specialist music journals that sprang up in this period.

★ ★ ★ ★ ★

Bizet was born in the heart of this musical mecca because his parents were musicians. His father, Adolphe-Amand Bizet, aged twenty-eight at the boy's birth, was born to artisan parents in Rouen where he entered the trade of wigmaker and hairdresser. At the age of twenty-five, according to Gallet,[3] he decided to become a musician. He could sing and he could compose, but where and when and even whether he received any instruction in these arts is not known. He was listed in 1837 as still living in Rouen and plying the wigmaker's trade, yet within three months, at

---

3. Gallet (1891), p. 3.

the time of his marriage in December 1837, he is described as a teacher of singing, with an address in Paris. Of his two sisters, Bizet's aunts, one lived in Blois.

His wife, Bizet's mother, Aimée-Marie-Louise-Léopoldine-Joséphine Delsarte, aged twenty-two at her son's birth, was from Cambrai, near the Belgian border. She was the daughter of an eccentric individual, variously described as a lawyer, café proprietor, inventor and doctor,[4] whose failure to provide for his family led to divorce. The four children went to live with their mother, whose death in 1837 caused Aimée to seek refuge with her older brother François, who was married and living in Paris. It seems likely that she met Adolphe Bizet through his shared profession with François, also a singing teacher, although it is possible to imagine a scenario by which they had met before they came to Paris and that Aimée introduced Adolphe to her brother when she learned that he wanted to set up in Paris as a singing teacher. Her mother's family were alarmed at Adolphe Bizet's lack of prospects, but François Delsarte vouched for his acceptability as a husband, and so they were married before the end of the year. Their only child, a son, was born within a year of the marriage, on 25 October 1838.

He was registered as Alexandre-César-Léopold Bizet, and perhaps they intended to call him Alexandre, or even César (Léopold was the name of an uncle who died young), but by the time the boy was baptised, on 16 March 1840, his name was plain Georges, and so he remained. Uncle François Delsarte lived with his wife Rosine (née Andrien) at 23 Rue Buffault, in the heart of the musicians' *quartier*.[5] Both were teachers of singing and both played a major part in their nephew's initiation into music. Through them the young newly-wed Bizets found living quarters at 26 Rue de la Tour d'Auvergne, a narrow street a few minutes' walk away, where a plaque today commemorates the composer's birth.[6]

From the day he was born Bizet was surrounded by musicians and music. Without siblings, he would have played in the street with children whose homes were organised around different walks of life, but no one nearby thought music a strange profession to be engaged in. For his parents it was not easy to maintain the necessities of life, for although his mother taught him how to read and how to play the piano, we do not know whether she had paying pupils as well. His father perhaps continued his earlier métier as hairdresser for a while, yet he was clearly determined to work as a musician. He was never a teacher at the Conservatoire but taught singing lessons at home, on which the boy Bizet eavesdropped from outside the door. His ear was so sharp that at an early age he could memorise and reproduce the

---

4. Curtiss (1958), p. 4; Lacombe (2000), p. 20.

5. *Agenda* (1836), pp. 59, 224.

6. The original building has been replaced. Although no. 26 is the usual address given, Lacombe reports that at the time of Bizet's baptism the family were at no. 22. See Lacombe (2000), p. 18.

pieces he had heard, and as soon as he was able, he would accompany his father's pupils in their lessons. As a mature musician he was an incomparable sight-reader, a gift that manifested itself very early and which enabled him to consume swathes of piano music and opera—whatever he could lay his hands on—with the same facility as reading books, an occupation he also ardently pursued. It might well have been hard to drag the boy from the piano and from his books even if his parents felt any urge or obligation to do so.

Of his father an image has come down to us of a good-looking man of moderate ability who could compose and who could teach, but who was unremarkable in every way. There is no sign that he ever performed in public. He composed some songs, a few piano pieces, and even a string quartet.[7] He was devoted to his talented son and outlived him by eleven years, long enough to witness the worldwide success of *Carmen*. His is a presence in Bizet's life that hovers in the background without exercising any powerful influence upon him. His mother's stronger personality guided Bizet's upbringing with deep affection and much common sense. If she escaped the eccentricity that marked her father and her brother, she was evidently dogged by ill health, and her early death in 1861 was a severe blow to her son; had she survived, her counsel might have more productively steered the course of a career that was, as Bizet himself admitted, full of uncertain turns and dashed hopes. It was her side of the family that was more generously endowed with intelligence and artistic sensibility, while his father provided the creative urge.

As long as his mother was alive, Bizet's uncle and aunt played a major part in his life. Delsarte was a well-known figure in Parisian music with leading composers and singers among his friends. Trained at the Conservatoire, his ambitions as a singer were hindered by vocal weaknesses for which the critics found a number of circumlocutions. He sang minor tenor parts at the Ambigu-Comique and the Opéra-Comique and was occasionally honoured by appearances at the courts of Louis-Philippe and Napoléon III, but his appearances in public were almost entirely given in the context of reviving forgotten French music of the seventeenth and eighteenth centuries and championing early music at a time when it was generally dismissed as unfit for a modern audience. This was not mere eccentricity in the style of his failed father but a real cause to which he devoted his energies, publishing an anthology of vocal music by Lully, Rameau, Campra, Gluck and others according to enlightened editorial principles.

Berlioz described his uncle as a singer "without much voice, but full of energy, soul and passion, who brings out the full emotion of great music by Gluck and others to the point where these masterpieces are made familiar to the least welcoming

---

7. Bizet *père*'s compositions are reviewed in detail in Lacombe (2000), pp. 40–49.

listeners and where the expression gets through to the dullest hearts."[8] Berlioz's own devotion to Gluck took a rather different slant, leading to passionate debates between him and Delsarte, always conducted in a civil and scholarly manner. Saint-Saëns described Delsarte's vocal teaching as "deplorable and destructive", but greatly admired his declamation and gestures when he was reciting Racine or La Fontaine and drawing a red handkerchief from his pocket with impeccable timing. Saint-Saëns recognised the debt his own generation owed to Delsarte for opening up the riches of French baroque music. "All who knew him recall one of the *illuminati*, a true apostle."[9]

With the painter Ingres and the composer Reber, Delsarte formed a little group dedicated to the classical heritage and implicitly opposed to the extremes of modern music and art. His wide circle of friends nonetheless included the composers Auber, Adam and Halévy (all of whom lived nearby), and his pupils included Jean-Baptiste Faure and Caroline Miolan, both later to play important parts in Bizet's career. Jenny Lind came from Sweden to hear him sing. At the Delsartes' apartment young Bizet would have seen well-known musicians and impoverished pupils endlessly coming and going, and he would have heard plenty of musical gossip.

He also had playmates there since the Delsartes had three boys a little older than himself with five more children appearing in the next dozen years. The atmosphere in the house was strange, since the Delsartes cultivated an ascetic style of genteel poverty and were also obsessively devout. Neither religious devotion nor an obsession with old music made any impact on Bizet's intellectual development, but the connection with other musicians certainly did, for Rosine Delsarte was herself gifted as both pianist and singer and she had taught solfège at the Conservatoire before her burgeoning family took over too much of her time. She was said to have married François at the age of sixteen against her will, but she shared her husband's mystical bent and was a devoted mother to her large family. Her sister, Thérèse Wartel, was an exceptionally fine pianist, married to Pierre-François Wartel, one of the Opéra's principal singers, and their son was to be a fellow-student with Bizet at the Conservatoire. Thérèse Wartel was also a composer and a writer who published a book on the Beethoven piano sonatas; she died relatively young in 1865.

In the homes of the Delsartes and the Wartels, not to mention his own, and in the daily business of the Ninth Arrondissement, young Georges acquired a musical culture and a familiarity with the nuts and bolts of the musical profession that any future composer might envy. As soon as he was old enough he would accompany the grown-ups to the music-sellers' shops to browse through the latest publications, especially piano music, which at that time flowed from the presses in torrents.

8. *Journal des débats*, 24 January 1841, reprinted in Berlioz (1996), t. IV, pp. 429–30.
9. Saint-Saëns (1913), pp. 243–249.

He would have sat in on rehearsals and later attended concerts performed by friends of the family. He would have heard discussion of the major musical events of the 1840s and the gossip that attended them: the arrival of Adolphe Sax's workshop in a nearby street and his newfangled instruments; Félicien David's *Le Désert*; Donizetti's last appearances in Paris; Verdi's first appearances; Berlioz's *La Damnation de Faust*; Duprez's ascendancy as the leading tenor at the Opéra; the constant speculation about Meyerbeer's *Le Prophète*; the endless succession of virtuoso pianists, including Thalberg, Dreyschock, Herz, Marie Pleyel, even occasionally Liszt or Chopin. If the 1830s had been a peak for French poetry in the hands of Hugo and Lamartine, the 1840s saw a surge of great novels from the pens of Dumas, Sand and Balzac. Because the French passion for cultural and political argument has never excused musicians from the obligation to be *au courant* with even the most trivial of new publications and current events, members of the narrowly focused circles in which Bizet was brought up would have unhesitatingly traded opinions on recent literature as they did on recent music. And when it came to politics, they would have been fully aware of the discontents brought on by industrialisation and the steady slide of popular feeling against Louis-Philippe's government.

★ ★ ★ ★ ★

Before he was nine Bizet began to attend the Conservatoire. Children could not be accepted before the age of ten, so a special case had to be made for him to sign on for the 1847–48 year. His talent was obviously exceptional and he had support from the singer Alizard (a friend of his father), the pianist Marmontel, and the horn-player Meifred (both friends of Delsarte) sufficient to waive the rule. When Meifred tested the boy's musicianship, Bizet identified every chord and every modulation correctly; whether or not he had perfect pitch, he had a remarkable ear and could reproduce everything he heard on the piano. He also had a prodigious memory.

At the Conservatoire Bizet encountered Paris's leading musicians, even if only passing them in the corridor. Many of them he would have seen before. The Director, Auber, lived comfortably on the fruits of his operas, which were played regularly at the Opéra-Comique and occasionally at the Opéra. He was sixty-five, with more than twenty years still to serve in a job to which he devoted less than his full energy, preferring his country home and his horses. Composition was taught by Bazin, a nonentity, and Halévy, whose part in Bizet's life was to be far-reaching. The piano was taught by Pierre Zimmerman, who retired in 1848 at the age of sixty-three, to be succeeded by his pupil Antoine Marmontel, aged thirty-two. Carafa taught counterpoint; Thomas and Reber taught solfège. Berlioz, never entrusted with any teaching responsibilities, held the derisory office of librarian and was occasionally to be seen in the building. During the early months of the year the Société des Concerts gave its performances in the Conservatoire hall every Sunday afternoon. These were invariably sold out to subscribers, but Conservatoire students were allowed to attend the final rehearsals on Saturday mornings.[10] Particularly valuable to Bizet was the opportunity to meet other students and to test his skills against musicians of the same age, some of whom would remain friends for the rest of his life.

It is not clear exactly what class or classes Bizet attended that first year. His name is to be found added in pencil to the official list of students, and according to Victor Wilder's lengthy obituary from 1875 he was permitted to sit in on Marmontel's piano class. Marmontel was not officially on the teaching staff, but he was substituting for Henri Herz, who spent more and more time abroad and was at this time on a long tour of the United States. It is quite likely that Bizet was also taking solfège (the skill of sight-singing while naming the notes ut, ré, mi, and so on, and learning intervals and clefs) along with many of the 356 men and 224 women who were listed as Conservatoire students that year, but the school offered no classes in what we would regard as general education. Happily Bizet was a voracious reader, so he was absorbing literature and history (though probably no languages) alongside the steady expansion of his musical horizons. He later reported that his parents concealed his books so that he should not be distracted from his musical studies.[11]

The year was in any case disrupted by the events of February 1848, which brought the July Monarchy to an end and saw the creation of the Second Republic. Throughout 1847 the injustice of a largely disenfranchised population and the severe limits imposed on political meetings guaranteed the eruption of civil disorder on the lines of the 1830 Revolution, which had forced the abdication of Charles X. Now it was Louis-Philippe's turn to face the reality of mob violence. Some noisy protests on 22 February 1848 were peaceful, but the following day, as the crowd faced troops on the Boulevard des Capucines, a single gunshot triggered a bloody cannonade that left fifty-two dead. After that, despite the cold, the dark and the rain, barricades were set up all over Paris, and it took a third day, just as violent as the second, to persuade Louis-Philippe to abdicate. The Boulevard des Italiens, one of Paris's main thoroughfares, was the scene of much of the action, but north of it, in the narrow streets that housed most of Paris's musicians, things were quieter. If the Bizet parents were sensible, they would not have let their nine-year-old son's curiosity lead him into areas of the city that were definitely unsafe. We do know that a year later they attended a meeting of freelance teachers planning to create some kind of union, and that young, well-behaved Georges went along too.[12] Years later Bizet referred to "that pointless, foolish, useless revolution".[13]

---

10. The history of these concerts is told in full in Holoman (2004).
11. Gallet (1891), p. 4.
12. Lacombe (2000), p. 71.
13. Imbert (1894), p. 175.

Theatres were closed for a week or so, and when the Opéra reopened it was no longer the Académie Royale de Musique but now the Théâtre National. Since the Conservatoire and most theatres were dependent on government funding, a change of régime could threaten everyone's livelihood. But artists of all stripes soon took heart when the poet Lamartine was acclaimed president of the new provisional government, and it became clear that under the Second Republic, which was officially proclaimed on 24 February, the musical world would continue as before even though finances would be tight for at least a year.[14] Universal male suffrage was introduced immediately and an election in April produced a moderate-to-conservative constituent assembly that only provoked further riots by working-class groups encouraged by revolutionary action almost everywhere else in Europe. The months of May and June 1848 were far from peaceful on the streets of Paris, but distant memories of the Terror left little sympathy for the radical left, and when a presidential election was held in December, it was won by a wide margin by Louis Napoleon, nephew of the first Napoleon. Monarchists and conservatives (including Berlioz, who reacted by writing a *Te Deum*) breathed a sigh of relief. Three years later Napoleon staged a *coup d'état* by dissolving the Republic and declaring himself Emperor Napoleon III. The nineteen-year-long Second Empire, under which Bizet spent the bulk of his short career, began. The Conservatoire became the Conservatoire Impérial de Musique and the Opéra became the Académie Impériale de Musique.

Bizet's studies at the Conservatoire began in earnest that autumn, 1848, just before his tenth birthday. On 9 October he competed with twenty-one other boys for admission to Marmontel's piano class, as Marmontel was now officially to succeed Zimmerman as principal piano teacher. Bizet was one of only two accepted, although another two were assigned to other classes. Marmontel was struck by Bizet's performance of Mozart sonatas and his preference for correct style rather than striving for effect; teacher and pupil became lifelong friends.[15] The class met three times a week at 11.30 A.M. following the solfège class. Since he lived only fifteen minutes' walk away from the Conservatoire, Bizet must have become thoroughly familiar with those streets in his ten years as a student, spending more and more time in the Conservatoire building and less and less time at home.

At the end of the year Bizet won a "Deuxième Premier Prix" for solfège, which he had been studying under Napoléon Alkan, brother of the reclusive virtuoso Valentin Alkan. We translate "prix" as "prize", but these prizes can best be viewed as grades or classifications since there was regularly more than one student awarded a particular

---

14. The first comprehensive history of these events (*Histoire de la Révolution de 1848*, three volumes, Paris, 1850–53) was written by Liszt's former mistress Marie d'Agoult under the pen-name Daniel Stern.

15. Marmontel (1881), p. 249.

prize. A Premier Prix was in effect a graduation from that class. A fellow-student in Alkan's class who won the same prize for solfège was Josef Wieniawski from Poland, who was only a year older and already a virtuoso pianist. He won a Premier Prix in piano the same year (Bizet did not achieve that for another three years) and went on to an international career, often accompanying his brother, the violinist Henryk. A Deuxième Prix in solfège was awarded to a boy two years older than Bizet, Léo Delibes. In 1848 another talented boy entered the Conservatoire: Camille Saint-Saëns was thirteen, already acclaimed as a prodigy by several Paris audiences and now intent on becoming an organist; he studied with the Conservatoire's respected organ teacher François Benoist. Many years later Bizet dedicated the six pieces that make up his piano work *Chants du Rhin* to six musicians all of whom had ties with him at the Conservatoire: they were Marmontel; Francis Planté (a year younger than Bizet); Félix Le Couppey, who taught solfège and piano; Charles Delioux de Savignac, a student of Zimmerman and Halévy; Charles de Bériot, son of a famous violinist and the diva Malibran; and Saint-Saëns. Ten years at the Conservatoire bred friendships that Bizet could count on for many years to come.

In 1850, when Bizet won no prizes, the piano prizes went to Planté and Jules Cohen, who was fifteen. In 1851 first prizes were awarded to Deschamps and Lestoquoy, while Bizet won a second prize. All of these were Marmontel's pupils. In 1852 Bizet, now thirteen, won a first prize along with Edmond Savary, aged seventeen, the set work that year being Herz's Piano Concerto no. 3, a brittle, showy piece that required long hours of practice, even for talented young boys such as those. The *Revue et gazette musicale* reported that "M. Bizet is a consummate musician, endowed with feeling and powerful expression; he played as if he were four or five years older than his rival when in fact it was the other way round."[16] At the Conservatoire's annual *séance publique* on 12 December 1852, with another student named Marie Colin, he played Thalberg's *Grand Duo sur les motifs de Norma* for two pianos, and a few days later he accompanied two violinists at a soirée given by Count Emilien de Nieuwerkerke, an aristocrat of Dutch origin and a leading figure in French cultural circles. His long liaison with Princesse Mathilde Bonaparte, Napoleon III's cousin, created one of the leading salons of the Second Empire. They liked Bizet; their salons were to be two of the few places where he would agree to play the piano in later years.

The following year Bizet entered Benoist's organ class. Benoist was the teacher of Alkan, Franck, Saint-Saëns and other eminent organists, and although he was no star player himself, he was a good teacher, according to Saint-Saëns, even if he was in the habit of composing ballet scores in class while his students played.[17] His new pupil

16. *Revue et gazette musicale*, 1 August 1852, p. 251.
17. Saint-Saëns (1913), p. 40.

remained in the class for three years and progressed steadily if not spectacularly, winning a Premier Accessit in 1853, a Deuxième Prix in 1854 and a Premier Prix in 1855. Surrounded by goodwill from all his teachers, Bizet must have contemplated a career as a pianist, or perhaps a career as an organist, and his family might have wondered if he would turn into a singer. His true direction, however, was already emerging in 1850, the year of the earliest Bizet compositions that have come down to us. We may attribute this appearance of buds on the young plant to the influence of Zimmerman, who was so impressed by Bizet's evident talent that although he was officially retired and in poor health he agreed to give him private lessons in counterpoint. He was a kindly and sympathetic teacher (as was Marmontel also) and was teased by his family for, as they thought, wasting his time with unpromising pupils.[18] Zimmerman taught him from Cherubini's counterpoint treatise and brought order into whatever the boy might have been improvising on the piano. Bizet was to write innumerable fugues and contrapuntal exercises in his student years, although in his mature compositions there is scarcely a fugue to be found anywhere.

A ten-page manuscript[19] contains a "Vocalise" for one voice and piano, followed by a "Barcarolle" for two sopranos and piano, both without words. The piano writing is plain but the vocal writing is elegant and assured, and both pieces are carefully shaped. Either piece (if it had words) might have come from an opéra-comique of the period. No less than four times in the manuscript Bizet wrote "J'avais 11 ans et 4 mois", assigning it to February or March 1850. The manuscript also contains the fragment of a cantata written a month later, still with no words but this time with indications of an intended orchestration and a certain dramatic energy that makes us regret that no more than thirty-nine bars have survived.

He was also composing piano music. A dozen piano pieces from the years 1851 and 1852 were published by Michel Poupet in 1984, and they give a vivid impression of Bizet's piano technique and taste. In class he was expected to study sets of variations and long concerto movements, but these published works are all short pieces with as yet no clear sense of style. His models were not Liszt and Chopin, whose music was in both cases too idiosyncratic, but the compositions of Zimmerman, Heller, Hünten and the swarms of composers who were putting out caprices, preludes, waltzes and etudes in those years for the amateur market. A second manuscript[20] headed *Compositions diverses par Georges Bizet premier prix du conservatoire de Musique* contains four extremely modest "Préludes" given the opus number 2, a "Thème", a "Romance sans paroles" with a wildly florid right-hand part, a

---

18. Curtiss (1958), p. 20.
19. F-Pn MS 422.
20. F-Pn MS 421.

"Valse", and a "Romance", which is of interest as being perhaps his first vocal piece with words (by Lamartine) and because the poem was also set by Bizet's father.[21] Each of three verses concludes with a change of time-signature and of mode, ending on a charming cadence (Example 1.1).

Example 1.1

Only one bar of the "Thème", notated on three staves and marked *Brillante*, is required to show its adventurous piano texture (Example 1.2).

21. F-Pn MS 3822.

Example 1.2

The most interesting of these early pieces are the two works entitled "Caprice original". Both were written in or before 1851 and both are found in this second manuscript and also copied into a third, larger manuscript collection now in Stockholm.[22] This is a book of over 160 pages in which Bizet has copied a number of works by other composers, including Dussek's piano sonata op. 9, the fugue from Mozart's *Requiem*, Scarlatti's "Cat's Fugue", and works by Herz, Czerny and Zimmerman. The first "Caprice" is in C sharp minor, the second in C major. Both are modestly ambitious works for a twelve-year-old. The first calls for some dexterous octaves in the right hand, and in the second one, thanks to the second manuscript (there is also a third), we can observe Bizet replacing simple harmony (Example 1.3) with something more adventurous (Example 1.4).

Example 1.3

Example 1.4

22. S-Ssm MMS 323:1.

Dated 13 June 1852, when Bizet was thirteen, is a curious "Étude", still unpublished.[23] It presents a melody accompanied by four independent parts with difficult rhythmic combinations and hand-stretches, as if intended to tease. He wrote on it: "a poor imitation of a Ries étude—worthless—it's antiquated and as idiotic as can be." The mystery is that no étude by Ferdinand Ries seems to have been published at that time.

★ ★ ★ ★ ★

If Bizet was alert to new music at this young age, he would have found a way to hear Meyerbeer's *Le Prophète*, whose long-awaited opening at the Opéra in April 1849 was the sensation of the year. The composer had done everything to ensure its success. Pauline Viardot and Gustave Roger in the principal roles established their leading status in that theatre, and the noisy presence of twenty-four saxhorns, visible on stage, made a strong impression on everyone (including Wagner). For the ballet the dancers put on roller skates to suggest skating on ice, even though this had no bearing on the drama. The other successes of 1849 were Ambroise Thomas's *Le Caïd* and Adolphe Adam's *Le Toréador* at the Opéra-Comique, restoring the fortunes of that theatre after the upheavals of the previous year and set respectively in Algeria and Spain. The latter opera is one of many French opéras-comiques in the ancestry of *Carmen*, this one with a bullfighter as the leading character. Each of these two composers had premières again in 1850 at the Opéra-Comique: Thomas's *Le Songe d'une nuit d'été*, in which Shakespeare is improbably represented as being in love with Queen Elizabeth; and Adam's *Giralda*, again set in Spain, with the twenty-two-year-old Caroline Miolan making her début in the title role. In addition to those by Adam and Thomas, new works were constantly appearing from the pens of Auber and Massé at this time, feeding a growing appetite for light, tuneful, Italianate music that enchanted the public but exasperated men of finer sensibilities like Berlioz. The most perceptive observers had already noticed a decline of Parisian taste in the 1840s, to be crowned by the imminent and triumphant appearance of Offenbach in the mid-1850s.

In April 1850 a little-known composer, Ernest Reyer, presented an "ode-symphonie" at the Théâtre-Italien entitled *Le Sélam*, modelled on Félicien David's *Le Désert* (which Reyer had never actually heard), and two weeks later *Le Sélam* and *Le Désert* were heard on consecutive evenings. Whether Bizet heard these exotic concert pieces then or later, they were to be a model for his own ode-symphonie, *Vasco de Gama*, composed ten years later. In October 1852 Parisians had a rare chance to hear Berlioz's mighty *Grande Messe des morts*, performed in the church of St-Eustache with the composer conducting. Bizet and his friends would surely not have missed such an opportunity as that.

23. S-Ssm, MMS 323:34.

Viardot's success in *Le Prophète* gave her the influence at the Opéra to persuade the management to accept an opera by the newcomer Charles Gounod, who had won the Prix de Rome in 1839 but had devoted himself almost entirely, since his return, to church music. *Sapho*, with a libretto by Emile Augier, was composed in 1850 and staged at the Opéra in April 1851. The critics, including Berlioz, had good things to say about it, but even with Viardot in the title role it had only a handful of performances, and a single performance in London in August was a disaster. Gounod soon began to play an important part in Bizet's life, but when they met is not certain. In May 1852 Gounod married Anna Zimmerman, daughter of Bizet's occasional teacher, so it may be presumed that the Zimmerman family was the link. Old Pierre was himself in rapid decline, and when he was unable to teach, he asked Gounod to stand in for him.[24] He was alarmed by the swarms of pianists that descended on Paris "like locusts". "It's terrible," he said, "everyone plays the piano nowadays and everyone plays it well." "That leaves just you and me," replied Berlioz, who was no pianist.[25]

Gounod was entering a highly productive period that culminated in *Faust* in 1859, and in most of his compositional enterprises Bizet was to play an important subsidiary part. Gounod was older than his protégé by twenty years. Like the Delsartes he was deeply devout, having thought more than once about entering the priesthood, but he was now a family man with his sights set on success in the theatre. He soon became the director of the Orphéon, a large choral group that grew steadily in size and importance, and throughout the 1850s, in the view of the critics, he was the composer to watch, as Berlioz had been twenty years before. His correspondence with Bizet, which survives from 1853 onward, has an avuncular, if not paternal, tone, for he was clearly aware of the boy's special talent and was glad to help him. In one letter he speaks of "mon enfant Bizet".[26] In return Bizet was glad to assist his mentor, as for example in the Salle Herz (just around the corner from the Delsartes' apartment) on 24 April 1855 when he played the piano for the first performance of Gounod's "intimate scene" *Deux vieux amis*. "You were the beginning of my life as an artist—I spring from you," Bizet told Gounod in later years after a period in which he showed the unmistakable anxieties of influence. It may be argued that Gounod's influence was not all good, for although Bizet was introduced to a style of music he found highly sympathetic, Gounod also plied him with work in the form of arranging scores for publishers when he might have better spent the time composing. We know that Bizet was taking piano pupils as early as

24. Pigot (1886), p. 4–5.
25. Berlioz (1972), t. IV, p. 301–302.
26. Lionnet (1888).

1853,[27] and there were few moments in his life when he could afford to refuse offers of paid work, never having a salaried job at the Conservatoire or elsewhere and never enjoying success in the theatre (in his lifetime) in the manner of Adam, Auber, Halévy, Gounod, Massé or Thomas.[28]

Although *Sapho* was not a success, Roqueplan, Director of the Opéra, had sufficient faith in Gounod to commission a second work from him. This was a Scribe libretto called *La Nonne sanglante*, based on the 1796 Gothic tale *The Monk* by Matthew Lewis. Berlioz had already embarked on a setting of the libretto but abandoned it in 1841. Gounod composed his score in 1852–53 and by October 1853 it was ready for rehearsal. Although Bizet's biographers claim that Bizet's first arrangement for Gounod was the music for Ponsard's play *Ulysse*, which opened in June 1852, that transcription was not by him: his first Gounod arrangement was the vocal score of *La Nonne sanglante*, 366 pages long, the printing being paid for by the Zimmerman family. Perhaps even earlier was the job of arranging Gounod's oratorio *L'Ange et Tobie* as a vocal score whose eighty-three pages Gounod also entrusted to Bizet. This score (renamed *Tobie*) was not published until 1866. A different kind of arrangement young Bizet took on was a set of a hundred very short extracts from the masters (Beethoven, Weber, Chopin, etc.) arranged for the "piano-scandé", an instrument invented by the piano makers Lentz and Houdart in 1853 which allowed the two pedals to be applied to single octaves at a time, thus allowing soft pedal in one register and sustaining pedal (or none) in another. Like so many inventions of the age, this instrument sank without trace.

La Nonne sanglante finally opened in October 1854. Although like *Sapho* it was not a success (Roqueplan's successor disliked it and struck it from the repertoire), the vocal score was reissued many times, first by the publishers Brandus & Dufour and then by a relatively new music publisher, Antoine Choudens, who was soon to assume the leadership in the publication of French opera. The name Choudens has become closely associated with Bizet's music, but young Georges can hardly have guessed that he was unknowingly passing his posthumous fate into the hands of a firm whose record remains to this day less than magnanimous.

Gounod's next work was a symphony, performed in February 1855 in the Salle Herz by the Société des Jeunes Artistes du Conservatoire, a new concert group conducted by an ambitious young musician, Jules Pasdeloup. Bizet was given the work to arrange for piano duet, published soon after by Colombier. A year later the

27. Wright (1988), p. 1.
28. For a detailed discussion of Bizet's relations with Gounod, see Gounod (1899), Poupet (1982) and Wright (1993).

same group introduced Gounod's Second Symphony, and this too was arranged by Bizet for piano duet and also for piano solo.[29]

★ ★ ★ ★ ★

In October 1853 Bizet became a member of the composition class of Fromental Halévy, the centre of his formal Conservatoire studies for four years. Since the highest aim for any young French composer was the Prix de Rome, which Bizet won in 1857, bringing this phase of his student years to a close, we will return to his work in the classroom later. Meanwhile his extracurricular activities included the composition of a variety of works with which he may not have troubled his busy teacher, perhaps showing them to Gounod instead (although neither older composer can have had many minutes of spare time in that decade). These include more piano music, more songs, his first works for orchestra, and his first two operas. In February 1854 the *Journal des loisirs utiles,* which proclaimed itself to be "l'ami des jeunes filles", included a "religious song" by Bizet entitled "La Foi, L'Espérance et la Charité", his first published music. The author of the poem, a former monk named Rousseau de Lagrave, who had a brief career singing tenor roles at the Opéra, was no doubt a friend of the Delsartes. Young Bizet, who later expressed a vehement distaste for religion, pulls out all the stops in asserting St. Paul's pillars of Christianity: all three strophes, set for bass voice and piano, end with a hugely forceful declaration of "Je crois en toi!".

Bearing the date September 1854 are two pieces for piano, the "Grande valse de concert" and the "Premier Nocturne". The waltz's length (476 bars) may justify the epithet "Grande", but it is built entirely on popular clichés such as one might find in any ballet music of the period and shows no evidence of individuality. Bizet performed it in January 1855 in a Montmartre church, and initially dedicated it to Marmontel (the dedication was erased).

The "Premier Nocturne" in F (Bizet later wrote another "Premier Nocturne" in D) is a different matter altogether, revealing a balance and sensitivity that may derive from Chopin as well as a fine control of harmony and piano figuration. Allowing triadic harmony to shift chromatically over a pedal bass note already reveals a daring mind. In the same year, 1854, he published two more songs, modest settings of poems by Olivier Rolland, who must have been a cousin on his mother's side. These were published by Madame Cendrier, whose music shop was next door to the Conservatoire building. Both songs have three strophic verses and both imagine flowers as living creatures: the first is a dialogue between a daisy and the young girl who is plucking its petals to divine the future, and the second imagines

---

29. These arrangements were published some years later by Choudens with no mention of Bizet's name. For evidence of Bizet's authorship, see the *Bizet Catalogue*, forthcoming.

a rose whose longing for love is fulfilled by the bee that settles in her embrace for the night. Like the "Romance" of three years earlier "Petite Marguerite" alternates G minor and G major, with the minor section offering more subtle music; the second song, "La Rose et l'abeille", is in the major throughout, yet still reveals subtle shifts of tempo and nuance. Both are accomplished compositions and give no sign of immaturity. Bizet inscribed a copy of "La Rose et l'abeille" to Gounod, signing off as "your devoted grateful pupil".

Sometime in his student years Bizet composed his first opera. This is a slight affair, to be sure, and its origin is not clear, nor is there any trace that it was performed at that time. It has no overture and was apparently never orchestrated. *La Maison du docteur*, in one act, has a libretto by Henry Boisseaux, a prolific author of opéra-comique; it was also set to music by an aristocratic amateur, the Marquis Paul de Richard d'Ivry and staged in Dijon in 1855.[30] When that score was published, it was dedicated to Gounod, so it is possible that Gounod suggested the same libretto to Bizet at the same time. With seven musical numbers shared by a cast of four and interspersed with extensive dialogue the work conforms precisely to the one-act format of innumerable works played at the Opéra-Comique, and the story—involving a young girl in love with an unknown stranger (the tenor), her father anxious to give her in marriage to a rich older man (the baritone)—is anything but original. The London setting was a favourite for such works (the rich man is a milord), and the happy ending mandatory. To add spice to the story, the father is a doctor who dabbles in poisons. The two numbers that stand out are the long "Trio" (no. 3), in which Eva's cantilena soars above the other voices, and the clever "Duo bouffe" (no. 6) for the rival suitors, the younger man furious, the older one disarmingly nonchalant in the face of an impending duel.

When it came to purely orchestral music, Bizet leaped ahead with astonishing assurance. In November 1855 he wrote his first symphony, well-known today as his Symphony in C. (Bizet's Second Symphony, incorrectly known as *Roma*, is also in C, so we refer to the earlier work as his First Symphony.) This venture was undoubtedly prompted by his experience arranging Gounod's first symphony just before, for there are many similarities between the two.[31] Whether or not Gounod suggested writing the symphony, Bizet was clearly under his spell, for the overall plan, the instrumentation and the clean classical tonality come from Gounod. For those who encounter the Bizet symphony without knowing the Gounod symphony the strongest impression is of its youthful freshness; it seems innocent of the advances

---

30. In fact the words of none of the seven numbers composed by Bizet correspond exactly to Boisseaux's libretto as set by d'Ivry, and two of them have entirely new words. See Girard (1990), pp. 16–21.

31. See Shanet (1958).

and expansion of the symphony apparent in Beethoven and his followers. With striking boldness Gounod shed the comfortable Romanticism of his two grand operas and the intimate religiosity of his sacred music and reached all the way back to Haydn. If he was following any trend at all, he had picked up an enthusiasm for Haydn from Narcisse Girard, who had conducted both of Gounod's operas and who warmly advocated Haydn in his programming as conductor, since 1849, of the Société des Concerts du Conservatoire.[32] There is no Beethoven, no Berlioz, not even any Mendelssohn in Gounod's symphony. While all those three composers left their mark on Saint-Saëns's Symphony in E flat no. 1, performed in Paris in December 1853 when Saint-Saëns was eighteen and warmly complimented by Gounod, Gounod himself was deliberately choosing a different path, different even from the dutiful classicism tinged with Romantic colour in the symphonies of Gouvy, David and Reber that form the tenuous link between French symphonies of the Revolutionary period (Méhul) and the new generation embodied in Saint-Saëns.

Bizet's symphony, at all events, is similarly free of earlier symphonic echoes. Apart from Haydn, this music might bring to mind Schubert's first five symphonies, but they were unknown at the time. Its bracing rhythms and triadic themes even anticipate Prokofiev's *Symphonie classique*. Bizet's dog-like care to tread in his mentor's footsteps did not prevent him from surpassing Gounod in many striking particulars or from displaying an individual voice for the first time. We hear it, for example, in two oboe melodies, one leading the second subject in the first movement, another being the main theme of the second movement. We hear it too in the horn's jumpy intervals that precede the recapitulation of the first movement and in the *moto perpetuo* passagework for violins in the finale. Like Gounod he introduces a fugato in the slow movement and like Gounod he imparts a rustic flavour to the scherzo's trio section.[33] He is fettered by the regularity of four-bar phrasing and very limited in his treatment of the lower strings; also, his timpani writing takes a somewhat random view of pitch, as it always did.[34] The most successful movement is undoubtedly the second, sustaining its broad pace with long-breathed melody, elegant orchestration and clearly balanced form.

Also for orchestra and probably dating from his student years is an overture without a title, simply headed "Ouverture". The style is different from that of the symphony and the orchestration richer, with the inclusion of trombones and ophicleide. The form is slow-quick-slow-quick and it has the feel of an opera overture in the manner of Flotow or Suppé, since the four sections are unrelated and might

---

32. See Holoman (2004), p. 197.

33. The modal sharpened fourth (B natural in the key of F) in the second half of the trio, found in the printed scores, is entirely out of character and should be corrected (as it is in many performances).

34. The printed score has corrected this in part, but many timpanists make further corrections.

be imagined as based on melodies from an opera. The cellos are generously treated and the harmony is full of the yearning appoggiaturas that the symphony so deliberately lacked, especially in the second slow section, which features the cellos in dialogue with a solo horn. The first three sections are full of interest, but the final Allegro is hampered by rigid four-bar phrases and a slackening of the invention, leaving only pace and energy to hold it up. One passage shows Bizet's trademark chromatic descent (Example 1.5).

Example 1.5

Neither the symphony nor the overture by Bizet were performed or published, whereas all the Gounod and Saint-Saëns symphonies contemporary with them enjoyed both performance and publication; there were enterprising conductors such as Seghers and Pasdeloup who might well have been glad to try Bizet's music, but he was perhaps reluctant to reveal himself so close to the hem of Gounod's garment. Perhaps he did not show the symphony to Gounod; it is even possible that the latter, having seen it, dissuaded Bizet from bringing his work before the public. At all events, Bizet never mentioned either symphony or overture again, and his friends and early biographers remained entirely ignorant of their existence.

The following year Bizet composed his second opera, his first to be performed. In a long article in *Le Figaro* on 17 July 1856 Offenbach, flushed with the success of his Bouffes-Parisiens, announced a competition for a comic opera. The preliminary round required the submission by 25 August of a *mélodie* for chorus and piano, a *mélodie* with orchestral accompaniment, and a piece for orchestra in full score. The second round required the orchestration of a song to be given to the candidates.

Seventy-eight candidates applied. The jury, consisting of Melleville, Halévy, Thomas, Scribe, Saint-Georges, Leborne, Gounod, Massé, Bazin and Gevaert under the chairmanship of Auber, shortlisted six candidates: Bizet and five others. The libretto *Le Docteur Miracle* was assigned on 28 September and the scores had to be submitted by mid-December. Two weeks later the jury awarded the first prize equally to Bizet and Charles Lecocq, who was six years older than Bizet but who had entered the Conservatoire at the same time. Lecocq later claimed that although Halévy taught both of them, he had unfairly influenced the jury in Bizet's favour.[35] But isn't influencing a jury what its members are supposed to do? Each winner received a prize of 600 francs and a gold medal worth 150 francs, and both works were staged: Lecocq's on 8 April 1857 and Bizet's the following day. Each work was performed eleven times. The company went directly afterwards to perform at St. James's Theatre in London, but they did not, it seems, take either version of *Le Docteur Miracle* with them. In Lecocq's case this was the start of a phenomenally successful career in operetta with over fifty such works appearing on Paris stages in the next fifty years. For Bizet it was vital encouragement on the eve of submitting himself for the Prix de Rome for the third time.

★ ★ ★ ★ ★

The young authors of the libretto, Léon Battu and Ludovic Halévy, were already active in the theatrical world and had collaborated on operas by Adam and Offenbach. Battu's career was cut short by his untimely death from tuberculosis a few months after *Le Docteur Miracle*; Halévy, the nephew of Bizet's teacher and only twenty-two, was later to be one of the librettists of *Carmen* and a close friend of the composer. Their tale was derived from a play by Sheridan, *St. Patrick's Day, or the Scheming Lieutenant*, dating from 1775, which had appeared in a French translation in 1841. Like *La Maison du docteur* it is in one act and has four characters, including a father (the Mayor of Padua) who wants to select a suitable match for his daughter Laurette, specifically *not* the soldier she loves. It consists of an overture and six numbers interspersed with dialogue. These similarities notwithstanding, it is a huge advance over the earlier opera in skill and invention. The libretto, for one thing, is compact and very witty, and although the Mayor is a conventional selfish blusterer, his wife Véronique is a sharply humorous character; the tenor, Captain Silvio, keeps the action moving swiftly along with two disguises, first as the clumsy country bumpkin Pasquin, who cooks a dreadful omelette, and second as the Latin-spouting Dr. Miracle, by both of whom Laurette is taken in, thus calling for two recognition scenes. The dénouement is engineered by Silvio, who informs the Mayor that he has been poisoned by the omelette and that only Dr. Miracle can cure him, in return for which he has to give his daughter's hand to his saviour. The quartet known as the "Omelette Quartet" is neatly farcical, including a parody of grand opera (the tempo is Adagio in 12/8 time) when the omelette is served, and a

---

35. Wright (1992), p. 220.

reminder of the First Symphony's moto perpetuo when they sit down to eat. Bizet's ear for comedy is admirable, for he has now learned to manipulate keys and silences while maintaining careful control of the pace of individual numbers. Laurette's "Romance", no. 2, for example, offers a delightful countermelody in the orchestra when the main section returns. More than once the composer seems to be careless with word stress, allowing the melody to override a natural declamation, but that is a common feature of Halévy's music also. It is certainly no surprise that *Le Docteur Miracle* has been revived more and more frequently in recent years, since it is a short opera full of character and humour, composed by an eighteen-year-old of more than ordinary competence.

★ ★ ★ ★ ★

The celebrity gained from this successful trifle won for Bizet entrée to a wider social milieu, including Offenbach's regular Friday evening soirées. At one of these he was responsible for a parody of *Il trovatore*, sung by Ludovic Halévy, Delibes, Offenbach himself and the author Edmond About. He was also introduced to the venerable Rossini, whose regular parties were held in his grand villa in Passy on Saturdays in the summer. With Saint-Saëns and Paladilhe, Bizet was part of the younger set that received regular invitations. Rossini gave Bizet an inscribed photograph of himself.[36]

A further handful of smaller works belongs to Bizet's student years. If it was through his father that Madame Cendrier, who had published some of Adolphe Bizet's songs, took two songs from Georges in 1854, it was also his father who introduced his son to the *Magasin des familles*, a monthly journal that offered occasional albums of music to its subscribers. In 1853 they put out five waltzes and a polka by Adolphe, and soon afterwards a "Méditation religieuse" for organ, harmonium or piano by Georges. With their December 1856 issue they also gave out two amiable but slight piano pieces by him: another "Romance sans paroles" and "Casilda", subtitled "polka-mazurka", actually a Chopinesque mazurka in 3/4 time, not a polka in the usual sense. The *Trois esquisses musicales* for harmonium exploit the instrument's special features, such as long sustained notes and the swell pedal which can effect a crescendo through a held chord. The three pieces are a "Ronde turque", with distinct echoes of David's *Le Désert*; a languorous "Sérénade" in D flat major; and a "Caprice", which has the sharpest character of the three, in the manner of Schumann or Grieg. These pieces were published in 1858 by Régnier-Canaux, self-styled "publisher of religious music", and dedicated to Lefébure-Wély, organist at the Madeleine, whom Berlioz described as "that pretty little organist with the rings,

---

36. Curtiss (1958), pp. 43–44.

cameos and gold-headed cane who *prettifies* everything he plays".[37] Régnier-Canaux followed this publication with medleys from three operas arranged by Bizet as duets for harmonium and piano. The operas were *Don Giovanni*, Grétry's *Richard-Cœur-de-lion* (which was revived at the Opéra-Comique in 1856), and *Il barbiere di Siviglia*. These pieces reflect the enormous popularity of the harmonium in France as a domestic instrument at this time; the first (domestic) version of Rossini's *Petite messe solennelle*, it will be recalled, was written for two pianos and harmonium in support of the voices.

★ ★ ★ ★ ★

Before we consider Bizet's participation in the Prix de Rome and his award of the Grand Prize in 1857 which brought his student years to an end, we need to observe the Parisian milieu in which the boy was growing to manhood. Threatened with an end to his non-renewable four-year term as President of the Second Republic, Louis Napoleon seized power with a smoothly executed coup d'état in December 1851. Tired of revolutions, France settled for the Second Empire and a new constitution, even if it meant a long period of authoritarian rule, censorship of the press, and the suppression of normal democratic processes; the Sénat established in 1852 was merely an advisory body. Napoleon III himself moved into the Tuileries Palace and married a Spanish beauty Eugénie de Montijo. A series of extravagant ceremonies, filling the streets with flags and triumphal structures, established the imperial style. The economy prospered, with France now belatedly catching up with Britain in the construction of railways and steamships. It was a good period for bankers.

A bellicose foreign policy brought a squabble with Russia in 1854 over the Crimean peninsula in the Black Sea, leading to a two-year war that ended in a largely favourable outcome for the French. In imitation of Britain's Great Exhibition of 1851 Napoleon launched the Exposition Universelle in 1855, held in the large new Grand Palais de l'Industrie on the Champs Élysées. Queen Victoria came to Paris on a state visit, marking an alliance between Great Britain and France after many centuries of hostility. The closing concerts of the Exposition, conducted by Berlioz and Gounod, involved huge orchestras and choruses, up to two thousand in number, in which almost every musician in Paris including many Conservatoire students must have been involved.

Notable musical events in this period include Halévy's *Le Juif errant* at the Opéra in 1852 and Verdi's *Les Vêpres siciliennes* at the same theatre in 1855. Verdi's Italian successes came one by one to the Théâtre-Italien: *Il trovatore* in 1854, *La traviata* in 1856, and *Rigoletto* in 1857. The Opéra-Comique introduced a steady stream of new productions by Auber, Halévy, Massé and others, and took a cuckoo into the nest

37. Berlioz (1972), t. IV, p. 553.

when Meyerbeer produced *L'Étoile du nord* in that theatre in January 1854 on a scale to which it was not accustomed. Another departure from tradition was Auber's *Manon Lescaut* in 1856, which abandoned the usual happy ending to allow for Manon's affecting death at the final curtain. This was a sign of things to come, for the Opéra-Comique was gradually to elevate the tone of its repertoire over the next fifty years, a trajectory in which *Carmen* was to play a decisive part. It was no coincidence that this upward trend coincided with the stratospheric success of Offenbach's Bouffes-Parisiens, which opened in 1855; twelve new shows by Offenbach appeared there in 1855, most of them of mind-numbing triviality; then eight in 1856, and seven in 1857, culminating with *Orphée aux enfers* in 1858.

A new theatre that Parisians watched with close interest was the Théâtre-Lyrique. Originally created as the Opéra-National before the 1848 Revolution, it reopened in 1851 in a theatre on the Boulevard du Temple, near what is now the Place de la République, some way from the centre of musical gravity around the Opéra. It successfully skirted the regulations that restricted repertoire at the other opera houses and made a point of presenting German and Italian operas in French (Mozart, Weber, Rossini) as well as works by French composers. Although its financial health was always perilous, in the nineteen years that it lasted, until laid low by the upheavals of 1870–71, it was to present some important premières, including two operas by Bizet and one by Berlioz. A new opera by Félicien David, *La Perle de Brésil*, appeared in 1851, once again tapping the mine of exoticism which he had made his own, and in 1854 Reyer produced his *Maître Wolfram* there.[38]

In the concert hall an event of considerable moment was the first performance in the Salle Herz in December 1854 of Berlioz's *L'Enfance du Christ*. He had not presented a new work in Paris since *La Damnation de Faust* in 1846, being disillusioned by what he took to be the indifference of Parisians and by the poor support for musicians in France, in contrast with healthier traditions of music-making in Germany. This new work was not at all what admirers of the *Symphonie fantastique* might have hoped, for its dominant tone is intimate, quietly narrating the story of the Massacre of the Innocents and the Holy Family's departure for Egypt. Saint-Saëns and the boy Massenet were among its many admirers, and in response to a favourable public Berlioz conducted it several more times in Paris in the following months. In 1855 he also conducted the first performance of his *Te Deum,* which he had composed in 1849. Requiring a solo organ with two large choruses and orchestra, it was put on in the spacious church of St-Eustache in Les Halles, using a brand new organ that had recently been installed. An indirect result of the success of *L'Enfance du Christ* was Berlioz's decision, against his better judgment, to compose the five-act opera *Les Troyens*. Absorbed in his big score, he gave no further

---

38. The full history of the Théâtre-Lyrique is told in Walsh (1981).

concerts in Paris in the years 1856 to 1858 and did his best to keep his preoccupation a secret. He became a less visible figure in and around the Ninth Arrondissement in those years.

We have little or no information about Bizet's attendance at any of these events. No doubt a gang of Conservatoire students was to be seen whenever an interesting new work was to be performed. Halévy arranged for Bizet to have free seats at the Opéra-Comique. His uncle François Delsarte continued to give occasional concerts always featuring Gluck and earlier French music, and occasionally reaching out into plainchant "from the fourth century AD". Bizet's parents had little choice but to continue their humble routine, more and more focused on their son and his widening successes. At some point in his childhood the Bizet family moved from the Rue de la Tour d'Auvergne a few yards away to no. 18 Rue de Laval, still in the Ninth Arrondissement.[39] Of Bizet's personality at this age we have barely a record, although by extrapolating backwards from the Italian years that followed, we can picture a plump, gregarious, unruly figure wearing a pince-nez, envied by all for his precocious facility in music, especially at the piano, casual in manner, perhaps disorderly in his daily organisation, passionate about literature as well as music, and not too concerned about his future. It seems that he was ready to turn his hand to any form of musical employment and to any genre of composition.

★ ★ ★ ★ ★

Returning now to Bizet's formal studies, this was the forum where he came into close contact with another man of great significance in his later career. The score of Gounod's *La Nonne sanglante* was dedicated "à mon ami F. Halévy", the composer who had taught him at the Conservatoire and who at the age of fifty-four became Bizet's teacher also. Like Gounod, Fromental Halévy had a considerable musical influence on his young charge, but unlike Gounod he took no personal interest in him. He was simply too busy. He had himself won the Prix de Rome in 1819 and quickly risen to prominence thereafter. He joined the Conservatoire teaching staff in 1827 and continued to produce operas of every kind with unfailing regularity. In 1853 he had already had sixteen works staged at the Opéra-Comique and nine works at the Opéra, including his greatest success *La Juive* in 1835, as well as a few at other theatres. He was an active member of the Institut and he led a busy social life, especially after his marriage to Léonie Rodrigues. Both Wagner and Berlioz admired him, with certain reservations. He was a man of broad culture who spoke many languages and took an interest in the entire world of the intellect, but he played less

---

39. In 1887 this street was renamed Rue Victor-Massé, an acute irony in view of Bizet's later contempt for Massé; the Rue Georges-Bizet is in the Sixteenth Arrondissement, some distance from any of his Parisian homes.

part than he could have done in opening up Bizet's mind to a wider culture than he had already been exposed to. According to Sainte-Beuve Halévy's well-balanced exterior harboured "an intimate sadness, a hidden wound. Halévy was too rich, too complex a nature, too open and communicative, too well organised in every sense, too susceptible to the pleasures of social and family life; he was a man with too many strings to his bow ever for any length of time to be profoundly unhappy."[40]

In the month that Zimmerman died, October 1853, Bizet entered Halévy's composition class, and he continued his studies with him for four years, an important period of adolescence and development. Halévy was too busy to give his teaching much attention (Saint-Saëns said he only went to the class when he had time),[41] but he achieved good results by focusing on the same two areas that he had himself studied at the hands of Cherubini, Auber's predecessor as head of the Conservatoire: fugue and dramatic vocal music. This curriculum, with the addition of the composition of a choral work, was designed for (and determined by) the requirements of the Prix de Rome, the summit of every student composer's ambition. Instituted in 1803 and administered by the Music Section of the Académie des Beaux-Arts, part of the prestigious Institut de France, this was a scholarship that brought music into line with painting, architecture and sculpture, for which prizes had been in existence since the eighteenth century. Winners were awarded up to four years' study at the Villa Medicis in Rome, followed in some cases by two years' study in Germany. Its purpose was to allow young talent to flourish without the constraints of the market-place and to imbibe the cultural masterpieces of Roman and Renaissance Italy. Preparation for the examination and fulfilment of its terms (when awarded) occupied a major portion of the early careers of Berlioz, Gounod, Saint-Saëns, Massenet, Charpentier, Debussy, Ravel, Ibert and many others, and left a mark, not always beneficent, on their music. Bizet too was to belong to this distinguished company as candidate, prizewinner and, later, examiner.[42]

Bizet had already studied fugue with Zimmerman and he continued to do so with Halévy. Perhaps he was proud of his work in counterpoint, for a great number of exercises in canon and fugue are preserved,[43] as well as the fugues he wrote for examinations each year from 1854 to 1857. Since the model was always to be Cherubini, not Bach, the fugues dutifully apply the techniques of stretto, augmentation,

---

40. Sainte-Beuve (1864), p. 243.

41. Saint-Saëns (1913), p. 42.

42. The history of the Prix de Rome has been exhaustively researched in Lu and Dratwicki (2011). For an account of Bizet's role in this history see Wright (1992) and Wright (2011).

43. F-Pn MS 479(B) contains about fifteen fugues, some incomplete, and more are found in F-Pn MS 471. F-Pn MS 479(A) is a collection of solfège and other exercises ascribed to Bizet and perhaps from an earlier stage of his studies.

double counterpoint at the twelfth and so on expounded in Cherubini's exhaustive *Cours de contrepoint et de fugue*. The other requirement of the preliminary stage was a short choral work.

Candidates were required to reside *en loge* at the Institut while taking the examination. If they passed the preliminary examination they went on to the second stage, which required a cantata for one, two or three voices and orchestra, conventionally divided into recitatives and arias on a text dictated to the candidates at the examination itself. Whereas the choral work was intended as training for opéra-comique, the cantata was to be in the elevated style of grand opera. Not only vocal writing but also dramatic imagination and orchestration were tested, skill in these arts being considered an essential prerequisite for success in opera.

Bizet had in fact competed for the Prix de Rome in 1853, before he became a member of Halévy's class. He was encouraged to do so by an over-optimistic Zimmerman. This must have been purely to gain experience, since at the age of fourteen he could not possibly have moved to Italy to complete his studies in the event of winning. On 7 May, with eight other students, he sat for the preliminary exam, which required a fugue on a subject by Onslow and a choral setting of the popular poem "La Brigantine" by Casimir Delavigne (Bizet's efforts have not survived). Six contestants went forward to the next round, not including Bizet. If he saw this as a setback, he also learned that he needed further study before he was ready to attempt the competition again.

According to Pigot, Bizet's first biographer, he was encouraged to repeat the attempt in 1854 by his new teacher, although this is unlikely, given Halévy's position as a member of the music section of the Académie des Beaux-Arts and an experienced member of the examining jury. So Bizet sat out the years 1854 and 1855, practising his skills on earlier cantata texts, which was Halévy's standard method of instruction, and entering simply for the fugue *concours*, at which he won the first prize in 1855. Halévy also assigned the texts of choruses by other composers as practice for the required choral setting—at least that is the evidence left by two Bizet works from his student years. One is a "Chœur d'étudiants", a new setting of a scene from Auber's *Le Lac des fées*. It is a rousing, boisterous piece for male voices in 6/8, in praise of women and the good life (Bizet changed "Vive la jeunesse" to "Vive la femelle") with some colourful orchestration to match. Parts for trombones and ophicleide have been covered over in the autograph, which suggests that it might have been performed, although we have no record of that. The other chorus is "Valse avec chœur", the words again by Scribe from *La Nuit de Noël*, an opéra-comique by another Conservatoire colleague, Henri Reber. Bizet's piece, dated 11 January 1855, is tuneful and lively and conforms precisely to the conventional opéra-comique style of the period, with block writing for the chorus, never too difficult to sing, and entirely in four-bar phrases.

In parallel with these works we have five attempts by Bizet at composing cantatas on texts previously set in 1819 (the year when Halévy himself won), 1840, 1843, 1847 and 1852; there may have been more. All but one of these are fragments only. Of *L'Ange et Tobie* (the 1847 text) just a few bars of recitative and part of a "Romance" survive with the orchestration partially filled in. For *Le Chevalier enchanté* (1843, on an Arthurian theme) Bizet prepared each page for full orchestra but wrote in only the voice parts, and only twenty pages, the last numbered 104, survive. Of *Herminie* (1819) sixteen pages from a score of over sixty pages survive, while of *Loyse de Montfort* (the 1840 text) some forty out of nearly two hundred pages survive, including a section for chorus that was not part of the original poem.

The only complete exercise cantata of this kind is *Le Retour de Virginie*, set for the examination in 1852 when Saint-Saëns, aged sixteen, was an unsuccessful competitor. Bizet's work is fully scored and displays a variety of moods and tempos, as it was designed to do. The text is by Auguste Rollet after Bernardin de St-Pierre's popular novel *Paul et Virginie*, published in 1787. Paul, tenor, longs for the return of his sweetheart Virginie to the island of Mauritius where they grew up together (Recitative and Air). He is comforted by his mother (soprano) who comes in with a letter announcing the boat's expected arrival (Recitative and Duo). A missionary (bass) warns of an approaching storm and the heavens duly cloud over. At the height of the storm time and the weather are held in suspense while the three sing a "Prière" invoking the aid of heaven. The gale resumes and the final scene portrays the dramatic events as a cannon shot is heard, warning of a ship in distress. Nothing can be done, and the body of Virginie is brought in and laid on the sand. They sing a final trio of grief, supported by wind and harps alone.

Bizet shows no sign of imperfect learning in his handling of voices and of a large orchestra. The treatment of each scene is conventional, certainly, but the storm gave him the opportunity for some bravura orchestral writing with shrieks from the piccolo, rumblings from the lower strings, rolls from the timpani, and plentiful chromatic scales, all ultimately indebted to Beethoven's Pastoral Symphony. The height of the storm is punctuated by fierce trombone chords. The two sections of the cantata's Introduction depict, first, an island idyll represented by softly shifting harmonies with divided strings, and, second, its exotic remoteness with the cor anglais intoning an angular tune supported by a "tamburino", by which Bizet intended either a tambourine, or perhaps the *tambourin*, a long provençal drum.

In 1856 he was ready to compete again, spurred no doubt by the accomplished symphony he had recently completed. Halévy was now Permanent Secretary of the Académie des Beaux-Arts, a position of great academic eminence, and the six-man music section consisted of Adam, Auber, Carafa, Reber, Thomas and Clapisson. Gounod took a close interest in the proceedings. On the very day they were due to receive the six candidates at the Institut for the preliminary examination,

Saturday 3 May, one of their number, Adolphe Adam, the very embodiment of mid-century opéra-comique, died at the age of fifty-two. A fugue subject by Reber was presented to the candidates and two stanzas from a poem by Lamartine, "Le Golfe de Baïa", for choral setting. Evoking the breeze and the gentle surge of waves in a bay near Naples, Bizet's setting provided a lilting background for a soprano soloist, unadventurous but effective, especially at the end when the orchestra drops out and the soprano's la-la-la floats over the chorus's softly pulsing beat. This gentle 6/8 Andantino character was to recur many times in his later music, as in "Sois la bienvenue" in the first act of *Les Pêcheurs de perles*. In *Ivan IV* he actually recycled a part of this chorus.

All six candidates were allowed to proceed to the cantata. They entered *en loge* on 17 May and were given a text by Gaston d'Albano (pseudonym of the poetess Julia Chevallier de Montréal), a somewhat sanitised version of the story in the first book of Samuel concerning Saul's hatred of David, with a trio of reconciliation at the end. Bizet handed in his completed cantata *David* on 9 June. Before considering their verdict the five musicians of the music panel had first to recommend a successor to fill Adam's chair, and at the head of their list they named Berlioz, who was somewhat desperately putting his name forward for the fifth time. By a majority vote his candidacy was accepted by the Institut and approved by the Emperor on 28 June. His very first duty as an Académicien was to review the six cantatas at a meeting on 4 July. Three singers were engaged, to be accompanied by all candidates in turn (assuming each one's competence as a pianist) in a play-through of their cantatas. Bizet's deft piano playing stood him in good stead, but even so no first prize was recommended. The voting procedure was open to all kinds of impropriety: the scores were supposed to be anonymous, yet they were signed by their composers who were in most cases seated in full view at the piano; four of the jury were teachers at the Conservatoire and would not only recognise their pupils' handwriting but would have a strong interest in promoting their success. Bizet could perhaps expect support from Auber, Reber, Thomas and Berlioz, but Carafa was known to favour only his own pupils and Bizet's dislike of Clapisson's music may have already been common knowledge, as it clearly was later.

The jury's votes had to be ratified (but were often overturned) by the full Académie. No first prize was awarded that year, but Bizet won a Second Grand Prize, along with Eugène Lacheurié, also in Halévy's class, whose later career left little trace. Every October the Institut's annual public session included a performance of the winning Prix de Rome cantata. Even though it had not won, the cantata *David* was performed on 4 October 1856, bringing Bizet's name to the attention of a group of music critics for the first time, although what they had to say about his music was predictably bland.

The music is efficient but not particularly distinctive. Bizet made a determined effort in *David* to organise the cantata's structure, using recurrent motives in different sections of the work and giving prominence to the two harps as David's instrument. The three characters each have a solo air, and there is a full duet for Michol (Saül's daughter) and David, slipping almost into the territory of operetta. Michol's "Invocation" is imaginatively scored, and Saül's entrance is sombre, full of bitterness at David's victory. The *Revue et gazette musicale* observed that Saül was more easily won over than the audience by David's strophes in the last section and by the harps' "golden harmonies".[44] Bizet finds it hard to escape the four-bar regularity imposed by the verse, but the variety of pace and mood, especially when the voices are not singing, goes a long way to alleviate that.

By the time he had to go through the rigmarole once more, in May 1857, Bizet had the cachet of recent performances of his *Le Docteur Miracle* at the Bouffes-Parisiens, although that would not in itself impress his judges. As winner of the previous year's second prize, and without Lacheurié competing, he also had some expectation of success. The six-man areopagus was the same as the previous year, and they selected a fugue subject by Thomas and a poem by Leconte de Lisle, *Chanson du rouet*, for the first round of the competition. The five candidates were confined *en loge* from 1 to 6 May. Of the three stanzas in the poem (supposedly addressed to her spinning wheel by a Scottish weaver) Bizet treats the first two with a jaunty tune of no special distinction, but the third stanza, where the weaver (soprano solo) recalls that the wheel will also make her shroud, strikes a more personal note, with an oboe melody over a distinctive dactylic rhythm that will come back in the song "Adieux de l'hôtesse arabe" and the "Ghazel" in *Djamileh*. At the words

Quand près de mourir et courbant l'échine
Je ferai mon lit éternel et froid.

Bizet slides a triad chromatically downward over a fixed bass, just as in Example 1.5, before returning to a repeat of the first two stanzas.

Once again all the candidates were allowed through to the next stage, which was held between 16 May and 10 June. The cantata text was *Clovis et Clotilde* by Amédée Burion recounting the fifth-century conversion and baptism of Clovis, king of the Franks, sponsored by his wife Clotilde and Archbishop Rémy. During the candidates' incarceration an incident was created by Gounod. Visitors were allowed during the dinner hour, but they were not allowed near the cells on the Institut's upper floors where the candidates were confined for the rest of the day. Gounod, who surely knew better, went up there to visit Bizet, whom he found in company with a guard and another candidate. There could not have been any impropriety, but nevertheless Gounod had to make a formal explanation, and Bizet was allowed to finish his score.

---

44. *Revue et gazette musicale*, 12 November 1856.

When the six judges met on 3 July they heard each candidate present his cantata and by secret ballot voted the first Premier Grand Prix to Charles Colin, a pupil of Adam and Bazin, and the second Premier Grand Prix to Bizet. The following day the candidates again presented their cantatas, this time before the full Académie (or at least twenty-eight members thereof, including Halévy). In their ballot Bizet got sixteen votes, Colin seven. Both were awarded the Premier Grand Prix. On 3 October, at the annual *séance publique*, the cantatas of both Bizet and Colin were played, to the annoyance of the critic Fiorentino, who observed that all Prix de Rome cantatas sounded the same anyway. Another critic, Édouard Fournier, saw a fine future for Bizet in the field of opéra-comique, since his talent was so "refined, flexible and clever".[45]

Whether these two cantatas were similar is impossible to say, since Colin's has not been traced, but Bizet's is a finely crafted work that unarguably merits its prize. He had proved himself to have the professional skills an opera composer needs: skill in writing for three different voices, skill in orchestration, skill in varying the pace and intensity of the action, and skill in displaying the difference between recitative, arioso, solo airs, and ensembles for two and three voices. If the music were signed by Halévy or Gounod we would not be disturbed, but since it is by Bizet we look for the spark that sets it apart, and we do indeed find it, twice in my judgment: the first is the clarinet melody in the Introduction that serves as a second subject and foreshadows part of the duet for Clotilde and Rémy, no. 2; the second is the Scène for Clotilde, no. 3, "Prière! Prière!" when Bizet writes a truly ravishing cantilena accompanied by muted strings alone. This is the gem at the heart of the work that should have reduced those twenty-eight Academicians to tears if Mlle Henrion sang it to them with all her heart and soul.

As Bizet approached his nineteenth birthday the first phase of his student career was over. Ten years at the Conservatoire had given him a thorough grounding in all musical techniques and a useful familiarity with all current practices in operatic and instrumental music. His tastes and opinions were well on the way to being formed. His family and friends would have been proud to see him join the distinguished list of Rome prizewinners and relieved that he had four or five years of financial support to look forward to. He took some lessons in Italian. But it would have been abnormal if he had not felt some misgivings about leaving the city he had grown up in, leaving his parents, his friends, and the professional opportunities that were beginning to open up, and setting out on a journey to a country far from home. On 21 December 1857, with a group of fellow prizewinners, he set off for Rome.

---

45. Fiorentino in *Le Constitutionnel*, 5 October 1857, Fournier in *La Patrie*, 5 October 1857, both cited in Wright (2011).

CHAPTER TWO

1858–1860: Don Procopio

WITH BIZET AWAY FROM HOME FOR NEARLY THREE YEARS, WE HAVE AN immediate view of his daily doings, of his likes and dislikes, and of some of the secrets of his mind, since he wrote a series of long informative letters to his parents from Italy.[1] After he returned in 1860 his letters became for the most part brief and business-like; if he reflected on his experiences and his surroundings, he rarely committed these thoughts to paper. But in Italy almost everything was new: the landscape, the language, the daily companionship of talented young men, freedom from financial cares, freedom to compose, freedom to absorb a world of literature, painting and history far broader than anything he had encountered so far, even the freedom to misbehave — and we sense his delight and his skill as a reporter. During some of his stay in Italy, too, he kept notes of places he visited and people he met.[2]

The party of five young men headed first for Lyon on the overnight train. Bizet's companions were a composer Charles-Joseph Colin, two painters, Charles-François Sellier and Jules Didier, and an architect, Eugène Heim. Bizet, at nineteen, was much the youngest of the party and the most susceptible to the extraordinary impact of new places. In Lyon they visited the museum, then continued at a slower pace in order to take in one town at a time. First Vienne, with its Roman remains, then Valence and its cathedral. Another night train took them to Orange and its famous Roman theatre, then on to Avignon, where they found themselves on Christmas Day 1857. They took a coach excursion to the Fontaine-de-Vaucluse

---

1. Published as Ganderax (1907).
2. F-Pn n.a.fr. 14383-4.

where water gushes in a torrent out of a spring. The next day they saw the astonishing Roman aqueduct Pont du Gard and the arena at Nîmes. Little knowing that the town would later feature in one of his finest works, Bizet then passed through Arles en route to Marseille.

His head full of architectural glories of the past, he was even more struck by his first sight of the sea. On a young man brought up entirely in the city it was the mountains, valleys, springs, and ocean that made the strongest impact in this adventurous week rather than anything man-made. The travellers took a boat out into the bay and felt the touch of the sea; they marvelled at the winter warmth; the group was also consolidating into a well-knit band of brothers as they got to know each other better. Bizet wore out two pairs of shoes on the rough mountain slopes.

They followed the spectacular coast road by coach, passing through Toulon, where they visited two navy ships, then across into Italy, which still at that time encompassed the city of Nice. In Italy he was immediately struck by the shabbiness of the buildings, the washing hanging out to dry, and the ubiquity of priests and beggars. From Genoa, where they spent a few days, they took the boat across the bay to Livorno, the train to Pisa, and then another train to Florence, where they arrived on 12 January 1858 and spent a week. Having cursed the cupidity of customs officers at every border-crossing and of porters who grabbed their luggage and then demanded a tip, they found life in Florence to be extremely cheap and agreeable. They went to see Verdi's *I Lombardi* ("very bad"); they took a trip to Siena and visited churches, museums, palaces and gardens at considerable leisure, noting the sad contrast between the glories of the Renaissance and the poverty of artistic life around them. In Florence they were joined by the twenty-six-year-old Joseph Tournois, the 1857 Prix de Rome winner in sculpture, and together they took the carriage the last part of their journey, arriving in Rome on 27 January.

Five weeks on the road had been an adventurous, eye-opening experience for all of them, but they had to adjust now to a more sedentary and stable life as students at the Villa Medicis, Bizet's home for the next two years. Set amid splendid gardens dotted with statuary and with a fine view overlooking the city, the sixteenth-century villa was acquired by the French government in 1803 and set up as a school for French artists and scholars administered by the Académie des Beaux-Arts. In theory the aura of Roman antiquity and of Renaissance art would provide an appropriate background for artists, whether painters or sculptors or architects, to perfect their craft before returning to France. Composers were included in the programme without any clear faith that Rome was the right place for them to study, but at least some had the option of further study in Germany or Austria; Gounod had studied in Vienna, Leipzig and Berlin under this arrangement. Rome in 1858 offered only a threadbare tradition of polyphonic singing at St. Peter's and had two opera houses, the Teatro Argentina and the Teatro Apollo, featuring mostly local composers and an occasional Verdi première, everything heavily censored by the papal authorities. Bizet found that the music of Rossini, Mozart and Weber was almost unknown.

Time and freedom to compose were nonetheless greater assets than the artistic environment of Rome, and most of the composer prizewinners at the Villa Medicis developed fruitfully there. There was an assignment for each year's productions, but otherwise the students were free to mix with their fellow-students, take trips to other parts of Italy, and work in their own time. Each occupied a private room of monastic simplicity containing a bed, a table, three chairs, and for the musicians a piano, and they shared public spaces for meals and gatherings of many kinds. Bizet's room had once been occupied by Ferdinand Hérold, whose spirit the earlier residents invoked in a practical joke played on Bizet as soon as he arrived. He took it in good spirit.[3]

The success of the whole enterprise rested largely on the director. Horace Vernet had been sympathetic to Berlioz's misbehaviour in 1831, when he had rushed off to Nice with murder on his mind. In 1858 the director was the painter Victor Schnetz, seventy years old, and serving a second term. He was thoroughly at home in Italy and was well known in the city; the students liked him, and he seems to have had a benign influence without recourse to severe methods of any kind. He was more ambitious on their behalf than he had ever been for himself. He didn't care for music, but Bizet liked him at once. His social gifts left their mark on the soirées he held in his salon, at which a pianist with any facility was always welcome so long as he played Italian music. Bizet's response was to play Chopin or Beethoven and say it was Verdi. The young pianist's arrival filled a gap at the Villa, where he was in great demand for his playing and for his evident social ease.

A community of Frenchmen in the heart of Roman society was vulnerable to the shifting political climate generated by Napoleon III's constant meddling in Italian affairs. This was a critical period in Italian history. Beneath the firm grip on northern Italy reestablished by the Austrians after the failed risings of 1848–49 in Milan and elsewhere, the separate northern Italian states—Piedmont, Lombardy, Veneto, Parma, Tuscany—set their hearts on independence and peaceful coexistence; a united nation-state of Italy was merely a dream nourished by a handful of radicals. Austrian armies enforced the Pope's rule in the northern part of the Papal States—Romagna and the Marches—while a French garrison watched over the city of Rome. The Pope and the priesthood were nonetheless the governing authority in those states, resulting in poor local law enforcement, as Bizet ruefully discovered. While Bizet had been in Florence, an Italian revolutionary named Orsini attempted to assassinate Napoleon III as he arrived one evening at the Paris

---

3. Champavier (1890), pp. 353–355.

Opéra. Bizet would have been anxious, since the attack occurred in a street he had known intimately all his life, and although the Emperor was unhurt by the explosions, there were many casualties among bystanders. The unexpected effect at the international level was to align Napoleon with Piedmont, led by their prime minister Cavour, since he was impressed by his would-be assassin's violent attachment to Italian nationalism and saw an opportunity to wield more influence in Italy if he could assist in the expulsion of the Austrians. The year 1858 brought uncertainty to the whole of Italy, with a sense that the country was a pawn in the larger game being played by the Great Powers, France, Austria and Great Britain. Before Bizet's stay in Italy was over, the country would be gripped by war and upheaval and transformed in ways that few could have foreseen.

He settled in quickly, making friends among the twenty-odd residents. Colin, who played the oboe, and Jean Conte, a previous prizewinner at the very end of his stay, were the only other musicians in the group. The food was simple but good, and the linen clean. He was at pains to reassure his parents that he was taking care of his health, which seems to have been one of their main concerns, perhaps on the basis of afflictions he may have suffered in adolescence. None of the correspondence in either direction between Bizet and his parents fails to express concern for the health of the recipient. His voracious reading accelerated during the Italian sojourn thanks to the Villa's well-stocked library. He attended the class in Italian that was provided. He wrote letters to many of his friends and bit by bit began to explore the city of Rome, holding back only because he was in a hurry to start composing again.

The requirements of his scholarship in the first year were the composition of a sacred choral work and a three-act opera in French or Italian on an existing libretto.[4] His first concern, though, was to write a piece he could enter for the Rodrigues Prize, worth 1500 francs and open to composers who had won the Prix de Rome. It was given by a cousin of Halévy's wife, Édouard Rodrigues, in order to encourage the cultivation of sacred music. Rodrigues felt that this branch of music was neglected both by institutional teaching and by the church itself, thinking wistfully of the Handel and Mendelssohn oratorios so beloved of English and German choruses. Bizet selected the *Te Deum* as a suitable text and studied a setting by Lesueur dating from the Napoleonic period. Either he found it harder than he expected or he spent little of his time at work, for it took him over three months to complete, a surprisingly long time for someone who was capable of writing quickly when required. The *Te Deum* was only half the length of the cantatas he had been composing in only a few weeks each. He was confident enough of his chances of winning

---

4. Dratwicki (2005), p. 108.

the prize to imagine spending the money on a trip to Switzerland or Germany. Even without it he reckoned he could travel to Germany and live in reasonable comfort "until I start having successes at the Opéra-Comique and the Opéra".

Social life at the Villa flourished under Schnetz's benevolent aegis. Embassy staff and other French residents in Rome knew that the Villa could supply talented young men for their dinner parties, and Bizet with his bright sense of humour and brilliant piano playing was quickly adopted as a regular guest. He was often invited to the table of Count Kiselyov, Russian ambassador to the papacy, who lived a luxurious and evidently idle life. Bizet's wide reading and love of art were additional marks in his favour. His letter home describing the thrill of seeing the Sistine Chapel and his thoughts on Michelangelo, Raphael and del Sarto give only a hint of the exuberance of his conversation in a social setting. When Schnetz gave a masked ball, Bizet, who described himself as chubby, went dressed as a baby. At carnival time a group of students went into the city and joined the throngs throwing confetti and whistling at the girls sitting in open windows. But the weather turned bad and Bizet developed a throat ailment that seems to have been tonsillitis. Confined to his room and visited by both Italian and French doctors he quickly recovered, encouraged by constant visits from his fellow students and Schnetz himself. Having described his illness in a letter home, he immediately regretted planting such anxiety in his mother's mind.

The *Te Deum* was drafted by mid-April and the orchestration finished a month later. The problem was that it really did not suit his mood or his temperament. He told his mother he was not cut out for church music. He had no church music in his upbringing and he was soon to declare his distaste for religion itself. The work is not without merit, however, and is not to be written off. Bizet divided the Latin text into four sections with the traditional panegyric at the beginning and end. The two central movements are the most interesting. The second, "Tu rex gloriae", is a lively solo for the soprano, prefaced by the same tune played on a solo trombone, while the third movement, "Te ergo", is a suave tenor solo, none the worse for being modelled on Mozart's *Ave verum*. The skillful writing here for the strings makes up for their unadventurous treatment elsewhere in the work. In the finale Bizet writes a fugue as a sop to tradition, although he had hardly benefitted from all those dozens of fugues he wrote as a student, and the return of the opening march-like hymn is welcome relief. A striking passage from the opening movement at "Pleni sunt coeli", with altos and tenors in octaves in the middle texture, was salvaged for *Les Pêcheurs de perles* some five years later.

A professional copy of the finished *Te Deum* was made and sent off to Paris. All the while he was itching to write an Italian opera, perhaps in order to show the Italians how it ought to be done. The regulations required a French or Italian opera, so he searched for a suitable libretto from the hundreds that had already been set by

Italian composers and planned to submit it the following year. His eye fell on *Parisina*, a *melodramma* by Felice Romani, the most successful Italian librettist of the previous generation, now living in retirement near Genoa. Set by Donizetti in 1833, the plot was based on Byron's poem *Parisina* (1816), full of intrigue and adulterous passion at the court of Ferrara in the fifteenth century. In June, soon after completing the *Te Deum*, he came to the conclusion that this libretto was not right for him, and after looking through hundreds more printed librettos he chose instead an *opera buffa* entitled *Don Procopio* by Carlo Cambiaggio (1798–1880), set by a team of six obscure Italians and performed in Trieste in 1844.

This work was to occupy him for the remainder of 1858. Meanwhile new friends arrived, among them the young composer Eugène Diaz, the symbolist painter Gustave Moreau at the end of a year studying Renaissance art (his tenor voice was a precious element in the Villa soirées), the painter Ernest Hébert, a former prizewinner who would one day be director at the Villa himself, and the prolific writer Edmond About, whom Bizet had met at Offenbach's home before he left Paris. About, who was thirty, had been sent to Rome by the French government to report on Italian affairs, but his articles in *Le Moniteur* were so scathing in their criticism of the Italians and so hostile to the Catholic Church that he left in a cloud of bitterness and his articles were discontinued. During his stay, however, he proved to be an admirable friend to Bizet, being greatly impressed by his musicianship and predicting that he would be the leading French composer of the next generation. He started on the libretto of an opéra-comique for Bizet, which the latter found "almost too funny", but although About had a reputation as a humorist, this piece was never written, nor did he ever write a libretto for anyone else. It was probably About who persuaded Bizet that he was better equipped to tackle a comic Italian libretto than a serious one. He also nudged him, if any nudging were needed, in the direction of anticlericalism.

With the *Te Deum* done and summer arriving, he and Eugène Heim took a couple of weeks off for an extended hike into the interior of the Roman countryside, visiting Tivoli, Frascati, Albano, Genzano and Norma, the last of which is some thirty-five miles from Rome. They had a chance to improve their Italian and they saw some characteristic sights, including a wedding and a burial. They visited a number of convents where Bizet invariably found the organ to be broken down. Unlike the city-dwellers, Italian peasants had no dislike of the French and were hospitable and friendly. Although Bizet promised his parents a detailed travelogue, his report was mostly about Italian women. "They are often pretty, sometimes ugly, but always dirty." His next letter was more revealing:

> What struck me most was the innocence of the country people. I say "innocence" rather than "ignorance" because for the women their virtue cannot compete with the offer of

two *paoli*, and nearly all the men are prepared to take on any job for a few sous. The same is true for the higher classes, except it's more expensive. There's not one woman in a hundred here who doesn't have a cardinal, a bishop or a priest, depending on her status. The virtuous Italian woman has my complete admiration. I value her and admire her more than Joan of Arc or Lucretia. I, who hoped when leaving Paris to see no more evidence of the flightiness of women, I have truly fallen! I'm sure you'll be furious with me at this, but what do you expect? You rare women who are truly virtuous, living in a devoted and loving family, you don't want to admit that you are a thousand times more deserving than all those saints and martyrs. You won't believe it, but fortunately we believe it for you.[5]

Living entirely in the company of men, Bizet can have had little notion of a social role for women other than as wife and mother. "I can see no purpose in the fair sex," he told his mother, "other than to satisfy one's *amour-propre*. I would gladly risk my life for a man, but I'd think myself very foolish to give a hair of my head on behalf of a woman."

On their return the travellers found many of the Villa's occupants gone and some down with the fever, which was rampant in Rome in the summer. Despite this, the sordidness of the city's streets, washing hanging in the windows, and the constant importuning of beggars were beginning to strike Bizet as picturesque rather than annoying. He liked all those statuettes of the madonna above doorways, the mud underfoot and the dung heaps in the squares. From the Villa gardens he loved to watch the sun setting over the city skyline. The Italians themselves were stubbornly unfriendly (except to Schnetz), and the presence of French troops sparked occasional violent incidents in the streets. He was reading the Greek and Latin classics in translation and plenty of French literature, including Voltaire, Beaumarchais, Chateaubriand, Lamartine and many others, catching up on the systematic education he'd never had and keeping notes on each book. During the summer months he made weekly excursions ("promenades monstres") out of the city, to Subiaco, Ostia, Rivoli and elsewhere. He complained about being woken in the middle of the night by About and two of the students completely drunk; they woke two more and settled into a game of cards. At other times he would work through the night, then wake his friends up and drag them off on a walking expedition.[6] Heim, already dogged by accusations that he owed his prize to his elderly father's prestige (and membership of the Académie), went off on his own to the island of Ischia, thinking it would cure his depression and persistent illness. Bizet

---

5. Ganderax (1907), p. 76.
6. Lacombe (2000), p. 213, citing François Oswald's obituary in *Le Gaulois*, 5 June 1875.

diagnosed his problem as homesickness, feeling sorry for architects since their work was "just geometry" while the painters, composers and sculptors could be limitlessly creative.

Bizet's mother was hoping, as mothers do, that her son would return soon, although she must have expected the answer she got: he was firm in his intention to stay at least a second year. There was talk of war, it was true, but at the Villa he was not exposed to danger and he had enough money to cover a longer stay. His opera would take several months, then he would embark on another large work. How could she expect him to abandon what he'd set his heart on, he asked. His record was clean. Since Schnetz was visiting Paris, why not ask him, he teased, whether I've murdered anyone? He sent her a photograph of the interior of the Villa to impress her that he was living in comfort and style.

At the end of September he learned that he had not won the Rodrigues Prize, but that it had gone to the only other contender Adrien Barthe, Prix de Rome winner in 1854, whose oratorio *Judith* was more substantial than Bizet's *Te Deum* and closer to what Rodrigues had in mind. It was undoubtedly a blow, but as he assured his mother, it wouldn't kill him. In any case he was happy working on *Don Procopio* and confident that it would be well received by the Académie. Except to plunder it for a passage in *Les Pêcheurs de perles*, he seems never to have given the *Te Deum* another thought.

"My life is so simple," he wrote home. "Work, interrupted occasionally by a good walk. That's all."[7] The autumn of 1858 was the most tranquil period of his life, and perhaps the happiest. He loved his surroundings and he had a small but close circle of friends. He worked steadily on *Don Procopio*, relishing the fact that he was not pressed for time and not, for the first time in his life, trying to do better than someone else. He saw his goal as simply to produce the best he was capable of, resisting his natural fluency and making time to revise his work thoroughly. He began to see the danger of facility, noticing that most of his fellow-students were naturally gifted but not sufficiently self-critical or original. He had written two comic French operas, but to write an Italian one he explored the best models, namely Mozart and Rossini. He came to believe that each of these was superior to the mightier figure who followed after: it was not fashionable to consider Beethoven inferior to Mozart, Meyerbeer inferior to Rossini, or Michelangelo inferior to Raphael, but this was the position he took, and it permitted him to compose music that was exactly measured to its purpose. Verdi, meanwhile, impressed him not at all, especially *Un ballo in maschera*, Verdi's latest opera, which he saw in Rome in November of the following year.

---

7. Ganderax (1907), p. 101.

The winter brought heavy rain and, in the city, floods, and the new year, 1859, saw the completion of his opera in draft. In reviewing his year at the Villa he felt he had not wasted his time. "I've read more than fifty books, both history and literature, I've travelled, I've learned a bit of art history, I'm quite a connoisseur of painting, sculpture, etc, and I've produced as much music as one can in four months of continuous work."[8] The opera was ready in time for Bizet to play it through to a new arrival, the latest composer to win the Prix de Rome, Samuel David. At twenty-two he was close to Bizet in age and a good friend from Conservatoire days, all the more welcome since Bizet had not found Colin the easiest of colleagues.

★ ★ ★ ★ ★

Don Procopio is, as Bizet intended it to be, a thoroughly expert opera, almost wholly in the Italian comic style most familiar to us from Donizetti, to whom it is clearly indebted. Bizet himself acknowledged certain similarities with *Don Pasquale* of 1843. He had clearly studied the genre in depth, since he adopts many of its mannerisms without falling into the vacuity that lesser Italian composers often betray. It is written for singers, both men and women, with strong techniques and fluent coloratura. The opera is incomplete since it lacks an overture, an entr'acte, and the recitatives that would link one number with another and give the essentials of the plot; perhaps, intending this merely as evidence of his progress to be offered to the Académie, he never wrote them. It is the longest work he had yet composed, consisting of twelve separate numbers divided into two acts.

Like many light operas of its type and its time, it concerns the attempts of a young lady's uncle and guardian (Don Andronico) to marry her off to an elderly miser (Don Procopio) rather than allow her to marry the young officer (Odoardo, a tenor of course) with whom she is in love. She, Donna Bettina, is supported by her brother Ernesto and her aunt Eufemia, and together they outwit Andronico and befuddle Procopio. By pretending to be sly and spendthrift, Bettina alarms the old miser to the point where he has no choice but to abandon his claim to her. The plot is slight, but it allows solo arias for Bettina, Ernesto and Odoardo, a duet for the lovers, a duet for Bettina and Procopio, two trios involving some action, and a little for the chorus.

The music is more polished than anything in *Le Dr Miracle*. There are occasional echoes of Mozart and plenty of Donizetti, but the tunefulness is Bizet's own and the scoring more resourceful than most Italian operas of the time. Sopranos might not thank him for packing so many acrobatics into Bettina's only aria so early in the opera, but tenors are eternally grateful for the Serenata that Odoardo sings to her at the beginning of Act II. If the guitar accompaniment recalls Ernesto's Serenata

---

8. Ganderax (1907), pp. 112–113.

"Com' è gentil" in *Don Pasquale*, the lilting rhythm and the key of A minor hark back to a similarly evocative melody in the slow movement of the First Symphony. It is not particularly Italian in style, but owes something to Félicien David, as we shall see. He liked this piece enough to insert it in *La Jolie Fille de Perth* a few years later as Smith's Sérénade (Example 2.1). In fact it is not a solo, for Bettina appears on her balcony and sings a delicious version of the melody in the major key and they close in harmonious thirds and sixths. Their other duet, "Per me beato appieno", the penultimate number of the opera, is equally beautiful in the same mood.

Example 2.1

When it comes to furthering the action, the two most impressive numbers are the duet for Bettina and Procopio in Act II, "Io di tutto mi contento", in which she taunts him with her pretended love of luxury, and the Trio later in the act for baritone and two basses, in which Ernesto and Andronico pile humiliation on poor ill-treated Procopio. The final chorus echoes the first-act finale, and the Marcia militare for the arrival (though not the appearance) of Odoardo is adapted from the second subject of the finale of the First Symphony.

In due course the opera was delivered to Paris and put before the music section of the Académie. Their report pointed out that Bizet's first submission should have been a sacred work, not an opera, although the regulation in force actually did permit a French or Italian opera. The *Te Deum* being an entry for the Rodrigues Prize, it did not count, for some reason, as an official submission, and Bizet never thought of it as one. Once they had got past their sniffy grumble about the regulations, the authors of the report liked the opera a good deal. "This work is distinguished by a fluent and brilliant touch in a young, bold style."[9] There was never any question of a performance, however.

★ ★ ★ ★ ★

While still at work on *Don Procopio* Bizet was looking ahead. He decided he would write a French opera using Victor Hugo's libretto for *Esmeralda*, an adaptation of his own novel *Notre-Dame de Paris* set to music by Louise Bertin and staged at the Opéra in 1836. This was to be his main work in 1859, and he would follow it with a symphony, as allowed by the regulations for the student's second year's work at the Villa. In his letters home, however, he is much readier to discuss his plans for a long holiday than for another composition. He was very excited by David's arrival and laid out a two-month trip they would take with Heim and Didier, taking in all the major cities of northern Italy, starting in Florence, then Bologna, Parma, Verona and Venice, and returning down the east coast. He would visit Naples, Sicily and Germany the following year.

Things did not work out as planned. David turned out to be less than the ideal companion and their musical tastes diverged, David affirming his admiration for Verdi while disdaining Mozart and the earlier Italians. Bizet found him selfish and indifferent to the concerns of others. Meanwhile Heim's health was still not good; he failed to complete his submission and decided to go back to Paris to recuperate. Within a month he had abandoned architecture altogether and resigned his scholarship.

Didier (and his dog) were still eager to make the trip, but larger forces intervened in April 1859 when the curious love-hate relationship between Rome and the French boiled over into street disorders that were contained by French troops only with difficulty. To his parents reading the news at home Bizet completely dismissed the dangers of his own situation, but he had learned not to risk alarming them. In May 1859 war finally broke out between Piedmont and France on one side and Austria on the other. A large French army commanded by Napoleon himself joined King Victor Emmanuel's Piedmontese force in Turin and defeated the Austrians in two major battles, the first at Magenta on 4 June, the second at Solferino on 24 June. Austrian troops stationed in the northern Papal States were recalled to Vienna. Napoleon called a halt to the conflict in July, troubled by lack of support in France and by the possibility that Piedmont might take over more of Italy than had been agreed on, including the Papal States. Bizet was thrilled by the French

---

9. Institut de France, AFR carton 64, "Rapport sur les travaux des pensionnaires de l'Académie Impériale de France à Rome, pendant l'année 1858." A different version of this text is found in Lacombe (2000), p. 242.

victories but struck by the little support that Piedmont had from the rest of Italy. Garibaldi, he noted, could raise only ten thousand volunteers. Italy resumed its unstable equilibrium while, unseen by our smiling composer, public enthusiasm for a united Italy continued to grow.

As in the previous May Bizet was again struck down with tonsillitis and an ulcerous throat. After a week in bed, he was well enough to set out with Didier and the dog and a new arrival named Pâris, perhaps a relative of the composer Claude Pâris who had won the Prix de Rome in 1826. They were two months on the road taking in churches and unusual sights, as recorded in Bizet's travel notes.[10] They spent the first week at Anzio, on the coast south of Rome, mostly bathing (Bizet always enjoyed swimming), and then moved further down the coast to San Felice and Monte Circeo, a promontory a little north of Terracina associated in legend with Homer's Circe. One of its caves gave Bizet the idea for a piece about Ulysses and Circe. This, he decided, would be his next submission. It would be an "ode-symphony", a concert form invented by Félicien David with *Le Désert* in 1844, and it would have four purely instrumental movements and five or six pieces for singers and chorus. David's work also employs a speaker, but this was not mentioned in Bizet's plan. In his mind he already picked the man to write its text, Victor Fournel, a literary critic living in Paris. He would need first to return to Rome, reread Homer, and work out a scheme for Fournel to flesh out. In the same letter that reports this plan Bizet mentioned the idea of a three-act opera to be called *Le Tonnelier de Nuremberg* based on a short story by E. T. A. Hoffmann, "Meister Martin der Küfner und seine Gesellen", written in 1817–18. The story is set in Nuremberg in 1580 and concerns the master-cooper Martin's determination to give his daughter Rose only to a member of the coopers' guild. All her three suitors have to take up that trade, but it is the silversmith Friedrich who wins her father's favour. The story contributed at least a little to Wagner's conception of *Die Meistersinger*. The idea of writing an opera on *Don Quixote* also came into his mind but did not lodge there when he read a report that Gounod was also planning such a thing.

Along with *Esmeralda* none of these works were written, but after the lassitude Bizet experienced following the completion of *Don Procopio*, it was encouraging that an energetic holiday and some congenial company could prompt new thoughts in the direction of music. Near Terracina, on 6 June, Bizet noted the strange sound of chanting by convicts on the beach accompanied by the rattle of their chains. Then Bizet, Didier and Pâris turned inland and headed for the mountains, visiting Sonnino, Piperno, Fossanova, Frosinone, Veroli, Ferentino, Alatri, Colle-Pardo, Anagni, Subiaco, Rieti, and as far north as Terni (which Bizet already knew from

---

10. F-Pn n. a. fr. 14354.

his travels in January 1858) before turning back south through Città Castellana to Rome. Without any instruction Bizet learned to ride a horse. Didier was already painting some of his finest landscapes. Pâris gave up half-way along and headed directly to Rome, while Bizet and Didier completed their wide circle and returned to Rome in mid-July in time to hear about the armistice signed at Villafranca. The Romans feared they would be swallowed up by Piedmont, now enlarged as the Kingdom of Sardinia, and they blamed the French.

Back in Rome Bizet took a closer look at the *Odyssey* and found the story of Ulysses and Circe to be unmanageable. In its place he suggested to Fournel something based on the *Lusiad*, the epic by the sixteenth-century Portuguese poet de Camões about Vasco da Gama's voyages. He must have known that Meyerbeer was at work on an opera on this subject, but after twenty years of rumours about it in the press the subject was surely free for anyone to take (*L'Africaine* was still unfinished at Meyerbeer's death in 1864).

When Fournel turned down Bizet's idea, the composer began to plan such a work himself, still using the template of the ode-symphony. His other idea, an opera on the *Tonnelier de Nuremberg*, could not be done until he was back in Paris. But he was not yet ready for serious work, having agreed to go on a trip to Naples with Didier and three others: two sculptors, Henri-Charles Maniglier (who later carved the images of Science and Art on the Palais Garnier) and Paul Dubois (who later carved the bust on Bizet's tomb), and a painter Pierre-Louis-Joseph de Coninck. Paul-Emile Bonnet, who won the Prix de Rome in architecture in 1854, was already there in Naples, where they spent the whole of August, swimming a great deal. In his *Mes Souvenirs*, Massenet described the Casa Combi, on the Via Santa Lucia in Naples where Prix de Rome students always stayed: "It was a tumbledown old house, its facade rough-cast in pink, with window-frames decorated with very skillfully painted figures."[11] They took a trip to the island of Ischia. But when Didier was laid low by typhoid fever, everyone except Dubois and Bizet suddenly vanished. Dubois suffered from boils but took care of the patient with Bizet, who felt in perfect health. The doctor advised them to go to Sorrento and stay in a decent hotel, which Bizet was sure that Schnetz would pay for (and he did). In Sorrento Didier happily recovered, so the party of three went on to look at Amalfi, Salerno and the ancient remains in Paestum. They then went back toward Naples and stayed at Pompeii, not in a hotel but in a farmer's house for three francs a day.

In October they were still in Pompeii in no hurry to return to Rome, a happy group of three friends. Having no text for the Vasco da Gama work, Bizet started to

---

11. Massenet (1992), p. 64.

compose a symphony, which he had earlier planned for his final year's work. The strong connection between the eventual Second Symphony and his travels in Italy has its roots in this trip, although which part of it came to him at this time we can only surmise. Then it was his turn to get ill. Influenza and more trouble with his throat struck him down just as they got to Naples for the return trip. They reached Rome at the end of October after a very successful and happy three-month trip, even allowing for illness.

The Académie's report on *Don Procopio* awaited Bizet at the Villa, and it gave him great satisfaction. It was rare that these reports were so generous. Then he looked through the score once more and decided it was extremely weak. Better than the veteran Auber could do, he thought, but still not good. He didn't like the little that he had written of his symphony either, and decided to start again. A second attempt pleased him no better, and that too was abandoned. Happily he found a French poet who was willing to write verses for *Vasco de Gama*. This was Louis-Michel-James Lacour-Delâtre (1815–93), the author of books of poetry and linguistic studies of Italian, German and Sanskrit who spent most of his life in Rome. Delâtre worked fast, so that Bizet was able to start the new year 1860, as he entered his third year in Rome, with a text in his hands. He was not impressed with the quality of the verse and had to rewrite some of it himself. "That's not funny: I realised with horror that my poetry is infinitely better than his."[12]

As in the previous year, the summer months were devoted to excursions and travel, the winter months to composition and the occasional walk. The symphony was still running through his mind. He had the finale taking shape at the same time as he was forging ahead with *Vasco de Gama*. He began also to think about an opéra-comique based on Molière's *Le Sicilien ou L'Amour-peintre* and wrote some verses for it, borrowing a rhyming dictionary from the Villa library as an aid. It cannot be a coincidence that an opera based on that play had been performed only two months before in a small theatre in the street where Bizet was born. No doubt his mother reported that its composer was a year younger than Bizet and trained as a painter: Félix Rossignol changed his name to Victorin de Joncières, went to study at the Conservatoire, and ended up as a music critic. Bizet may even have composed some music for his own version, but within a few weeks he reminded himself of the Académie's report and its thinly veiled disdain of "productions légères" and dropped it.

Samuel David was no more congenial company than before, but Bizet had a new musician to look forward to in Ernest Guiraud, the 1859 prizewinner and a friend from the Conservatoire only a year older than himself. He arrived in February and

---

12. Marmontel (1881), p. 260.

immediately became Bizet's close companion. He was an excellent pianist and they played duets together. *Vasco de Gama* was drafted by the end of that month, with the orchestration still to do. The autograph describes the work as an ode-symphony in three parts, but only Part I has come down to us. Were it not for the poverty of the verse, he told his mother, he might have carried on. The orchestration was finished in March and the score copied.

★ ★ ★ ★ ★

Whereas Reyer's ode-symphony of 1850, *Le Sélam*, was modelled on Félicien David's very successful *Le Désert* of 1844, Bizet's *Vasco de Gama* was modelled on David's second work in this genre, *Christophe Colomb*, first performed in 1847.[13] Bizet must have heard it when it was performed at the Conservatoire on 23 September 1855, when he might well have been a member of the double men's chorus. A narrator speaking over the music, a chorus of sailors setting sail, a bass voice for the title character, a *morceau caractéristique* for a young male sung by a soprano, the sea becalmed, a prayer to the Almighty, a powerful storm, the return of calm, the happy arrival at a new and exotic land—all this is common to both works, although Bizet's work is half the length of David's, which is divided into four parts.

Bizet's action covers the departure of Vasco da Gama's 1497 expedition from Lisbon. When the ship is finally under way the giant Adamastor appears and causes a storm to threaten the ship. The giant warns the Portuguese to turn back. Calm returns, but fear remains. Vasco calls the men to prayer. They pray to the God of Moses and sail on. Land is espied and they all rejoice.

Bizet was still avoiding the styles of Gounod and Halévy but not ashamed to adopt some of David's mannerisms, such as a fondness of the "lazy bass", the tonic note held in the bass while the harmony shifts above it. The song for Fernand in *Christophe Colomb*, "Adieu, ma belle" (A minor, 6/8 rhythm), was no doubt the model for Odoardo's aria in *Don Procopio* (see Example 2.1), especially as it devolves into a duet in the major. David's Chanson du mousse, sung by a soprano cabin-boy, is similarly the precedent for the Boléro, "La marguerite a fermé sa corolle", sung by Léonard (soprano), a junior officer on Vasco's staff, although nothing by David equals the verve and character of this superb piece. The nearest precedent might be Berlioz's *Zaïde* (Example 2.2).

A countermelody to the second verse outlines the melody of "Les tringles des sistres tintaient" from the Chanson bohème in *Carmen*, and the end of the song matches the end of Carmen's Séguedille with a thrilling high B. Picked out for

---

13. A helpful study of the *Ode-Symphonie* may be found in Laudon (2012).

Example 2.2

salvage like Odoardo's Serenata, Bizet retrieved Léonard's Boléro for the opera *Ivan IV*, as if to confirm that this is the best piece in the work.

Only the characters Vasco and Adamastor are found in Camões; Léonard and Alvar (tenor), Vasco's brother, are newly created. After an introduction hailing the two continents, Europe and the East, a chorus of sailors (men and women) in a 6/8 Andantino is followed by a chorus of soldiers (men only) in a martial 4/4 rhythm. With an obvious doff of the cap to the soldiers' and students' chorus in Berlioz's *La Damnation de Faust*, Bizet then presents both choruses simultaneously with the addition of some plaintive cries of "Adieu!" from Léonard. It must be said that the combination is short and not very strict, but the effect is impressive, as it was meant to be, and the close of the scene is beautifully handled. The excuse for Léonard's Boléro is that it is the song his lover Inès used to sing to him every day. A storm brews and the dreaded voice of the giant Adamastor is heard threatening the Portuguese with destruction. Yet calm returns, so Vasco urges his crew to their knees for the Prière. This outclasses even the Prière in *Clovis et Clotilde*. Starting as a five-part unaccompanied chorus, it soon becomes an ensemble of extraordinary power when the soloists and orchestra join in. If it were in an opera this piece would stop the show. Here in *Vasco de Gama* it occurs after rather than during the storm from which they are all praying to be saved, but even so its effect is breathtaking. After that the Finale can only seem commonplace, with the harp welcoming the sight of land and a brief banal march celebrating the success of the voyage. Clearly Bizet had once intended to fill out this scheme with scenes in whatever exotic shore the Portuguese had reached, but he was convinced that the idle members of the Académie preferred short works. "Reber says nothing, Berlioz isn't there, Auber's asleep, Carafa and Clapisson—alas!—listen. The only one is Thomas, and he's so lazy!"[14] (There was scarcely a musician in Paris who thought either Carafa or Clapisson merited their exalted Institut chairs.) If *Vasco de Gama* had been completed and revised, it might have become a successful concert work, but its single performance in Paris in 1863 was not enough to persuade Bizet to pay it any further attention.

★ ★ ★ ★ ★

Thinking he ought to submit a sacred work, he decided next to set not the Christian Mass but Horace's *Carmen saeculare*, in the hope that a pagan religious text would serve. This is a seventy-six-line hymn in sapphic metre commissioned by the Emperor Augustus to mark the *ludi saeculares* (secular games) held in Rome in 17 BC. It is an ode to Apollo and Diana, to be performed by two choirs, one of twenty-seven boys, the other of twenty-seven girls. The poem also celebrates the achievements of Augustus and the glory of Rome. Having started it, Bizet realised that the style was probably too pagan for the music section of the Académie and that it would be a tough challenge to compose, but he carried on nevertheless, at least for a while.

After reviewing *Vasco de Gama* and finding it to be "good, very good even",[15] he sent it off to Paris. Finally, after some years of doubt, he felt he was truly a composer with a future, with many better works to come. Looking around at the competition he felt only Gounod was in the field; as for Italian music, it was beyond redemption since Verdi "will surely never again have those flashes of genius you find in *Il trovatore, La traviata*, or the fourth act of *Rigoletto*".[16]

No more was heard of the Horace work. Bizet idled away his time reading and walking, waiting for 1 July, when he and Guiraud were free to set off on their planned trip to the cities of northern Italy. While 1859 had seen fighting in the north, 1860 was the year of upheaval in the south. Piedmont-Sardinia had now ceded Nice and Savoy to France, under an earlier agreement, and the French were wary that Cavour would move to take over the Papal States. Meanwhile popular support for the idea of a united Italy was rapidly taking root, especially when in May Garibaldi landed in Sicily with his famously few "Thousand" and soon

---

14. Ganderax (1907), p. 247.
15. Ganderax (1907), p. 254.
16. Ganderax (1907), p. 255.

defeated the island's Neapolitan rulers. Bizet's patriotism and admiration for Napoleon III were never stronger.

His grant money for July arrived a month late, so the travellers could not leave Rome until the end of July, heading for Venice. By that time he had made a decision not to return to Rome for the autumn months and complete his third year of residency but to go directly to Paris after their northern ramblings. He loved Rome too much, he told his mother; he had to leave. There is no reason to doubt the sincerity of his assertion that "it's not good to be too happy". Not even his attachment to a young lady noted as "Zeph" was strong enough to keep him there. His recent rush of self-confidence must have given him the strength to re-enter the Paris musical arena with good prospects for getting his works accepted at the Opéra-Comique and elsewhere. Guiraud, who as a student had played the timpani at that theatre, already had a work accepted there, and Bizet must have felt he could equal that. Having abandoned the *Carmen saeculare* he had no clear assignment ahead; an unproductive two months might well have persuaded him that life at the Villa was alluring but no longer helpful to the career that was beckoning to him from the boulevards. Guiraud had been idle too.

After a tearful farewell to all the inhabitants of the Villa and to his Roman friends the pair set off. Bizet again took notes, this time recording the books he was reading as well as the sights they saw and revealing much more of their escapades than his letters ever did.[17] There is a remarkable dissonance between his almost obsessive delight in the architecture and art of old churches and the appetite for female flesh that seized him every evening. Thoughts of Zeph exercised some restraint at first, but not for long. Their goal was Venice, but they started on the west coast, taking trains where they could, travelling elsewhere by stagecoach: through Civitavecchia (for a swim), Viterbo, Orvieto, where he played the organ in the cathedral, Città della Pieve, where "having cast a covetous glance at the hostess's daughter" they slept until noon. At Chiusi the hostess's sister not only resisted their suggestive banter but stole from them, a discovery they made as they travelled on in a stuffy carriage to Perugia. They spent three days there (8–11 August), looking closely at works of Bizet's beloved Raphael. The nightly search for women was unsuccessful, so they moved on to Assisi to take in the Giotto frescoes.

From there they crossed to the Adriatic coast and spent some time in Rimini, lured by the sea. Bizet dragged Guiraud out of bed every morning to teach him how to swim. He wrote a long letter home and started to plan his next work, evidently a continuation of the symphony he had tried to get started the previous winter. This version of the symphony was to comprise four movements entitled

---

17. Entries in this journal were first cited in Curtiss (1958).

"Rome"—"Venice"—"Florence"—"Naples", with "Venice" the slow movement and "Florence" the scherzo. Rimini's antiquities were disappointing, but not, one hopes, the night he spent there with an unidentified woman, perhaps one he did not have to pay. The same two activities occupied them in Ravenna, up the coast. Bizet was becoming more critical, for their next stop was Bologna, inland, whose Fountain of Neptune by Giambologna (1567) with its four sirens "pressing streams of water from their breasts" struck him as "cochon". In Ferrara he considered the cathedral of San Giorgio "an ugly Gothic curiosity". He was still in a critical mood that evening when they visited the local brothel and the girl he was assigned was "a little on the skinny side". He added, cryptically: "O Berlioz, why weren't you there?"

In Padua they admired the Giottos in the Scrovegni Chapel and on 4 September they reached Venice. They had allowed themselves a month in the city of St. Mark to be followed by a two-month itinerary, carefully worked out. Arriving in Venice on the Tuesday they hurried to the Piazza San Marco, the "most marvellous of all marvels", as Bizet described it. They then took a gondola to the post office and there found three letters from his mother, the most recent written from a hospital. On seeing the name of the hospital he panicked and lost his temper with the gondolier. Guiraud restrained him, but the shock was severe, and the next day he realised that he might have to return to Paris at once. He wrote almost identical letters to his father and his mother begging for more news. There was also a letter from Gounod awaiting him in Venice, commiserating with him on parting from Rome, a city that Gounod, the ardent Catholic, had loved. Gounod was clearly willing to remain the younger man's mentor and guide on his return to Paris.

As an uncanny pre-echo of Camus's *L'Étranger*, Bizet's anxiety about his mother did not curb his nocturnal pursuits. "Went on the hunt without success," he wrote the same day, and the next day, 6 September: "we trawl the brothels. I tangle with a gorgeous girl. She wants ten francs—if you please!" Whether any further news arrived or not, they did not linger in Venice. The long informative letters home and the detailed travel notes come to an abrupt end, and the planned visits to Milan, Siena and other cities were abandoned, unless Guiraud went there on his own on his way back to Rome. A week later Bizet passed through Nice (now part of France) where his friend Heim was attempting to find a cure for his persistent maladies. On Bizet's route north from Nice he shared a carriage between Chambéry and Ambérieu-en-Bugey with the physicist Gaston Planté (later the inventor of the lead-acid battery), who, with a remarkably steady hand, made a charming sketch of the bearded, lorgnetted Bizet. In Mâcon Bizet had to run an unidentified errand for his father, and by the end of the month he was home.

September 1860, the month that ended his long absence, was also the month when Garibaldi occupied Naples, when Cavour sent troops to occupy the Papal

States (with Napoleon III's backing), and when the unification of Italy under King Victor Emmanuel was all but complete, for it would be another ten years before Rome itself was absorbed. Bizet would have enjoyed the excitement of those events, but after two and a half years at the Villa he had had enough of the limited circle of friends of his own age and the lack of musical stimulus in his surroundings. Being without a teacher had forced him to choose a direction for his work, which he did not find easy, and although he mistrusted Parisian opinion, he would have been glad of some constructive criticism beyond the rejection of the *Te Deum* and the bland compliments handed down on *Don Procopio*. He did not lack confidence in himself and he knew he wanted to be a composer, not a pianist, but he was without any clear view of the path ahead and dangerously inclined to indolence when life was so easy. Gounod urged him to develop the habit of working hard and to go to Germany for a spell, but he showed no enthusiasm for that. Paths contemplated but not taken are no blot on a young composer's record, but three works completed, two of them quite short, is not impressive for such a period when the complete absence of any other obligation is taken into account. He had enjoyed his freedom, taken many important steps toward maturity, and learned much about friendship and independence. He loved art and good food but was convinced that the Italians knew nothing about either. If he had loved the Italian people as much as he loved their landscape he would certainly have wanted to stay longer.

Being out of touch with Paris's music had troubled him from the start. We have almost no correspondence between Bizet and any of his Paris friends, but he surely had first-hand reports of important premières such as Gounod's *Le Médecin malgré lui,* Halévy's *La Magicienne*, Gevaert's *Quentin Durward*, David's *Herculanum*, Meyerbeer's *Le Pardon de Ploërmel*, Berlioz's revival of Gluck's *Orphée* with Pauline Viardot, Gounod's *Philémon et Baucis,* and Wagner's three concerts in early 1860, heatedly discussed by *le tout Paris*. He missed all these important events, although Gounod sent him a score of his *Le Médecin malgré lui* and wrote caustically about *La Magicienne*. Most of all he was troubled by missing the opening of Gounod's *Faust* at the Théâtre-Lyrique in March 1859, and it turned into a complicated issue of loyalty since his admiration for Gounod was enormous and his instinct that the opera would be a success was right. Yet a pupil of Bizet's father and a good friend, the tenor Hector Gruyer, having originally been assigned the leading role, was replaced within three weeks of the première when it became obvious that he was not up to it. Bizet felt the blow personally, especially on his father's behalf, and allowed a certain chill to enter his relationship with Gounod, mostly dissipated by the letter Bizet picked up in Rome. But the decision was probably right, and although the unfortunate Gruyer was cast as Faust for the revival in September he withdrew after four performances and his career never took off. Bizet had profound respect for his father's teaching and once called him the only teacher who really understood the art of singing. Allowing for filial loyalty, this was a fine thing to say, and while it was his mother to whom most of the letters from Italy were written, he preserved a cool but respectful regard for his father. He was undoubtedly happy to see his parents again and he looked forward to throwing himself into the whirlpool of Parisian life and testing his abilities against the competition, come what may.

CHAPTER THREE

1860–1863: Les Pêcheurs de perles

HE PARIS TO WHICH BIZET RETURNED IN SEPTEMBER 1860 WAS UNDERGOING the most far-reaching transformation the city had ever known. Under the feverish energy of the Préfet de la Seine, Baron Haussmann, many of the cramped streets around the Louvre had been cleared and a wide new north-south boulevard, the Boulevard de Sébastopol, connected directly across the Île de la Cité to the Boulevard St-Michel. The Bois de Boulogne had been redesigned and the city's sewage system modernised. A start had been made on the spectacularly grand design of a new opera house in a wide open space with a broad avenue to connect it to the Louvre. Nearer to Bizet's own stamping-ground in the Ninth Arrondissement a series of boulevards were opened up to give access to the railway stations and to improve traffic circulation. The Rue de La Fayette was extended south-west to the Rue du Faubourg Montmartre by 1859 and reached all the way, straight as an arrow, to the back of the new Opéra by 1862. Constructing the Rue de Mauberge and the Rue de Chateaudun nearby also required extensive demolition of old buildings, so that Bizet's walk down the hill from his home in the Rue de Laval to the Conservatoire or the opera houses took him through and around an endless series of building sites. Such ambitious public works depended on the very visible prosperity of the city and the confident glitter of Second Empire society, although the extravagance of all that building eventually caught up with the city's masters when the Second Empire itself ran out of steam and money.

Bizet moved back with his parents in the Rue de Laval. From Rome he had explained at length his plan for living with them but independent from them, preferably in the same apartment or the same building, but with the freedom to come and go as he wished. This would enable him to assist his father in caring for his ailing mother. How well he adjusted to such a narrow and mournful ménage after his carefree years in the company of clever young men under Italian skies we can only guess. His mother's condition filled him with anxiety, which may be why Reyer reported that he was very irascible on his return from Italy. His short fuse had been displayed in the case of the Venetian gondolier, and it would be tested again from time to time in later years.

There is little documentation to record his daily activities in the next few years since his surviving letters are few and terse and he was not yet in the public eye. He was permitted to spend the fourth year of his Prix de Rome in Paris, so he had a modest income at least until the end of 1861. There was no urgency to find employment, yet he certainly would have weighed his options. He would have liked to have an opera accepted at one of the lyric theatres, but failing that he had a wide choice of *métiers*, and he may have filled his week with any or all of the following activities: giving private piano lessons; teaching piano in a school; acting as accompanist for singers in private salons and for singing teachers; acting as rehearsal pianist; playing the organ in a church; conducting ballroom or theatre orchestras; conducting amateur choruses; writing piano reductions of vocal works and operas for publication; writing band and orchestral arrangements of piano music to be played in balls and theatres; proof-reading for music publishers; and scoring operas for composers who lacked the skill or the will to do it themselves. We know he had no ambition to be a virtuoso solo pianist: "Nothing on earth would make me want to play in public," he wrote in 1867.[1] He probably hated to practise, and besides, he knew that virtuoso pianists were not thought to understand opera and were not welcome in its world, as Saint-Saëns attested: "Bizet would never dare to play the piano in public for fear of making the situation worse."[2] And although a recent letter from Italy had speculated that he could write about music as well as many critics he knew, his name appears in no journals under reviews or articles (except once in 1867).

None of these forms of employment open to him would normally leave any written record except when vocal scores of operas named the arranger, which was not always the case. His piano teacher Marmontel simply reported that he taught piano, harmony and singing on his return from Italy, without any details,[3] and occasional letters tell of slogging across Paris to give lessons. Gounod, for example, recommended him to Turgenev as a piano teacher for his daughter: "My young friend Georges Bizet, a very talented young man, a superb musician who plays the piano to perfection and has a charming personality and a refined and cultivated intelligence, will be the man you need, I believe."[4] Gounod added that the charge

---

1. Malherbe (1951), p. 50.
2. Saint-Saëns (1913), p. 23.
3. Marmontel (1881), p. 231.
4. Vente Alde, Paris, 15 April 2013, p. 51.

would be ten francs an hour. Although Bizet worked extensively as an arranger and transcriber throughout his career, he certainly did far more of this work than we know. To give some idea of the extent of this: whereas he published, in his lifetime, about 1500 pages of his own music, he published at least 6200 pages of music by other composers in arrangements of every kind, including reductions of his own operas, but not including arrangements that carried no name. He had already done the vocal score of *La Nonne sanglante* for Gounod and might have been assigned *Le Médecin malgré lui*, *Faust*, *Philémon et Baucis* or *La Colombe* if he had not been away; in compensation Gounod arranged for him to write the piano duet version of *Faust* for the publisher Choudens, his first employment by that firm. He did not have the opportunity to see the opera until December 1862 but he was very anxious to study the score; transcribing it for piano duet was the best way to get to know it well. At the same time Choudens engaged him to do the vocal score of Ernest Reyer's opera *La Statue*. Normally a publisher would want the score arranged and engraved as soon as possible after the first performance, so he would have been busy with the Reyer job that first winter in time for its opening at the Théâtre-Lyrique in April 1861.

Since the publisher Choudens features so prominently in the Bizet story, we should observe his first connection with the founder and proprietor Antoine Choudens, who set up in business in the 1840s but did not rise to a competitive position in Parisian music publishing until he signed up Gounod. Previously published by Colombier and Brandus & Dufour, Gounod accepted Choudens's bold offer of 10,000 francs outright for *Faust*, a deal that kept the publisher in comfortable prosperity for a full century, especially after *Carmen* joined the stable. Choudens lived long enough to see the latter opera's worldwide success. He apparently had little taste for music (he did not care for *Faust*), but he had a hard business head, having realised that an opera's success depended on foreign and provincial opera houses taking it up, and he worked hard to make that happen. He published all Gounod's later operas (except *Cinq-Mars* and *Polyeucte*) and the four Bizet operas performed in his lifetime. With the publication of Offenbach's *Les Contes d'Hoffmann* in 1881 his triumph was complete. Despite some furious exchanges, Bizet and Choudens became close friends. Choudens had faith in him when many other publishers would have written him off. Of his two sons, Antony was later Bizet's pupil.

The introduction to such a man was valuable for Bizet's career, and it seems that Choudens was rarely without some kind of commission to offer him. No sooner was Reyer's *La Statue* done than Gounod's next opera, *La Reine de Saba*, was ready. Bizet worked on this three-hundred-page vocal score in 1861 and also helped Gounod with the orchestration and with rehearsing the chorus. He was thus absorbing four of Gounod's latest works at once, as well as the Gluck *Orphée* with

Pauline Viardot and Halévy's 1848 opéra-comique *Le Val d'Andorre*, both revived the month after his return, both at the Théâtre-Lyrique, the theatre that offered the most eclectic and interesting repertoire at this time. In December 1860 Bizet must surely have taken note of an opera called *Les Pêcheurs de Catane*, with a libretto by Michel Carré, one of the librettists of *Faust*, and music by Aimé Maillart. This piece (which was about fishermen and had a character called Carmen) was a flop, but its heroine dies at the end, taking another step in the gradual progress of opéra-comique toward sentiment and tragedy.

Maillart was by no means a nobody. His *Les Dragons de Villars* was one of the most successful operas of the period, drawing large audiences to the Théâtre-Lyrique every year from 1856 to 1863. If Bizet, from his Italian ivory tower, thought he would face little competition from French composers other than Gounod on his return, he was forcefully disillusioned when he saw opera contracts going to such well-known names as Massé, Deffès, Lajarte, Caspers, Semet, Dufresne, Rivay, Hignard, Sellenick, Lacombe, Debillemont, Clapisson, Ymbert, Reyer, Prince Poniatowski, Gastinel, Pascal, Leblicq, Paliard and Grisar; works of all these composers were performed at the Opéra-Comique or the Bouffes-Parisiens. His contemporaries Saint-Saëns and Delibes, neither of whom were Rome prizewinners, were also competing for the palms of success. Saint-Saëns seems to have been happy with his new position as organist at the Madeleine, and Delibes was chorus-master at the Théâtre-Lyrique while writing a string of operettas for the Folies-Nouvelles; he also arranged the vocal score of *Faust*.

During his first year in Italy Bizet had written: "My friends say I am amusing, but modesty forbids me to believe them. They all say no obstacles stand in my way and my career is all set. I wish it were true, but I am scared of coming back, I'm scared of dealing with theatre directors and librettists (I can't bring myself to call them poets). I'm scared of singers, I'm scared, in a word, of the tacit civility of people saying nothing disagreeable to your face but stubbornly making sure you get nowhere. It's in Providence's hands, in fact, not mine."[5] These insecurities passed, but the Paris scene to which he returned was bound to discourage him. At least the Académie appreciated his gifts. Their report on *Vasco de Gama*, released soon after his return, was very positive: "Elevated style, large-scale form, fine harmony, rich colourful orchestration—these are the qualities to which we wish to draw attention in this work. We would advise the composer, however, to be on his guard against a certain harmonic audacity which might be considered harsh. Otherwise, this work would seem to presage a brilliant future for the young composer."[6]

5. Ganderax (1907), pp. 104–105.
6. Institut de France, AFR, carton 64, folio 16.

The single caution—to avoid advanced harmony—can only have made Bizet smile, since he knew exactly which members of the music section were incapable of handling even the simplest chromaticism in their own works, and he knew well the powerful effect of harmonic audacity in his own, in the Prière of *Vasco de Gama* above all. When, over two years later, *Vasco de Gama* received its first performance by the Société Nationale des Beaux-Arts conducted by Bizet himself, it was the very intensity of the Prière that offended the critic Adolphe Botte, recorded in the *Revue et gazette musicale*.

In theory the Prix de Rome brought with it an engagement to write a one-act opera for the Opéra-Comique, but in practice this depended on the whim of the theatre's director. The new director, Alfred Beaumont, had already turned down a proposal Bizet had sent him from Italy[7] and was not inclined to engage him until the composer had at least a libretto and preferably a score to offer. Without an opera libretto to work on and without any engagement to set one, his only obligation was to complete a submission as a record of his third year in Italy. This was to be his Second Symphony, and he worked on it sporadically during his first year back in Paris. Unlike the First Symphony, it did not come at all easily. At the deadline in the summer of 1861 he had only the two middle movements ready, a Marche funèbre and a Scherzo, pleading that special circumstances, probably his mother's illness, prevented him from finishing the whole symphony. With these two movements, which received bland notes of approval from the examiners, he sent in an overture entitled "La Chasse d'Ossian", of which we know nothing except that the Académie found it to have "interesting orchestration, an elevated style, and poetic colour."[8] We shall return to the mystery of Ossian's Hunt when we consider the finished symphony later, but since the Marche funèbre was not retained in the final version, we must take note of one more remarkable piece by Bizet that has escaped performance and publication. The Académie found in it only its "fine character", overlooking the fact that it is an unusually shaped piece displaying great inventiveness in its orchestration. It has a sixteen-bar theme rigidly divided into four balanced phrases of four bars each, but although this theme is heard four times, it is not varied or developed, only progressively rescored to culminate in a grand, solemn conclusion. There is a secondary theme, but it too is in clear four-bar phrases and structured very like the first. Four times in the course of the movement trumpets and drums sound a formal bugle call, so that the entire piece takes on the character of a grand military solemnity. The first half of the main theme found its way into the closing scene of *Les Pêcheurs de perles* two years later (Example 3.1).

---

7. US-NHb Koch 914, letter to Ludovic Halévy, 5 November 1860.
8. Institut de France, AFR carton 64, folio 23.

Example 3.1

An important figure whose acquaintance Bizet made within months of returning to Paris was Jules Barbier, aged thirty-five, playwright and librettist, who with his usual partner Michel Carré had already provided the librettos for three of Gounod's operas (including *Faust*), as well as *Le Pardon de Ploërmel* for Meyerbeer and *Psyché* for Thomas, among many others. Bizet was probably introduced by Gounod, whose most recent opera, *La Colombe*, also by Barbier and Carré, had been performed at the Baden-Baden festival the previous year. The librettists would have been visibly involved in the rehearsals of Reyer's *La Statue*, which they wrote as a shameless transferral of the Faust story to an Arabic setting. As arranger of the vocal score, Bizet was almost certainly needed for rehearsals too. The opera opened at the Théâtre-Lyrique on 4 April 1861. It was a huge success, supported by spectacular sets depicting the ruins at Baalbek. Reyer was a shy, sympathetic man aged thirty-seven who had acquired a strong musical technique without attending the Conservatoire. He shared Bizet's admiration for Berlioz, and despite his enthusiasm for Wagner his music belongs firmly within the stylistic circle generated by David and Gounod, at least in his earlier years. Bizet was not ashamed to learn from him or to work with him. *La Statue* gave him his first experience of working within the Théâtre-Lyrique on the production of an opera, mixing with composer, librettists, singers and the director, and putting his formidable musical skills to good use.

At the Opéra the repertoire had stagnated into revivals of the three Meyerbeer staples and Halévy's *La Juive*, with very few new works in sight. The building in the

Rue Le Peletier, dating from 1821, was itself in limbo since all eyes were focused on plans for the new house to be erected in the huge open space created at the conjunction of the Boulevard des Italiens and the Boulevard des Capucines as part of Baron Haussmann's grand plan. The design was put out to competition and an impressive, extravagant design by Charles Garnier was the winner. Construction started almost at once, with an impossibly optimistic schedule for completion since more than a dozen years would pass before it opened. The grand imperial carriageway at the left side of the building was never to see the arrival of a grand imperial carriage.

But the Opéra could not be accused of skirting controversy when it mounted Wagner's *Tannhäuser* in March 1861, a month before *La Statue*'s opening at the Théâtre-Lyrique. Such was Wagner's reputation across Europe that every dinner table in Paris resounded with anticipatory judgments for and against, and when the opera finally suffered the ignominy of being booed off the stage, the critics, the know-it-alls and the public were horrified, confused or delighted—or some mixture of the three. The scandal had many dimensions: to some it was an example of political meddling, because the wife of the Austrian ambassador had leaned heavily on the Emperor to open the doors of the Opéra to Wagner. To others it was payback for Wagner's arrogance in demanding an extraordinary number of rehearsals and expecting the impossible from singers and management alike. To others it was divine retribution for claiming that this was the "music of the future" (the claims came from Wagner's supporters, not from the composer himself). To a brave few it was the shameful condemnation of a great work, and not a very recent one at that, which had not been given a fair hearing. The opera was performed only three times before Wagner withdrew his score and headed back to exile in Switzerland uttering maledictions of all kinds. Whether Bizet attended is not known. What is clear is that the epithet "Wagnerian" took on new defamatory force in the language of French music criticism, and that composers who dared to strike out along new paths were ruthlessly tarred with the Wagnerian brush, whether their music had any Wagnerian qualities or not. Bizet was to suffer this indignity many times, even though an honest assessment of his music would not identify more than a few traces of Wagner's DNA anywhere in it, not enough to prove even distant kinship, let alone a deliberate attempt at cloning.

Only a year earlier Bizet had expressed the view that Wagner had no personality and no originality and that he preferred Verdi or Adam, both of whom he heartily despised.[9] He had missed the Paris performances of the *Tristan* prelude in 1860, and if his view of Wagner ever softened from greater familiarity with the scores (he possessed, eventually, all the opera scores up to *Tannhäuser*), it would have been from

---

9. Lacombe (2000), p. 268, citing part of Bizet's letter to his mother of 2 March 1860 not included in Ganderax (1907).

conversing with Wagner's admirers, such as Reyer or Pasdeloup, the young conductor who boldly included Wagner on the programmes of the Société des Jeunes Artistes. Bizet arranged a Wagner song for piano, but was never a Wagnerian in any sense, and he did not meet Wagner during his long stay in Paris.

In contrast, Liszt came to Paris very soon after to visit his mother and his daughter Blandine, so on 24 May, in his honour, Halévy hosted a soirée in his grand official residence at the Institut. In his 1886 biography Pigot tells the story, with plenty of sensational detail (which suggests that he was not there himself), of how Liszt played one of his pieces after dinner, declaring that only he and Hans von Bülow were capable of surmounting its extraordinary difficulties. Halévy nodded in Bizet's direction, prodding him into going to the piano and repeating certain passages from the same piece from memory. Liszt then produced the full piece, which Bizet sight-read with such ease that Liszt was forced to admit: "I was wrong. There are three of us, and to be fair, the youngest of us is perhaps the most brilliant."

Most of the few letters from Bizet that survive from 1861–62 were addressed to Barbier. When Barbier's play *Cora* was staged at the Ambigu-Français in August 1861 Bizet wrote him a letter full of admiration and warmth.[10] But the whole year after his return from Italy was darkened by his mother's illness, the nature of which was, like so many at that time, unclear even to the doctors.[11] Bizet was alarmed by her condition when he arrived back in Paris, but she clung to life for almost a year. She died on 8 September 1861 at the age of forty-five. Thanks to all those long letters from Italy, we know how much she meant to her son and how sincerely he depended on her for warmth and approval. They exchanged all sorts of quotidian details like very close friends, although there was probably much he did not tell her. Without her his life lost one of its guiding hands, and one that his father was unlikely to replace. He was not now rudderless since he had acquired new friends, mostly older than himself, but if it is ever appropriate to apply the word disorder to his life, this is the point at which such a charge might begin to take on some meaning.

Aimée Bizet was nursed through her illness by a girl from Alsace, Marie Reiter, who, willingly or not, allowed herself to be seduced by Georges. It would be generous to ascribe this event to their need for mutual consolation, but we have seen that in the only period for which we have his confessional notes Bizet's sexual antennae were on constant alert, so there is no reason to suppose that he ever abandoned the eternal chase, at least not until his marriage. Paris, after all, offered even more varied and enticing attractions than any of the small Italian towns he passed through the previous summer. We hear of him going to a seedy theatre with his

---

10. Vente Drouot, Archive Barbier, 29 November 1990.
11. Wright (1988), p. 6.

Rome friend Félix Giacomotti,[12] and many other such adventures may be presumed to have escaped the record. He told Gounod in August 1861 that he was managing two love affairs at once.[13]

Nine months after Aimée's death Marie gave birth to a son, Jean, and both mother and son remained in the Bizet household, it being generally supposed, by the boy himself too, that Adolphe Bizet was his father. Marie remained a devoted member of the household, working for Adolphe until his death in 1886 and for Bizet's widow for the rest of her life. It is not impossible that she was Adolphe's mistress too. Just before her death in 1913 she revealed to her son that his father was not Adolphe but Georges, and although she might have wanted to bestow an illustrious paternity on him, the claim undoubtedly has the ring of truth. Jean held his real father in great respect and treasured belongings which came down to him.[14] Soon after his mother's death Bizet was living at 14 Rue de Bruxelles, not far away,[15] but he eventually moved with his father to a third-floor apartment at 32 Rue Fontaine St-Georges, just around the corner from their previous home in the Rue de Laval.

In the winter months that followed his mother's death we cannot be sure that Bizet was composing any music at all. He was obliged to submit a fourth score to the Académie and he intended it to be an opera. Pigot and Curtiss claim that he was already composing *La Guzla de l'Émir* a year earlier, but there is no reason to think it was started any sooner than the summer of 1862. Meanwhile he was working with Gounod (and Barbier and Carré) on *La Reine de Saba*, a full-scale work in five acts for the Opéra; it eventually opened after a long period of rehearsals on 28 February 1862.[16] This included arranging the ballets for two violins, which was for some reason what the dancers rehearsed to. Based on a story by Gérard de Nerval using biblical characters (King Solomon, the Queen of Sheba, Adoniram), the libretto devised several grand ceremonial scenes and a second act that culminates in the explosion of a huge kiln built for the casting of a bronze vessel, hurling flames and debris on the crowd gathered round. Faced with the insuperable difficulty of making this happen, the Opéra cut the second act entirely. In any case, despite many scenes that unquestionably exhibit the best of Gounod, the work was a failure, savaged by the press. Berlioz said privately "How am I to stand up for something that has no bones and no muscles?"[17] With this fiasco following that of *Tannhäuser*, the Opéra retreated into an even more cautious repertoire of the tried-and-true.

12. Lacombe (2000), p. 267.
13. Gounod (1899), p. 691.
14. Malherbe (1951), p. 53.
15. Gounod to Turgenev, 6 March 1862, Vente Alde, Paris, 15 April 2013, p. 51.
16. Bizet's copy of the vocal score, inscribed by Gounod, is at US-Wc M1503.G711.R3 Case.
17. Berlioz (1972), t.VI.

Halévy was not there to witness his friend Gounod's public embarrassment. His health had been failing for several months due, many claimed, to overwork. He spent the winter with his wife Léonie and two daughters in a large rented villa in Nice, hoping to finish his opera *Noé* (another biblical subject) on a libretto by the ever-productive St-Georges. But his strength failed him and he died on 17 March 1862. A week later his funeral took place in Paris with an imposing cortège leading from the Institut to the Jewish section of the Cimetière Montmartre. As Permanent Secretary of the Institut, Halévy had been one of the most prominent figures in French academic life, so the funeral was attended by everyone of note and eight eulogies were delivered. Five composers, all Halévy's pupils (Gounod, Massé, Bazin, Cohen and Jonas), contributed a *De Profundis*,[18] and a large orchestra played the funeral march from *La Juive*. On the second anniversary of his death, 17 March 1864, a life-size statue of Halévy was unveiled at his grave. His widow, suffering a nervous breakdown, was unable to attend, but his daughters Esther, aged twenty, and Geneviève, aged fifteen, were there. A month later Esther died, leaving Geneviève under the sole guidance of her unstable, complicated mother. Bizet surely attended the ceremony, perhaps the first time he set eyes on his future wife.

★ ★ ★ ★ ★

Pierre Berton, a gossipy man-about-town who published his memoirs in 1913, left an evocative description of Bizet in his early days back in Paris:

> Broad-shouldered and rather plump, he seemed to have a strong physique. Beneath a thick crop of wavy hair his forehead was broad, his nose long and straight, his small eyes blue with a sincere, piercing look always behind a permanent lorgnette. All this was framed with a frizzy beard as fair as his hair. He usually looked very serious, and a detail of his dress seemed to add to his age: at a time when our shirt-makers left the neck fashionably open, he wore a high collar and cravate to protect his delicate throat, like the previous generation.[19]

The high collar might have been a sign that he was fighting the return of the recurrent angina or quinsy that he had reported from Italy. Earlier, Berton had observed the social Bizet:

> He went around with a gang of sympathetic admirers such as I have never seen. He did not pay for his success with coolness on the part of his friends. Whenever he was the subject of conversation the joking stopped. Friends who had been on the closest terms with him at the Conservatoire for ten years held him in the greatest respect. They already

---

18. Jordan (1996), p. 198, includes Bizet in the list, although there is no reason to think he was involved.
19. Berton (1913), pp. 214–215.

treated him like a master. I don't recall hearing a single discordant note in the concert of universal praise that his name provoked. What makes my report all the more precious is that I was not yet his friend then. I did not know him. Evil-spirited tongues could safely discharge their bile at me, but no, there were none. The greatest of his qualities was his perfect naturalness: he was passionate about anything to do with music, enthusiastic about what he admired, inexhaustibly funny about what he despised, and he had some fine fits of temper which he came to suppress later on. His real nature never changed and he remained to the end extremely sensitive, often to his cost.[20]

In 1862 Bizet's life began to take on the hectic condition from which he was rarely ever to escape. If it had been only composition that took his time he would have been delighted, but he was forever ensnared in the double pressure of composing to meet a deadline and not being able or willing to refuse employment as pianist or arranger. He started work on the comic opera *La Guzla de l'Émir* as his final submission as winner of the Prix de Rome just at the moment when summer engagements were coming in. The most demanding of these was Reyer's opera *Érostrate* commissioned for the new theatre in Baden-Baden. Reyer was recommended for this by Berlioz, who for some years had been giving annual concerts at the Baden-Baden festival, in part as a refuge from Paris, where his concerts had dwindled to nothing. He was generously supported by the festival manager Edouard Bénazet and was the first choice as a composer to inaugurate the new opera house which opened that year. In frustration at the prospect that *Les Troyens*, which he completed in 1858, would never be performed in Paris, he gladly accepted the commission for a comic opera in two acts, knowing that it would be well received by his faithful Baden-Baden audiences and well performed. It was to be followed in the same season by operas by Reyer and Litolff.

Bizet hoped that a commission from Baden-Baden might one day come his way too, so he was eager to oblige Reyer and also to attend the festival itself. Reyer went to Baden-Baden to compose, leaving Bizet in Paris to take care of everything. He later wrote: "My young colleague Georges Bizet took on the rehearsals with a generosity and devotion for which I will always be extremely grateful. I sent him the final pages of my score as soon as they were ready."[21] Reyer probably completed most of the orchestration and required only the piano arrangement for the vocal score, but in some cases Bizet was left to orchestrate Reyer's draft, arrange it for piano too, and deliver everything to the copyist. He then had to rehearse the singers in the Opéra building, the star being Marie Sasse, who had sung the role of Elisabeth in the recent *Tannhäuser*.

The libretto of *Érostrate* was by Joseph Méry, a fertile lyric poet who once said he could write verse quicker than prose, and Émilien Pacini, a veteran confectioner of

---

20. Berton (1913), pp. 211–213.
21. Reyer (1875), p. 375.

French librettos. Curiously for the composer of the recent *La Statue*, *Érostrate* concerns two statues, one of them being the Venus de Milo, whose arms are struck off by the jealous goddess Diana. The opera ends in the general conflagration of Diana's temple with the lovers engulfed within it. At the end of July, with only a couple of weeks to go before the opening, Bizet received the conclusion of the main Trio, about a hundred pages. This must have been a draft score needing to be orchestrated, since Reyer added: "There is no accompaniment at the end, just a few chords to guide you. I didn't see the need to send you any more than that." "What shall I do about an overture?" he added, perhaps hoping that the obliging Bizet would throw one together for him.[22]

Inevitably the opening of *Érostrate* was postponed, and Bizet was kept in Paris waiting for the parts to be copied. He therefore missed the ceremonial opening of the new Baden theatre and the first performance of Berlioz's *Béatrice et Bénédict* on 9 August. But he had been able to hear a run-through at noon on 26 July at the Théâtre-Lyrique, along with a number of Berlioz's friends who were unable to go to Baden-Baden. "We'll have a real treat and give ourselves a whole week's happiness," he wrote in anticipation,[23] being a devoted admirer of Berlioz's music and sympathetic to his isolated position in Parisian music. Bizet may have reached Baden-Baden in time for the second performance on 11 August. Berlioz left on 15 August, and both he and Bizet feature with Gounod and Reyer in a facetious and perhaps fictitious tale told a year later by the journalist Benoit Jouvin, no admirer of Bizet's music.[24] At another dinner, it is recounted, Pacini, one of the librettists of *Érostrate*, remarked in Gounod's presence that *La Reine de Saba* had "died a natural death". Bizet, enraged, leaped up and challenged Pacini to a duel. Gounod acted the peacemaker saying that his opera was alive and standing; it was only himself who was laid out on the ground. During a long visit to Rome Gounod had indeed been meditating on his future, thinking that he was in a process of "demusicalisation". The plan of his next opera, *Mireille*, however, was already taking shape in his mind.

Bizet had travelled to Baden-Baden with Choudens, who arranged to publish Reyer's vocal score, although when it came out Bizet's name was not to be found in it. *Érostrate* finally opened on 21 August and was well received, although no performance followed in Paris until 1871, when it failed miserably at the Opéra, perhaps because the final conflagration was cut. There is no further mention of Bénazet inviting Bizet to write an opera for Baden-Baden, and after returning to Paris he never trod German soil again.

He had *La Guzla de l'Émir* to finish. This one-act opéra-comique had a libretto by Barbier and Carré previously offered to Maillart. Unfortunately the following exchange between Barbier and Bizet carries no date. Barbier: "The piece is therefore yours

---

22. Lacombe (2000), p. 284.
23. Berlioz (1972), t.VI, p. 317n.
24. *Le Figaro*, 8 October 1863.

[Maillart having renounced it]. I'm delighted to give it to you since I think it's not bad." Bizet: "I trust our collaboration will have a good future. I'm getting to work on our *Guzla* at once."[25] The action is set in Tunis in Babouc's house. Bakbarah (Le Cadi) wishes to marry Babouc's sister Margiane, but the latter throws a fit whenever marriage is mentioned. The only thing that will calm her is a song accompanied by the guzla (a kind of Arabian zither), which she heard once played by a mysterious stranger in the street. The singer is of course Hassan (L'Émir) who is brought to the house to cure her while she is obliged to pretend to be an old aunt. Later he comes disguised as an old Jewish doctor. Margiane is eventually cured and all misunderstandings are cleared up.

The names and situations come from *1001 Nights*, as they did for *La Statue* and dozens of other operas and plays set in the Middle East, and like most one-act operas it contained an overture and seven numbers, three solos for the protagonists, a duet, two trios and a final quartet. There was no chorus. Bizet submitted it to the Académie in September and their judgment was handed down on 4 October, remarking upon "a Prelude acting as an overture, nicely shaped and delicately orchestrated, some *couplets* [solo airs], a duet which includes an elegant Serenade accompanied by a harp and an attractive melody on the flute, an air for the tenor, and finally an extremely graceful song, followed by a theatrically effective trio."[26]

This report is precious since none of the music has survived. The libretto was later passed to Théodore Dubois, whose setting was performed at the Théâtre-Lyrique (at that time playing at the Athénée theatre) on 30 April 1873. It is likely that much, probably all, of Bizet's score was absorbed by *Les Pêcheurs de perles*, perhaps by *Ivan IV*, *Djamileh* or other works. The mention of a guzla in the stage direction of no. 8 (Nadir's Chanson) of *Les Pêcheurs de perles* is perhaps an indication that this piece was originally the Air (no. 4) in *La Guzla de l'Émir*; and the Institut's description of the Duo contains more than a hint that this was the original form of the duet for Nadir and Zurga in Act I of *Les Pêcheurs de perles*, with its distinctive colouring of flute and harp.

The Académie's report went on to consider Bizet's record as a whole. Along with a tendency to be too clever and to sacrifice vocal interest to rich orchestration they found elevated feeling, technical assurance and a lively style, "in a word, the serious qualities of which M. Bizet has already furnished proof and which today guarantee a brilliant future." Once again the reference to his cleverness must have amused Bizet, since it was precisely that which gave him the edge over the stuffed shirts who sat in judgment on his work.

---

25. Les Autographes, Catalogue 72; Lacombe (2000), p. 287.
26. Institut de France, AFR, carton 64, folio 31.

In fact the brilliant future seemed no nearer than ever. Verdi complained of being a galley slave in his early years, but at least his operas were played; Bizet was thinking the same fate had befallen him, but without the prospect of any operas being seen on the stage. Choudens began to send anything and everything his way. The publisher attempted to get *Béatrice et Bénédict* from Berlioz: "I'm leaving Paris for ten days," Choudens wrote, "and before going I'd like to give Bizet the pieces that are not arranged for piano so as to have them done when I get back." It did not go unnoticed that Berlioz had written the libretto, composed the music, conducted the performances, arranged the vocal score, and paid for its printing all himself. He declined Choudens's offer and had the opera published by Brandus & Dufour the following January. Bizet's sense of oppression, meanwhile, emerges clearly from a long letter to Choudens that seems to belong to the declining months of 1862:

> I wish I was in a position not to have to raise these arguments about money, which I hate....The day will surely come, and come soon, when my courage and my talent will be rewarded, and then you will be able to depend on a conscientious composer and a good friend in everything that concerns your publishing business. Meanwhile I am experiencing great difficulties and I would be extremely obliged if you would help me get out of them. The sum you offer is not enough; my minimum is 1800 fr., that's to say my board and lodging in my father's house. I ask you for this amount in the conviction that I am capable of making it from our business. If we want to sort out our finances strictly, we would come to a total a little higher than I myself thought. For example:
>
> | | |
> |---|---:|
> | *Érostrate* | 200 |
> | *Le Cabaret* | 100 |
> | The symphony for piano duet, two weeks' work, i.e. what none of your friends would take on for | 200 |
> | Ditto, piano solo | 100 |
> | Then fixing up the Italian score of *Faust*, of *Philémon*, proof-correcting at 2 francs an hour, this would amount to much more than | 100 |
> | not to mention the *Merry Wives*, for which I did over sixty pages of orchestration, which ought to be paid at the rate of | 100 |
> | | 800 |
>
> You must understand that I am not asking for this....I'll undertake anything—polkas, redowas, quadrilles, proof-correcting, transcriptions signed or unsigned, arrangements, derangements, transpositions and scores for two flutes, two trombones, two cornets, even two pianos, I promise you. Between us we'll do well.

As for the contract, this is what I propose: we'll begin on January 1st and we will deduct the 400 fr. already received. I'll tell my father that our arrangement will not begin until 1 July and I will ask you to advance me the 500 francs remaining from the first six months. It's not possible that I am not worth 1800 francs a year. Please reply quickly, otherwise I'll go to the person you know....It's urgent. Do not write, in case the letter falls into my father's hands.[27]

Apart from its disturbing evidence that Choudens was working him too hard and paying him too little, and that relations with his father were not good, we learn from this letter that Bizet must have arranged the vocal score of Prosper Pascal's *Le Cabaret des amours* (Opéra-Comique, 8 November 1862, libretto by Barbier and Carré) as well as *Érostrate*. He had various cleaning-up jobs on editions of *Faust* and *Philémon et Baucis*, he did some unspecified proof-reading, and he wrote both piano solo and piano duet arrangements of a symphony. This must have been Gounod's Second Symphony, first performed in 1856. Neither publication (they did not come out for another three years) names the arranger. On top of that, Bizet had been given at least a scene from Nicolai's *Merry Wives of Windsor* to orchestrate, for unstated reasons, a revival of which was announced at the Théâtre-Lyrique in 1863, even though the performances did not take place until May 1866. There may have been a performance in Bordeaux in 1864.

Since there was no sign of a commission from Baden-Baden despite Reyer's and Gounod's efforts, the renown of *La Guzla de l'Émir*'s two librettists and the approval of the Académie might convince the director of the Opéra-Comique to accept the opera for production. But the management of that house was changing hands. Beaumont's term as director ended quickly in financial disaster, so Émile Perrin was brought in in January 1862 to sort things out, which he did very successfully, partly by picking a winner in Félicien David's colourful and charming *Lalla Roukh* in May 1862 and partly by reviving Boieldieu's eternally popular *La Dame blanche* from 1825, a work of which Bizet thoroughly disapproved. In August Perrin put on Pergolesi's *La Serva padrona*, introducing to Paris a young star, Marie-Célestine Galli-Marié, the future Carmen. In December 1862 he was moved up to the Opéra, while the Opéra-Comique was put in the charge of Adolphe de Leuven. Pigot asserts that *La Guzla de l'Émir* was not only accepted by the Opéra-Comique but also put into rehearsal, but there is no evidence to confirm this. Bizet knew that the success of the exotic *Lalla Roukh* would work against him, and *La Guzla de l'Émir* remained just another unheard score while he continued to work on other people's music. That same December Ambroise Thomas approached him with a request to take on the completion of Halévy's last opera, *Noé*, a task that Halévy on

---

27. Lacombe (2000), p. 289. Copy in F-Po.

his deathbed had asked to be assigned to Gevaert.[28] Pauline Viardot was ready to play the main role.[29] Then with both Gevaert and Thomas unwilling to take it on, Madame Halévy suggested Bizet. Perhaps he turned it down. Eventually he did undertake the completion, but in 1862 it is unlikely he would have done so unless there was a prospect of the opera's performance, so the project fell into limbo for a number of years.

In December 1862 Bizet had his first chance to see *Faust,* revived at the Théâtre-Lyrique amid great fanfare because the company had just moved into its splendid new theatre in the Place du Châtelet, opposite the equally new Théâtre du Châtelet, both of which still face each other in dignified grandeur today (the Lyrique is now named the Théâtre-Sarah-Bernhardt). The rehearsal of Berlioz's *Béatrice et Bénédict,* which Bizet attended in July, was actually the last performance in the old theatre on the Boulevard du Temple before it was demolished. The star of the revival was Madame Miolan-Carvalho, the original Marguerite, now in great demand. She was the wife of Léon Carvalho, the theatre's director, although he was only able to book her for his own theatre when her other engagements allowed. The title role was now sung by Jules Montjauze. The opera was still then sung in its original version with dialogue.

Bizet's own music was suddenly to be heard in the concert hall. At some unknown date, probably in 1862, the Scherzo from his unfinished symphony was played by the Cercle de l'Union Artistique under Deloffre, the resident conductor at the Théâtre-Lyrique.[30] This prompted Pasdeloup to include it on 11 January 1863 in one of his Concerts Populaires, which were presented in the large Cirque Napoléon in front of huge audiences. Not to be outdone, a third organisation, the Société Nationale des Beaux-Arts, invited Bizet to conduct the Scherzo himself exactly a week later. Saint-Saëns reported that it was "badly played, badly received, met by general inattention and indifference, and showed no sign of life next morning".[31] This in turn led to the first (and only) performance of *Vasco de Gama,* also performed by the Société Nationale des Beaux-Arts, also conducted by Bizet himself. This took place on 8 February. The timing was not good since there had been a revival of David's *Christophe Colomb* by the same organisation only two months before, so the press was all too ready to pounce on the similarity of Bizet's work to the David model, inevitably favouring the earlier work. The appalling Scudo (whose entire career seems to have been devoted to denigrating the music that we most value today) described *Vasco de Gama* as a feeble imitation of *Christophe Colomb*:

---

28. *Le Figaro*, 20 March 1862.
29. Vente Ader, Paris, 21 February 2013, p. 88.
30. *Le Ménestrel*, 11 July 1875, p. 250.
31. Saint-Saëns (1899), p. 173.

"M. Bizet has talent but no trace of originality. The entire score is derivative, even the *Boléro*, which has a pretty accompaniment." This was enough to eliminate *Vasco de Gama* from any prospect of acceptance or further performance.

This succession of concerts brought Bizet's name to a certain prominence, but it did not lead to any other hearings. The Société des Concerts, which performed at the Conservatoire on Sunday afternoons for a season between January and April, was wedded to the music of dead German composers. Originally founded in 1828 with the laudable aim of bringing Beethoven's music to Paris audiences, it had settled into the routine of playing Haydn, Mozart, Beethoven, Weber and Mendelssohn, and rarely risking music by the living. In April 1861 the Société was brave enough to include some extracts from Berlioz's *La Damnation de Faust* and in 1863 they included the most successful number from *Béatrice et Bénédict*, the Duo-Nocturne, but young French composers knocked at their door in vain. Not until the last few months of his life did they play any of Bizet's music: the *L'Arlésienne* suite, twice, in February 1875.

In the spring of 1863 Bizet's fortunes turned, probably not because of these concerts but because of the old-fashioned mechanics of the network. Bizet was introduced to Carvalho by his uncle Delsarte, who had taught his wife, the soprano Caroline Miolan-Carvalho. He would have met him in any case through Choudens, Gounod, Reyer, Barbier or someone else. Carvalho was a colourful character with plenty of charm who played a leading part in the operatic history of Paris for over forty years, beginning in 1856, when he abandoned his career as a singer and took over the direction of the Théâtre-Lyrique. With a two-year gap from 1860 to 1862 he held the reins there until 1868. His achievements in that period were impressive enough, but he had a second career as director of the Opéra-Comique from 1876 until his death in 1897 (with a four-year gap), which was similarly momentous in the production of new works and also momentous for the fire that destroyed the theatre in 1887. He was hospitable, generous, devoted to good wine, and always short of money. Bizet was the composer who perhaps most, after Gounod, benefited from Carvalho's impulsive managerial style, which was hands-on to the point where Berlioz, after *Les Troyens à Carthage* was staged in the same season as *Les Pêcheurs de perles*, had nothing but bitter invective for him in his *Mémoires*.

Since as the director of the most adventurous opera house in Paris Carvalho was a target for every aspiring young composer, strong support was needed to give an approach any clout, and Bizet was sufficiently well connected for Carvalho to take note. He had perhaps been offered *La Guzla de l'Émir*; we don't know. In April he accepted the proposal for a three-act opera, originally entitled *Leïla*, with a libretto by Eugène Cormon and Michel Carré and music by Bizet. This was to be *Les Pêcheurs de perles*. Carré was taking a break from collaborating with Barbier, and Cormon was a busy dramatist who wrote comedies, dramas and librettos in profusion. The commission reached Bizet at least by the beginning of April,[32] so it was good fortune that the minister of state, Count Walewski, as a parting gesture on leaving office soon after, decreed an annual subvention to the Théâtre-Lyrique of 100,000 francs, relieving at least temporarily Carvalho's almost permanent financial distress. In the new administration the functionary responsible for theatres was Camille Doucet, a playwright himself and a friend of the arts who added as a condition to the subvention that each year a three-act opera be staged by a Prix de Rome winner who had not previously had a work staged in Paris. Except for the fact that *Le Dr Miracle* had been performed at the Bouffes-Parisiens in 1857, which everyone conveniently forgot, Bizet was precisely the kind of composer Doucet had in mind.

It was while he was composing *Les Pêcheurs de perles*, inevitably getting advice from uncle Gounod, that Bizet had his best opportunity to get to know Berlioz and his music, since he was engaged as rehearsal pianist for a performance of *L'Enfance du Christ* to be given in Strasbourg in June but rehearsed with the soloists in Paris. He also worked with Mlle Morio, originally cast as Cassandre when Carvalho was still planning to mount the complete *Les Troyens*. This is enough to suggest that Bizet continued to work with Berlioz in rehearsing *Les Troyens à Carthage* right through the period when he was busiest with his own opera. Reyer envied him his free access to Berlioz's rehearsals which he himself was denied.[33] Berlioz had good reason to mention Bizet's brilliant piano playing in his notice of *Les Pêcheurs de perles*.

★ ★ ★ ★ ★

The sequence in which librettists, composer and subject of *Les Pêcheurs de perles* were selected and approved is unknown to us. Carvalho liked to be involved in every decision, and no doubt he was. The choice fell on an exotic setting, originally Mexico, an opéra-comique format with separate numbers interspersed with dialogue, and a story about two men's rivalry for the love of a native woman. Public enthusiasm for the Indian setting of David's *Lalla Roukh* and a recently published book by Octave Sachot, *L'Ile de Ceylan et ses curiosités naturelles*, caused Mexico to be replaced by Ceylon as the location for the action. With the production scheduled for early September, Bizet set to work.

The story of *Les Pêcheurs de perles* springs from two vows: the first is a vow of friendship made by two young men, Nadir (tenor) and Zurga (baritone), who find themselves in love with the same unknown woman; the second is the vow taken by

---

32. Gounod (1899), pp. 695–697.
33. Reyer (1909), p. 303.

Leïla (the unknown woman) as priestess in the service of a Brahmin temple. By falling in love with one of the men, she is drawn into breaking her vow in a manner familiar from earlier operas, notably Spontini's *La Vestale* of 1807, where a vestal virgin is in love with a Roman captain, and Bellini's *Norma* of 1831, where a Druid priestess has broken her vows with a Roman pro-consul. By falling in love, Leïla and Nadir, in the Bizet opera, are simultaneously breaking their own vows. The libretto has inconsistencies and ambiguities, but it was designed to highlight the exotic setting and provide a balance of solo and ensemble numbers for the principal singers. The ending has proved to be a topic of debate.

The Prélude is a foretaste of the music that accompanies Leïla's first entry, a beautifully shaped melody over a constant viola phrase acting as an inner pedal. Bizet's model was a *mélodrame* in the first act of Gounod's *Philémon et Baucis* of identical length and character. The curtain rises on the pearl fishermen's encampment on the shore where the people are busy setting up camp and dancing with abandon. Percussion and a steady beat hint at jungle drums, and the minor key allows some effective modal shifts. They dance to standard-issue French ballet music. The men are proud of their craft, diving for pearls, as we hear from one of the loveliest pages in the opera, never repeated: they sing "Voilà notre domaine" in four parts in an entirely non-savage style.

The first character to be introduced is Zurga, who invites the people to name their chieftain. They choose him without hesitation with the third fine melody of the opera, again never repeated. Nadir then appears. Zurga recognises him at once as his friend of long ago. The chorus greet him with "C'est Nadir, le coureur des bois", despite the fact that they have never seen him before. Still pouring out good melodies, Bizet gives Nadir a solo, in unison with bassoon and cellos, recounting his years roaming wild in the jungle. A second *couplet* was removed in rehearsal. Nadir is welcomed into their community and they close the introductory scene with a reprise of the G minor music for the chorus, who then leave the stage to some delicate exit music.

During rehearsals in August 1863 the title of the opera was changed to *Les Pêcheurs de perles* and the five passages of dialogue were hastily replaced by recitative, causing a good deal of explanatory matter to be removed.[34] In their first conversation, which follows at this point, Nadir and Zurga reveal that long ago they were close friends, living by their wits and hunting dangerous animals. Twenty times they had saved each other's lives. Zurga had taken up pearl-fishing as a refuge from the vow they had made; Nadir has been cast ashore in a storm. Nadir is distinctly taciturn, but we do not yet know why. They recall how long ago, in Kandy, far from the

---

34. These changes are fully set out in Wright (1986), pp. 27–45.

shore, they attended the temple of Brahma and both fell in love with the priestess who for a moment had lifted her veil. Fearing that a rivalry would come between them, they vowed to forget her and remain eternal friends. The scene is recounted in the famous duet that follows, "Au fond du temple saint", now one of Bizet's best-known melodies.

What is the secret of its success? The music perhaps came from *La Guzla de l'Émir*, as we have seen, and the pairing of flute and harp was already a familiar formula, normally suggesting the ancient world. It seems to have originated in Gounod's *Sapho* in 1851 and was also familiar to Bizet from the trio for two flutes and harp in Berlioz's *L'Enfance du Christ*. Saint-Saëns, Massenet and Debussy were later to adopt it. Here in *Les Pêcheurs de perles* it suggests the holy sanctum of the Brahmin temple and also the divine beauty of the "goddess" the two men catch sight of there. The tune itself is mostly harmonised with root-position chords, a crude device by the standards of Beethoven or Schubert, but strongly effective here. Bizet had already given a foretaste of this style in his Conservatoire cantatas and in *Don Procopio,* and if it is not his fault that New Age music of our own time shares a fondness for root-position harmony, it helps to explain its current appeal. The success of this tune has contributed much to the continued popularity of the opera.

Following the flute's statement of the tune, which we may call a "vow theme", the two men share it, but only once through. The delicate placing of *piano* entries and the fact that the tune is not repeated is a masterstroke, for the glimpse they had of the beautiful vision is all over in a trice, and the melody's function from here on is to remind us, usually in high violin tremolos supporting a flute, of their vow and their inability to forget or forswear the priestess. The posthumous version of the opera normally adopted today that recapitulates the big tune at the end of the scene misses the point that the tune, like the goddess, should be tantalisingly beyond reach. What Bizet actually wrote next is a duet in which the two men confirm their promise of eternal friendship and loyalty in waltz-like music that is stronger in its middle section than in the rather conventional main refrain.[35]

The recitative that follows replaced more dialogue in which Zurga explained the pearl fishermen's ritual by which a young girl is brought each year from a distant land to preside over the fishermen's fortunes and keep away evil by singing and praying all night on a rock overlooking the shore. The dialogue/recitative ends where the music recalls the Prélude, now in its pristine form played *pianissimo* by a string quartet and clearly a description of Leïla's veiled virginal beauty. The flute

---

35. This correct ending to the scene is to be heard as an Appendix on Michel Plasson's 1989 recording on EMI.

and high strings immediately tell us and Nadir, who knows, that it is *she*, the object of the two friends' vow, while the chorus ironically whisper "C'est elle!", welcoming their new priestess.

The chorus sing a pretty chorus of welcome in A major, "Sois la bienvenue", whose awkward accentuation ("Daigne ac-cepter nos présents", "Les es-prits de l'on-de") suggests that it might have been salvaged from *La Guzla de l'Émir*. Zurga recites her duties, to each of which she swears obedience. Warming to his task, Zurga explains with a certain passion (and a grand vocal flourish) that if she is faithful she will receive the finest of pearls, but if she betrays her vows the punishment will be death. Nadir gasps with horror and in that moment Leïla recognises him with an impulsive "Ah! c'est lui!" How she knows him is not explained. Nadir knows who she is, but keeps silent. Tremolo violins mark the moment with their second recall of the fateful vow theme. Zurga catches only her sudden alarm and offers her the chance to leave if she wishes. No, she affirms, she will stay and do her duty.

Originally at this point the chorus repeated their lilting chorus of welcome, but with masterly judgment Bizet replaced it with a solemn hymn to Brahma whose powerful final phrase (with the second sopranos and tenors in octaves) was taken from the *Te Deum* composed during his first year in Italy. (This piece was already in place at the end of Act II.) The crowd then disperse while Leïla is led away to her rock by the priest Nourabad (who has yet to sing), the orchestra replaying her innocent theme from the Prélude for the third time.

Zurga goes off with a group of fishermen, leaving Nadir alone. (In the original libretto, he offers Nadir a place in his tent for the night, and Nadir's private confession is spoken, not sung.) He should have confessed to Zurga, Nadir admits, that far from forgetting the vision in Kandy he has in fact been following Leïla. But love trumps guilt at this moment, for his Romance is a beautifully sentimental song in two verses, pitched high in the voice, lingering over the memory of the one and only time Nadir has seen her before. As in the Serenata in *Don Procopio* (see Example 2.1), the key of A minor and the 6/8 pulse bring out a distinctive Bizetian charm. The word-setting is this time exemplary, even if Bizet has had to invert the order of "Doux rêve" and "Folle d'ivresse" at the end of each verse to ease the phrasing at the expense of the rhyme.

Nourabad had led Leïla away purely to give Nadir the stage to himself, for now they return and she is set on her chosen rock. Behind Nourabad's brief instructions runs a superb stretch of very animated music, symphonic in feeling and hinting at the primitive instincts of the natives. It acts as a foil to the stillness and solemnity of Leïla's formal diegetic Air that follows, the song with which she has to drive away evil spirits and protect the fishermen, who can be heard in the distance singing in three parts beneath her increasingly elaborate melismata. Nadir, watching, creeps close to the rock and exclaims when she leans toward him and briefly opens her veil, "Dieu! c'est elle!"[36] Leïla and Nadir are content to feel each other's presence as the first act ends in a haze of nocturnal tranquillity.

Act II is set in the ruins of a temple surrounded by cacti and palm trees forming a different aspect of the rock on which Leïla was left at the end of the previous act. In the original dialogue at this point Nourabad instructs Leïla in her obligation to watch through the night. Her singing has brought the fishermen home safely, so she now has to pray and guard her secret identity. She knows she can keep a promise, she tells him, since long ago she rescued a fugitive from marauding Indians who, as a token of his thanks, gave her a bracelet to keep for ever. Nourabad assures her that the place is well guarded and leaves.

Recitative, beginning at "Les barques ont gagné la grève", was composed to replace this, allowing Nourabad to borrow the tune with which Zurga had explained to her the reward for good behaviour. Leïla's narration of her rescue of the fugitive is set to strongly dramatic music depicting the marauders and her solemn promise. Nourabad and the guards then leave her alone. At some point, perhaps even after the opera had opened at the Théâtre-Lyrique, the authors decided to insert a chorus before this scene, "L'ombre descend des cieux", sung off-stage at the start of the act to create a suitable atmosphere. Constantly repeated la-la-las in the basses and a tambourine provide an exotic backdrop, while two piccolos suggest the call of night-birds. The song is heard again as Nourabad leaves.

Once left alone, Leïla feels a frisson of terror yet knows instinctively that Nadir must be nearby. Her Cavatine is a full, elegant solo in a gentle 9/8 rhythm, featuring a solo horn, occasionally two, and an elaborate cadenza at the end. The middle section, which is equally carefully crafted, features a gurgling clarinet as proposed by Berlioz in his *Traité d'instrumentation*. The close over a pedal fifth F–C is particularly affecting.

A guzla is heard in the distance. It is doubtful if Cormon or Carré knew or cared what kind of instrument that was; Bizet here simulates it with an oboe, obedient to Leïla's response: "Ô chant mélodieux!" which was in the libretto but not set to music. Nadir has to put it down in order to sing his Chanson from far in the distance, accompanied by an offstage harp. The words were originally intended for David's *Lalla-Roukh*, a permissible theft since Carré was one of the librettists of that opera too.[37] Bar-lengths shifting from 9/8 to 12/8 and some vocal *agréments* enhance the oriental flavour of the music. He gets closer as he sings and suddenly he is there in full view, on the terrace beneath her rock.

---

36. In some editions of the vocal score, his words are placed *before* she opens her veil, which makes no sense.
37. See Lacombe (2001), pp. 113–114.

A long duet inevitably follows, breathless with excitement at first, then calm and sensuous, then tense as a storm gathers, leading to the disaster of discovery. Bizet's muse is in full flood. Consider the suavity of the melody that pours out of Nadir in his ecstasy (Example 3.2).

Example 3.2

The music moves to B flat minor for the slower section as Nadir sings "Ton cœur n'a pas compris le mien" to yet another ravishing tune, so alluring that Leïla starts her verse before Nadir has quite reached the end of his. The middle section moves a little faster, then the lovers join in octaves and sing the main tune in the major key with the full orchestra behind them. The librettists planned a longer build-up here, with a storm rumbling in the distance, but Bizet, or perhaps Carvalho, moved the action quickly forward. The earliest libretto has Zurga alerted by footprints near the temple and seeing a man, whom he does not recognise, with Leïla. He summons the camp and Nourabad and others run up. A second version has Nourabad, not Zurga, discover the lovers, although he gives no reason for coming to the place. In the final version, as Nadir and Leïla promise eternal devotion, with their duet melody lingering in the background, they are interrupted by a rifle-shot heard from offstage. With Nourabad's earlier appearance removed, no explanation is given that it is he who fired the shot; at all events it sends Nadir scurrying away while Nourabad comes on the scene (again) and sets off a general alert before going in pursuit of Nadir.

The chorus enter too, wondering what is going on. They are immediately aware of the breaking storm, although in their cry of "Ô nuit d'épouvante" over surging C minor figures in the orchestra they seem to be more disturbed than desperate. Nourabad returns with guards holding Nadir, and the significance of the music behind his original instructions to Leïla is now clear as it supports with some ferocity his announcement that a man has been caught in the sanctum. The chorus hurl threats at the lovers, for the priestess's broken vow will bring disaster on them all, and in a furious ensemble, which has all the feel of a cumulative finale, they call for the death of the guilty pair.

The dramatic value of holding Zurga's entrance back is now clear, for at the height of the clamour he steps boldly in and orders the crowd, as their chieftain, to desist. He tells Leïla and Nadir in a whisper to flee at once, while the flute and tremolo violins tell us that he is obeying his vow of eternal friendship with Nadir. Out of curiosity Nourabad then tears the veil from Leïla's face. Zurga recognises her and immediately turns in fury on the pair, and the chorus take up their bloodthirsty calls with even more vigour than before. Finally they all sink to their knees and repeat the hymn to Brahma from the first act.

Act III starts with a scene for Zurga alone in his tent, wracked by conflicts within himself, as many operatic baritones have been before and since. A strong Beethovenian introduction sets the scene, for he has to condemn Nadir to death even though he dearly loves him. When he begins to reflect, the ripeness of this music is unmistakeable (Example 3.3).

Example 3.3

This is a great scene for a dramatic singer. It was followed in the original libretto by the appearance of Nourabad and the fishermen, and a cabaletta for Zurga in which his inclination to spare Nadir's life is shouted down. In the opera itself his thoughtful mood at the end of the Cavatine is broken instead by the appearance of Leïla, led in by two fishermen. The shadowy vow theme is heard again in the flute and tremolo strings as memory plucks at his conscience. There is a stiff duet which they sing *à part*, as in a baroque opera, before coming to the point. She has come to plead for Nadir's life to be spared. She knows her own culpability, but Nadir has not broken the fishermen's laws and he came there, she tells him, purely by chance. By lying to save his life she persuades Zurga to think that Nadir has been faithful to their vow. But as her plea extends into a plaintive section in the dark key of E flat minor, Zurga picks up her hints that the passion is not purely on Nadir's side; she loves him, too, and pleads that a pardon for Nadir would help her confront her own death. Zurga's jealousy is violently aroused, for he too loves her, he tells her, though she cannot know why. The scene ends with conventional high-voltage operatic exchanges, Leïla swearing eternal love for Nadir, Zurga intent on ordering his death.

Nourabad enters to lead her away. As she goes out she hands a necklace to one of the fishermen standing by with the request to see that it is given to her mother. The return of the vow theme at this point, now more heavily scored, makes little sense since its origin and presumably its import is the vow that binds Nadir and Zurga. She does not know that it was Zurga who gave her the necklace, but he recognises it, snatches it, and rushes out after her as the curtain falls.

The final scene is set at a place of execution with a statue of Brahma looking on. The prisoners are due to die at dawn. Nadir is already there. This is the moment for some ballet in the form of a Chœur dansé, the dances being ritualistic and savage, the chorus singing a bloodthirsty invocation to Brahma to bless their tribal justice. Leïla is led in to the solemn tread of the music that Bizet had entitled Marche funèbre in the incomplete symphony he wrote in 1861 (see Example 3.1) and is here designated as a funeral march in the printed libretto. She rushes to Nadir's arms and they sing a rather sanctimonious hymn entrusting their souls to the divinity. Harp chords emphasise its stiffness in the manner of Gounod. The ensemble builds to a huge ending, at which point a light is seen in the distance. The crowd takes this to be the long-awaited dawn. Zurga rushes on just in time to avert the execution, telling them that it is not the dawn, it is a fire in the fishermen's camp struck by lightning. Abandoning their grim purpose, everyone rushes off to save what they can, so Zurga can cut the rope that binds Nadir and Leïla, telling them that he has deliberately set the fire. Now he tells Leïla that it was he whom she saved from his pursuers long ago and who gave her the necklace. In gratitude he will now set them free, pointing toward a safe route for their escape. After a strong "Adieu!" the lovers give us a reprise of the vow theme in octaves, while Zurga observes that he has done his duty. Whose tune is it? Once it was the men's, now it is the lovers'; in the end it can only stand for the delicate triangular relationship of Nadir, Zurga and Leïla, since Bizet was entirely free to apply it in whatever way he wished. Perhaps the question should not be asked. The curtain falls.

The opera thus has a happy ending for the lovers, while Zurga remains behind unsuspected and unpunished. Regardless of the changes imposed on the opera in posthumous revivals,[38] there were many revisions in the course of rehearsals and performances in 1863, the only performances in Bizet's lifetime. Pleasing though it would be to attribute all sensible decisions to Bizet, we cannot know whether to credit them to manager, librettists, composer, or perhaps the singers or the set designer. This was normal in those times, especially when Carvalho felt free to assert control in his own theatre. It is said that when the librettists could not think how to end the opera, Carvalho said "Just throw it in the fire", planting the idea of Zurga's fire as the device by which to free the lovers. But Eugène Cormon, one of the librettists, later regretted that they had saddled Bizet with such a "bear" of a libretto. The plot is clumsily spring-loaded with two important incidents that have happened before the curtain rises, connecting Leïla with each of the two men. Zurga was involved in both incidents, but somehow, when he was a fugitive sheltered by Leïla, he did not recognise her as the veiled girl that he and Nadir had already forsworn. If not her face, he does recognise the bracelet, which thus becomes the contrivance that turns his fury into forgiveness in the final scene.

Bizet had never embarked on such a large undertaking, and it came exactly at the time when his musical imagination was ready to take wing. The score owes a very great debt to both Gounod and David and occasionally recalls Halévy, but he here displays a richer melodic invention than before, more assured harmonic control and variety, and a sharper sense of musical phrasing, particularly in longer movements, than he had had an opportunity to exploit before. He has fully matured as a musician. *Les Pêcheurs de perles* is deservedly a popular opera today, for the deficiencies of the libretto are unimportant and the music rarely falls below a new high standard that Bizet has risen to. Some of this may have been accomplished in *La Guzla de l'Émir*, but *Les Pêcheurs de perles* at last gave him an opportunity to compose an opera with a distinctive colour and to pace the action over three acts. It was a major achievement.

★ ★ ★ ★ ★

After a fortnight's delay caused by the soprano's illness, *Les Pêcheurs de perles* opened at the Théâtre-Lyrique on Wednesday 30 September 1863, a few weeks before Bizet's twenty-fifth birthday. Leïla was sung by Léontine de Maësen, Nadir by François Morini, and Zurga by Jean-Vital Ismaël. De Maësen and Ismaël were both singing in Paris for the first time, recruited by Carvalho after promising careers in Belgium and the French provinces. De Maësen was Belgian herself. Their next assignments at the Théâtre-Lyrique were to be as Gilda and Rigoletto before the end of the year. Morini sang in *L'Enfance du Christ* in Strasbourg that June, so he

---

38. See Chapter Ten.

had worked with Bizet already. He sang for Carvalho again in *Mireille* in 1864, along with Ismaël (Berlioz reported that they both sang sharp), but whereas Ismaël's career flourished, Morini's seems to have faded soon after. Louis Deloffre, Carvalho's resident conductor, was on the podium. There is good reason to believe that in the course of rehearsals and performances Bizet became involved to some degree with his leading soprano, Léontine, a relationship that turned later into an affectionate and lasting friendship.[39]

At the end of the first performance Bizet was brought in front of the curtain by the singers to take a bow. Louis Gallet, later an accomplished librettist, remembered him as looking "rather dazed, with his head down so that we could only see a forest of thick curly fair hair on top of a round rather childlike face; this was enlivened by the glint in his eye chasing around the theatre looking both delighted and confused."[40] This action brought the fury of the press down upon his head, or at least of those members of the press who were not prepared to like his music. It has been said that only Berlioz's notice in the *Journal des débats* was positive in its admiration for what Bizet had achieved, but that is far from being the case.[41] Berlioz's endorsement was very precious: "The score of *Les Pêcheurs de perles* does M. Bizet great honour", with several other compliments, but the cadre of music critics at that time was filled with clever writers with little or no musical training who loved to cut upstart composers down to size with accusations of Wagnerism or Verdiism, which in Bizet's case were nonsense, or with an inability to sound like Rossini or Offenbach, with which Bizet would have been perfectly content. The libretto was widely condemned, but the score elicited a variety of responses, sometimes treating what we think of as a great gift, his orchestration, as "noisy" or "too colourful". One of the favourable critics was the young Emmanuel Chabrier, who learned much from Bizet.

The judgment of the public is reflected in the eighteen performances the opera received, closing on 24 November after dwindling receipts. This was better than many other new operas presented at that theatre, but fewer than the run of successes enjoyed by *La Statue* in 1861 or *Mireille* in 1864. Gounod missed the first night, being treated at the time by Dr Blanche for one of his periodic bouts of depression, but he was back in time for the second or third performance. Meyerbeer went to see it twice but made no comment. After five performances it shared the bill with Grétry's *L'Épreuve villageoise*, an opéra-comique in two acts, an arrangement that could only be achieved by drastic cutting of Bizet's score.[42] Bizet himself was

---

39. Lacombe (2000), pp. 357–358.
40. Gallet (1891), pp. 1–2.
41. For a full analysis of the opera's reception, see Lacombe (1996).
42. The list of cuts is found in Lacombe (2001), pp. 320–321.

disappointed, and the real test of success was whether an opera was revived in later years or played anywhere other than Paris. *Les Pêcheurs de perles* enjoyed neither, and it thus disappeared into a dark corner of Bizet's workroom, not to reappear for another twenty-three years. He called it an "honourable and brilliant failure, but a failure nonetheless".[43] At least the vocal score was published. In August Choudens had let it be known that he had bought the rights to the opera—before he had reached any agreement with the composer, who was quite reasonably annoyed. But Choudens did soon draw up an agreement, thus obtaining a prize that would prove golden in the distant future. Bizet himself wrote the piano reduction and saw it through the press for publication in late October or November.

By that time Carvalho had launched his second new opera of the season, Berlioz's *Les Troyens à Carthage*, which opened on 4 November. Whereas for Bizet a production at the Théâtre-Lyrique provided an enviable opportunity at the start of his career, for Berlioz to have his greatest work rejected by the Paris Opéra for which it had been intended and to be played with lamentably insufficient resources at Carvalho's theatre was an indignity that contrasted painfully with the excitement his music had aroused in Paris thirty years before. Carvalho treated him as if he were a novice, eliminating the first two of five acts and then cutting freely at the rest until all that was left was, in Berlioz's words, "a score lying dismembered in the window of a music shop like a carcass on a butcher's stall". It was a bitter experience for the senior composer, and it soured his already cantankerous opinion of Parisian music for the rest of his life. He took no further interest in the music of younger composers, not even Bizet's, we are forced to record.

Bizet wrote Reyer a long enthusiastic account of the dress rehearsal and was doubtless present at the first night. He received an intemperate letter from one Victor Chéri, in charge of music at the Variétés, suggesting, on the basis of a perceived personal insult, that he refrain from applauding Berlioz's work. Bizet took it, tongue-in-cheek no doubt, as a challenge, and replied: "Sent two seconds to V. Chéri (Nephtali Mayrargues and Ernest Guiraud). V. Chéri gave his word of honour that he had nothing to do with this dastardly action." The story is amusing for it shows Bizet for once being the calm, not the hot-headed, disputant, and being a true admirer of Berlioz, as we already knew.[44] *Les Troyens à Carthage* was barely more successful than Bizet's opera, for it came to an end on 20 December and the year ended with *Rigoletto* in French at the Théâtre-Lyrique, setting out on its triumphal run hand in hand with another revival of *Faust*. Bizet's three principal singers were now otherwise employed.

---

43. Imbert (1894), p. 162.
44. The story was first told by Curtiss (1958), p. 144.

CHAPTER FOUR

1864–1865: Ivan IV

APOLEON III'S SUCCESSES IN THE CRIMEAN WAR AND IN HIS ITALIAN CAMPAIGN IN 1859 reinforced his taste for military adventures abroad, a weakness that would eventually bring the Second Empire to a humiliating end. But in the early 1860s Parisians were more inclined to take note of the country's continuing prosperity at home and of the partial relaxation of the Emperor's authoritarian rule than of attempts to expand French influence in distant lands, so long as they were not actually unsuccessful. This is when France took control of Cochin-China, for example. It was in 1862 that the Emperor began interfering in Mexican politics, almost immediately facing military defeat at the hands of General Zaragoza on the Fifth of May. For the next five years the French had to contend with stubborn guerilla resistance against the Emperor Maximilian I, brother of the Austrian Emperor Franz Josef, imposed on the Mexicans by Napoleon III. Even less interesting to Parisians amid these faraway events was the American Civil War, whose blood-soaked course continued through 1864 with the Confederacy, which Napoleon supported, gradually losing ground to Union forces and finally surrendering in April 1865.

On 6 January 1864 the Emperor signed a decree granting an end to the special privileges enjoyed by the main Parisian theatres. These were in effect restrictions on other theatres that had been imposed in 1807 by the first Napoleon and had been widely circumvented by clever managers, at the Théâtre-Lyrique and the Bouffes-Parisiens among others. In practice the Opéra and the Opéra-Comique continued to present much the same repertoire as before, although the enforcement of dialogue at the latter theatre was gradually overlooked. Other theatres and other companies now attempted to present opera, as, for example, the upstart Grand Théâtre Parisien, which in October 1865 staged a five-act opera about Joan of Arc composed by the great tenor Gilbert Duprez. The Bouffes-Parisiens reopened after some major rebuilding and continued to mount Offenbach's flow of operettas despite his recurrent disputes with the theatre's management.

Opera remained the focus of Bizet's ambitions. If *Les Pêcheurs de perles* felt to him like a failure, it was successful in one important respect. In a letter of 1867 to a Belgian correspondent he recounted that "the fate of my poor *Pêcheurs* was not brilliant enough to extend my reputation beyond the city limits….Carvalho immediately commissioned an *Ivan IV* in five acts."[1] It is important to quote these autobiographical words, so rare from Bizet, because they have consistently been disregarded by Bizet's biographers ever since Winton Dean put forward the notion that *Ivan IV* was proposed and started in 1862 after discussions with Gounod in Baden-Baden and that there were two versions of the opera.[2] This theory has been endorsed by Robert, Stricker, Lacombe and Wright.[3] In fact there is no known document that links this opera with Bizet earlier than 10 March 1864 when *Le Figaro* announced that Bizet's *Yvan le Terrible* would be staged at the Théâtre-Lyrique after Gounod's *Mireille*, which was then in rehearsal. If, as Bizet said, *Ivan* was commissioned immediately after *Les Pêcheurs de perles,* that is, in about December 1863, he would have set to work at once since Carvalho would have had a slot in mind at the end of the 1863–64 season. Bizet was given a libretto which had been for some years on Gounod's desk but not renounced by him until 6 June 1863, at a point when he, Gounod, was fully absorbed in the composition of *Mireille* and Bizet in *Les Pêcheurs de perles.*

The libretto—which concerns the marriage of Ivan IV, first tsar of Russia, widely known as Ivan the Terrible, to his second wife Maria Temryukova in 1561—was by François-Hippolyte Leroy, actor and stage manager at the Opéra, and Henri Trianon, translator, librarian and prolific author of librettos. They had previously collaborated on the ballet *Orfa* by Adam in 1852, and in 1855 Crosnier, Director of the Opéra, gave their new piece to Gounod who probably set to work at once. In November 1857 he played through what he had written to Royer, the new Director of the Opéra, but the latter took alarm at a story that includes a conspiracy against an emperor and turned it down, wisely perhaps, in view of Orsini's assassination attempt a few months later. Gounod moved on to *Le Médecin malgré lui* and *Faust* instead. At the suggestion of his old friend Ingres, Gounod transferred a chorus of Cossacks into *Faust* as the now famous Soldiers' Chorus. He also drew on his unfinished *Iwan le terrible* for the Queen's March in *La Reine de Saba* and the Shepherd's Song in *Mireille*.[4]

1. Malherbe (1951), p. 50.
2. Dean (1955).
3. Robert (1965); Stricker (1999), p. 79; Lacombe (2000), pp. 325, 327; Wright (2005).
4. The history of Gounod's *Iwan le terrible* is given in Condé (2009), pp. 464–465.

For Carvalho to entrust this libretto to Bizet was a bold step since it was designed for the Opéra with its grand historical setting and five acts. By far the greatest part of the Théâtre-Lyrique's repertoire was made up of operas in one, two or three acts. Four acts were rare (*Figaro, Rigoletto*), and so were five (*Faust, Mireille,* and Semet's *Gil Blas*). Even though Bizet must by now have been aware of the blend of wild optimism and artistic butchery that Carvalho thrived on, he would have been foolish not to take up this new offer. From a surviving manuscript copy of the libretto, heavily worked on, it is clear that he collaborated functionally with the librettists, although the basic outline is not too different from Gounod's.[5]

While Bizet's work on *Ivan IV* went steadily ahead, Gounod's *Mireille* was being rehearsed. For a run-through in Gounod's house Bizet and Saint-Saëns provided the accompaniment on piano and harmonium. The opera's opening at the Théâtre-Lyrique on 19 March 1864 was an important date in the social calendar, such was Gounod's *réclame*. "Duchesses, baronesses and bankers were all contending for the best boxes," reported the *Musical World*, "and if tickets could have been auctioned the direction would have recovered part of its expenses from that very first evening." But the opera's reception was mixed; it had a total of thirty performances that year, with eleven more in 1865, by which time Gounod had begun an extensive series of revisions, including the provision of recitative to replace the original dialogue. Bizet's Nadir, François Morini, was the country boy Vincent, while the role of Mireille, originally intended for Léontine de Maësen, was sung by Carvalho's wife, Mme Miolan-Carvalho, now established as the definitive Marguerite in revivals of *Faust* and causing swoons with the brilliance of her coloratura.

Bizet was involved in preparing much of the material; a letter of January 1864 from Gounod to Choudens reported sending the overture to Bizet, presumably for reduction, so he may have made the piano reduction for the vocal score even though no arranger was named in the published version, and he was probably acting as rehearsal pianist. He would certainly have been eager to get to know the music, which exploited the regional exoticism of Provence since the epic poem on which it was based, *Mirèio*, was written in the Provençal language (published with a parallel translation in French) by Frédéric Mistral. Carré supplied the libretto. Gounod had spent many weeks the previous year in Provence in order to capture a genuine sense of locale in the music, which contributed in no small way to the ultimate success of the opera. There is much that Bizet would have admired, for the locations are not the faraway Ruritanian setting of most operas but a distinctive area of France that many Parisians knew. Bizet had been there himself en route to Italy, and he would have had *Mireille* vividly in mind when he composed the music for *L'Arlésienne* eight years later. The stamping Farandole and the shapely Chanson de

---

5. The libretto is at F-Pn Th.B. 4849(1).

Magali have a strongly local character, and the bull-tamer Ourrias is a prototype of the bull-fighter Escamillo, especially when his *couplets* "Si les filles d'Arles sont reines" are compared with the much better known Toreador's Song. Bizet would have been far less taken by the plot's reliance on sorcery or by the sanctimonious flavour of the opera, and we may guess that its closing scene, when Mireille is received into celestial bliss in an ecstasy of devotion, would have horrified him. Backstage the opera was nicknamed *Mirieleison*.

Shortly before the opening of *Mireille*, on 14 March, the elderly Rossini, who composed very little in his later years, brought out his *Petite messe solennelle*, which turned out to be neither *petite* nor very *solennelle*. He called it "a mortal sin of my old age". It was given before a very select audience at the home of the Comtesse Pillet-Will in its original version for twelve singers, two pianos and harmonium. Meyerbeer, Auber and Thomas were there, but not, apparently, Gounod. To the second performance a larger audience was admitted, still by invitation only. If Bizet ever had the chance to hear this disarmingly appealing work, he would have preferred its light-hearted treatment of the sacred text to Gounod's cloying religiosity in *Mireille*. In any case he had long been a great admirer of Rossini's music. Rossini and his French second wife Olympe usually spent the summer in their villa in Passy, one of the newest and smartest *quartiers* of Paris, and the winter in a huge apartment at the foot of the Rue de la Chaussée d'Antin, close to the Boulevard des Italiens, the Opéra and his favourite restaurants. Invitations to their Friday night salons there were greatly sought after, but whether Bizet ever played for the old maestro is an unanswered question.

On 2 May 1864 Paris was transfixed by the dramatic news, "Meyerbeer n'est plus!" It is hard for us now to grasp the centrality of Meyerbeer in French music of the mid-nineteenth century and the overwhelming sense of loss his death brought about. No composer had so effortlessly commanded the loyalty of the French public for over thirty years or aroused such interest in his every move. He was adept at winning the press to his side, but it was a genuine fear of failure, not calculation, that kept him from releasing his later works until he was completely satisfied with the compositions themselves and with the singers and the production they would be assigned. *Le Prophète* had been in gestation for a dozen years before its triumphant première in 1849, and *L'Africaine*, the subject of excited anticipation for well over twenty years, had only recently been delivered to the Opéra when the composer died. Indeed he had been supervising preliminary rehearsals up to his last few days.

Meyerbeer was a chronic hypochondriac and his fear of being buried alive was so great that he gave instructions that his body should remain unmoved for four days before being prepared for burial, in contravention of Jewish practice. So on 6 May the hearse drawn by six horses moved from his apartment near the Champs-Élysées to the Gard du Nord whose almost new facade had been heavily draped in black for a ceremony of farewell in which all the highest dignitaries of French culture took part. The eulogies outdid each other in superlatives, and the funeral train then set off for Berlin, where he was buried in the Jewish Cemetery. It was a cliché of the day to raise Meyerbeer to the same level of genius as Aeschylus, Dante, Michelangelo and Beethoven, no less.[6]

Carvalho's plans for the end of the 1863–64 season fell into confusion. It must have been obvious that *Ivan IV* was not going to be ready. Another project was a libretto by the faithful Carré, *L'Esclave*, with music by Félicien David. This was to alternate with the Paris première of Reyer's *Érostrate*, but neither opera was played, *L'Esclave* because it was withdrawn at the last minute with everyone's agreement and *Érostrate* for unknown reasons. So following the success of *Rigoletto* Carvalho decided to put on Donizetti's *Don Pasquale*, then replaced it at the last minute with a distinctly under-rehearsed *Norma*, by Bellini, with de Maësen singing Adalgise.

Assuming that Bizet had any time left over from working on his score and running between rehearsals, he would have been anxious to hear the one-act *Le Docteur Magnus* at the Opéra in March, since the librettists were Cormon and Carré, the pair responsible for *Les Pêcheurs de perles*. The composer was Ernest Boulanger, later in old age to father two brilliant daughters, Nadia and Lili. He would have been equally eager to see Maillart's three-act *Lara*, based on Byron's poem, at the Opéra-Comique because that too was written by Cormon and Carré. Galli-Marié was singing the leading female role, with unusual energy, it seems, since she twice had accidents on stage, in one case falling through an inadvertently opened trapdoor. In May Bizet's friend Guiraud, back from his sojourn in Rome, had a one-act piece, *Sylvie*, played at the Opéra-Comique. Of this work Félix Clément wrote: "It's said that former Prix de Rome winners have access to a store piled high with inoffensive patched-up librettos written in ink of easy virtue, poorly concealing their age, like a theatre wardrobe full of old costumes which can quickly be brushed down and thrown at the singers. Poor unwanted prize-winners! They wait fearlessly, they wait for ages, if not for ever, and in their starved state accept the crumbs so generously thrown down for them."[7] Bizet had not been so lucky. In fact Guiraud had been promised this opportunity when as a Conservatoire student he played the timpani at that theatre. The libretto was indeed absurd and the opera short-lived.

During that summer of 1864 Bizet and his father took possession of two cottages at Le Vésinet, a community about ten miles west of Paris situated in the embrace of one of the Seine's many loops. The recent arrival of a train service greatly enhanced the value and utility of this attractively wooded area, and it was being

---

6. For example Blaze de Bury (1865), p. 181.
7. Clément (1877), p. 644.

rapidly developed into the suburb that it is today. Adolphe Bizet bought a plot at 10 Route des Cultures in October 1863 and had two cottages built side by side, divided by a garden. Georges must have contributed to this plan since it closely matches his dream of together-but-separate living quarters that he had outlined in letters to his mother before he returned from Italy. The front was a row of railings, while behind were a lawn, a shrubbery, and a vegetable garden in which Adolphe liked to work. In the right-hand cottage was Adolphe's bedroom, dining room and kitchen; on the left was Georges's study with the piano, three chairs, a table, a small cupboard and a bust of Halévy, with his bed behind a partition. This was to be his modest haven in many summers to come where he could work in peace and to which his friends would be invited for music-making, walking along the river and talking.[8]

At the end of July the *Revue et gazette musicale* confirmed that Bizet was at work on *Ivan IV* for the Théâtre-Lyrique. Perhaps Carvalho's enthusiasm was waning, for he started to work at the same time on an opera called *La Prêtresse*, whose origins and history remain, like many of Bizet's unwritten and unfinished works, cloaked in mystery. It was intended for the Baden-Baden festival of 1865 and its librettist was Philippe Gille, a prolific librettist for Delibes, Lecocq and others; Gille worked as secretary for Carvalho at the Théâtre-Lyrique and also wrote a regular column in *Le Figaro*. The only surviving fragment of this work, a fifty-four-bar sketch for soprano and accompaniment, is a hymn of love addressed to Phoebus, which suggests that it might have been based on a classical myth like Reyer's *Érostrate* or Gounod's *Philémon et Baucis*.[9] In an undated letter to Gille Bizet wrote: "I'd like to finish *Ivan* and *La Prêtresse*, that's to say for February and August 65." In another he wrote, "What's happening with *La Prêtresse* I would like to know.... The orchestration of my *Ivan* is almost finished and this is the moment to finish *La Prêtresse*."[10]

The chronology is slightly clarified by a report in the *Revue et gazette musicale* of 20 November 1864: "We learn that, following a recent decision, French opera will not be included in future Baden-Baden programmes. In succession to [the French composers who had been played there, listed] there were to be works by Léo Delibes, G. Bizet [and six others] which seemed to be assured of as great a success as theirs." No further work on *La Prêtresse* would be required after such a decision, so the idea was dropped. Bizet later discussed with Gille the idea of an opera on the Borgias and worked with him also on *Clarisse Harlowe*, although none of these plans came to fruition.

So he kept going at *Ivan IV* with the expectation of a production in February 1865. In October Gounod wrote to Hébert: "Lo Bizetto del Vezinetto: he's still

---

8. Descriptions of the house are found in Galabert (1909), pp. 6–7, and in Marix (1938), p. 146.
9. The sketch is in a private collection; a copy is found at US-NYp (Mina Curtiss papers).
10. The correspondence with Gille is at F-Pmlm.

working on his *Ivano quarto, ossia il terribile !!!*"[11] Carvalho found that Italian opera brought in the crowds more effectively than French, so he put on *Don Pasquale* and *La traviata*, both sung in French and both stolen from the current repertoire of the Théâtre-Italien, where Adelina Patti was all the rage. In *La traviata* he introduced a new star, the Swedish soprano Christine Nilsson at the outset of her career. Still preferring old or foreign operas he staged the *Magic Flute* in French with Nilsson singing the Queen of the Night and sets recycled from *Les Pêcheurs de perles* and *Les Troyens à Carthage*. This was followed by the French première of Verdi's *Macbeth*, for which Verdi at Carvalho's request introduced a number of substantial changes to his 1847 opera, including a ballet. Ismaël sang the title role. With only fourteen performances it was regarded as a failure, to Verdi's chagrin. He did not attend in person. One French critic enraged him by observing that he did not understand Shakespeare, which made him even more mistrustful of Parisian music than he already was after his experience with *Les Vêpres siciliennes* in 1855. The only substantial French work introduced by Carvalho in the 1864–65 season was *L'Aventurier* by Prince Poniatowski—senator, aristocrat, and singer—whose four-act *Pierre de Médicis* had been staged at the Opéra in 1860. The first night, attended by Paris's high society, even brought out Rossini, who hardly ever went to anything, but the opera did not survive beyond ten performances, partly because its Mexican setting struck a sensitive nerve in political circles. Throughout the season Carvalho must have been prevaricating with Bizet about when *Ivan IV* would be staged.

In any case the Théâtre-Lyrique could not hope to compete with the Opéra when Meyerbeer's *L'Africaine* opened after nearly thirty years of speculation from critics and public. Its first night, 28 April 1865, was exactly a week after that of *Macbeth*. No Parisian could afford not to see it, especially with its sensational sets, one of which presented an ocean-going ship in cross-section. With *Ivan IV* on his desk Bizet would have had many reasons to see Meyerbeer's final opera: the leading soprano was Marie Sasse, whom he had coached for *Érostrate* in 1862, and the main character is Vasco da Gama, whose story was the subject of his own "ode-symphonie" of 1859. Geographical precision was not the opera's main strength, for although much of the action takes place in Africa, the slave Sélika herself appears to come from Madagascar and the gods invoked are definitely Indian. Within a year *L'Africaine* attained its hundredth performance at the Opéra and was staged in ten foreign cities. With success on that scale, the grand opera formula as perfected by Scribe and Meyerbeer must have seemed to any ambitious French composer exactly the right model to adopt.

The summer of 1865 came round with no certain prospects for Bizet's own grand opera. We are fortunate that a figure entered Bizet's life at this time who has

---

11. Lacombe (2000), p. 327.

left us correspondence and reports that greatly enhance our picture of the composer in the next three years,[12] in sharp contrast to the years immediately after his return from Italy, for which we have little information other than what was publicly circulated. Edmond Galabert was the young son of a wine grower in Montauban, in southwest France, who aspired to become a musician, perhaps a composer. From 1865 at least until 1870 he came to Paris for a month every summer to study with Bizet, to whom he was introduced by one of Adolphe Bizet's pupils named Lécuyer. Some of this instruction was conducted in person and some by correspondence, which reveals much about Bizet's methods as a teacher. Like Halévy, he gave his pupil basic contrapuntal exercises so he could learn harmony and part-writing, and also had him set Prix de Rome texts from earlier years, starting with the 1859 text whose setting by Guiraud was the winner in that year. Galabert admired Bizet and possessed a mild and patient temperament. Bizet evidently refused a fee for his teaching, but he did accept deliveries of wine in lieu. Guiraud, Galabert, and Bizet became a group of friends who met when they could in Paris or Le Vésinet, with Guiraud also contributing to Galabert's education and also partaking of the wine.

With *Ivan IV* mostly complete Bizet turned his attention to other works. Galabert was with Bizet in Le Vésinet that year when another visitor was Ernest Dubreuil, a minor dramatist and librettist, who came to discuss a possible project on the subject of Nicolas Flamel, the fourteenth-century writer and teacher who amassed a considerable fortune from, according to legend, his successful practice of alchemy. This opera was never written, probably never started, and the libretto was later set by one of Bizet's fellow-students at the Conservatoire, Edmond-Marie Chérouvrier. It was perhaps ironic that an opera by Chérouvrier to a libretto by Dubreuil, *Le Roi des mines*, opened Carvalho's 1865–66 season at the Théâtre-Lyrique. It survived only five performances.

Galabert also recalled that Bizet was invited that year to compose a piece for a Belgian choral festival. He could not remember the city from which the invitation came, and it appears that by 1867 Bizet was acquainted with choral societies in Brussels, Antwerp and Liège.[13] On the other hand Galabert may have been thinking of Cambrai, which, though close to Belgium, is in France and which Bizet visited on 20 August 1865 as a member of a twenty-five-man jury judging choruses, wind bands and brass bands from all over Belgium and northern France. His mother and uncle were brought up in Cambrai, and it was reported that Delsarte apparently, though improbably, took Bizet on more than one occasion to visit the Benedictine Abbey at Solesmes nearby.[14] The work, *Saint-Jean de Pathmos*, was a setting for

12. These were published as Galabert (1877) and Galabert (1909).
13. Imbert (1894), p. 176.
14. François Semaille, *Comœdia*, 3 April 1925.

unaccompanied male voices of a visionary passage from Victor Hugo's *Contemplations* putting words in the mouth of St. John of Patmos, author of the book of Revelation. The opening is impressive (Example 4.1). The piece's 233 unaccompanied bars would put a severe strain on any but the most accomplished male-voice choirs, for it modulates freely and includes a severe fugue in the middle on the words "Continuez, grands, petits, jeunes, vieux" as if prompted by his schoolwork with Galabert. When the end recapitulates the opening section, St. John's vision seems to close down rather than open up, as if Bizet were responding more to the demands of the musical structure than to those of the text.

Example 4.1

Choudens published a Bizet song that summer, his first for many years and the start of a steady stream of song-writing. The "Vieille Chanson" has proved to be one of his most popular. It was evidently at the centre of some playful teasing. There are two autographs, the first inscribed: "Words by Millevoye, music by Alfred de Neufchâtel (1807) collected and arranged for the taste of the day by Gaston de Betzi!... (1839), recovered and offered to Madame Carvalho." Alfred Neufchâtel (1807) might be an allusion to Alfred-Émilien, Comte de Nieuwerkerke, born in 1811, at whose salon Bizet frequently played, while Gaston de Betzi (1839) is clearly an anagrammed version of himself, although he was born in 1838. He was later to take this version of his name as his pseudonym when one was needed. Most probably he accompanied Madame Carvalho in this song, whose published version is dedicated to her. The charming pastoral tale by the Empire poet Millevoye is delightfully told, with some warblings and trills for Madame Carvalho in the middle to depict the little bird that escapes its cage.

Bizet also undertook what turned out to be an enormous project for the publisher Heugel. In September 1865 Heugel's house journal, *Le Ménestrel*, announced the appearance of a set of twenty-four Italian opera arias transcribed by Bizet for piano under the general title *Le Pianiste chanteur*. These were intended as preliminary study before going on to *L'Art du chant appliqué au Piano: transcriptions des célèbres œuvres des grands maîtres*, twenty-four pieces of vocal music transcribed by the famous virtuoso Sigismund Thalberg for solo piano and published between 1853 and 1863. Hence its generic title *Introduction à l'art du chant de S. Thalberg*. Bizet's transcriptions are anything but simple, in many cases. He selected the pieces himself mostly from familiar operas by Rossini and Bellini with a few by Cimarosa and Paisiello and one Italian duet by Lully. By November the set had increased to twenty-five pieces. Whether or not Bizet knew how extensive the undertaking would be, it eventually ended up by the end of 1866 as six series of twenty-five transcriptions each, two Italian, two French, and two German, a total of 150 pieces filling over seven hundred pages. The French series included little-known pieces by Grétry, Dalayrac and other eighteenth-century composers, and the German series included Mozart, Weber and Schubert.

No. 43 in the French series was the "Ave Maria" by Gounod, his famous melody superimposed on the first Prelude from Bach's *Das Wohltemperirte Clavier*, which first appeared for piano, violin and organ in 1853. The words of the Ave Maria were added in 1859, a copy of which Gounod presented to Bizet in that year.[15] Bizet's transcription for solo piano is plain and straightforward, but Heugel at the same time published a separate arrangement by Bizet which is grand and extravagant. Later still, in response to the piece's unstoppable popularity, Bizet arranged it for four hands.

Perhaps he found it congenial or profitable to work for Heugel, for there was more in the same vein. Thalberg's *L'Art du chant appliqué au piano*, op. 70, had been published by Heugel in 1853 in two series, comprising twelve pieces. A simplified edition and a piano duet version of the first two series were made in 1856 by the legendary Carl Czerny, who died the next year. This was followed in about 1862–63 by two more series comprising a further twelve pieces, and it was these that Bizet was engaged to simplify for piano solo in a similar manner and to arrange for piano duet. The solo set appeared in 1867–68 and the piano duet version a year later.

In July 1865 *Le Ménestrel* announced that a work by Bizet would be featured in the coming season at the Théâtre-Lyrique. Carvalho was still giving him hope. In December the theatre found itself with a new hit on its hands—Flotow's *Martha* with Nilsson—but by this time Bizet, after endless promises not kept, had lost patience with Carvalho. He decided to approach the theatre that was, after all, better equipped to present *Ivan IV* than any other: the Opéra. Even with *L'Africaine* drawing the crowds, that theatre was always on the lookout for good grand operas. Their mechanism for selecting works for acceptance set the quality of the music low on their list of priorities, for they judged new works first by the "poème", then by the reputation of the librettists and composer, with good connections in high places an important element in their discussions. Bizet might have invoked the Princesse Mathilde; in fact he had a friend in Adrien-Théodore Benoît-Champy

---

15. F-PnVm7 61056(3)A.

(1805–72), lawyer and politician, who served in the Assemblée after 1848 and since 1856 had been Président du Tribunal Civil de la Seine. It was little help to call on Gounod, since his record at the Opéra was dismal, and Halévy was not there to help him. His own reputation rested thinly on one not very successful production at the Théâtre-Lyrique. Of the librettists neither Leroy nor Trianon carried much weight in such circles (Leroy worked at the Opéra, but only as a stage manager), and the director, Perrin, though thoroughly familiar with the intricacies of Parisian opera, had many competing interests to hold in balance. He received Bizet's proposal politely, but his recommendation to the ministry that gave their subvention was not favourable. Camille Doucet, in the Ministry of Fine Arts, wrote to his Minister on 11 December:

> This work [*Ivan IV*] has been accepted at the Théâtre-Lyrique and will perhaps be played there before the end of the theatrical season (June 1866). M. Bizet is now thinking that he would have a chance of seeing his work played earlier and in better circumstance if he took it to the Opéra. This is what M. Benoit-Champy told me this morning. M. Bizet is wrong. The Opéra has works by Verdi and others and some ballets which will keep them busy even beyond 1866. I would add that this *Ivan IV*, because of its subject, has more chance of success at the Théâtre-Lyrique than at the Opéra. To make his début at the Opéra M. Bizet, being still young, would need a work that offered more guarantees of success there. With *Ivan IV* he would probably succeed at the Théâtre-Lyrique; at the Opéra he would run the risk of failure. I have spoken to M. Perrin and that is what he advises; he is not inclined to set up a rivalry with the Théâtre-Lyrique that would be damaging for the Opéra and for the young composer who will be able to present himself on that stage at a later date with more certain armament and in more favourable circumstances.[16]

The language is the unmistakable jargon of the bureaucrat unburdening himself of a problem he has no wish to deal with. Berlioz had faced the same stony rejection at the Opéra with *Les Troyens*. Verdi's *Don Carlos* was in the works, but "other works and some ballets" in prospect should not have precluded a closer look at *Ivan IV*. If the Théâtre-Lyrique had really undertaken to mount the opera before the end of the season Bizet would not have had to approach the Opéra at all. But to argue that the work was better suited to a different theatre shows only that Doucet (and perhaps Perrin) had not looked at it closely. If they had, they would probably have raised the question of whether a conspiracy to murder the tsar would be acceptable to the imperial censors, the problem that had caused Royer to reject the libretto in 1857. Bizet's problem is deemed to be his age, not his music, which he was not even asked to play through.

16. F-Pn n.a.fr. 14346 f. 34–35.

A curious feature of *Ivan IV* is the scoring of the offstage band required in the third act. The large number of extra brass, including saxhorns, seems to be designed for the resources of the Opéra, whose repertoire since Niedermeyer's *Robert Bruce*, played in 1846, had repeatedly called on the assistance of Adolphe Sax and his new range of brass instruments. The presence of saxhorns in *Les Troyens* is a clear indication that Berlioz had the Opéra in mind for his great epic. When it came to trimming that work for the Théâtre-Lyrique in 1863, the saxhorns were deleted. Then Carvalho had let it be known that Sax instruments would be heard at the Théâtre-Lyrique for the first time in *Macbeth* in March 1865, and perhaps they were, in which case Bizet could have scored for them while still expecting his opera to be mounted by Carvalho. Otherwise he must have revised his score in order to bring it into line with the Opéra's noisier repertoire.

Any adjustments he made to enhance the work's appeal to the Opéra were in vain: the 936 pages of *Ivan IV* joined *Don Procopio* and *Les Pêcheurs de crevettes* (Shrimp Catchers), as he now called it,[17] on that high shelf of unwanted operas.

★ ★ ★ ★ ★

The reader should be warned that no printed score of *Ivan IV* presents the opera as Bizet wrote it, while recordings and revivals have been incomplete and rare.[18] It is nonetheless a work of considerable merit that was never given the chance that all operas need: to be worked on and heard in the theatre. It is Bizet's longest work, and though not quite complete, it can be compared to the best grand operas of its time within the conventions with which Bizet was thoroughly familiar in the works of Meyerbeer, Halévy, Gounod, Verdi and others.

When the first wife of Ivan IV of Russia died in 1560, he took as his second wife Maria Temryukovna, daughter of a Muslim prince from the Caucasus. The opening scene of the opera, which has no overture, shows the seventeen-year-old Marie with a chorus of Caucasian girls drawing water in preparation for the hunters' return. Of all the female choruses that open operas of this kind, this is one of the most enchantingly beautiful, reminiscent of the Nadir-Zurga duet in *Les Pêcheurs de perles* in its steady harmonic progressions, as if Bizet were intent on throwing one of his finest pearls to the audience at the start. Caucasians, they proudly sing next, are children of the sun, to a tune close to Gounod's "Chanson de Magali".

A young Bulgar (sung by a soprano) appears. He was following his master but got lost in the mountain mist. Marie tenderly invites him to stay till the next day, and they join in a duet of delicious elegance, the two sopranos bouncing phrases off

---

17. Undated letter to Choudens, copy at F-Po, p. 61.

18. For the posthumous history of *Ivan IV*, see Chapter 10. Some of the material missing from the printed scores may be found in Wright (1981).

each other like love-birds (with a duet cadenza!). The style suggests Meyerbeer, who had a similarly deft touch with duets of this kind, and the music reappeared in the Prélude to *La Jolie Fille de Perth* a year or two later.

A stranger enters supported by *pesante* scoring: he is obviously a figure of some importance (Example 4.2). The young Bulgar recognises him as his master but is hurriedly told not to reveal who he is. Marie invites him to drink at the well, which he does to a strong, almost too strong, melody in the clarinet, then strings. When he thanks Marie by giving her a flower, however, he adopts the gentle ostinato (by *Philémon et Baucis*, out of *Les Pêcheurs de perles*) in the violas that had introduced Leïla in the earlier opera. The two men leave while Marie tries to contain her excited response to the stranger, while the girls reprise their lovely opening chorus—as the operatic convention for opening scenes required.

Example 4.2

A solo cello recitative introduces Temrouk, Marie's father. She welcomes him with infinite grace, but his mood is sour. A Caucasian runs in with news that the Russians are near. With fearful threats a Russian officer demands that Temrouk hand over his daughter, on the orders of the Tsar. The Caucasians are gripped by horror (a slow 12/8, the convention, superbly done), and when Temrouk starts to defy the officer Marie rushes forward to give herself up. After a short hectic ensemble, she is led away.

The next scene is a powerful lament for Temrouk supported by the old men of the tribe in a solemn unison, "Ah! c'en est fait", after which the hunting party, which includes Temrouk's son Igor, returns only to learn that the Russians have abducted Marie. Igor reacts with a defiant call to arms, and the men are about to leave to rescue her when Temrouk reminds them that they must obey the word of Allah. They have to draw lots for who is to be sent to win her back, and the men's choral invocation to Allah over a throbbing inner pedal is a passage of great power, only twelve bars long, but conveying a rare intensity. It is Igor's ring that is drawn out of the cap, so he is chosen for the great task. A vigorous chorus and an echo of *Lohengrin*'s Act III Prelude brings down the curtain.

Act II takes us to Moscow, where the boyars are celebrating a Russian victory over the Tartars. A sombre roll of drums from outside disturbs their mood, but Tsar Ivan enters to explain that the sound simply indicates that justice is being done—nothing to be alarmed by. The three-octave-deep extension of Example 4.2 tells us what we have probably guessed: that the stranger in the Caucasus was the Tsar himself, although why he was there in the company of a young Bulgar we are not told. Victims of his justice are heard pleading for their lives, but there is no reprieve. Yorloff, Ivan's right-hand man, enters to report the executions. Ivan then turns to the young Bulgar and bids him sing a song from his homeland. This is where Gounod, in his version, wrote a tune that he recycled as a shepherd's song in *Mireille*, and it is where Bizet recycled a tune from *Vasco de Gama*, there called a Boléro but here called a Serenade, with new words. As "Ouvre ton cœur" this song has enjoyed some currency outside the context of the opera, especially as a striking foretaste of *Carmen*. The tambourine adds to the Spanish flavour.

Ivan dismisses this as effeminate entertainment and offers a more manly Cossack song, of which three versions exist.[19] The first suggests the stamping of heavy Russian boots, or perhaps Mephistopheles's blasphemous song in *Faust*; the second has some contrast and even tenderness, and the third is set as two identical verses with several shifts of tempo and key. All have hearty interventions from the chorus, and each version is a little shorter than the previous one.

Ivan announces that he intends to select a suitable bride for himself, and a parade of feminine beauty, with all the women veiled, comes in to a seductive melody on the flute. Yorloff mutters that if his daughter is not chosen, woe betide the Tsar! In a gentle 6/8 and the key of A minor (a combination with a special resonance for Bizet) the girls lament their far-distant homeland. The Tsar orders them to unveil, but Marie recognises the voice as that of the stranger she met before, and the melody that accompanied the drink she gave him is heard in the orchestra. She insists that as the daughter of a prince she cannot appear unveiled before the assembly. With a defiant challenge to his authority she declares that his infamous cruelty is an offence to his God. Amid the uproar this causes she unveils, to the consternation of the Tsar, since she, he realises, was the girl he had fallen in love with in the Caucasus, while she reluctantly admits she had felt the same. Four cellos encapsulate the tension of the moment, and Marie leads off with a marvellous cantilena worthy of Verdi, full of longing for her family and her homeland, and a great ensemble grows out of it, rich in harmony and passionate expression.

The Tsar now offers Marie the throne beside him. Yorloff is furious. So too is Marie, refusing ever to marry him. Ivan orders her to be taken to the Tsar's chambers. At that moment Ivan's sister Olga appears with a group of nuns suavely invoking the Virgin to the sound of the organ, as if this were a Gounod opera. She takes Marie under her wing, and when Ivan attempts to grab her back Olga defies him by brandishing a crucifix; the full ensemble takes up the nuns' chant, which might be banal were it not for the thrilling climax Bizet builds up, joined at the close by the organ.

19. The first two versions were published in Wright (1981), pp. 403–436.

Act III is set in the Kremlin's grand square where the people are vigorously celebrating to a Chœur dansé in waltz time, drenched in intriguing orchestral detail. A herald announces that the Tsar is about to present his new queen for coronation. The stand-off at the end of the last act has evidently been resolved, for, willingly or not, Marie has agreed to be his wife. The grand procession, using plenty of extra brass, passes into the cathedral. Marie's brother Igor appears, gloomy at his poor prospects of getting close enough to the Tsar to assassinate him. He hears a voice nearby which turns out to belong to his father Temrouk, whom he believed to be home in the Caucasus.

They break into a joyous duet whose rhythms too faithfully reflect the jaunty metre of the verse, but the main section is short with a stirring close. Temrouk had been eight months without news of his children, so he and the others whose daughters had been taken resolved to set off for Moscow themselves. The account of his arrival is coloured by the orchestra as if they had reached the Holy City itself. Igor in turn recounts his journey and his privations before reaching, again gloriously, the Kremlin. The jaunty duet is reprised.

Yorloff, who should perhaps have been attending the ceremony in the cathedral, then appears, accompanied by sinister orchestration and a gloomy theme on the cellos that Winton Dean has with good reason compared to Sparafucile's music in *Rigoletto*. Igor rather rashly tells Yorloff that he is seeking vengeance against the Tsar for the abduction of his sister. Yorloff's reply is a masterly repeat of the sinister background music in the lower instruments, rising to a climax as he reveals his own ambitions for his daughter and his rage that she was passed over in the Tsar's selection. "Why have you not already killed him?" asks Igor. In the brisk trio that follows, Yorloff lays out his plan to kill both Tsar and Tsarina that very night, a plot both Igor and Temrouk accept, still unaware that the Tsarina is Marie.

The organ is heard as the people come out of the cathedral. Over acclamations of the Tsar and his new bride Yorloff whispers his plan to open the door of the nuptial chamber for Igor to enter and to murder both victims on the stroke of two.

Act IV takes us to the bridal chamber where Marie, now Tsarina, is listening to a Barcarolle sung in the distance by the Young Bulgar supported only by the chorus's la-las, an exquisitely charming piece based on Bizet's chorus written for the Prix de Rome in 1856, the *Golfe de Baïa*. This was not inserted simply to gratify Bizet's desire to salvage the music; Gounod's libretto has a Barcarolle at this spot too.

Marie now has a solo scene in which she explains how Olga took her to Olga's brother Ivan when he was suffering from one of his fits of depression. Marie took pity on him, and we recall that she was irresistibly drawn to him the first time she saw him in Act I. "Ivan our enemy, Ivan our oppressor, Ivan is ruler of my heart!" is the cue for a beautiful sicilienne for woodwind in A flat minor leading to a perfectly crafted Andantino air, "Jamais l'aspect de nos montagnes", which concludes with coloratura tracery as she recalls her happy childhood. An expressive phrase in her air is a good illustration of Bizet's fondness for approaching the dominant with alternating seventh chords followed by rising chromatics in sixths (Example 4.3).

Example 4.3

The cabaletta is a burst of soprano energy in E flat major, confirming Marie's love of Ivan despite everything she has left behind. Ivan then enters to bid her join the festivities outside. The music is full of tenderness, with yet another inner pedal, this time on the horns. She leaves, but Ivan has picked up a note which, as Yorloff, entering at that moment, helpfully mutters, is from him. Ivan asks Yorloff to read it. It recounts the story of Judith seducing Holofernes and cutting off his head. Ivan leaves (to the sound of Example 4.2) in a suspicious mood, convincing Yorloff that the trick has worked. The theme from the conspirators' trio in the previous act is heard on the clarinet as Igor enters to receive final instructions from Yorloff, whose sombre theme sees him out.

It is time for a solo scene for Igor. His tranquil ternary Cavatine in 9/8, "Pourquoi revenez-vous", recalls the happiness of his childhood, a perfect offering for the lyric tenor voice. A snatch of the Barcarolle is heard in the distance followed by loud acclamations of the Tsar and Tsarina on whom Igor calls down a fearful curse.

Marie was not far away, perhaps on a balcony overlooking the square, for she now comes in to the same melody with which she left a little earlier. She is unaware that Igor is there. Suddenly he reveals himself, to her great joy. Still unaware that she is the Tsarina, he longs to spirit her back to the mountains of their home. Their duet is passionate and impetuous.

He then confesses to Marie, to a superbly agitated accompaniment, that he has sworn to strike down Ivan, "your abductor". "No, no," she cries, "you can't do that" and pleads with him to spare his life. "Why does he mean so much to you?" he asks. "He is my husband and I love him!" she replies, unleashing intense shock from Igor and a passionate protest from Marie that she is ready to die if need be; her marriage to Ivan is a commitment for life. Igor then threatens to kill her too.

Marie lowers the temperature by reminding Igor, to a plaintive throbbing rhythm, that their mother made him promise to protect her at all times. Igor, overcome by emotion, joins Marie in a tender but intense duet. Coming to his senses he declares he will abandon his vow, and they rejoice in a disappointingly commonplace, but short, duet.

Ivan and Yorloff now enter with enough followers to form a chorus. Yorloff has clearly overheard the previous scene and learned that Igor is Marie's brother. Feeling betrayed, he is determined to kill him. So he tells this to the Tsar, who sees Marie as the Judith preparing to murder him in his sleep. Finales such as the one that now unfolds conventionally began in a broad 12/8 tempo, in which all give vent to their various dilemmas and tensions. Ivan launches this one with a bitter reminder of how much he loved Marie. In the ensemble she begs him to be merciful, Igor affirms his brotherly love, Yorloff is appalled at the Tsar's weakness, and the chorus is shocked to see the Tsar in tears. The music builds and builds, then settles on a quiet cadence.

An officer rushes in with the news that Temrouk and his friends have attacked the Kremlin and set it on fire. Everyone turns in fury on Igor and Marie, calling for their deaths. Ivan, in recitative, orders them to be buried alive, but as he relishes the thought of their punishment he falters and collapses. "Pray for the Tsar," they mutter, "the Tsar is dying."

Act V has to resolve the action, but it can hardly be said to have been satisfactorily handled by the librettists; Bizet's failure to finish the last two scenes other than the voice parts and a section of the orchestration suggests that he may have had misgivings himself. The first scene takes place outside the citadel with a light-textured March in the middle of which an officer tells a sentry that the Tsar is dead and that Yorloff has taken over. The model seems to be the Marche nocturne in Berlioz's *L'Enfance du Christ* in which a march provides similar background for two soldiers' exchanges. This music would reappear in *Jeux d'enfants* a few years later.

Temrouk appears, enraged that his two children are condemned to death when Ivan is the real culprit. Ivan himself staggers on stage, not dead, clearly, but at the mercy of the crowd that has turned against him, presumably at Yorloff's bidding.

He has killed his guards and escaped, begging Temrouk, who does not know who he is, to help him, the great Ivan, once the feared leader of his country. They join forces to save Marie and Igor.

The second scene shows Yorloff proclaiming his authority and confirming the sentence passed on brother and sister. Marie and Igor sing in octaves the melody from the first scene, yearning for their homeland. As Yorloff tears off the Tsarina's symbols of power, Ivan and Temrouk appear. General consternation ensues. Yorloff is condemned and the Tsar and Tsarina are gloriously restored to their thrones.

In all but the last act Bizet was composing *con amore* and with great care. His attention to detail is exemplary, for interesting figures and counterpoints are constantly appearing. The orchestration, which owes something to *Les Troyens à Carthage*, is varied and always subtle. Ivan has a motif (Example 4.2), but it is used sparingly; otherwise musical interconnections are recalls, not persistent motifs. There is little suggestion of local colour other than Ivan's Cossack Song. Bizet knew that a success with this work would project his career from the level plain where *Les Pêcheurs de perles* had left him, so he was clearly putting a special effort into it. The fact that the new opera occasionally echoes the previous one was used by Dean as an argument for its earlier composition on the grounds that Bizet would not recycle a published work.[20] But these are echoes, not borrowings, and furthermore Bizet had no expectation that *Les Pêcheurs de perles* would ever be revived (very few operas of the time ever were). *Requiescat in pace*: his own words.[21]

Opera thrives on the chance meetings, misunderstandings and changes of loyalty that motivate the plot of *Ivan IV*, which only falls down in the last act and in the bizarre entry of Olga's nuns in Act II. Casting the leading soprano and tenor not as lovers but as sister and brother adds a special appeal. Ivan himself is a cruel tyrant with a soft heart and an addled brain, a perfect complexity for opera, and although Ivan and Marie are strongly taken with each other, they have no love duet. The Young Bulgar is a gift of a role for a soubrette soprano (like that of Oscar in *Un ballo in maschera*). Two different styles of exotic décor and costumes are required, Caucasian and Russian, and the lack of an overture and a ballet would have been rectified, probably balanced by cuts elsewhere, if the work had ever got close to production.

Apart from the lack of a proper published score, the only factors that prevent a wider appreciation of this work are its incomplete state and its genre. The former problem can be and has been overcome, but the whole world of French grand opera presents almost insuperable problems in a modern culture that scorns spectacle and grandeur for their own sake and resists operas of great length unless they are

---

20. Dean (1955), p. 82.
21. Letter to Gounod, 1866, copy in F-Po, Dossier Bizet, p. 61.

by Mozart, Berlioz, Verdi or Wagner. Bizet's *Ivan IV* is certainly the equal of any of Meyerbeer's operas, and it contains more fine music than any of his own operas except *Carmen*. Yet it is today treated as operatic refuse, left behind by the march of history. For all their devotion to Bizet, both Winton Dean and Hervé Lacombe treat it harshly, and *The Cambridge Companion to Grand Opera* found no space in its 490 pages even to mention it.

CHAPTER FIVE

1866–1867: La Jolie Fille de Perth

ALTHOUGH PERSONAL REMINISCENCES OF BIZET WRITTEN AFTER HIS DEATH ARE numerous and enlightening, we have few details of the intricacies of his daily life in the 1860s, which is only normal for a composer in his twenties not yet famous. The musical press mentioned him intermittently and some correspondence survives, but we would like to know more. Who were his friends? How much was he teaching? How well did he get on with his father? Did he keep up with his Delsarte cousins after his mother's death? How well did he manage money? Did he have a favourite café, as we imagine all Parisians do? Did he ever go out of Paris? If so, what for? What was he reading? Did he go to the theatre or to art exhibitions? Did he follow political affairs? Was the womanising constant, or were there more serious affairs? If so, with whom?

The answer to all these questions is that we have little idea. Of the composers of his own age he was certainly friendly with Guiraud, Saint-Saëns, Delibes, Paladilhe, Joncières, Marie Vicomtesse de Grandval, Massenet and others, but what degree of intimacy existed can only be guessed. A number of his friends were pupils of his father or uncle. It is hard to tell whether he remained on close terms with Gounod and whether he attended the frequent performances of his works. He worked a lot with singers and must have acquired many as his friends. He had a friend named Nephtali Mayrargues (there were Jewish bankers of that name), but who he was and how close they were is a mystery. As for artists, we have an invitation from Eugène Isabey, who was considerably older than Bizet,[1] but no sign of friendship maintained with all the painters he knew in Italy—not even Didier, who nearly every

---

1. Lacombe (2000), p. 342.

year was exhibiting in the Paris Salon pictures either painted or conceived during his travels round Italy with Bizet as his companion.

Relations with his father must have been good enough for them to continue to live together, even if the arrangement was primarily financial. His father "opens my letters, reads them, forgets them and loses them, unless he doesn't forget them and doesn't lose them, which is much worse."[2] There were many matters he did not wish to share with his father. Money was never abundant: he was a musician, after all. Perhaps things were even desperate at times, since we have a letter, apparently from 1865, in which he is begging for a loan of 1500 francs.[3]

As for politics, we hear a cry of protest in a letter from July 1866 following the battle of Sadowa in which the Prussians roundly defeated the Austrians: "When a so-called civilised society, in the middle of the nineteenth century, tolerates and even encourages the stupid, pointless horrors and outrageous slaughter that goes on in front of our very eyes—and in which our noble Frrrrance will probably soon take part—men of decency and intelligence ought to club together and share their understanding, their love and their knowledge to take pity on the 99.9 per cent of the idiots, crooks, bankers and swindlers that cover our poor globe!"[4]

A missing archive that would shed a most revealing light on these years is the correspondence that passed between Bizet and Carvalho. Bizet was so closely involved with the Théâtre-Lyrique that the constantly shifting sands of their relationship would come into clear focus if only we had the documents to show them. Carvalho was generous but exasperating, optimistic but perennially broke. What Bizet went through with hot-and-cold, now-you-see-it-now-you-don't expectations for *Ivan IV* would drive even Job to despair, and we can only guess at Bizet's state of mind at the end of 1865 when his hopes for the opera seemed finally dashed. He probably swore never to have anything to do with Carvalho again. Carvalho was doubtless equally displeased with Bizet for offering the Opéra a work he thought was his. The only record we have of their exchanges is not pretty: on 28 December 1865 Bizet went to the Théâtre-Lyrique to hear a rehearsal of *La Fiancée d'Abydos* by Adrien Barthe (who had won the Rodrigues prize when Bizet submitted his *Te Deum*) and ran into Carvalho, who said in an unfriendly voice "Well well, it's you!" Bizet turned to leave, but Carvalho pulled him back.

"People as rude as you stay at home. Here you are *chez moi*."

"Excuse me," Bizet replied, "but I believe I was invited by M. Barthe."

---

2. Lacombe (2000), p. 327.
3. Lacombe (2000), p. 327.
4. Galabert (1909), p. 63.

"Leave, and don't set foot here again." A crescendo of abuse led to Bizet shouting "Carvalho, I'll kill you!" to which Carvalho rather feebly replied "Or I'll kill you!"[5]

He had plenty of work from the publisher Heugel, for as well as the colossal *Pianiste chanteur* series he was also transcribing the complete *Don Giovanni* for piano solo without voices, 223 pages altogether, to accompany the almost simultaneous revival of the opera at three different theatres—the Théâtre-Italien (1 March), the Opéra (2 April), and the Théâtre-Lyrique (8 May). The claim on the title page that the music had been carefully reviewed and fingered, showing details of the orchestra and singers, is reflected in the generous fingering found along with detailed indications of the vocal entries and the instrumentation, not normally supplied in such publications. Bizet also arranged the overture for piano duet.

Happily Heugel was prepared to publish Bizet's own music as well as his transcriptions, perhaps as part of a quid pro quo. He brought out two of Bizet's main piano works at the beginning of 1866. If Bizet had wanted to be a pianist in the public eye, he would have composed much more for the instrument, but the list of his solo piano works, apart from many smaller pieces composed when he was a boy, is not long. Bizet told Galabert that he was inspired to compose piano music after hearing the virtuoso Delaborde playing an Erard pedal-piano,[6] although he never composed anything for that rare instrument. The "Chasse fantastique", for the standard piano, calls for an accomplished player (it was dedicated to Bizet's piano teacher, Marmontel, who had recently dedicated one of his *24 Grandes Études* to Bizet) and it has the élan of a swift 6/8 tempo, but its unlovely sound and repetitive figuration goes some way toward explaining why Bizet had little sympathy with virtuoso pianism. A secondary theme expands too quickly into hysteria and never returns; we hear Bizet's orchestra in the textures more readily than a characteristic piano sonority. One might wish he had written a truly virtuoso piano work with Chopin's stylishness and Liszt's brilliance, but this is not it. There is perhaps a programmatic idea behind it, but he gave nothing away about its origins. Heugel's title-page shows a demented horse galloping through an infernal forest while his rider is tormented by devils.

The other piano work is quite different, and much more appealing. *Chants du Rhin* is a collection of six pieces each based on poems by François-Joseph Méry, who appears to have written them specifically for this collection. A preludial verse evokes the Rhine and its history, a topic dear to Méry's heart, and the sequence loosely outlines a day's journey enacted in the course of the six pieces. "L'Aurore"

---

5. Wright (1988), p. 10.
6. Galabert (1877), p. 10.

is a graceful melody with an arpeggiated accompaniment that continues unbroken for nearly two hundred bars, strongly suggesting Mendelssohn's *Lieder ohne Worte* and accounting for the set's subtitle *Lieder pour piano*. After the dawn comes the departure. "Le Départ" shows a group of young country boys singing as they row down the river. The water ripples throughout and the piece passes through a long crescendo from *pianissimo* to a resounding climax at the end. "Les Rêves" sounds innocent as the theme arises bit by bit, but it soon spreads into something much more heroic, all the while built on repeated notes in the middle texture. This is both melodious and perfectly crafted, and if it is supposed to represent its poem it enters the dreams of the rowers no longer rowing but dreaming of German history.

No. 4 is "La Bohémienne", the gypsy girl who dances by the water's edge to the sound of her tambourine. Her step is forthright and provocative, not least in the games Bizet plays with surprise modulations, all the while maintaining the rhythm of the dance. The final return adds a countermelody in the inner texture calling for the "third hand" technique beloved of Thalberg and Liszt. This piece needs some deft piano playing since the nuances are constantly changing and the notes often lie uneasily under the (two) hands.

No. 5, "Les Confidences", is the slow movement of the set. The wind nudges the sail and the oars resume while the song of the sybil (presumably the Lorelei) hangs in the air. The elegant sixteen-bar melody is heard twice, the second time at a higher register, and a coda draws the piece out slowly to its close. As one might expect, "Le Retour", the final piece, exudes joy and satisfaction at the end of the day. It is a rondo with a very attractive theme and a semiquaver motion that never lets up until the final resounding chords.

It is doubtful if Bizet had any higher ambition when writing these pieces than to charm. They are unmistakably directed at the same domestic audience as Mendelssohn's pieces, with the intermediate influence of Stephen Heller, whose music Bizet much admired. They were dedicated individually to six of Bizet's pianist friends, including Saint-Saëns, who received the final piece of the set and performed it in the Salle Pleyel in May 1868. It is recorded that on 16 March 1866 Bizet himself played nos. 2 and 6 at a soirée given by the Comte de Nieuwerkerke in the Louvre, and a month later, breaking his determination never to play in public, he played nos. 2 and 4 at a concert given by the Société Philharmonique in Beauvais, north of Paris. In January 1867 we read a report of him even playing some Chopin at a soirée hosted by Mme Gaveaux-Sabatier.[7]

★ ★ ★ ★ ★

---

7. *Le Ménestrel*, 27 January 1867.

Heugel's commitment to Bizet now produced a set of six songs under the title *Feuilles d'album* and composed in the summer of 1866. "I've just written six songs for Heugel at top speed," he wrote to Galabert. "I think you'll like them. I chose the words with care: *Adieux à Suzon* and *À une fleur* by de Musset, Lamartine's *Le Grillon*, an adorable *Sonnet* by Ronsard, a graceful little amusement by Millevoye, and Hugo's crazy *Guitare*. I've not omitted a single verse, everything's there. Composers have no business mutilating a poet's work."[8]

These are some of Bizet's best songs, but they are not well known because Heugel later allowed them to go out of print. They are a collection, not a cycle, and are not intended for a single voice. Bizet's choice of poems is broad and eclectic, and there is a balance of mood and style in the set. The first two songs take poems from the same de Musset source, his *Poésies légères* of 1850, and though each contains forty lines, the style and effect are entirely different. "À Une Fleur" is a pretty poem addressed by a lover to a flower sent and delivered, and the music is neither dramatic nor demanding, with the same piano pattern throughout. It was set by Lalo a few years later in a much more adventurous manner. But perhaps Bizet intentionally opened the collection mildly in order to make more impression with the second song, "Adieux à Suzon". Here the vigorous piano part is determined by the horse evoked in the third stanza: "Paf! c'est mon cheval", as the lover rides reluctantly away from his Suzon (there was a real Suzon in de Musset's life). The music of all four verses is different but with a similar refrain for each. Dramatic harmonic shifts, ritardandos, portamentos, and extreme dynamics are constant, and it ends with a drawn-out goodbye. This is a man's song, the only one in the set to be dedicated to a man, Hermann-Léon, the son of a more famous singer of the same name. It is perhaps the best song in the set and, strangely, it has never been recorded.

The two central songs were dedicated to the daughter and wife, respectively, of Manuel Garcia, brother of Maria Malibran and Pauline Viardot, all singers and singing teachers like Bizet's own family. Maria Crépet, the daughter, was a soprano who died aged twenty-six on 4 April 1867, just after the songs were published. The Ronsard "Sonnet" is a plea on behalf of animals who sing and happily play while "you are cold", with a real frost in the last couplet. Bizet has divided the poem into two almost equal parts, but Ronsard's long alexandrines cause Bizet to play havoc with word stress which, as Halévy's pupil, he had never wholly respected. This is a hazard for the singer but not a blot on the music itself, which veers between minor and major modes and returns to F minor just in time for the bitter last two lines. A plaintive tone is what the listener takes away from this song.

---

8. Galabert (1909), p. 77.

"Guitare", the fourth song, is completely different, being another piece in Spanish style, in fact a Bolero like "Ouvre ton cœur" in *Ivan IV*. Hugo's short lines and tight rhyme-scheme dictate their musical effect, and Bizet has extended the song with regular "Tra-la-las" and some repetition of the lines. The final line of each of the three short verses, the girls' response, goes from *pianissimo* to *fortissimo* with a great flourish and requires a singer of some agility. This song was also set by Bizet's father[9] and by Lalo, but neither with the panache that Bizet brings to it.

"Rose d'amour" is slow in pace and low in tessitura, tracing Millevoye's endearing sympathy for the rose buffeted by the north wind but caressed and loved by the south wind. The first two verses murmur gently on, but the third brightens with new textures and a more declamatory style. The dedicatee was the mezzo-soprano Marie Trélat, the wife of a surgeon, who had a salon in the Rue Jacob on the left bank and was a good friend to Bizet. He took part in many performances in her house in the years to follow and corresponded extensively with her.

Finally, as one might expect, "Le Grillon", about the cricket on the hearth, is a *tour de force* for a brilliant soprano, fittingly dedicated to Mme Carvalho. Lamartine's poem, from his *Harmonies poétiques et religieuses*, trips along to a scherzo pulse and the music ends on a trill and a high E flat. Again, how can this marvellous piece never have been recorded?

An interesting counterpart to the six piano pieces of *Chants du Rhin* is the set of six Gounod choruses arranged for piano and published not by Heugel but by Choudens later in 1866. These are transcriptions that make severe demands on the pianist since Bizet tends to put in orchestral detail regardless of whether it falls comfortably within reach of the player's hands. We get a good sense of his skill as a sight-reader of orchestral scores or as an opera coach, since singers like to hear everything that's going in the accompaniment. His arrangement of the Soldiers' Chorus from *Faust*, for example, conveys the dynamic impact of that piece in the theatre, so does the Chœur dialogué: Les Juives—Les Sabéennes from *La Reine de Saba*, an opera for which he had already written the vocal score. In addition there are two transcriptions from the music for *Ulysse* in this collection, one from *Philémon et Baucis*, and one from *Mireille*. Choudens now finally brought out some of Bizet's Gounod transcriptions, which he had probably made some years earlier: the vocal score of the oratorio *Tobie*, and the two arrangements (two hands and four hands) of the Symphony no. 2.

A curiosity among all these arrangements and transcriptions published in 1866 is Bizet's edition of Handel's "Harmonious Blacksmith", as the Air from his E major harpsichord suite has been popularly known. The edition is little more than a

---

9. F-Pn MS 3823.

fingered edition for pianists published by F. Lambert, whose activities as a publisher are otherwise unknown. This was evidently Lambert's first and perhaps only publication. How many such jobs did Bizet take on? As long as he was paid for fingering or editing or transcribing a piece, did he care whether he was credited on the music itself? Would he sometimes prefer not to be named? "On Saturday," he wrote to Choudens in 1866, "I hope to give you the orchestral arrangement of Gounod's *Noël*."[10] How many other such tasks did he take on? We know of only one occasion on which he worked for the publisher Lemoine, for example, writing an orchestral arrangement of a popular piano piece, the "Mazurka des traîneaux" by Joseph Ascher, first published in 1854. Is this the tip of an immense iceberg? We would know nothing of this had not a set of proofs survived, which they rarely do for pieces such as this.[11] If Lemoine engaged him once, why not again? And again? He once mentioned having orchestrated someone's "dreadful waltz":

> I made the scoring more vulgar than usual, with the cornet screaming like in a madhouse, the ophicleide and bass drum thumping the first beat of each bar with the bass trombone, cellos and basses while the second and third beats are beaten to death by the horns, violas, second violins, first two trombones and the snare drum. Yes, the snare drum! If you could only see the viola part! Like this all the way through:

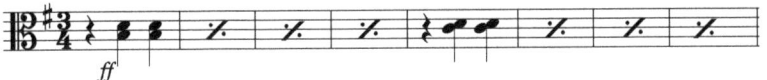

> Ten pages of that! There are people who spend their whole miserable lives playing mechanical stuff like that. Horrible! They could be thinking about something else, if they can still think.[12]

★ ★ ★ ★ ★

The breach with Carvalho over *Ivan IV* in December 1865 left Bizet in a bitter frame of mind. The doors of both opera houses where his music might be played were now closed, and it was opera on which his career had until then been built. It made sense now to diversify his portfolio and compose piano music and songs when a reliance on opera proved to be so hazardous. He also had a problem in his

---

10. Copy at F-Po.
11. US-STu MLM 13.
12. Galabert (1909), p. 76.

relations with Choudens, although what triggered the following letter from Bizet is not recorded. It is known that on 6 January 1866 Choudens signed an extremely generous contract with Gounod for the publication of *Roméo et Juliette*, on which Gounod had been working in the previous year. Could it have been then that Gounod agreed to have the vocal score arranged by Hector Salomon, not Bizet, and a whisper of this reached Bizet's ears?

> I have never done any harm to anyone. I have always entered into relations with everyone with great good will and in some cases, which includes you, with true friendship and no ulterior motive. Having no influence I cannot help my friends, but I try to be friendly to them. If I don't succeed, it's not my fault. I embarked on this career with an open mind and a confident heart. I am sometimes brusque in manner and my tongue has a crazy way of obeying my nerves rather than my mind, but I know no one on earth who could reproach me for having knowingly caused harm to anyone.
>
> I'm learning a tough lesson at the moment. Rebuffs and refusals pile up around me, yet I know not why. Yes, I'll put up with it all, I keep struggling. …
>
> I had not expected you know what! I write all this without any anger or bitterness. I only ask you to be loyal and open with me.
>
> What do you have against me?
>
> You are not a child. I don't believe you are capable of a thoughtless action. Choudens, I'll believe whatever you tell me. I am counting on the truth. The issue is neither wounded pride nor posturing nor politics. I just feel there's something going around that I don't know about. Once again, be sincere, tell me everything. If discretion is called for I give you my word of honour not to repeat anything you tell me. Don't come to my house, not because I wouldn't be very glad to see you there, but for a reason that I'll explain later. Write to me or give me an appointment.
>
> I am astonished, dumbfounded and mostly annoyed.
>
> I will expect a reply from you and will be glad if this reply will allow me to remain your friend as before.[13]

Choudens noted on the letter that he replied on 8 January 1866 (we have a number of letters from Bizet to Choudens, but none of the replies). Three months later Bizet was still troubled by Choudens's behaviour. Again, his forthright language deserves to be quoted:

> Yesterday I was thinking. Our conversation convinced me of this: somewhere around in matters that concern me there's a pile of shit. I can smell it, I can guess it, I'm plagued by it. Where is it? What's its shape and its colour? That's what I don't know. Why do people hide it from me? Does no one think me serious enough to accept responsibility for my

---

13. Copy at F-Po.

share in some offence? That would be a mistake. I don't deserve this mistrust. Whatever's the case, I'll lie low and make no move whatever for fear of immediately putting my foot in the aforementioned stuff. *I trust you.* I'm convinced that if the slightest suspicion were to touch my reputation as a man of *irreproachable delicacy*, you would give me the wherewithal to make a thorough clean-up of the whole situation, *no matter what the consequences of that clean-up might be*. I have the right to demand this of your friendship on which I totally count on this occasion.[14]

We would not be surprised if Choudens was double-dealing, given the nature of the music publishing business and the number of egos he had to satisfy. That is a more likely explanation than paranoia in Bizet's mind. Only three weeks later Bizet was begging Choudens to assign him the arrangement of *Roméo et Juliette*, which had probably already been assigned to Salomon without Bizet being told. Or the problem could have been something entirely different.

It may have been some form of consolation that Choudens gave Bizet another opera to arrange. This was by his friend Saint-Saëns, who had entered for the Prix de Rome in 1864 at the age of twenty-eight. He had previously entered twelve years earlier, but he was no more successful this second time despite his manifestly superior musicianship. His failure was the occasion of Berlioz's *mot* "He knows everything, but lacks inexperience." In consolation Auber, who admired Saint-Saëns, persuaded Carvalho to give him a libretto to set. A libretto that was ready at hand was a remarkable story of metamorphosis and mysterious devilry by Barbier and Carré called *Le Timbre d'argent,* which Saint-Saëns then set, while Choudens agreed to publish it and Bizet undertook the vocal score. Carvalho's promises once again vanished into thin air and it was not performed and published until 1877, two years after Bizet's death.

The passage omitted in the first letter quoted earlier suggests that Bizet had quickly made it up with Carvalho, for it refers to a visit in early January to the Carvalhos' house and the joy of again seeing friends "who I'd thought were quite lost to me" and the joy of seeing Mme Carvalho too. It would be entirely within Carvalho's mercurial character if he picked up with Bizet again and started hinting that he might commission another opera. *Ivan IV* was history, and there were many reasons why Carvalho was never able to stage it. But something perhaps that would be less ambitious to stage, tailored for his roster of singers?

In March 1866 Paris received a visit, the first for five years, from Liszt, who now lived principally in Rome. His purpose was to clear up his mother's affairs—she had died in February—and to conduct a performance of the "Gran" Mass in the church of St. Eustache at the invitation of the Mayor of Paris. Liszt spent over ten weeks

---

14. Copy at F-Po, p. 87.

there and was the centre of gossip and public attention, as he had always been. He was now an abbé, garbed in soutane and clerical collar. Relations with Berlioz, once very close, had unfortunately soured, but he saw a good deal of Gounod and Saint-Saëns and a group of younger admirers, perhaps even Bizet. On 7 March he attended one of Pasdeloup's concerts in the Cirque Napoléon which included the March from *Tannhäuser* and the Septet from Berlioz's *Troyens*. Not having been sent a ticket, Berlioz paid three francs for a seat high up at the back. When his piece was encored, he did his best to hide, but someone spotted him and he was forced to acknowledge the applause. On 1 April the Société des Concerts at the Conservatoire performed Berlioz's *La Fuite en Égypte*, another tiny breach in their long and nearly total ostracism of Berlioz's music, and a week later, at Auber's request in honour of Liszt, they played the March from *Tannhäuser*, the first time they ever admitted Wagner's music to their programmes.

The performance of Liszt's Mass on 15 March, attended by many high-ranking officials, was not a success; a military detachment inside the church was being given stentorian orders, according to an English witness, during the performance. The chorus was weak and the orchestra put together from other groups, and the press were mostly determined to suggest that Liszt was the ally of Wagner (which he was) and therefore the purveyor of intolerable music, which was not at all the case. But the church was full, and therefore much money was made for the local charity.

A few days later the composer Clapisson died. There would have been no tears in Bizet's eyes since he had always regarded Clapisson as an impostor ever since he succeeded to Halévy's chair at the Institute in 1854 on the strength of a long series of opéras-comiques aimed at the least sophisticated audiences. His appointment as professor of harmony at the Conservatoire in 1862 compounded the fraud since his command of harmony was demonstrably infantile. Before he left for Italy, Bizet had improvised a piece known as "Clapisson's Interment" or sometimes "Beethoven's Reception of Clapisson in the Elysian Fields". He never wrote it down. Pigot described the piece as follows:

> It represented Clapisson's burial, accompanied by a series of the so-called great man's feeble themes treated as a funeral march. It started with the procession of members of the Institute following the hearse, then the arrival at the cemetery, with official speeches from Baron Taylor, Ambroise Thomas, etc., and finally the departure of guests. The second part was the apotheosis. Clapisson's soul flew up to the abode of the elect. Surrounded by famous composers the Almighty Father was there to receive the new arrival. Beethoven was first to speak, beginning with the Fifth Symphony. At the fifth bar Clapisson interrupted him and played a theme from *La Fanchonnette* [a Clapisson success from 1856], Beethoven then resumed his symphony, but Clapisson wouldn't let him continue. More

themes from *La Fanchonnette* drowned out the master's voice. It then turned into a fight. While the improviser's left hand kept going with famous passages from the sublime symphony, the right hand sneered back with Clapisson's most awful tunes trying to silence Beethoven. In the end Beethoven let it go. After that *La Fanchonnette* reigned supreme, closing with brilliant cascades in a grotesque apotheosis greeted by gales of laughter from the audience.[15]

This performance was a popular hit with the occupants of the Villa Medicis during Bizet's time in Italy. It need hardly be added that Bizet's extraordinary gifts as pianist, improviser and humorist were all on spectacular display on those occasions.

Bizet objected most that such a poor musician should be sitting on the Prix de Rome jury, but then Clapisson was not the only nonentity elected to the Institute in those years. Nor would Berlioz have shed a tear, having been gravely hurt when, as a candidate in 1854 (his fourth attempt), he was decisively rejected in favour of Clapisson. For a third composer it was also good news, since Clapisson's death created a vacant chair at the Institute, soon to be filled by Gounod. On 19 May Gounod hosted a celebratory dinner in his apartment on the Rue de la Rochefoucault.

Clapisson's legacy was in fact richer than a bunch of mockable tunes, however. He had put together a large collection of old musical instruments which he sold to the state in 1861. As its curator he spent his last years living with his collection in the Conservatoire building, and this eventually became the nucleus of the great collection now known as the Musée de la Musique.

Assuming that Bizet ceased to be *persona non grata* at the Théâtre-Lyrique, he would have followed its repertoire as before. Following the success of *Orphée* in 1859, Carvalho planned to revive Gluck's *Armide*, not with Pauline Viardot but now with Madame Charton-Demeur, Berlioz's favourite mezzo, who had sung in the premières of *Béatrice et Bénédict* and *Les Troyens à Carthage*. Gluck's music had been in Bizet's ears since childhood, thanks to François Delsarte, and *Armide* had not been revived for many years, but for some reason the project was abandoned in March after Mme Charton-Demeur had had several sessions working on her role at Berlioz's house with Saint-Saëns at the piano.

Still mining the eighteenth-century seam, Carvalho decided on *Don Giovanni*, rather tardily setting up a competitive rivalry with the Théâtre-Italien and the Opéra. It was generally agreed that although the Théâtre-Italien had Adelina Patti as Zerlina, Carvalho held the stronger hand with three magnificent sopranos for Anna, Elvira and Zerlina in Mmes Charton-Demeur, Nilsson and Carvalho. Berlioz went to hear it eight times and was seen to "cover his face and weep like a child" at

15. Pigot (1886), pp. 332–333.

the Maskers' Trio in the Act I finale.¹⁶ Bizet might have been disappointed that his Leïla, Léontine de Maësen, was not singing, as first intended, but she was now Madame Rabaud and "in a state of health that would render her appearance in the part of Donna Anna impossible".¹⁷

One more non-French work was introduced that season: Nicolai's *Merry Wives of Windsor*, for which, as we have seen, Bizet had been engaged to orchestrate some sixty pages more than three years earlier. Jules Barbier wrote the French translation and Ismaël (Bizet's Zurga) sang the role of Falstaff.

It is possible, even likely, that Bizet was involved in two Gounod works not heard before in Paris. The oratorio *Tobie* was performed in Versailles on 4 June with a friend of his, Mme Ernest Bertrand, singing the soprano solo, and the opera *La Colombe* opened at the Opéra-Comique on 7 June. Based on a fable by La Fontaine and with a libretto by Barbier and Carré, this exquisite two-act opera was first performed in Baden-Baden in 1860 when Bizet was in Italy. The vocal score had been arranged then by Emile Périer, but Choudens now issued a new piano solo version which may have been assigned to Bizet. Caroline Girard, who had sung the part of Léonard in the only performance of *Vasco de Gama* in 1863, sang the role of Sylvie in *La Colombe*.

★ ★ ★ ★ ★

Summering, as he now did, in Le Vésinet, Bizet was reluctant to travel into Paris more than once a week if it could be avoided. His father spent all day gardening, and a big dog called Zurga stood on guard. Saint-Saëns, visiting one day, sang the Romance from *Les Pêcheurs de perles* in the street since he was not sure which house to call at. Another time, Gallet, the librettist of *Djamileh*, described finding Bizet there strolling around in a straw hat and a large jacket, smoking a pipe with the comfortable ease of a country gentleman. He would receive his friends there with his usual bantering bonhomie, eat and drink in the garden, and go for walks along the Seine.¹⁸

Any friend of Bizet's would have been delighted to get a note like this: "You get up at five, or four thirty if you like. You wait till it's time for the train—9.35 from the Gare St Lazare—St Germain line—Vésinet station—you get to Vésinet station at 10.10 or perhaps 10.15. You ask for the church—if you're polite they'll tell you where it is—you'll get to the church porch—you pause a moment—you go in—you see nothing! you wait. Melodious sounds suddenly fill the church up to the

---

16. *The Orchestra*, 19 May 1866, cited in Walsh (1981), p. 209.
17. *The Orchestra*, 21 April 1866, cited in Walsh (1981), p. 206.
18. Gallet (1891).

rafters. It's one of my friends singing. I'm at the organ. You feel weak because you're hungry. When the music's over you go out, you wait. I appear!!!!!!!! Lunch. If you want to spend the day with me—thankyou—you'll stay for dinner—and you'll leave late."[19]

A new friend in Le Vésinet that summer was a famous courtesan known as Céleste Mogador, although she was officially the widow Mme la Comtesse de Moreton de Chabrillan. With an adventurous past that included humble origins in the outskirts of Paris, official registration as a prostitute, love affairs with de Musset and a collection of aristocrats, engagements as a dancer at the Bal Mabille and as an equestrian at the Hippodrome, and three years as manager of the Bouffes-Parisiens, Céleste had also spent a period in Australia with her husband Lionel (the Count). She earned her soubriquet Mogador after her partner at the Bal Mabille commented that it would be easier to defend the Moroccan city of Mogador than to fight off her admirers. She was forty-two years old, now concentrating on a career as a novelist and successful playwright despite never having learned to spell. Céleste and her mother acquired a villa close by the Bizets' little houses, and her voluminous memoirs written some years later recall a friendship with Bizet (always platonic, she insisted, although few of Bizet's biographers believe that) warm enough for her to be invited to Bizet's little cabin as the only woman when his usual guests were normally men. In return, he was able to spend time at her house where a large room with a higher ceiling gave the piano more resonance and he could work in peace. Relations were not so good with her mother, who once threw a pot of water over his head when he knocked on Céleste's window after getting back on the late train. Her memoirs describe him as an "aristocratic savage" who was never very cheerful.[20]

In Le Vésinet that summer of 1866 he had started to work again on the symphony which had occupied him in Italy. Perhaps Pasdeloup had offered to programme it in the winter season of Concerts Populaires. When Galabert came for his annual visit in May he was put in the other cottage to work on his counterpoint exercises (Adolphe Bizet being away) while Georges worked on the first movement in his own. He found the work unusually difficult, the very opposite of the fluency with which he composed his First Symphony in 1856. The Second proved to be intractable, although bit by bit it came into being. "I have a real soft spot for it, even though it's a devil of a job."[21] In July he told Galabert he still had more work to do on it.

★ ★ ★ ★ ★

19. Letter to Emmanuel Jadin, 2 June 1866, Vente Drouot, 16 October 1991.
20. Marix (1938), pp. 147–148; Moser (1935), pp. 223–227.
21. Galabert (1909), p. 65.

Things took a marked turn for the better at the beginning of July. Every organisation in Paris was beginning to plan for the crowds that would be pouring into Paris for the Exposition Universelle announced for 1867. Carvalho already had Gounod's *Roméo et Juliette* signed up, and now, at the mercy of his conscience, he turned to Bizet for a new opera as compensation for the débâcle over *Ivan IV*. Whoever had the idea to convert Walter Scott's *The Fair Maid of Perth* into an opera, it was surely not Bizet; it more likely came from one of the librettists, Jules Adenis or the prolific Jules-Henry Vernoy, Marquis de Saint-Georges, the latter now a celebrated dandy aged sixty-seven with a huge catalogue of librettos to his name. He had written for almost every composer active in France in the previous thirty years, including Halévy (*L'Éclair*), Donizetti (*La Fille du Régiment*) and Flotow (*Martha*). Adenis was a journalist and dramatist more familiar with the spoken theatre than with opera. He wrote the libretto for Guiraud's *Sylvie*. Bizet had not collaborated with either of them before. Adenis probably worked out the scene-by-scene action, leaving Saint-Georges to do the versification.

The contract once signed, Bizet set to work. The seclusion of Le Vésinet was needed for the pile of work that now confronted him. He finished drafting the symphony before starting work on the opera, but he still had other commitments: "I'm required by contract to deliver my score by the end of December, and I've only written one act," he wrote in September. "On top of that there's a symphony which is driving me mad, all to be orchestrated for next month, three songs to write for Choudens, six songs for Heugel [to proof-read], and piles of transcriptions for Heugel which require me to read about five hundred pages of proofs. This will give you an idea of what I'm up against."[22]

Act II of *La Jolie Fille de Perth* was finished in October. Bizet admitted that he hated the Scott novel on which it was based, but he liked the libretto more and more as he got further into it, and felt satisfied with the characters. In the pressure to finish his opera he abandoned any idea of orchestrating the symphony, which disqualified it from being performed that winter. In October he put his name forward for the vacant post as chorus-master for the Société des Concerts du Conservatoire, but he was narrowly defeated by Auguste Charlot, winner of the Prix de Rome in 1850.[23] Back in Paris for the winter season he was working fifteen or sixteen hours a day to meet his deadline. This he did, delivering the score of *La Jolie Fille de Perth* to Carvalho on 29 December.

The sensation of the season was the opening of Thomas's *Mignon* at the Opéra-Comique on 17 November. Thomas had been composing operas for thirty years

---

22. Lacombe (2000), p. 360.
23. Holoman (2004), p. 219.

and had been a member of the Institute since 1851, but he had still not enjoyed real success and had never been heard at the Opéra except as the composer of ballet. He was a far more accomplished musician than many who were regularly heard at the Opéra-Comique (Clapisson comes to mind), so with *Mignon* he was able to give solid evidence of his gifts and enjoy the fruits of success. He was already engaged on a *Hamlet* for the Opéra. In *Mignon* Barbier and Carré offered Thomas a version of Goethe's *Wilhelm Meisters Lehrjahre* much as they had adapted *Faust* for Gounod.

Part of its huge success was attributed to Célestine Galli-Marié who played the part of Mignon. Her voice and demeanour were perfect for the child Mignon, "neither boy nor girl", as she is introduced in the first scene. The original version of *Mignon* had Mignon die at the end, and in this form it was first performed in 1866.[24] In the novel too Mignon dies, but in circumstances far too complicated for transference to an opera. Although Manon Lescaut had expired in the last scene of Auber's opera of that name ten years earlier, in 1866 there was still an expectation at the Opéra-Comique that the two leading characters would be happily in each other's arms at the final curtain, so the ending was altered, and to this Barbier attributed the work's enormous success.

Once *La Jolie Fille de Perth* was finished and delivered Bizet could catch up on the backlog. At the beginning of 1867 he hoped to complete the orchestration of his symphony, but he was overwhelmed with work for Heugel and Choudens. On top of that he was meeting Carvalho and Saint-Georges every day to discuss *La Jolie Fille de Perth*, which was supposed to be ready for performance in April—and he had lessons to give. At least Choudens was asking for some compositions as well as arrangements. The three songs he had promised were "Adieux de l'hôtesse arabe", "Après l'Hiver" and "Douce Mer", which were issued separately, not as a collection, in March, all three in two alternative keys for high or low voice. The first of them has become the best known of all Bizet's songs and has been recorded many times. Hugo's characteristically colourful poem—in eight stanzas, of which Bizet set just four—imagines an Arabian woman watching her European lover depart across the desert. Bizet incorporates the conventional Middle Eastern augmented second in the opening line of his melody, and the insistent rhythm of the piano part suggests the beat of a lap-held drum; but the exoticism is natural, not forced, and the expressiveness of the vocal part is exemplary. It was dedicated, like "Le Grillon", to Mme Carvalho, a high soprano, but the lower version of the song, in A minor, is perhaps the more evocative. There can be no better illustration of Bizet's deft handling of chromatic harmony than the second half of the strophe, which contains examples of his favourite chromatic passages in contrary motion and of his alternating chords of the seventh (Example 5.1).

24. Rogeboz-Malfroy (1994), pp. 209, 214.

Example 5.1

"Après l'Hiver" is also a setting of Hugo, this time a gentle love poem linking love to the euphoria of awakening nature. Bizet's setting is equally gentle, with a constant semiquaver figure in the right hand running through three strophes with a melodic episode before and after each and barely a trace of chromaticism. Its dedicatee was Mme Fanny Bouchet who was probably an amateur singer heard in the salon and not the theatre.

For the third song, "Douce Mer", Bizet selected the first three stanzas of an eighteen-stanza poem by Lamartine entitled "Adieux à la mer" and included in his *Nouvelles Méditations poétiques* (1830), written, according to Lamartine, on the island of Ischia in 1820. Bizet's title comes from the second line of the verse. The accompaniment unmistakably suggests a calm sea with a repetitive figure in the piano's right hand. A common failing of Bizet's songs is his inclination to keep an accompanimental figure going beyond the point where the ear seeks a change. In this case the figure does change, but only slightly, not enough, for the middle section, and in addition the left hand is static too. This song was dedicated to a young tenor, Victor Capoul, whom Bizet had accompanied at one of the Comte de Nieuwerkerke's receptions in the Louvre in March and who had also sung the main tenor role in *La Colombe*. At the moment when this song came out he was at the centre of a dispute at the Théâtre-Lyrique since Gounod wanted to cast him as Romeo when he was under contract to the Opéra-Comique. In the end the role was sung by Michot.

Example 5.1 Continued

Choudens had earmarked Saint-Saëns's *Le Timbre d'argent* for Bizet to arrange, but he had another opera that had to be done first: Massé's *Le Fils du brigadier*, a three-act work that opened at the Opéra-Comique on 2 February. No doubt that was quickly done. Meanwhile Heugel, who engaged Auguste Bazille to arrange the vocal score of *Mignon*, was sensing a success on his hands. He needed a piano solo version, so he turned to Bizet for that and at the same time engaged him to oversee all the *Mignon* publications. Bizet was soon proof-reading six hundred pages of full score twice over as well as eight hundred pages of orchestral parts, and checking the vocal score. Within a year Heugel was even moved to order a piano duet arrangement of the entire opera from Bizet, a mere 283 pages.

It must have become very quickly obvious to Bizet that with the Exposition Universelle opening on 1 April Carvalho's plan to mount *La Jolie Fille de Perth* as well as *Roméo et Juliette* in the same month was another of his pipe dreams. If it was to be a choice, there was no doubt that Gounod's opera would be the one chosen. In February Carvalho had engaged Christine Nilsson for a three-act opera *Sardanapale* by Victorin Joncières, who was a year younger than Bizet and seeing his first opera professionally staged, as Bizet had with *Les Pêcheurs de perles*. It was about as (un)successful as that opera too. The *Troyens à Carthage* sets reappeared on stage once again. Whether it was promised or merely hinted, Bizet had been led to expect that Nilsson would be the leading soprano in his opera too. Any delay would put that in jeopardy since she was much sought after at the Opéra and in London and could not commit herself to the Théâtre-Lyrique very far ahead. Once an April opening was given up, Carvalho scheduled it for late May, to be followed by a two-month gap while Nilsson was in London, resuming in August. A new contract was signed. "This time he'll honour his engagement or we'll *kill* him," Bizet told Galabert.[25]

★ ★ ★ ★ ★

The Exposition Universelle of 1867 was an extravagant display of Napoleon III's *folie de grandeur*, which would register in history as nearer to the successful affairs in London in 1851 or Paris in 1855 if the Second Empire had not been slipping closer and closer to the chasm that engulfed it just three years later. Although international trade was fostered and promoted, the Exposition cost the French government an unimaginable sum of money. To all appearances things were going well. Baron Haussmann had transformed the city and filled it with elegant tree-lined boulevards, and the grand facade of the new Opéra was revealed for all to see (the rest was well behind schedule). The Exposition was planned to draw the attention of the world to the glories of French commerce and culture and to attract the possessors of titles, wealth or curiosity in great numbers. With an official opening on 1 April, the city put on its best show.

Eiffel built not a tower—that would come for a later Exposition in 1889—but an immense iron and glass pavilion in the Champ de Mars (where his Tower now stands) with hydraulic lifts by the Otis brothers carrying visitors to the roof. The Bateaux Mouches began their sightseeing trips along the Seine. Nadar, the photographer, took up twelve tourists at a time in his double-decker balloon. A large-scale model of the soon-to-be-opened Suez Canal was shown, complete with ships passing through it. The Japanese exhibit proved to be very popular, leading to a

---

25. Galabert (1909), p. 102.

craze for *japonaiserie*. The United States exhibited surgical instruments, artificial limbs and a submarine, while Victorian England sent biblical tracts, agricultural implements and a school. From Vienna the younger Johann Strauss brought a new waltz, the *Blue Danube*. From Essen Herr Krupp brought the largest artillery in the world.

Only a year earlier Napoleon III had brokered an uneasy peace after nearly half a million Prussians, Saxons and Austrians had torn each other apart on the battlefield of Sadowa. Now he was playing genial host to the King of Prussia and his wily chancellor Bismarck, who was already planning the deadly blow that would soon bring France to its knees. Napoleon was also trying to offer a smile for Emperor Franz Josef of Austria, especially when news of his brother Maximilian's ignominious execution arrived from Mexico in the middle of June. Most of Europe's leading royalty came to Paris, including the Tsar of Russia, Ludwig II of Bavaria, the King of Belgium, and the Prince of Wales.

It is estimated that the capital had ten million visitors from the provinces and abroad during the seven months that the Exposition was open. All Paris's theatres vied to entertain this captive audience, not least those that offered opera. First off the ground, surprisingly, was the Opéra, with the première on 11 March of *Don Carlos* by Verdi, who, since the death of Meyerbeer, was now widely regarded as Europe's leading composer. This early opening was surprising because the problems that Verdi encountered in the course of rehearsals were almost insurmountable, and the performance went ahead only after large cuts and alterations had been made. Marie Sasse was Elisabeth (she had been Wagner's Elisabeth too) and Jean-Baptiste Faure was Posa, both previously the star singers in *L'Africaine*. Despite the huge effort that went into the production, it failed to attract the crowds and disappeared from the Opéra's repertoire after 1869. French high culture was perhaps not best displayed in the form of a German play about Spain set to music by an Italian composer. Bizet found it "exhausting", judging Verdi to have avoided displaying his weaknesses but not showing enough of his strengths.[26]

A month later, on 12 April, the Théâtre des Variétés on the Boulevard Montmartre opened its doors to *La Grande Duchesse de Gérolstein*, Offenbach's special contribution to the festivities. With a libretto by Meilhac and Halévy, who had already found Offenbach's vein of gold in *La Belle Hélène*, *Barbe-bleue* and *La Vie parisienne*, this new opéra-bouffe satirised all those medal-laden generals and admirals who were almost as overdressed as the tsars and kaisers they served. In the character of General Boum, who takes gunpowder for snuff and walks bandy-legged in oversized boots, they created a ridiculous figure who is quite believably overshadowed by the humble soldier Fritz promoted from the ranks.

---

26. Curtiss (1958), p. 190.

It was the sensation of the season. Everybody laughed, including the Emperor himself. He came to the show again and again, blind to the fact that his own military prowess was not that of his uncle. Offenbach had a secret weapon in the shape of Hortense Schneider, who as the Grande Duchesse conquered all hearts and became the centre of Parisian gossip. So many grand visitors to her dressing-room and to her house in the Avenue de Versailles were assumed to be her lovers that she was maliciously referred to as the "Passage des Princes".

Last but not least, on 27 April the Théatre-Lyrique unveiled Gounod's *Roméo et Juliette*, and this too became a hit. Mme Carvalho was Juliette with a part precisely tailored for her voice; Pierre-Jules Michot was Roméo; the indefatigable Deloffre conducted. Like most of Gounod's operas it was to undergo radical revision in the course of the next few years as performances proliferated in many cities of the world. Barbier and Carré's libretto is reasonably faithful to Shakespeare, except that it ends with the lovers' deaths in conformity with a common performance tradition in the theatre. From the same tradition Juliet wakes from her drugged sleep before, not after, Romeo dies, so they have a fourth and last duet together. Gounod's music was widely admired, even by Verdi, and among the crowds that flocked to hear the opera were many grandees from the international aristocracy. Gounod dedicated his opera to the King of Sweden. There were eighty-nine performances before the year was out.

How much Bizet was involved is an open question. His biographers have freely attributed both the vocal score and a piano duet version of the opera to him, but those scores were in fact by Hector Salomon and Adolphe Schimon respectively. The piano solo arrangement was by "Ant. Berel", the pseudonym of Antony de Choudens, the son of Bizet's publisher. He attended rehearsals, after one of which he wrote to Adenis to report Gounod in a rage with everyone. But he was not a staff repetiteur for the theatre, and if he worked with the singers it would have been privately at his or at Gounod's house. One letter to Choudens mentions possible cuts and corrections in the score;[27] another sets out sixteen "morceaux séparés" to be spun off from the vocal score, presumably a job that Gounod had no desire to take on himself.[28] For the Entr'acte before Act II he wrote ten lines of verse as a "Rêverie de Juliette" beginning "Ô beau nuage blanc dont les bords argentés", adding "If you don't like my lines you can use the thing written by Carré, though I think these are as good as the poor stuff by those gentlemen." In fact his lines do not fit the Entr'acte in question, so perhaps he had different music in mind. For the chorus that followed, Bizet added his own words. He corrected the proofs of the

---

27. Copy at F-Po, p. 75.
28. Copy at F-Po, pp. 65–71.

orchestral parts.[29] For the revivals at the Opéra-Comique in 1873 Bizet would again be called in to help.

Another product of the Exposition Universelle was the Ministry's plan for two competitions: one for a hymn and one for a cantata. A panel of twelve judges was named under the honorary chairmanship of Rossini and the executive chairmanship of Auber. The panel included Berlioz, Thomas and Verdi. The words of the hymn were also put out to competition, and the two winning poems were published on 6 April. The compositions had to be submitted by 1 June (later extended to 6 June) and identified only by a motto, with the author's name and address attached in a sealed envelope. Bizet and Guiraud decided to enter for both competitions, Bizet choosing to set the three-verse hymn by Gustave Chouquet, beginning "À l'appel viril de la France". They left it to the last minute, arriving with their pieces at the Commission office half an hour before the deadline. The functionary on duty was overwhelmed: "Sacrebleu," he cried, "is everyone in the world a musician?" The authorities had not anticipated being inundated with entries and had suggested that the hymn should be set in a simple, popular style. In fact more than eight hundred entries were received[30] and most entries consisted of four-part hymn-tunes to be repeated for each verse. While Alkan's entry covered only three pages, Bizet's was perhaps the most elaborate of all, 118 bars long, scored for four-part chorus and a heavy brass ensemble consisting of six saxhorns, six saxtubas, four trumpets, four horns, two cornets, four trombones, ophicleide and contrabassoon! Bizet had Galabert copy the score so that his handwriting would not be recognised, and he used the pseudonym Gaston de Betsi and Galabert's home address in Montauban. Each entrant had to identify his piece with a motto, Bizet's being "Fù il vincer sempre mai laudabil cosa", the first line from Canto XV of Ariosto's *Orlando furioso* (1516): "To win was always a splendid thing".

The judges were overwhelmed. Bizet reported to Galabert that the three judges who actually took part (we can be certain that Berlioz and Verdi were not among them) looked at the stack of entries and threw up their hands. No prize was awarded.

The cantatas, settings of a poem entitled "Les Noces de Prométhée" by Romain Cornut, had to be in for the same deadline, but of these there were only 103. A first short-list of fifteen included settings by Bizet and Guiraud, and Guiraud's cantata was included in the list of four finalists. The prize was awarded to Saint-Saëns, with Massenet and Weckerlin making up the final quartet. Bizet's cantata has not survived, perhaps because he was anxious to conceal the fact that he had entered. (The

---

29. Galabert (1909), p. 117.
30. All now preserved at F-Pan F^{12} 3097–3099.

cantata might have survived somewhere, of course, miscatalogued as by the composer de Betsi.) He wrote to Saint-Saëns: "A thousand compliments, my dear friend. I'm sorry I didn't compete: I would have had the honour of being beaten by you."[31] The winning cantata was supposed to be included in a grand festive concert in July, but Rossini had composed his last work, a *Hymne* for vast forces that took so much time and effort to rehearse that Saint-Saëns's cantata was summarily removed from the programme.

Massenet's success in the competition reflected his growing presence in Parisian music since he returned from Italy at the start of 1866. His first opera, *La Grand' Tante* was played at the Opéra-Comique on 3 April 1867, just before the opening of *Roméo et Juliette*, and he had already had his *Première Suite* played by Pasdeloup's orchestra in March, initiating a series of orchestral works that would greatly extend his fame in the next few years.

Bizet is listed in the archives as a member of the jury judging the competition for Orphéons, amateur choral groups, as a part of the Exposition, but he seems not to have signed any of the reports and perhaps did not participate at all.[32]

★ ★ ★ ★ ★

With the Exposition still running, the Théâtre-Lyrique had no summer closing that year. By July *La Jolie Fille de Perth* was in rehearsal at the theatre, but without Christine Nilsson, who on returning from London in August elected to sing in *Les Bleuets* by Jules Cohen instead. Three years older than Bizet and the son of a Jewish banker, Cohen had studied at the Conservatoire and had had operas staged at the Opéra-Comique in 1861 and 1866. Bizet was already resentful of Cohen's easy access to opera managements and always referred to him as the "usurer Cohen". Nilsson's decision—or perhaps it was Carvalho's—reinforced his annoyance that his own opera had been so long delayed. The replacement soprano, Jeanne Devriès, was only seventeen and had been over-promoted as the "new Malibran", yet she had a bright, agile voice and Bizet was pleased with her. As late as December the librettists wanted Mme Carvalho to sing the role, but Bizet would have forfeited, he claimed, ten thousand francs from his takings if she had sung, so he was content with Devriès.[33] A successful dress rehearsal took place on 23 September, but although an opening night was expected to follow, none took place. According to *Le Ménestrel*, "it was unanimously agreed that the score was too unusual to be staged during the Exhibition and that it should await the return of the Parisians—which means the

---

31. Letter in the Musée de Dieppe.
32. F-Pan F[12] 3101.
33. Imbert (1894), p. 180.

month of November."³⁴ A more potent reason was the imminent departure of Mme Nilsson to the Opéra, which made it imperative to open Cohen's opera as soon as possible. It did open, but not until 23 October, so only nine performances could be given before her contract expired.

A small Bizet composition that bears the date 1867 is a short simple song, "Notre Rosa" for unison voices and piano, setting two verses by the animal sculptor Auguste-Nicolas Cain, father of Massenet's librettist Henri Cain. This was composed in honour of the painter Rosa Bonheur, well known for her magnificent animal paintings and for her defiantly feminist way of life. On 10 June 1865 she was decorated with the order of Chevalier de la Légion d'Honneur by the Empress Eugénie at the Château de By, near Fontainebleau, where Bizet's manuscript is still to be seen. How he made her acquaintance is unknown, unless he had been to nearby Barbizon earlier than the 1870 visit (see Chapter 6).

Before we return to *La Jolie Fille de Perth,* whose first night eventually came round on 26 December 1867, we must pause to consider Bizet's unique contribution to musical criticism and a few other events of the year. Etienne-Eugène Crépet, recently widowed by the death of the singer Maria Crépet-Garcia, and editor of the *Revue nationale et étrangère,* invited Bizet to take on the job of music critic for his journal. No doubt thinking he would write something every month, he in fact wrote only one article, published on 3 August 1867, under the pen-name Gaston de Betzi, in which he declares his principles and defines the duties of a critic, as he saw them.³⁵ His stance is unimpeachable, for he argues strongly that it is not only permissible but right for musicians to criticise music, and by implication wrong for non-musicians to do it—an echo of the pain he had suffered at the hands of critics who were unqualified to judge. The critic's sole job, he insists, is to distinguish between good and bad, and to be able to award grades in between without resorting to jargon or technical language. He is against the idea of "systems" in musical style, for music must be judged by what it is, not by what it stands for. "Let us be unaffected and genuine, not demanding from a great artist the qualities he lacks, but learning to appreciate those he possesses." And he concludes with a *cri de cœur*: "I tell you in all truth, composers are the pariahs and the martyrs of modern society....O music! What a splendid art, but what a dreary profession!"

His article was well received, but two months later Crépet was succeeded as editor by Gervais Charpentier. When Bizet submitted his next article to him, some sour comments on fellow-critic Azevedo (a thorn in the flesh of all major composers

---

34. Walsh (1981), p. 233.
35. The article, entitled *Causerie musicale,* has been republished in French in Robert (1965), pp. 7–16, and in English in Dean (1965-1), pp. 248–252 and Dean (1975), pp. 283–287.

of the time) were censored and a section on Saint-Saëns was cut.[36] Bizet's response was "9679III" (mirror-writing for "merde"); he withdrew his article and wrote no more for the journal. In any case he may have found the task of writing a regular article of two thousand words much less congenial than he expected.

In 1867, in addition to Galabert, with whom he continued by correspondence to exchange fugal subjects and answers, sound musical advice and informative chat, he acquired a new pupil in the person of Paul Lacombe. The son of a wealthy manufacturer in Carcassonne in southwest France, Lacombe was the same age as Bizet and well advanced toward becoming a composer of some standing. Having seen a score of *Les Pêcheurs de perles* he was determined to learn from its composer. He submitted a collection of works that impressed Bizet, who agreed to take him on at fifteen francs an hour. The benefit for us is a series of letters written by Bizet over the next seven years and published in 1894;[37] like the Galabert correspondence we have only Bizet's contribution, not any letters addressed to him. To begin with, Bizet's letters were almost entirely taken up with observations on Lacombe's music, but as the years went by a friendship developed and the letters became more informative. Lacombe started sending full-length sonatas accomplished enough for Bizet to observe that he could give advice but scarcely be his teacher. Lacombe's Violin Sonata op. 8, when published, was dedicated to Bizet, who urged him to come to Paris to meet leading musicians and get his music played. On that advice Lacombe had a number of his symphonic and instrumental works played in Paris, especially in the 1870s. He lived to a great age but never attempted opera or dramatic music.

Just as he was fully occupied with rehearsals of *La Jolie Fille de Perth*, an additional chore came Bizet's way when Heugel asked him to arrange Mozart's *L'oca del Cairo*, an opera buffa written in 1783–84 but not completed. The opera was freely adapted and completed by Victor Wilder, who also wrote a new libretto. All the surviving music was included, with additions taken from other Mozart works, and it opened at the Fantaisies-Parisiennes on 6 June. Bizet had to arrange this composite score for solo piano.

An even more unusual task was arranging a group of six folk songs from the Pyrenees. The assignment seems to have come from a publisher in Pau in the Pyrenees named Taldoni, by way of Jules Ruelle, secretary at the Théâtre-Lyrique. Ruelle provided French versions of the local dialect while Bizet supplied piano accompaniments for the tunes. The arrangements were published in December with each song dedicated to a different lady, two of them singers whom Bizet knew, Mme Bouchet and Mme Trélat, and two of them members of the aristocratic Duchâtel family, perhaps acquaintances of Ruelle.

---

36. See Galabert (1909), pp. 127–128.
37. In Imbert (1894).

Then just as *La Jolie Fille de Perth* was approaching its opening night at the Théâtre-Lyrique, a minor boulevard theatre, the Théâtre de l'Athénée, put on an "opéra-bouffon" called *Malbrough s'en va-t-en guerre* and written by Paul Siraudin and William Busnach, both experienced men of the theatre. Busnach was a member of the extensive Rodrigues family. From the printed libretto we learn that the flimsy story requires Malbrough to exchange costumes with his minstrel Galaor, whom he sends off to war while remaining at home to observe the courting of Mme Malbrough by the unscrupulous Lord Boule-de-Gomme and the tricks played by her page Bouton d'Or. It was very successful.

The composer of the music was supposed to be kept secret. Delibes told the full story in a letter to Mme Trélat:

> At first I had been asked to write the music for this piece of nonsense. I was worried about the theatre's future and I was only half interested in the play, so I hesitated. Meanwhile Bizet accepted the task on condition that no one would know it was his. Carvalho found out about it, however, and made it clear that just when his opera was due to be done at the Théâtre-Lyrique, it would leak out and that would be damaging. Bizet took the point and gave it up, though he left the first act, not yet scored (I did all that later). Then two other composers were called in but evidently not in time, since one fine morning I had a visit from Busnach who asked me to do him the favour of writing the fourth act in a few days. My name would not be given out, but once I'd finished those few pieces I wanted them played as well as possible. My writing was recognised so I didn't hide the fact that I was the composer of part of this masterpiece. That's how I was credited with the whole thing. Frankly, I cannot accept the paternity of Act I, which is by Bizet, and orchestrated by someone or other....The conductor wrote the overture, Jonas the second act and a M. Legouix the third act.[38]

The only section of this motley score to have survived is by Bizet. The song "Il n'faut pas vous gêner" was much applauded and separately published for voice and piano by the publisher Heu, the music being there wrongly attributed to Delibes.

Example 5.2

---

38. Curtiss (1958), pp. 208–209; Lacombe (2000), pp. 392–393.

The song is witty and tuneful, and at least two bars foreshadow a familiar phrase in Carmen's Chanson bohème (Example 5.2).

★ ★ ★ ★ ★

La Jolie Fille de Perth opened at the Théâtre-Lyrique on 26 December 1867. Anyone expecting to find some useful guidance in Scott's *The Fair Maid of Perth* will be disappointed, for connections between the opera and the novel are slight. Scott's rambling story has nothing operatic about it except the highland setting, which Bizet made no attempt to evoke, the celebration of St. Valentine's Day, and two leading characters, Catherine Glover and Henry Smith, who fit well as soprano and tenor leads. Catherine's father and the Duke of Rothsay are taken from the novel, and Ralph, Glover's apprentice, is perhaps based on Conachar, but the gypsy Mab is a newly invented character at the centre of most of the intrigue, and the two plots move along entirely different lines. The libretto has always been ridiculed and blamed for the scarcity of revivals since 1900, but in fact the motivations are as strong as in any opéra-comique, and careful staging can make it all clear. The gilded rose that causes misunderstanding is a common feature of such plots, as is the mistaken identity of guests at a masked ball. The motif of one girl at a window pretending to be another when serenaded from below is familiar from *Much Ado About Nothing, Ariodante*, perhaps *Don Giovanni*, although it is awkwardly included in *La Jolie Fille de Perth* as a way of drawing Catherine out of her madness at the very end. Mab's part in the story is critical; she is a gypsy in order to justify a gypsy dance as divertissement, but in her voice and character she needs to be clearly distinguishable from Catherine. The men are represented by a tenor, a high baritone, and two basses.

After *Ivan IV* the tone of this opera will strike the listener as belonging more to the world of opéra-comique, light and flexible for the most part. It was always designed for continuous music, without dialogue. It breaks conveniently into separate numbers, even so, with linking music where necessary. It is important to present the action here in detail since the available vocal scores give widely divergent versions of the opera with few stage directions. The following synopsis with commentary is based on the original vocal score of 1868 and the libretto printed at the same time.[39]

The opera is set in the town of Perth around 1400. The Prélude is lightly scored, with one rich passage for the strings but mostly given up to a charming rescoring of the duet for two sopranos from the first act of *Ivan IV.* Act I opens in the workshop of the armourer Henry Smith (tenor). His workers are making weaponry and

---

39. The gestation of *La Jolie Fille de Perth* is studied in depth in Wright (1981), pp. 226–331.

armour at the forge with the anvil struck on the first beat of each bar emphasising the music's strongly rhythmic character. Smith enters and tells his men they will be free to celebrate the carnival that evening, the eve of St. Valentine's Day. They reprise their work-song briefly, then leave as the orchestra fades to silence. Left alone, Smith hopes that tomorrow his love, Catherine Glover (soprano), will finally accept him, and he gives in to a melodious reverie. Hearing a disturbance in the street, he looks out and sees a woman being harassed by a group of men. He opens the door to a frightened woman whom he helpfully identifies for us as Mab (soprano), the queen of the gypsies. She was being pursued by some characters from the court. Being kissed at the right time by the right man is fine, she says, but under duress, never! To repay Smith she offers to read his fortune.

Here she sings her Couplets, in which she sees Catherine as a flirt who enjoys being admired by all and sundry and who will make her lover jealous. Her second verse then assures Smith that in the end she will choose him for her Valentine and that he should not be jealous. The tune is pretty and the accompaniment neat, and it calls for a soprano who can sing with agility and assurance and not be upstaged by the coloratura that Catherine will shortly unleash.

There is a knock on the door, which causes Smith to worry that Catherine might be jealous if he were found there with Mab, so he pushes her into the next room. Without any introduction Catherine Glover, her father Simon Glover (bass), and his apprentice Ralph (baritone or bass) enter and sing as a trio that they have come to celebrate with their friend Smith, who welcomes them. Catherine and Smith exchange teasing lines. Ralph, whose slow wits are represented by low, thick chords, watches them uneasily. Glover heartily announces that he has brought some venison, some well-aged whiskey and a pudding. Catherine hints that there are other pleasures one might think of, which leads her into her Air, a brilliant display of vocal acrobatics in Polonaise rhythm in which she rejoices in the delights of winter and carnival, especially the flowers (which would normally be hard to find in Perth in February). The music is subservient to the needs of the voice, but Bizet compensates by modulating wildly in the middle sections, and at the end the three men join in behind her ever more stratospheric roulades reaching as high as top F sharp in her final flourish.

Glover, contriving to leave Smith and Catherine alone, takes Ralph off to help get the meal. Ralph says someone is loitering outside showing interest in Catherine. Smith defiantly replies that he can protect her and needs no help from Ralph, who is clearly jealous. Now the lovers are alone and their Duo—set in G flat, the ultimately rich key for love duets—is the first music in the opera to rise above the more routine style of opéra-comique music we have had so far. Smith is the ardent lover while Catherine is more inclined to say "We'll see…" He gives her a silver-gilt rose, which she accepts as a gage of their love as their duet settles into its serene close. They then agree: she will abandon her teasing and he will stop being jealous.

A stranger enters, wrapped in a heavy coat. He has followed Catherine to her house and walked through the open door. He tells Smith that he needs an armourer to repair a damaged dagger. A Trio begins immediately, simultaneously showing three reactions with irresistibly neat music: Catherine sees a chance to make Smith jealous, Smith is troubled by the intrusion, and the philandering Duke of Rothsay (for it is he, a high baritone) observes the "treasure" Smith keeps in his house. The Duke makes an immediate move on Catherine, not unnoticed by Smith who sets to work, hammering louder and louder. Catherine's warm response to the Duke is embodied in a suave melody she shares with him, for while Smith is otherwise engaged, the Duke reveals who he is and invites her to a masked ball at the palace that night. At the height of the Duke's wooing, Smith, enraged, raises his hammer to strike him when Mab, who has been listening from the next room, steps in to stop him. Both Catherine and the Duke are dumbfounded at the presence of a woman in Smith's house.

Operatic convention calls for an ensemble of dismay at this point. What they each say scarcely matters, for the Quatuor is a gem, almost frivolous in tone, executed with the lightest touch and with a memorable melody first heard in the middle, not at the start.

The Chanson et Scène Finale that follows is not long and it sets up the action without recourse to recitative. There is much ingenuity in the orchestral thread behind the exchanges. Catherine demands an explanation from Smith for the presence of Mab, and the Duke doubts that there is an honest one. Catherine's rage is interrupted by the arrival of her father and Ralph bringing in the dinner, which they proceed to set up, apparently unaware of the situation in the room. Glover is singing a folksy (but not Scottish) song about a pleasure-loving king, and breaks off when he sees first Mab and then the Duke there. How convenient, Glover says, I was going to seek an audience. "Tomorrow," mutters the Duke, making a hasty departure.

Catherine, standing apart, throws down the rose Smith gave her earlier, and Mab picks it up. Glover does not let his daughter go but sits her down at table where she turns her back on Smith. Ralph sees a chance for himself. The act closes with a brief ensemble for the five singers in which Glover's folk song provides the bass line.

Act II is set in Perth's main city square with houses around. Glover's house is on the right, a tavern on the left. As an echo of Act V of *Ivan IV* (and indirectly of *L'Enfance du Christ*) the Marche et Chœur makes a gradual crescendo as the citizens' patrol, led by Glover, approaches carrying torches. The sound of maskers carousing in a nearby street alarms the patrol, who take to their heels. When Glover realises his men have deserted, he flees too.

To a steady build-up in the orchestra the revellers stumble in, with the Duke riding in a waggon, all singing lustily. At the Duke's orders and to the sound of the cornet's bland arpeggios, a giant cup is produced. Over slithering phrases in clarinet and violas he offers the title of Chevalier of Pleasure to whoever can down the cup in one draft. As the Duke leads the menfolk into a boisterous Chanson à Boire, they pass the cup around with little attempt by any one reveller to drain it.

Some random pizzicato chords answered by slithering woodwind accompany the arrival of Mab and a group of gypsy girls. The Duke invites them to perform, so to the accelerating pulse of the Danse bohémienne they swirl and twirl. The dance opens with the suggestive combination of flute and harp, then with infinite subtlety the other instruments gradually join in, a model of skillful orchestration.

The return of the theme that accompanied the Duke's wooing brings us back to the plot. Afraid that Catherine will not go to the masked ball, the Duke asks Mab to make sure that Catherine rides in the Duke's litter at midnight, masked. Somewhat shocked, Mab agrees and launches into her second set of Couplets, which comment on the ephemeral nature of love in the Duke's circles, promising to keep these things to herself. The music is pure opéra-comique, without distinctive traits.

The Duke thanks her, but she privately promises to be avenged "for this betrayal", referring to the fact, as yet unmentioned, that she has herself suffered at the Duke's hands. His masked supporters appear with the waggon, and to a reprise of their boisterous chorus they all go out. The handling of the orchestra's diminuendo at the end and the gradual dissolve into the next scene is masterly. As Smith appears, a group of cellos paint an expressive picture of his solitary thoughts. He now sings the beautiful Sérénade, refashioned (though still in A minor) from the Serenata in Don Procopio (see Example 2.1) and addressed to Catherine's window. Instead of an immediate second verse a free-roaming clarinet outlines her silhouette in the window. But no: she doesn't hear him. The second verse is set to a quite different tune, in a different key, F major, and it is possible that this was originally Bizet's plan for the Sérénade, later realizing that he could aptly recycle the earlier Serenata for the first verse, thus combining both melodies. As he concludes on a fading high A, midnight strikes, so he turns despondently to go home, supported by declining echoes of the A minor melody.

He is accosted by a workman who recognises him and understands why he is there. The workman too has been stood up, so he suggests they both go to the tavern opposite, which they do. Another clock strikes midnight as Ralph appears; he is drunk and carries a flask of sherry. His Air is an interesting character study, not of a blustering old fool, as he would be in many operas, but a bass with a heart, even though the solution to all his troubles is drink. The low-pitched orchestration is particularly imaginative. He collapses on a bench.

The Duke's majordomo enters with four men, two of them carrying a closed litter, the others with torches. A murky version of the Duke's wooing theme tells us why they are there. The majordomo asks Ralph which is Catherine Glover's house. Ralph can only mutter her name. A woman wearing a domino and mask crosses the square and calls to the majordomo. She is helped into the litter and carried out. Ralph calls upon sufficient brainpower to realise (wrongly) that Catherine has been abducted. He calls for Smith, who appears from the tavern. Smith runs off in pursuit of the litter while Ralph, sluggishly following, is stopped in his tracks by the voice of Catherine. She appears in her window echoing the strains of Smith's Sérénade, now magically transfigured in the major key.

For Act III we go to an elegant boudoir in the Duke's palace, leading off from the great hall, whence can be heard musicians playing. Another scene of merriment is in progress with the Duke and his friends now at the gaming tables. The Duke lets slip a few hints about an anticipated conquest upon which he reflects dreamily in a Cavatine. The melody is smooth and eloquent, but what gives the piece its class is the constant interplay of instruments in the accompaniment, never overshadowing the voice, but adding colour and richness. The Duke ends on a sustained high A flat.

His wooing theme tells us that he expects Catherine now to appear. When a woman is brought in, the Duke begs her to unmask, but she (Mab) tells him she will unmask only for him in private. As the music is heard again from the other room, the courtiers politely withdraw and the servants remove all the candles but one. The Duo that follows is entirely accompanied by the stage music, which carries the melody throughout, leaving the Duke and Mab to converse over it. (This piece is better known as the Menuet arranged for the second *Arlésienne* suite, where it has no business to be.) Once again, as in the Danse bohémienne, a flute and a harp lead off and the other instruments join one by one. The calm course of the music counterpoints the brief, tense exchange between the Duke and Mab, who, as promised, removes her mask, but only after snuffing out the only candle in the room. Mab is offended when his smooth words are the same as she herself has heard from him before. When he tries to grasp her, his hand falls on the silver rose attached to her belt. At this point the musical exchanges are polite, concealing Mab's rage, barely contained. The Duke attempts to catch her in the darkness, but she escapes through a side door closely pursued by the Duke.

The theatrical effect of this number is extraordinary, for the off-stage music is entirely independent of the active scene before our eyes. It was not unique in opera, but it was the first time Bizet had attempted anything so precisely dramatic. There were precedents in *La traviata,* for example, which may have been in his mind.

Smith suddenly enters through the door at the back, looking dishevelled. He is close to despair, but the music of his Air is slow and contained, the clue to his tense state being supplied by the twisting chromatic phrase in the violas that marks every bar. Just for four bars in the middle do his true feelings come out before the apparently calm music resumes.

The rest of the act is a lengthy Final which builds to an ensemble in which tensions and misunderstandings reach a point of crisis. Having given up his pursuit of "Catherine", the Duke returns with his friends, at the sight of whom Smith hides behind a curtain. We are to suppose it is now morning. When one of the lords asks the Duke how he got on with his masked visitor, he says she fled at break of day. Smith is horrified to hear this.

The majordomo comes in to announce the arrival of Glover, who was promised an audience. He is not alone, for Catherine has come with him. In somewhat fawning tones, Glover has come to tell the Duke that his daughter has chosen Henry Smith as her Valentine and that she intends to marry him. The Duke tells Catherine he thought they had quarrelled. Only for a moment, she replies, and today she is sorry about it. The wedding is to take place the next day.

A brilliant, light ensemble follows in true Bizetian style, Catherine hoping the Duke will now learn not to pursue her, and the Duke thoroughly confused about her loyalties. Smith then decides to emerge from hiding and is introduced to the Duke by Glover as his daughter's intended husband. When Catherine says she is his, Smith reacts violently, accusing her in a low voice of spending the night in the palace. He wants to leave, but Catherine insists that he stay, announcing to the company what she has been accused of. She asks the Duke to exonerate her from the charge, to which he replies in a whisper that he will never divulge the secret of their "heavenly night" together.

Grand finales such as this generally proceed from a slow section to an Allegro accelerating to the final curtain, but this one launches directly into an Allegro molto with everyone singing at once. They lapse into silence when Catherine comes forward to launch the slow section of the ensemble with an impassioned plea to Smith to believe her. Beginning softly, all the voices join in behind her in an impressive series of harmonies (the top line rising, the bass falling) and concluding with the closing bars of her plea richly scored and a stunned quiet ending.

To everyone's surprise Smith confesses that he does believe her, but then immediately rebuffs her, pointing to the gilded rose the Duke is wearing on his doublet. This confirms Smith's suspicions and seals her despair as the curtain falls.

The last act is in two tableaux, the first taking place at some wild spot outside the town. Duo et Chœur: Smith is in sombre mood. His workmen and Ralph have come to convince him of Catherine's innocence. Ralph asserts that she spent the night in her own house, to which Smith replies that he, Ralph, had told him otherwise, referring to his drunken alert when he saw the litter leaving the square. "I was wrong," Ralph replies, "and I have proof" (for some reason Ralph does not say what it is). Ralph and the workmen are enraged that Smith persists in his belief that Catherine is the Duke's mistress, and the exchanges become heated. The issue can only be solved by personal combat, to take place on the banks of the Tweed ("close by"!) at the bugle's call. This leads to an exaggerated and vacuous display of chivalric pride on both sides. Ralph and the workmen leave.

Alone, Smith wishes it was the Duke he was going to fight, not Ralph. But he is resigned. He is about to rush off when Catherine appears, pale and trembling. She feels she is dying and has come to see him for the last time. Smith is touched. In the Duo she likens herself to a flower that fades and dies too soon, singing a shapely melody without a trace of ornament or coloratura. Smith responds with the same melody, and the second part of the duet lingers romantically on thoughts of love and tears and loss, without any recrimination on either side.

One of Smith's workmen comes up to tell him that the signal has been given. The workman tells a horrified Catherine that Smith and Ralph are to fight over her honour. Smith calmly assures her that her honour will be untarnished when he dies in the fight and rushes off. Catherine fails to hold him back and falls fainting at the foot of a tree.

The scene changes to Perth's main square at daybreak on St. Valentine's Day. The young men are all decked out with buttonholes and bouquets and the music is particularly fresh in Bizet's most characteristic manner. The boys sing to the girls, and the girls at their windows reply, all promising to pair off appropriately with their Valentines. Each boy gets a kiss from his girl, who gets a bouquet. More people gather in the square.

Pushing through the crowd Mab hurriedly searches for Glover to tell him that when she learned about the fight she persuaded the Duke to intervene. The misunderstandings have all been cleared up, it seems. Alas, no, replies Glover, since Catherine has now lost her reason. Having been the cause of Catherine's distress, Mab will now make recompense, and she whispers her plan (which we do not hear) to Glover.

Catherine is now heard from off-stage warbling with the traditional high-altitude gyrations heard in operatic mad scenes, particularly associated with Scottish ladies (Donizetti's Lucia and Verdi's Lady Macbeth, for example). Glover hustles everyone out of the square as Catherine comes out of her house singing a disconsolate love song that dwindles to a series of ornamental Ah's and La's. Over mysteriously gloomy harmony she sings the Valentine song, but because Henry Smith is dead, she will never be his Valentine. She falls to her knees and seems to be praying. Glover then brings Smith forward. He steps up behind Catherine unseen and quietly sings the first strain of his Sérénade. Catherine hears it in some bewilderment, and when Smith responds with the second strain addressed to her window she remembers it well enough to sing it herself. So Henry Smith is not dead! Smith then sings the Valentine song to the window where Mab now appears, dressed as Catherine. "Don't believe it!" Catherine cries, and after uttering that old operatic standby "Où suis-je?" falls into Smith's arms. Glover advances with the townspeople, who sing the praise of St. Valentine once again.

★ ★ ★ ★ ★

Apart from Smith's Sérénade, which is so effectively brought back at the end, there is only one melody that recurs throughout the opera, the theme that links Catherine to the Duke of Rothsay. The Sérénade does not quite rival the Nadir-Zurga duet in popularity, yet the music of *La Jolie Fille de Perth* has as much vitality as that of *Le Pêcheurs de perles* and the plot is more credible. There are some numbers that do not rise above the opéra-comique standard of the day, but Bizet's melodic invention is extremely rich, and the orchestration is as always inventive and apt. There is a real flair in the Prélude, in the St. Valentine chorus, in the night patrol, in the Trio and Quatuor in Act I, in the Sérénade, in the scenes in the Duke's palace, all showing Bizet's special gift. He was pleased with the music. Treating Catherine as a coloratura and giving her a mad scene has a respectable pedigree in nineteenth-century opera, but Bizet came to see this aspect of his opera as a flaw. When the critic Johannès Weber accused him of sacrificing to the "false gods of the quadrille, the *roucoulade*, and to several others, because they are false gods in which he himself does not believe," he replied: "I have made some concessions which I regret; I could say a lot in my defence. Imagine: the flon-flon school, the school of roulades and lies is dead, quite dead! Let us bury it without a tear, without regret, without emotion, and let's move on."[40]

Devriès proved to be more than adequate in the part of Catherine. The tenor, Massy, whom Bizet had travelled to Bordeaux to engage, was also good as Smith. Wartel, Delsarte's brother-in-law, sang the part of Glover. Lutz, as Ralph, made a big impression with his drunken scene in Act II. Deloffre was once again the conductor. If Nilsson had sung as Bizet once imagined she would, the opera might have had a better run than the eighteen performances it lasted, the same number as *Les Pêcheurs de perles* four years earlier. It was a very cold winter, which also depressed attendance, and Barré, who sang the Duke, became ill. The critics were mixed, as usual, though on the whole favourable. Some raised the eternal issue of Wagner (whose influence on the opera is nil) and some observed Bizet's genuine gifts. Some expected more savagery in a story based on Scott. Bizet was himself disappointed that the opera did not do better.

40. Wright (1988), p. 18.

"This second disappointment," wrote Pierre Berton some years later, "was harder to bear than the first. Without expecting a triumph that would make his fortune, Bizet felt he was sure of a real success....He stiffened himself against injustice, took refuge in work, and prepared for a struggle which he never imagined would be so bitter. He said goodbye to his earlier joviality and the bright confidence of his youth, and from that time on I saw a worried look on his brow that never left him."[41]

---

41. Berton (1913), pp. 229–230.

1 Jules Didier, *Watering Place in the Mountains, Italy,* Musée des Beaux-Arts, Pau.

2 Gaston Planté, drawing of Bizet, September 1860. Bibliothèque Hachette.

3 Caricature by H. Meyer. *Diogène,* 28 September 1863. Braam Collection, Munich.

4 Bizet in the Garde Nationale, 1870. Photograph. *La Revue musicale*, 20 (1939), p. 66.

5 Célestine Galli-Marié in May 1875, photograph by Liébert. Institut de France, Paris.

6 Photograph of Bizet by Carjat. John Knowles Paine, Theodore Thomas and Karl Klauser, *Famous Composers and their Works* (Boston: J. B. Millet Co., 1891), vol. 3, opposite p. 697.

7 Letter to Ambroise Thomas. Stiftelsen Musikkulturens Främjande, Stockholm, MMS0393.

ravi l'autre soir. — C'est toujours jeune et spirituel... et quelle main !...

Croyez, mon cher maître, aux sentiments affectueux et dévoués de Georges Bizet

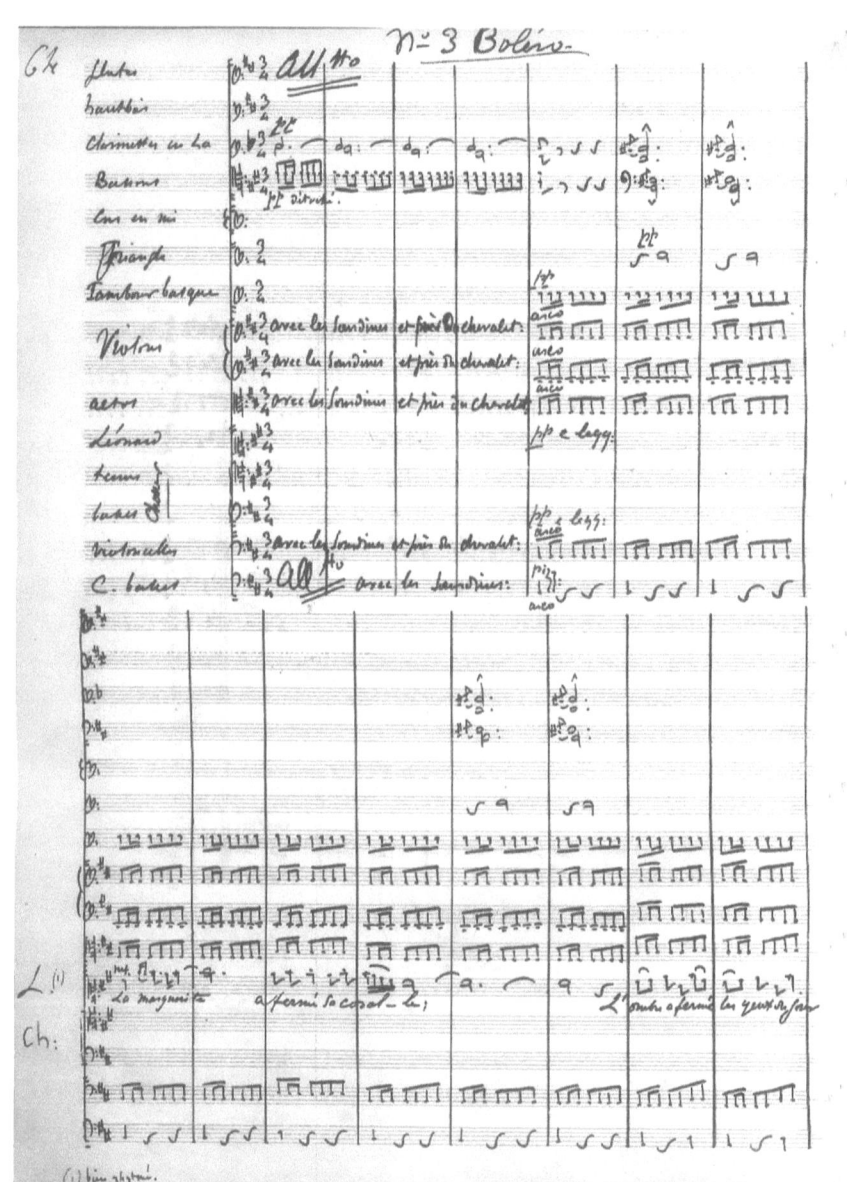

8 The *Boléro* in *Vasco de Gama*, autograph full score. Private collection.

CHAPTER SIX

1868–1870: *La Coupe du Roi de Thulé*

THE CLOSING YEARS OF THE SECOND EMPIRE WERE SEEN BY MANY FRENCHMEN AS the culmination of the nation's mission to provide prosperity and pleasure for all. The gilded decorations that adorned new buildings, the fantastic wardrobes that wealthy women sported, the bustle of the boulevards, the vitality of Paris's theatres and *guingettes*, the wonders of mechanical science (balloons and bicycles), the steady liberalisation of the political system, the apparent sense of going eternally onward and upward—these all contributed to France's self-satisfaction and complacent optimism.

But many people, and most foreigners, saw all this as disturbingly parallel to the luxury and decadence that swept away the civilisation of ancient Rome. We would now perhaps compare it to dancing on the *Titanic*. A closer look would reveal that all was not well, starting with the Emperor himself, whose health was steadily failing although he was at pains to conceal it. His relations with the Empress Eugénie were strained, since his mistresses were known to line up for admission to the Tuileries and because her own influence increased just as his declined; her sympathies were much more with conservative Catholic principles than with his growing espousal of the idea of a liberal autocracy. Republicanism, never dormant, was spreading in the corridors of government itself, and satirical magazines proliferated, mocking the hollow facades of Empire. A journalist named Rochefort published one of the most biting of these, *La Lanterne,* which Bizet enthusiastically read. Baron Haussmann, the very symbol of the regeneration of Paris, was revealed to have been borrowing on an unmanageable scale with 40% of the municipal budget going to pay interest on the debt, all carefully concealed in the public accounts. The bonhomie engendered by the Exposition Universelle did not carry over into international relations but merely reinforced a false image of France's prosperity at home and influence abroad.

Bizet started the year 1868, once the run of *La Jolie Fille de Perth* came to an end, with bleak prospects. Since his return from Rome he had composed four operas, only two of which had been staged, with little prospect of either being revived. He had no more commissions in hand. In a sense he was better off than Saint-Saëns who had composed two operas, neither of which would be staged for another ten years (*Le Timbre d'argent* was actually in rehearsal at the Théâtre-Lyrique but was about to fall victim to Carvalho's excesses). But Saint-Saëns was a striking public figure who played piano concertos, was organist of a prominent church, conducted concerts, and travelled abroad, while Bizet had no desire to do any of those things—and with his stocky frame, heavily bearded countenance and brusque manners, he was not a glamorous figure in the public eye.

In January he went to Beauvais, where he had given concerts before, to accompany Mme Carvalho and Hermann-Léon in recital. This was reported in the press,[1] but there may have been many other engagements of this kind that went unnoticed.

While Bizet was working on the piano duet version of *Mignon*, Thomas came out with another formidable success, this time a grand opera in five acts at the Opéra. *Hamlet*, with a libretto by the ever reliable Barbier and Carré, opened on 29 March, with Christine Nilsson as Ophelia and Faure as Hamlet. Thomas originally wrote the part for a tenor but rewrote it for baritone once it was known that Faure was available. As Ophelia, Nilsson was singing all the elaborate coloratura that Bizet might have had her sing in *La Jolie Fille de Perth*. Her closing scene, with the beautiful Ballade "Pâle et blonde, dort sous l'eau profonde", and the sound of off-stage harps as she sinks beneath the water, contributed to the opera's success. Bizet wrote warmly to Thomas on the occasion of an award: "It was expected! I don't say it was merited, because all the medals on earth will never be worth as much as the Esplanade scene."[2] For all the scorn thrown at the libretto's happy ending with Hamlet acclaimed king, the libretto is strong in dramaturgy and characterisation, and it includes a great role for Hamlet's mother. The ending Thomas casually put together for Covent Garden, to satisfy English sensibilities about Shakespeare, is musically much inferior. *Hamlet* in fact offers an excellent illustration of the principles by which Barbier and Carré worked, which were not to present Shakespeare (or Goethe) in operatic dress but to write a strong opera that satisfied the tastes of Second Empire France, and in this they were highly successful.

The vocal score of *Hamlet* was arranged by Vauthrot, chorus-master at the Opéra-Comique, but once again Heugel turned to Bizet for the piano solo reduction. This was done by May, and then he had to arrange the entire opera once again,

---

1. *Le Ménestrel*, 26 January and 2 February 1868.
2. Wright (1988), p. 44.

this time for piano duet, which came out in September. It is likely that he was also charged with proof-reading on the same scale as his labours with *Mignon*.

The vocal score of *La Jolie Fille de Perth*, meanwhile, had been published by Choudens before the end of the opera's run, arranged not by Bizet himself, surprisingly, but by Hector Salomon, principal repetiteur at the Théâtre-Lyrique. The reduction was also available as eighteen separate extracts. Choudens then succeeded in arranging another production of the opera at the Théâtre de la Monnaie in Brussels. There was a close relationship between the opera houses of Paris and Brussels, where a number of French composers were heard when they had no luck with managements in Paris. Probably for these performances, though perhaps earlier in the course of the Paris run, Bizet introduced a number of changes, mostly cuts. The first of three performances was given on 14 April conducted by Charles-Louis Hanssens, who had been conductor at the Monnaie for twenty years. The Catherine was Mme Danieli, on the roster of the Monnaie's leading sopranos, and the Smith was Pierre-Marius Jourdan, the Monnaie's principal tenor, who had sung in the first performance of *L'Enfance du Christ* in 1854. Bizet went to Brussels to attend the final rehearsals and the first night. What he saw in rehearsal horrified him. "I'm in despair. Nothing is going well.... The chorus just quack, the conductor gets the beat wrong, the main singer has a dreadful cold."[3] The orchestra was very good but the production left much to be desired and most of the tempos were quite wrong. "It was not really my work that you heard," he wrote to one of the Brussels critics.[4] He told Lacombe the performance was "monstrous", but that it was nevertheless a success.[5] Bizet wrote to a friend: "They say the *Jolie Fille* was a success in Brussels. I didn't go! But I saw the Rubens in Antwerp!"[6] This is a strange remark, since he did at least go to Brussels for the dress rehearsal, and he could hardly have gone to Antwerp without going to Brussels.

Back home the most worrying news came from the Théâtre-Lyrique, where Carvalho was floating downstream ever closer to the cataract. He started the year expanding his activities to the Théâtre Ventadour, home of the Théâtre-Italien, where in addition to daily performances at the Lyrique, he began to mount his larger productions, including his two Gounod hits, on evenings when the Italiens themselves were not playing. Suddenly on 1 May it was announced that the Lyrique would cease to give performances, and a few days later Carvalho was declared bankrupt with liabilities said to reach one million francs. Both theatres went dark. His creditors, which included many of the musicians who had performed for him

---

3. Lacombe (2000), p. 422.
4. Wright (1988), p. 19.
5. Imbert (1894), p. 187.
6. F-Pn, n.a.fr. 14345 f. 338.

for years, were left unpaid. Mme Carvalho went off to Brussels to sing Juliette, while Carvalho's career suffered no more than a jolt. He even announced that he would stage Saint-Saëns's *Le Timbre d'argent* and Wagner's *Lohengrin* at the Théâtre de la Renaissance that autumn, remote though the possibility of mounting either of them was. He still had many years of successful enterprising management ahead of him, some of it to Bizet's advantage. For all Carvalho's endless history of prevarication, Bizet still owed him a great deal. Whatever sympathy he may have had for the man, Bizet's feelings for Carvalho's wife amounted to unqualified admiration and affection. He must have regretted that she never appeared in any of his stage works.

In his private life change was in the air. During the autumn of 1867 when rehearsals of *La Jolie Fille de Perth* were going well, Bizet wrote to Galabert: "I'm on track! Forward, now! I must keep moving up, moving up! No more evenings out! No more dissipation! No more mistresses! That's all over! Completely over! I'm serious. I've met an adorable girl and I adore her! In two years time she'll be my wife! Between now and then nothing but work and reading; thinking—that's living! I'm serious! I'm convinced! I feel sure of myself! Good has vanquished evil! Victory is won!"[7]

He was speaking of the daughter of his composition teacher: Geneviève Halévy. She was now eighteen, Bizet twenty-nine, and she did indeed become his wife two years later, as promised. She was a competent musician and composed a little. He might not have known her when her father was alive, but he had many contacts with the family; it may have been her cousin William Busnach who brought them together when his farce *Malbrough s'en va-t-en guerre* was in rehearsal at the Théâtre de l'Athénée. Her adored father's death five years earlier and her sister Esther's death two years after that had thrown her life into confusion since the family was inexplicably short of money and had to be shored up by the Rodrigues, Rothschild and Péreire families. Her mother Léonie's mental balance, never good, deteriorated, leaving her dependent on male relatives and friends. After Esther's funeral in 1864 Paladilhe wrote: "The mother has been mad for several months, and Bébé [the family name for Geneviève which Bizet adopted too], who is now a woman, is more and more unbalanced."[8]

In Bizet's next letters to Galabert his hopes have been dashed by a family that was exercising its rights, and his spirits were low.[9] When the question of marriage was raised in the Halévy family it would certainly require consultations with Léonie's brother, Hippolyte Rodrigues, a financier and writer, known in the family

7. Galabert (1909), p. 126.
8. Curtiss (1958), p. 245.
9. Galabert (1909), pp. 130, 131.

as Hippo, also with her in-laws Léon Halévy, Fromental's brother, and Ludovic, Léon's successful librettist son. The idea of this pretty young daughter of a wealthy Jewish family marrying the not very successful composer Bizet, whose prospects were at best uncertain, was unacceptable.

It has always been supposed that their refusal was based on religious grounds: that Geneviève ought to marry a Jew, not a Gentile. Bizet's financial situation was certainly an issue too. But equally likely to have created an obstacle was the suggestion that the suitor's way of life was anything but salubrious. If Bizet was a habitual womaniser, as seems most likely, whispers of the sort of Bohemian company he kept would quickly circulate in theatrical, if not in banking, circles. The French have always taken a lax view of personal morals, so that if a young man was regularly seeking out chorus girls and dancers, even women of the street, no particular stigma was attached. In Bizet's case, this was probably the scenario, since we know of no romantic passions in those years and no steady attachments, although a conversation with Céleste Mogador is suggestive. When she was discussing with him the state of their own relationship, she said:

"My heart has never dreamed of inhabiting a heart which is like a bed-and-breakfast hotel."

"I could get rid of my other lodgers," replied Bizet.

"No, there's one with a lease, your best friend's wife."

"I think her lease has expired. I don't love her any more."

"You love her less, perhaps, but finish your time with her and we'll see what we can do with our nice open friendship." Respectability apparently prevailed.[10]

Who was his best friend's wife? Guiraud was not married, nor was Galabert. As Touchstone says, "Many a man has good horns and knows no end of them."

We might suspect Ludovic of knowing a little too much about the seamier side of Parisian life and Bizet's part in it. Ludovic had once been engaged to his cousin Esther and was devastated when she died. Now he was about to get married himself. He seems to have been firmly on Bizet's side, however. "In the midst of all my troubles," Bizet told him, "I've not had time to thank you for all the support and for the excellent friendship you continue to show me."[11]

So starting in 1867 Bizet promised no more dissipation, no more mistresses. Whether he ever kept these promises is of course an open question, but at least for the time being he was committed to the straight and narrow, learning to be a respectable citizen and a worthy son-in-law. When Lacombe sent him some erotic pictures in August 1868 he replied that he had not thought about a woman for three days. "I'm indulgent towards such sins, and for good reason. Just go to

---

10. Moser (1935), p. 226.
11. US-NHb, Koch 914.

Capua!"¹² We can only guess what he and his friends got up to in Capua on their trip to Naples in August 1859. But now, since the Halévys' objections had to be surmounted, his love for Geneviève was strong enough to instill in him a real determination to change his ways.

★ ★ ★ ★ ★

After an unproductive half-year Bizet was composing again in the summer of 1868, no doubt encouraged by the solitude of Le Vésinet. The symphony was causing a headache, for although it was fully drafted he still had revisions to make and the orchestration was not done. Smaller works, however, were taking shape with some regularity, if not always to his satisfaction. "Dear Madame," he wrote that summer, "I've burnt four songs. I'll tell you all about it this week."¹³ Happily there were songs that were spared. He made the acquaintance of a new dynamic force in Parisian music in the form of Georges Hartmann, who had recently set up as a music publisher close to the Madeleine church. Although as a publisher his name disappeared in the twentieth century, unlike those of Heugel and Choudens, he offered a serious challenge to both. He was also impresario, librettist, composer and above all *animateur*. He was someone who could make things happen and who provided the means by which new music could be heard.¹⁴ Pougin remembered:

> About forty years ago there was to be seen at no. 19 Boulevard de la Madeleine a music shop of modest external appearance but of extraordinary interior design, which seemed, in contrast with its glamorous neighbours in this rather fancy and elegant part of Paris, to refuse to make any special effort to draw the attention of the passing public. After this long span of time I can still see that shop with such a singular ground-plan, stretching a long way back, more like a lengthy passageway leading to a kind of meeting-room where the regulars could meet and chat about art, poetry, and especially music and opera. This modest establishment had been founded a few years earlier by an enterprising, energetic, intelligent and bold young man named Georges Hartmann who, driven by true artistic taste and by confidence in the future vitality of the new French school that was beginning to make itself felt, and finding himself in possession of a certain inheritance, decided to become a publisher with the clear aim of putting the works of unknown young composers before the public. The idea was bold, but Hartmann had the drive and the persistence to bring it off.¹⁵

---

12. Imbert (1894), p. 183.
13. F-Pn, n.a.fr. 14345, f. 350.
14. See Macdonald (2009).
15. *Rivista musicale italiana*, 19 (1912), pp. 916–917.

Hartmann was firmly dedicated to the promotion of young French composers, nearly all of whom were habitués of his shop, and he published works by most of them. His list included Bizet, Franck, Lalo, Saint-Saëns, Paladilhe, Delibes, Guiraud and Joncières, and his star property was Massenet, all of whose works until 1891 were published by Hartmann. A set of six songs by Bizet composed in July 1868 and published in the autumn were some of the first pieces he brought out.

For "Ma vie a son secret", the first song, Bizet went to a well-known poem by an obscure poet, the "Sonnet" of Félix Arvers, published in his *Mes heures perdues* of 1833. Whether Bizet deliberately altered the first line from

> Mon âme a son secret, ma vie a son mystère

to

> Ma vie a son secret, mon âme a son mystère

is not clear, for there are minor substitutions elsewhere that seem to be from a faulty memory, not from an intentional modification. It was probably a poem he had learned in his childhood. The sonnet breathes a passionate love, surely an echo of Bizet's feelings for Geneviève at this point in his life. The last two lines are

> Elle dira, lisant ces vers tout remplis d'elle :
> « Quelle est donc cette femme ? » et ne comprendra pas !
>
> She will say when she reads these lines so obsessed with her:
> "Who is this woman?" and will not understand!

Bizet divides the poem into verses of eight and six lines, so that the second strophe is modified to accommodate a shorter text. Each verse gets louder and faster to a passionate climax, receding to the cadence, and each verse is followed by an eloquent interlude in the piano. Originally composed in the low key of D flat, he published it later in two higher keys, E flat and F.

For "La Coccinelle" he turned again to Victor Hugo with a poem twenty lines long and, as always, cleverly rhymed. The music makes a delightful scherzo-waltz for the poet's youthful folly in taking too much notice of the ladybird sitting on a girl's neck and missing the kiss on her lips. For the last verse, which carries the moral of the fable, Bizet abandons the speedy tempo and the tuneful piano part and turns to painful regret, adding the words (not in Hugo): "Hélas ! j'aurai dû !...j'aurai dû !...", "Alas, I should have..."

The third song, "Pastorale", takes a song from the final scene of *Le Bal*, a comedy in one act by Jean-François Regnard (1655–1709). The song is sung by a valet, Merlin, and a shepherdess. Regnard's works were reprinted many times in the nineteenth century and were enthusiastically praised by Sainte-Beuve and Jules Janin. His plays were still occasionally revived. Bizet's setting of this two-verse pastoral dialogue is utterly charming, with a folk-like lilt and static harmony at the start. Between the lines of the song little would-be-oboe figures are heard. Each verse goes from minor to major, but in the second verse it has all the smiles of a happy ending since the shepherdess has said to her shepherd, "You don't have to steal a kiss, I give it to you!"

"Berceuse sur un vieil air" is a lullaby by the popular poetess Marceline Desbordes-Valmore, who died in 1859. The original has nineteen verses, of which Bizet set only ten, slightly rearranging the order, with two strophes absorbing five verses each. The "old air" is the French folksong "Dodo, l'enfant do", familiar from Fauré's *Dolly* suite and Debussy's "Jardins sous la pluie", which appears in the piano marked by accents in the introduction and between verses. The monotony of the cradling motion in the left hand is broken by the ingenuity of treating the folk song in various different ways (Example 6.1 and Example 6.2, for instance, and at the very end in the bass) and by setting the second strain a tone higher while still preserving the tonic bass. The song was supposed to be dedicated to Léontine Rabaud, née de Maësen, Bizet's Leïla, who was now living in Marseille and had, according to Lacombe, commissioned the song for her baby daughter Gilberte. The publisher mistakenly gave the dedication to Mme Trélat. According to Curtiss it was she who chose the poem, not Léontine Rabaud, who received the dedication of "Rêve de la bien-aimée" instead.[16]

Example 6.1

Example 6.2

Next Bizet chose a poem by a contemporary, Louis de Courmont, "Rêve de la bien-aimée", which he found in a recent anthology entitled *Rimes et idées*. The imagined beloved dreams that she is a spring and her lover is a bird of paradise; that she is the dawn and he a butterfly; that she is a corpse and he her shroud; that her

---

16. Curtiss (1958), p. 219; Lacombe (2000), p. 359.

lips are an open pomegranate and he a gentle breeze; that her breast is an oasis and he the traveller in its shade; finally that her soul is wandering amid eternal shades and he is the angel that carries her to God. Initially calm and in a steady tempo, the music changes radically for the third verse where she dreams she is a corpse, and breaks out into a melodramatic climax. The whole process is repeated for the last three verses, so that the beloved goes to heaven in a glorious fortissimo, the only song in the set to close with such force. Nonetheless there is a certain banality about Bizet's setting, especially in the accompaniment of the opening section which suffers, like many of his song accompaniments, from repetitiveness.

Finally another virtuoso Hugo poem, "La Chanson du fou", sung by the madman in Act IV of his play *Cromwell*. The madman is full of wisdom. Bizet's setting is simple at the beginning, but the second strophe is given a complicated accompaniment that he can only have imagined in orchestral dress. Would that he had made orchestral versions of this and "La Coccinelle", indeed of many of his songs!

These six songs were not intended as a set. They were sold separately, and we should not read too much into the four love poems among the six. All but one are in a steady Andante tempo, at least to start with, so there is too little contrast if all six are sung together. As with the Heugel set, *Feuilles d'album*, all but one are dedicated to female singers, the last being assigned to Emmanuel Jadin, perhaps the grandson of Emmanuel Jadin, composer of Revolutionary hymns and for some years a teacher at the Conservatoire.

When they were finished he wrote to Mme Trélat: "I'll bring you my songs tomorrow. I especially beg you not to assume that you'll find them attractive. I am not sure of myself, and I need some honest advice. If I publish something bad, it will be your fault."[17] Hartmann paid him generously for the songs, which, Bizet confessed, was his main reason for writing them. Hartmann was prepared to publish piano pieces too, three of which came out that year, very different one from another. The first is entitled "Marine", the allusion of the title unexplained unless the gentle melody and rocking accompaniment are intended to suggest a sea voyage. The well-shaped melody is in the left hand (tenor range) and after a full statement minor switches to major for a new broader melody, still in the tenor. Suddenly the music builds in tempo and dynamic and hurtles into a massive pile-up in a remote key, as if this had all along been a narrative, perhaps of a shipwreck. But then the agitation subsides and the closing bars are luminous and calm. Bizet left no clue as to what, if anything, this attractive piece alludes to, although the original title was "La Chanson de matelot—Souvenir d'Ischia", which Bizet had visited in 1859.

Almost in the same breath he composed a Nocturne in D for the piano, strangely entitled "First Nocturne" when he had written another work so named many years

17. Wright (1988), p. 20.

before (in 1854; see Chapter 1) and there never was a second. This piece is harmonically rich and infused with widespread arpeggios in the left hand, almost suggestive of Fauré, and the right hand is decorated with trills and parallel thirds and sixths like garlands of flowers.

The major work of the set is the "Variations chromatiques", a strange and challenging work unique in Bizet's output and unusual in France at that time. His theme is a chromatic scale that rises an octave C to C, and then descends the same octave, rise and fall each filling eight bars of 3/4 time. Seven variations are in the minor, seven in the major, all with the same time-signature, the same rise-and-fall, and the same length. The fifteenth is free, leading into a coda.

Within these restrictions there is a wide variety of texture, tempo and difficulty. The plan is unadventurous but the resourcefulness required to handle chromatic harmony is remarkable. Unfortunately, although many fine pianists have been drawn to this work (including Marmontel, who reviewed it warmly, and Glenn Gould), the layout of the hands is often uncomfortable, and problems of pedalling and balance are acute. No player will ever find this comfortable (see Example 6.3).

Example 6.3

Galabert recalled Bizet playing Beethoven's Thirty-two Variations in C minor, hinting that Bizet was consciously tracing his own variations back to that source. Variation 4 is fiery and massive, *con fuoco*; variations 8 and 9 are delicate and melodious; variation 11 recalls the Chopin *Nocturnes*; variation 13 introduces the love theme from Gounod's *Roméo et Juliette* in an inner voice adapted to 3/4 time; and the coda rounds off the set in elaborate style. Bizet dedicated the "Variations chromatiques" to Stephen Heller (who lived a little way down the same street) and he himself performed this difficult work on 23 December 1871 at a concert of the newly formed Société Nationale de Musique.

★ ★ ★ ★ ★

Throughout the year 1868 Bizet and Geneviève Halévy appear to have been out of touch if not out of mind. Her journal for the year mentions Bizet only once, saying "With all my soul, I love my beloved Georges."[18] Not surprisingly she was more inclined to see the darker side of life: "Each day brings more suffering. I am nineteen years old, and I would need to live through only very few more experiences before my death to have run the full gamut of misfortune.... I dread the future, for the past was hardly such as to give me confidence."[19] Meanwhile, as he approached his thirtieth birthday, Bizet was maturing, thinking harder about his own career and about wider issues, and determined to reform. A return of his troublesome angina in the summer accentuated this frame of mind, and he repeatedly sank into gloomy thoughts about his prospects. At the same time he forced himself to be positive: "An extraordinary change is happening to me. I am changing my skin, both as artist and as man. I am undergoing purification and becoming better, I can feel it! I'll find some good in myself if I look hard enough."[20] He undertook a study of the history of philosophy from the ancient Greeks to the present, discarding almost everything not based on impartial observation and proof. He found spiritualism, idealism, eclecticism, materialism, scepticism and other -isms all useless. Positivism was for him the only rational philosophy. "It's strange that the human mind has taken almost three thousand years to reach this point."[21] While guiding Galabert in his musical studies, Bizet was seeking guidance in philosophy from him in exchange. "What should I read by Littré and Comte?" he asked him, settling on the leading exponents of positivism in recent years.

★ ★ ★ ★ ★

Along with this broad attempt at moral regeneration Bizet was conscious of a radical change in his musical outlook too. The "Variations chromatiques" certainly opened up a bold new path, explored in "La Mort s'avance" and "Tarantella" composed soon after, and in *La Coupe du Roi de Thulé*. If he was to develop a new style it would have to prove itself in opera, since his thoughts were never far from that world. The greater difficulty he had with his symphony, the easier he found it to plunge into the world of the theatre. All his training and all his instincts led him to persist in the search for the right libretto and a management willing to stage his

---

18. Curtiss (1958), p. 248, in a penetrating chapter on the Halévy family and their troubles.
19. Curtiss (1958), p. 249.
20. Galabert (1909), p. 147.
21. Galabert (1909), p. 151.

work with the best singers. He was always curious about operas by other composers, especially those he respected. Félicien David's *Herculanum*, widely regarded at the time as his best opera and certainly his most extravagant, was revived at the Opéra in July 1868. It had originally been performed when Bizet was in Italy.

Bizet was in discussion with Perrin, director of the Opéra, who proposed a libretto for him to be written by Leroy and Sauvage. Hippolyte Leroy wrote librettos for Adam and Membrée, worked for the administration of the Opéra, and was a librettist of Bizet's own *Ivan IV*, while Thomas Sauvage was the author of many plays and librettos, especially for operas by Ambroise Thomas. At seventy-two he had effectively retired from libretto writing, was in bad health, and was an unlikely collaborator for a young composer. Neither the subject nor the libretto's title is mentioned in any correspondence, and no other composer appears to have set a libretto by these two, so the project, like so much else, remains wrapped in mystery. Bizet referred to it as his "grande affaire" and his "machine" and had considerable hopes for it. In October 1868 the libretto's first act was written. Bizet liked it, but in February 1869 the finished libretto was rejected by Perrin, and the project lapsed. This was the second time he had knocked without success at the door of the Opéra.

In addition to the Leroy/Sauvage libretto, which he expected to be given to set, he had a less than exciting proposal from the Théâtre-Italien that went nowhere since the libretto did not appeal to him. Pasdeloup, who had taken over the management of the Théatre-Lyrique, said he was interested in reviving *La Jolie Fille de Perth*, although he never did. More promising were plans for an opera with a libretto by none other than Geneviève's uncle Léon. Léon Halévy, the composer's younger brother, was a classical scholar and philosopher who wrote poetry and was deeply interested in the theatre. He had written a one-act libretto for his brother nearly forty years before, but very few since then. He now offered Bizet two subjects entitled *Vanina* and *Les Templiers*, the former based on a Stendhal story. "I'm impatient to tell you," Bizet wrote to him in September 1868, "how excited I am about your plan for *Les Templiers*. It's *superb*! I've spent a week on this outline and I think I have a good grasp of it."[22] The plan was to have the expert St-Georges write the verse, as his name would enhance the opera's prospects. Bizet raised the topic with Perrin at the Opéra, but the latter could not make any commitment until he saw the libretto. That libretto was evidently never written, for no more was heard or said about it, at least not until Victor Wilder, in his obituary of Bizet in 1875, mentioned it as one of his works. It is doubtful if St-Georges ever got round to writing it. The subject was evidently drawn from the history of the ever-popular Crusades, as displayed in Prosper Pascal's opera *Les Templiers* on his own libretto from 1867; Massenet

22. US-NHb.

wrote part of an opera called *Les Templiers* on a libretto by Jules Adenis in 1873, and Litolff set the same libretto, or something like it, in 1886.

As a residual legacy of the 1867 Exposition Universelle three competitions were announced with invitations to compose operas for the Opéra, the Opéra-Comique or the Théâtre-Lyrique, the operas to be submitted by August 1868. The choice of libretto for the Opéra was announced in April 1868: *La Coupe du Roi de Thulé* by Louis Gallet and Edouard Blau, published soon after. The libretto for the Opéra-Comique was *Le Florentin* by St-Georges, and for the Théâtre-Lyrique the composer was free to choose his own. Deadline for the compositions was then re-set as 30 April 1869 and later extended to 1 September 1869.

Bizet suggested to his pupil Galabert that he set the first two acts of *La Coupe du Roi de Thulé* as an exercise, so we have Bizet's detailed response to Galabert's efforts and his thoughts on how the libretto ought to be set. With the Leroy/Sauvage opera in the air he hesitated to enter the competition himself, reasoning that if he did not win the prize, Perrin would think less of him; if he won, it would delay the other project; if he did not enter and the other project fell through, he would fall between two stools. Perrin in fact encouraged him to enter, hinting that he would win—which Bizet interpreted as meaning that Perrin counted on having at least a Bizet score to fall back on if there were no better ones to choose from. In August he told Lacombe he had composed the first act "on his walks", but had decided not to enter the competition. He did not tell Galabert he had decided to enter until October, when while orchestrating his symphony at top speed he revealed that he had written the first two acts and was thoroughly pleased with them. The opera would be his main preoccupation throughout the winter, once the symphony was orchestrated and launched.

On 13 November 1868, in his villa in Passy, Rossini died at the age of seventy-six after a prolonged illness. He was regarded by all Parisians as their Grand Old Man of music, much liked for his conviviality and for his adoption of the city as his home. The church of the Madeleine was too small for the funeral, so it was transferred to the church of the Sainte-Trinité at the top of the Rue de la Chaussée d'Antin, a major addition to the landscape of the Ninth Arrondissement completed only the year before. In the presence of a vast crowd of mourners Patti, Alboni, Nilsson, Tamburini and Faure all sang, and the Funeral March from Beethoven's piano sonata, op. 26, which had been played at the funeral of Beethoven himself, was heard in an arrangement for four saxophones. Rossini was buried in the cemetery of Père Lachaise near Cherubini, Chopin and Bellini, although he remained there only until 1887 when his embalmed body was transferred to the church of Santa Croce in Florence, leaving his wife behind at Père Lachaise.

It was not long before the funeral of another senior composer was held at the same church, that of Berlioz, who died at his home on the Rue de Calais on

8 March 1869 aged sixty-five. Overlooking the years of disdain and neglect that his music had suffered in Paris, an impressive delegation of leading musicians and members of the Institute attended, and his own *Symphonie funèbre* was appropriately heard. At the graveside in the Montmartre cemetery four speeches were delivered, one of them by Gounod. Another was by Antoine Elwart, a musician of little talent to whom Berlioz had once said, "If you are going to make a speech, I'd rather not die." Listening to his speech, Bizet was driven to a fit of outrage when he heard Elwart refer to Berlioz as "our colleague".[23]

Hartmann drew three more smaller pieces from Bizet that winter, all published in 1869. *La Mort s'avance* is a strange work whose origin is obscure. Bizet selected (or was given) a text from the *Cantiques spirituels* by the Abbé Pellegrin, a cleric and tragedian who had written the libretto for Rameau's *Hippolyte et Aricie*. He set two verses for chorus and orchestra and called the piece a "meditation on two Études by Frédéric Chopin", whose name is printed in larger type than Bizet's on the title page. The melodic outline and harmonic framework of the piece are derived from the Études op. 25 no. 12 in C minor and op. 10 no. 1 in C major, while their elaborate keyboard figuration is completely replaced. The outline of the first of these Études can be seen in the opening bars for the voices (Example 6.4).

Example 6.4

The first verse in the minor key is for men's voices; the second verse in the major key, based on the major-key Étude, is for sopranos, gradually joined by the tenors, then the basses. The ingenuity and originality of the plan are nothing if not bold, perhaps illustrating what Bizet referred to when he said he was striking out in a new direction in music. He copied out a set of orchestral parts himself, perhaps for a performance in September 1869 suggested by a letter which comments on Chopin's name sharing a concert bill with his own.[24]

The second composition was a song, "Tarentella", a breezy setting of an Italian popular verse which he probably brought home from Italy. It was written for

23. Boschot (1912), p. 661.
24. Curtiss (1958), p. 254.

Christine Nilsson and is clearly fashioned as something with which she might bring the house down at a private soirée. The singer is given plenty of trills and runs with a middle section where the vocal line is calm and smooth as respite from the rapid tarantella before and after. Bizet seems to be pushing his harmonic language forward to allow casual collisions which his Conservatoire teachers would have forbidden. When putting together his collection *Vingt Mélodies* in 1873, Bizet adapted this music to a French poem on the fleeting essence of love, taken from Edouard Pailleron's collection *Amours et haines*, and he later orchestrated it.

Hartmann must have expressed a preference for sacred texts, for Bizet's third vocal work for his list was "Esprit saint", a setting for voice, piano and optional harmonium of "Invocation à l'Esprit Saint" from the *Cantiques de Saint-Sulpice*, a widely circulated compendium of hymns. There is nothing churchy about Bizet's setting, however. The melody is broad and powerful, and the relentless figuration in the piano's right hand above a striding bass suggests an intense religious fervour that Bizet could plainly express, if not himself share. The song was dedicated to the Viennese Marie-Gabrielle Krauss, a leading soprano at the Théâtre-Italien from 1866 to 1870.

Hartmann, like Choudens and Heugel, offered Bizet work as an arranger also. Two Saint-Saëns works fell to his lot. The first was the Second Piano Concerto in G minor, today the best known of the five, of which Saint-Saëns had given the first performance on 13 May 1868. Bizet's assignment was to arrange the orchestral part for piano so that the work could be issued for two pianos; in this form, though now published by Durand, it is still available today. Three years later, when Durand, Schœnwerk & Cie had taken over the concerto from Hartmann, Bizet wrote an arrangement of the scherzo movement for solo piano, combining both solo and orchestral parts, and it is possible that he in fact arranged the entire work for solo piano, although the outer movements did not appear in print until 1894. The second Saint-Saëns work was the well-known violin solo "Introduction et Rondo capriccioso", first performed by Sarasate on 4 April 1867, for which Bizet supplied the piano reduction of the orchestral part. This is another Bizet arrangement that has been in continuous use to this day. Soon afterward Hartmann sold the Saint-Saëns arrangements to Durand and the songs to Choudens and published no more Bizet at all.

★ ★ ★ ★ ★

Bizet approached the performance of his symphony with a certain nervousness, for he expressed an unusual level of anxiety when working on it, a task he had more than once postponed. Pasdeloup had conducted the scherzo in January 1863 and continued to express interest in performing the entire work. Now that it was finally ready, Pasdeloup found a place for it in his concert on 28 February 1869, one of the Concerts Populaires—which were truly popular concerts—given in the large

Cirque Napoléon. The enterprising Pasdeloup, though by common consent not a brilliant conductor, presented works which other bodies, notably the Société des Concerts, would not consider, and in the weeks before Bizet's symphony was heard he had conducted Rubinstein's "Ocean" Symphony, Mendelssohn's "Reformation" Symphony, and Gade's Symphony in B flat. Forgetting or denying his brilliant Symphony in C from 1856, Bizet always referred to this new work as his "Symphony", sometimes as his "First Symphony", and he ended up naming it his "First Suite"; it has been known to posterity as "Roma", a title he never gave it. We will hereafter call it his Second Symphony, another title he never gave it but which might bestow on it the dignified status it deserves.

As the concert date approached, Pasdeloup or Bizet decided to omit the scherzo, and the work was billed as *Souvenirs de Rome, fantaisie symphonique* with the movements headed (I) "Une Chasse dans la forêt d'Ostie", (III) "Une Procession", and (IV) "Carnaval à Rome". There is no reason to think Bizet came up with these titles. Galabert could not recall him ever speaking of the work as having titles of this kind, and the *Revue et gazette musicale* in its review of the concert thought they could not be his choice.[25] In 1911 Octave Séré astutely suggested that "Une Chasse dans la forêt d'Ostie" sounds suspiciously like "La Chasse d'Ossian", linking the first movement to the overture submitted to the Institute in 1861.[26] Ostia is the port of Rome, in whose forested vicinity there was probably more hunting in Bizet's time than in the pages of Ossian. The main Allegro of the first movement adopts the 6/8 time-signature and prominent horns essential for all evocations of the hunt, and if "La Chasse d'Ossian" were recycled, not destroyed, in 1861, this is where we should look for its reincarnation. A letter to Galabert of 1868 describes the main theme of the Allegro as "l'ancien thème",[27] and there is no reason to think this first movement was not originally conceived in Italy, perhaps with the title "Rome" and finished in Paris in 1861. The same letter reports that he had abandoned "the variations", referring to the funeral march heard in 1861, which was now replaced as the slow movement. The finale has the character and tempo of a saltarello or tarantella from Naples, as Bizet originally planned it. The plain heading "Carnaval" is the only part of these titles to survive in the printed score. There are two autograph orchestral scores of the complete work, neither bearing any descriptive titles, one bearing the main title 1ère *Symphonie*, while the other is headed 1ère *Suite*, op. 11.[28] This is

25. Galabert (1909), p. 23; *Revue et gazette musicale*, 7 March 1869.
26. Séré (1911), p. 33.
27. Galabert (1909), p. 138.
28. Private collection. In the first autograph, which has been subjected to heavy revision, the Scherzo ("No. 3") is a survival from the 1861 submission. The second autograph is a neat fair copy, probably intended for the engraver.

curious since very few works composed between 1854 and 1874 bear any opus number at all, and since nowhere in his correspondence did Bizet refer to the work as a suite.

The Second Symphony is strong and well written, scored with Bizet's usual imaginative skill. The first movement is compact, since instead of recapitulating the Allegro in the usual place the music returns to the slow introduction. At the opening, four horns present a broad hymn-like tune; but before the Allegro arrives a storm grows out of nowhere and turns the music to the minor key for a direct lead-in to the Allegro. This has something of the same restless C minor vigour as the first allegro in Saint-Saëns's better known Third Symphony. Horns and hunting rhythms are prominent. A long melody on the clarinet provides a contrasting subject in E flat. Once the development arrives, the movement is given over to continuous development, never restating the main C minor theme or even returning to that key. The horn's opening melody is heard in the strings in E major against scurrying rhythms in the lower voices, and it returns finally at its original slow speed in its original key of C major. Bizet was right to regard this as a new treatment of traditional form, here abbreviated into something closer to a ternary design, with a highly exploratory allegro featuring brisk 6/8 rhythms and some exposed writing for—besides the ever-present horns—clarinets, bassoons and violas.

The Scherzo is one of Bizet's brilliant inventions, comparable to the scherzo in the First Symphony. It is cast as a swift fugue with a broad theme in the Trio that suggests Italian opera. The slow movement looks forward to the *L'Arlésienne* music, strongly melodic and interestingly scored with the double basses sounding higher than the cellos. The middle section offers a chorale-like theme scored for flute, cor anglais and bassoon each an octave apart and supported by the harp. It is hard to argue that this is a satisfactory foil to the beautiful outer sections of the movement, but the theme will return in the last movement with much more potent effect, contributing an exultant close to an energetic movement full of carnivalesque life and colour.

Bizet reported that at the concert there was much applause and some boos, "in sum, a success."[29] The reviews were favourable, but the only further performances in his lifetime were, once again, partial: Saint-Saëns conducted a performance of the scherzo for the Société Philharmonique de Paris on 25 April 1872, and not long before this, on 23 December 1871, at a concert presented by the newly formed Société Nationale de Musique, the Finale was heard in Bizet's arrangement for eight hands at two pianos, played by Saint-Saëns, Guiraud, Alexis-Henri Fissot and

---

29. Galabert (1909), p. 183.

Bizet himself.[30] It has been claimed that Bizet revised the work in 1871,[31] but there seems to be no evidence of that, only the hope expressed, sometimes with false confidence, that Pasdeloup would programme it again in his winter concerts. Shortly after the performance of the Second Symphony Choudens undertook to engrave the score and to have a piano arrangement made, although in fact he did not publish it until a few years after Bizet's death.

★ ★ ★ ★ ★

In Pasdeloup's hands the Théâtre-Lyrique came alive again, although he had little experience of management and inherited many unsolved problems from Carvalho. He was determined to stage some Wagner, filling in meanwhile with revivals of older successes including *Rigoletto* and *Don Giovanni*. In March 1869 he dug up a one-act opera by Guiraud, *En Prison*, which had been the theatre's property for many years and therefore proof against Guiraud's protests that it was an immature work that he did not wish to see performed. The Wagner Pasdeloup successfully staged was *Rienzi*, which opened on 6 April. It was not a failure, but it ran into a storm of abuse from the anti-Wagnerians mocking the idea of a twenty-eight-year old opera being the "music of the future", and not such good music at that. Pasdeloup would have done better to choose *Der fliegende Holländer* or *Lohengrin*. Bizet went to the dress rehearsal, which lasted from eight o'clock until two in the morning. "Bizarre, bad style," he wrote, "music more of decadence than of the future. Chaotic genius, but genius nevertheless," was his confused reaction.[32]

Camille Du Locle, Perrin's nephew, hoping to take over the Opéra-Comique, offered Bizet a libretto by Du Locle himself and the popular playwright Victorien Sardou, *Grisélidis*, on a story by Boccaccio. This was for the future, and in any case he had *La Coupe du Roi de Thulé* to finish, a preoccupation he kept largely to himself. We know that he told Guiraud, Galabert, Hartmann, Léontine Rabaud and perhaps others that he was composing it, but it is likely that he did not want everyone to know. In August 1868 he told Lacombe "on my walks I've composed the first act of the *Roi de Thulé*, but I've decided not to compete." It was not until October that he told Galabert that he too was composing the opera, and in October 1869, a year later, he told Lacombe he had not composed anything for thirteen months, which was patently untrue. We are reminded that he told Saint-Saëns he did not compete in setting *Les Noces de Prométhée* in 1867, which was also untrue.

30. The autograph parts of this arrangement, which has never been published, are at F-Pn MS 10601, entitled *Final de la 1ère Symphonie*. An eight-hand arrangement of the Scherzo by Emil Kronke was published by Steingräber, Leipzig, in 1909.
31. For example by Curtiss (1958), pp. 310–311.
32. Galabert (1909), p. 185.

He might have had good reason to finish the opera in good time (it was not due to be submitted until 1 September), because another well-kept secret came abruptly into the open when on 6 May 1869 he and Geneviève Halévy announced their engagement. The family's attempt to arrange a match with a wine merchant from Bordeaux named Desoria having failed, other obstacles laid in the lovers' way were somehow overcome. They found opportunities to meet and renew their commitment to each other. As Mme Halévy was in a sanatorium at the time, the Halévy family approval came from Léon Halévy, and the couple were married on Thursday, 3 June at the Mairie of the Ninth Arrondissement. There was apparently no religious ceremony, neither Jewish nor Christian. Besides Léon Halévy the witnesses were Bizet's father, Hippolyte Rodrigues (Mme Halévy's brother, who strongly supported Bizet's claim), Emile Péreire the banker, Adrien Benoit-Champy, and Adolphe Franck, a philosopher, probably a friend of Léon's. The Delsartes were apparently absent.

On hearing of the engagement Paladilhe's father wrote to his son, "I'm glad it's Bizet, not you, who's marrying Mlle Halévy, even though she is your teacher's daughter. Even when I knew her as a child it was not difficult to recognise the seeds of a mental instability that did not bode well for the future."[33] Bizet had no such warning from his own family; indeed he was clearly and boundlessly happy. She brought a dowry that Bizet estimated as 150,000 francs now, plus 500,000 later, which would make any young composer happy. Ludovic Halévy noted in his diary: "Today Geneviève married Bizet. How happy she is, the poor, dear child!"

They went to Rodrigues's house in St-Gratien, a little north of Paris, for their honeymoon, Rodrigues henceforth becoming an indispensable friend to them both. He had been a stockbroker but was now writing a long series of books, including poems and plays. He was a helpful stand-in for his sister in taking what care he could of his niece. The couple had an apartment to move to in a new building at 22 Rue de Douai, a continuation of the street in which Bizet was born and literally around the corner from the Rue Fontaine-St-Georges where he had been living with his father for the last few years. A little to the north was the Place Pigalle, soon to become a regular meeting place for artists and men of letters. They took possession of their new home in the middle of October and busied themselves, as young couples do, fitting it up to their liking. Bizet already had a substantial library of books and music to find room for.[34] They still kept the two little houses in Le Vésinet for the summer. No doubt Bizet had to rein in his habit of working late into the night.

He was without any certain commissions, but he had several tasks ahead of him. That July he was coopted to serve on the examining board for the Prix de Rome,

---

33. Curtiss (1958), p. 248.

34. A full description of the apartment is given in Lacombe (2000), pp. 460–463.

following the new practice of opening up juries to musicians other than professors at the Conservatoire, a sensible move since teachers had always unfairly favoured their own pupils. He was late with some work for Choudens, perhaps correcting the proofs of the Second Symphony, perhaps an arrangement of some kind. He asked Choudens to approach Henry Litolff, who was planning some concerts at the Opéra, with the offer of some extracts from *La Jolie Fille de Perth*, but he insisted he would not conduct them himself, even if they were programmed (which they weren't). "Je suis un chef-d'orchestre de *carton*," he said, a *cardboard* conductor, adding that he hated exhibitionism.[35] He could not offer Litolff his symphony since he was keeping that in case it would be played again in one of Pasdeloup's concerts (which it wasn't).

He was tempted by a libretto on the Gaulish warrior Vercingetorix by Emile Delerot, director of the Bibliothèque de Versailles. The trouble with it, he said, was how to make Julius Caesar sing. "Those emperors are usually so unmusical—Caesar, Charlemagne, Alexander, Napoleon."[36] He might have added Napoleon III to his list of unmusical emperors, he who in 1865 had published a two-volume life of Julius Caesar.

Whereas for many years Bizet had been closely associated with the Théâtre-Lyrique and its director Carvalho, he now moved more and more into the orbit of the Opéra-Comique, with du Locle taking over the role of occasional benefactor. Du Locle was a poet and librettist with an eye for novelty and talent. He was one of the librettists of Verdi's *Don Carlos* and had played a part in the genesis of *Aida*. He had sufficient faith in Bizet to entrust him with Sardou's *Grisélidis*, and at the same time he came up with a project to compose an opera on Mistral's story *Calendal* with a libretto by Paul Ferrier, a young writer still unversed in the ways of opera. This was clearly intended to exploit the Provençal vein of Gounod's *Mireille*, also a Mistral story, even though that opera was still not enjoying the success that later came its way. The Sardou libretto *Grisélidis* was not ready, and he was soon thinking about an opera on Richardson's *Clarissa*, encouraged by du Locle, who was hoping to be named director of the Opéra-Comique and was indeed so appointed at the end of the year. None of these ideas were yet ready for the work of composition. In fidelity to his late father-in-law Bizet undertook to supervise the republication of his 1838 opera *Guido et Ginevra* which the Théâtre-Italien was about to revive (in Italian) and which the publisher Lemoine was planning to reissue. He was similarly consulted by Ludovic and by Lemoine about alterations that might be needed in Halévy's *La Reine de Chypre* (1841) if Marie Sasse were to sing it in a revival at the Opéra. This did not take place, however.

35. Copy at F-Po, p. 73.
36. Curtiss (1958), pp. 254–255.

As another filial duty he undertook a task that had been waiting for seven years: the completion of Halévy's opera *Noé*, left unfinished at his death.[37] There could be no better way to repay his debt to the family and to earn their gratitude. Pasdeloup undertook to produce it at the Théâtre-Lyrique, a strong incentive to move forward. It was a huge task. Halévy left the vocal parts complete and the bass line indicated in many places, but there was no harmony and only a few hints at orchestration. Bizet described the first three acts as "almost done", which implies that Halévy had not begun to compose the substantial fourth act shown in the manuscript librettos. It is likely that Halévy left the Introduction and the recitatives undone. What survives is a total of nearly five hundred pages of full score in Bizet's hand, but which sections were composed by him is not easy to determine. Two sections of the opera were published as his compositions in 1883 in the posthumous collection of *Seize Mélodies*: the central section of the Duo no. 3 under the title "Pourquoi pleurer?" and part of the Duo no. 14 with the title of its first line "Qui donc t'aimera mieux?" It is certain that the Duo no. 8 is his, since it is adapted mostly from *Ivan IV*. The Entr'acte before Act II includes a passage borrowed from *Vasco de Gama*. Dean has observed that there is "no doubt that Bizet's work on *Noé* was greater than is commonly supposed," citing the end of the Scène no. 9bis as distinctive of Bizet's style.[38] In their contract with Pasdeloup the family retained the right to withdraw the work if the right singers were not available. This was in fact the case, Pasdeloup's troupe being significantly short of good singers, and in January 1870 it was announced that the plan had been abandoned. Here was yet one more case of many hundreds of hours of work wasted on an opera that would not be performed.

★ ★ ★ ★ ★

Another such case was *La Coupe du Roi de Thulé*. On 19 November 1869 the results of the competition were announced. Forty-two scores were submitted; the judges were Bazin, Boulanger, Duprato, Gevaert, Maillart, Massé, Saint-Saëns and Semet, with Perrin ex officio. The list of candidates was reduced to twenty-one, then to seven, including Bizet, then to five. The grand prize was awarded to Eugène Diaz de la Peña, who spent a month with Bizet at the Villa Medicis in April 1858 although he never won the Prix de Rome. Massenet was second, Guiraud third, Barthe fourth and Prince Poniatowski fifth. It is customary to deride Diaz as an amateur and to repeat Paladilhe's malicious remark that his cantata was partly the work of Massé, one of the judges. But Diaz had a full Conservatoire training under Halévy and had had an opera *Le Roi Candaule* very successfully staged at the Théâtre-Lyrique

---

37. Galabert (1909) and Pigot (1886) claim that he started work on *Noé* in 1868, but there seems to be no other evidence for that.

38. Dean (1975), p. 193.

in 1865. He and Bizet were good friends; according to Gallet he had even consulted Bizet and Guiraud about the orchestration.[39] Diaz's opera was eventually performed at the Opéra on 10 January 1873 with Faure in the part of Paddock, and revived later the same year.

La Coupe du Roi de Thulé was Bizet's fifth full-length opera, whose fragmentary survival is one of the saddest of the many misfortunes that have bedevilled his life and subsequent fate.[40] Having submitted it for the competition he must have known that if it failed to win it would have no chance of being staged, since the winner's opera would preempt any performance of a different setting of the same libretto. He knew, in other words, that he was very likely to be wasting his time, and it is possible that he concealed his participation from the Halévy family, even perhaps from his wife, for that reason. It is significant that in his publication of Bizet's letters Galabert started making substantial cuts at the point where Bizet's engagement to Geneviève is announced, since Bizet was confiding things which his widow, still alive in 1909 when the book came out, might not want to read. Bizet evidently put it about that he did not finish the opera and that he abandoned any plan to submit it for the competition. Galabert, Wilder and Pigot all believed that. Even Dean, in his extended study of the opera in 1947, supposed that Bizet gave up. But complete it and submit it he did, and having done so he exchanged the envelope that contained his name and address for two envelopes, one stating that in case of not winning he did not wish his name to be known, the second giving his name and new address just in the event that he was the winner.[41] He was unusually silent about the results when they came out, the more to conceal the fact that he had actually taken part.

Massenet transferred much of his score to later works, while Bizet extracted three sections as songs later published in the collection *Seize Mélodies*. About 130 pages of autograph score survive out of perhaps five or six hundred. The fragmentary state of the autograph suggests that missing portions were adapted for music he composed after 1869.

Knowing it was a risky undertaking when he decided to compose the opera, therefore, he must have found the libretto all the more appealing and its musical possibilities well suited to his gifts. Often in his letters to Galabert we can hear Bizet thinking aloud about how to set certain scenes and develop certain characters. Despite being described by Clément as an "amphibian opera, neither fish nor fowl",[42] the libretto of *La Coupe du Roi de Thulé* is a well-crafted story taking as its

39. Gallet (1891), p. 61.
40. A longer study of *La Coupe du Roi de Thulé* is found in Dean (1947), although he was unaware of three more fragments of the opera in private hands.
41. Curtiss (1958), p. 256.
42. Clément (1877), p. 839.

starting point Goethe's ballad as sung by Gretchen in *Faust* in which the king's fidelity to his long-lost love is embodied in the cup he hurls into the sea just before his death. Gallet and Blau, the authors of the libretto, suppose that the king received the cup from Claribel, immortal queen of the ocean, and that on his deathbed he has to give the cup to whomever he chooses to be his successor. He is dying for love of Myrrha, who has betrayed him with his favourite, Angus, who nonetheless expects to be named his successor. A young fisherman, Yorick, is also in love with Myrrha. The king, whom we do not see, calls his jester, Paddock, into his presence, and gives him the cup. Paddock hurls it into the sea. In the consternation that follows Myrrha promises to give herself to whoever will bring the cup back. Yorick plunges after the cup into the sea.

Act II takes place in the watery kingdom where Claribel and her sirens are surprised to find the cup. Claribel has always been in love with Yorick, who comes in in quest of the cup. Claribel offers him immortality if he will love her, and she even shows him a vision of Angus and Myrrha cooing amorously to each other in a barge, but Yorick is determined to return to Thule to claim Myrrha. If that fails, Claribel tells him, he must drink from the cup three times and she will come to his rescue.

The first tableau of Act III shows the people led by Paddock in revolt against Angus who has claimed the throne without the old king's blessing. Yorick returns with the cup and detains Myrrha, reminding her of her promise. She is defiant. In the second tableau, the people are appeased and Angus and Myrrha are enthroned. All drink from the cup. When it is Yorick's turn, he sings in praise of Claribel and drinks three times. The palace collapses consuming Angus and Myrrha, while the sea rises with Claribel and the sirens claiming Yorick for their own.

There are many operatic opportunities here: in the contrast between the regal scenes on earth and the fairytale underwater world; in the tension, Tannhäuser-like, between Yorick's love of an earthly woman and the enchantments of a nymph; in the ballads and legends sung by Myrrha, Paddock and Yorick; and in the cataclysmic ending in which the usurpers are punished and immortal love is rewarded. There are good scenes for both the men's and women's choruses, and a fitting place for ballet in the underwater scene. Angus is clearly a villain and a bass, Yorick a diffident tenor hero, and Paddock the canny foil to all of them, perhaps derived from Rigoletto. The two women are nicely contrasted: Myrrha beautiful, ambitious, and unscrupulous; Claribel pure and unselfish. (Why they were all given such inappropriate names is a mystery.) The verse is good, mostly in short lines and free of operatic cliché.

The most complete section of music to have survived is the Prélude, a tense and sombre piece, full of acerbic harmony in Bizet's new style, presenting the theme of Myrrha's "Légende" at the opening, Claribel's "Siren song" in the middle section, and representing in its final mood the alarm felt in the kingdom of Thule in anticipation of the king's death. The first surviving fragment of the opera itself is from the end of the Introduction where a five-part chorus is already richly displaying the new harmony (Example 6.5).

Example 6.5

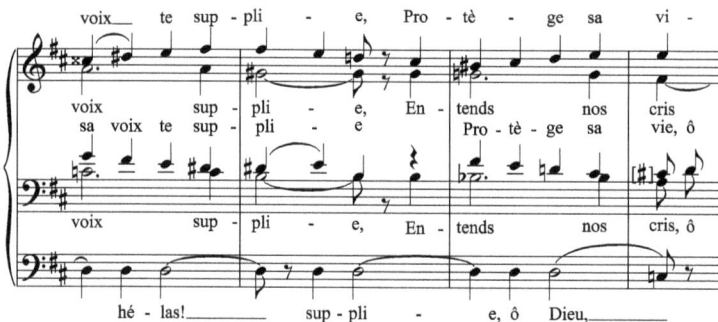

This is followed by the music for Paddock's first entry, still in D major, with the melody scored for clarinets, first violins and cellos all in unison, and we have his complete Air "Quand la nuit te couvre", an impassioned lament in B major, sung alone on stage, for his dying king. Paddock is not the only operatic jester to be lamenting when he should be jesting, but this is certainly one of the most expressive of such solos, over rich deep harmony with cellos and basses on independent lines.

We have no music for Yorick's entry and only the last nineteen bars of his duet with Paddock. Nor do we have Myrrha's first entry, which is unfortunate since Bizet told Galabert to attach great importance to this moment in order to delineate her character as an ambitious, catlike "courtesan from the ancient world".[43] We have Yorick's presentation of the pearl, and from later in the same scene Myrrha's "Légende", darkly coloured with two cors anglais. The first verse ends on a rapid diminuendo replaced in the second verse by a stirring choral climax with two notes (its only contribution) from a contrabass trombone. Paddock's entry with the cup is a formal melody in march tempo, not unlike his entry at the beginning of the act. His song about the lion and the monkey is preserved as the song "N'oublions pas", evidently transposed, in the posthumous *Seize Mélodies*, where new words by Barbier replace the original. It has a strong dramatic quality derived from the constant dissonance, although the rhythms are mostly unchanging. The end of the song is operatic in character, certainly, and the piano part suggests an orchestra (Example 6.6), with a tremendous orchestral climax at the end.

43. Galabert (1909), p. 165.

Example 6.6

In the surviving remnant of the first-act finale, when Yorick calls on Myrrha to uphold her vow, Bizet introduces a phrase that was to come back at the end of Act III of *Carmen* (Example 6.7). Winton Dean has rightly drawn attention to the dramatic as well as musical kinship of this scene in *La Coupe du Roi de Thulé* with *Carmen,* for the tenor is begging the soprano to be true to her word when no one doubts that that is not in her nature.

We do not have the sirens' chorus at the beginning of Act II, but Claribel's lines dismissing them call for an off-stage group of two clarinets, piano, harp and harmonium, following a similar off-stage line-up in Gounod's *Philémon et Baucis*. In the scene that follows, where one of the sirens, her confidante, urges Claribel to find love, Bizet must have been thinking of the scene for Anna and Dido in the opening scene of Berlioz's *Les Troyens à Carthage*, where some of the lines are similar. Only the last sixteen bars survive, leading into Claribel's Romance which survives with different words as the song "La Sirène" in the collection *Seize Mélodies*. Restoring the original

Example 6.7

Example 6.8

words and imagining, say, a sustained horn note on B flat, the following passage gives a good idea of the harmonic collisions which Bizet's new style permitted (Example 6.8).

The full music of the vision that Claribel shows Yorick to prove that Myrrha is not worthy of him survives in a duet "Rêvons", the accompaniment of which Bizet arranged for piano himself, although when it was published in 1887 it was supplied with new words by Barbier. It is a languorous duet with the voices often a tenth apart and a flowing barcarolle accompaniment. The middle section works up to a strong climax over a long tonic pedal, and one can well imagine the impressive effect of this scene if only we had Bizet's orchestration. Part of this scene was adapted as a solo song "Aimons, rêvons!", also published posthumously.

In the third act Myrrha, like Lady Macbeth, is bolstering Angus's faltering resolve in the face of Paddock's insinuations. Myrrha then has a solo scene, at the end of which the clamour of the crowd is heard outside. More alarming still is the sound of Yorick's voice singing "Myrrha, la brise est forte" (Example 6.7). After Myrrha has taken the cup from Yorick and handed it to Angus, Yorick is horrified, and the chorus file out, mocking Yorick with a four-square tune that was arranged as a quintet by Choudens for one of the many posthumous versions of *La Jolie Fille de Perth*. Otherwise only fragments give any idea of the final scene, although the recurrence of certain ideas, in addition to Example 6.7, show that Bizet was ready to link one scene with another in a constructive fashion. Of the pacing and dramatic effect of the whole there is too little to form a judgment, although the care with which the manuscript materials have been prepared, not to mention the thoughtful discussions with Galabert, show that Bizet put his heart into it. Signs that he was working out a new harmonic language are all the more tantalising since he wrote no major work after this for over two years and seems to have left this style behind for a different kind of maturity.

The libretto indicates a number of set pieces whose music has disappeared. These include:

Paddock's Couplets, Act I: "Pourquoi veut-on que je pleure ?", two verses.
Yorick's Romance, Act I: "La nature entière me semble", two verses.
Paddock and Yorick, Duo, Act I: "Démon ou femme".
Myrrha, Couplets, Act I: "De ton âme troublée", two verses.
Sirènes' Chœur, Act II: "Nous sommes les sirènes".
Claribel's Air, Act II: "Tombez, flot courroucés".
Claribel and Yorick, Duo, Act II: "Enfant, tu connais mon empire".
Seigneurs, Chœur, Act III Tab 1: "Ah! quel audace!".
Yorick's Invocation, Act III Tab 2: "Au pauvre insensé qui tremble", two verses.

It is not impossible that some of these may be identified with music in *Djamileh* or *Carmen*.

★ ★ ★ ★ ★

Reyer observed that Bizet was transformed by his marriage, leaving behind the impulsive, excitable young man and "surprising all those who had no idea how much honesty, sensitivity and delicacy there was in that charming personality."[44] Whatever happiness he derived from his new domesticity was tarnished by the deteriorating political situation on which he comments from time to time with bitter incredulity at the folly of the country's leaders and dismay about the disaster that threatened them all. Elections at the time of his marriage brought heavy gains to the opposition, forcing the Emperor to concede to many of their demands. On 2 January 1870 Émile Ollivier, Liszt's son-in-law, was appointed to head the government, and in May 1870 the Emperor called a plebiscite that strongly endorsed the parliamentary system recently put in place. Paris, alone with Marseille, voted no. Ollivier, however, was preparing reforms that favoured the right, which only exacerbated the simmering unrest in the capital, whose streets were no strangers to disturbances led by ever-increasing numbers of radicals savouring the scent of revolution.

It is not clear what Bizet was doing while the world around him was falling apart. He had at least three operatic projects—*Calendal, Clarisse Harlowe* and *Grisélidis*—but he had little incentive to begin work on any of them, nor did he have any transcriptions to complete that we know of. A report in the *Télégraphe* in January 1870 mentioned yet another opera he claimed to be engaged on. This was entitled *Rama* with a libretto by Eugène Crépet, whom we encountered in 1867 as editor of the *Revue nationale et étrangère*. The opera was to be based on the Indian epic *Ramayana*, in which Rama wages war against the giant Ravan, the fierce enemy of gods and men who carries off Rama's wife, Sita, and who is slain by Rama. All we know of this work is that by the summer of 1871 Bizet had too many other works in hand to continue with it (or perhaps begin it) until later.[45]

The opera houses had few new and interesting productions to offer. The Opéra subsisted on *L'Africaine* and *Hamlet*, while the Théâtre-Italien narrowed its repertoire to four works which have remained to this day at the centre of the world's notion of what Italian opera is: *Don Giovanni, Il barbiere di Siviglia, Rigoletto* and *La traviata*. Pasdeloup continued to promote Wagner by including the *Faust* overture and the preludes to *Lohengrin* and *Die Meistersinger* in his concerts. From his other rostrum at the Théâtre-Lyrique he made up for the non-performance of *Noé* by mounting a revival of Halévy's *Charles VI*, dating from 1843. Saint-Saëns brought his Third Piano Concerto in E flat to the Salle Pleyel, having given the first performance in December 1869 in the Leipzig Gewandhaus. In May the Opéra mounted a ballet that would prove immortal: Delibes's *Coppélia*, marking the composer's transition from an obscure producer of operettas to an important figure in French

---

44. Reyer (1909), p. 304.
45. Letter to Crépet at F-Pn W8, 10.

music with serious achievements ahead of him. Bizet was not in the news. No doubt he had lessons to give and occasionally an engagement to play for someone's salon. In addition to his wife's unpredictable state of mind and body he was getting used to the demands of in-laws whose social level was higher than his own and whose behaviour was everything from highly polished to madly eccentric.

No doubt he and Geneviève spent the start of the summer at Le Vésinet, though a rewarding departure from routine was the time they spent in the village of Barbizon, near Fontainebleau, in July 1870. It was here in 1824 that François Ganne opened an inn, the Auberge Ganne, which became a centre for landscape artists from Paris who were for the first time determined to leave their studios and work in the open air. For several generations the École Barbizon continued to attract painters as celebrated as Corot and Théodore Rousseau, and paved the way, in many respects, for the early impressionists. Bizet's connection was surely Eugène Diaz, whose father, Narcisse Virgilio Diaz de la Peña, the one-legged landscape painter of Spanish extraction, was one of the luminaries of the École Barbizon. His works were widely exhibited. Bizet planned to spend four months there, taking the librettos of *Grisélidis, Clarisse Harlowe* and *Calendal* with him, and he made considerable progress with the first of these. The Bizets visited Paris on July 2nd to hear Guiraud's opera *Le Kobold* at the Opéra-Comique, in which the title role is played by a dancer. The performance was interrupted by unprompted singing of the *Marseillaise*. Bizet was still in Paris for the examination of Prix de Rome cantatas that year, the final meeting of which was held on 5 July. In Barbizon Geneviève found the heat very uncomfortable, and events soon began to disrupt their plans. Early in July a diplomatic dispute with Prussia arose over the succession to the Spanish throne—recalling the style of sixteenth-century monarchical affairs—and an imagined slight conveyed in the "Ems telegram" caused the French legislature to vote funds for war. Ollivier, perhaps reluctantly, accepted the vote, and the Emperor, no doubt intending to force the King of Prussia to back down, saw military success as a way to consolidate his faltering Empire. War was declared on 19 July.

These events were swiftly brought home to the Halévy family when Anatole Prévost-Paradol, Ollivier's choice as ambassador to the United States, shot himself in Washington on 19 July at the age of forty. He had been violently attacked by the Republican party. He was the illegitimate son of Léon Halévy, the fruit of a liaison with the singer Lucinde Paradol, and was brought up in his father's family as a brother to Ludovic and cousin to Geneviève. He had developed his career as a writer and journalist and had consistently opposed the Empire in its earlier years. Bizet proposed going to Rodrigues's house in St-Gratien for a few days, but nothing could really lighten the gloom. While most Frenchmen were confidently expecting a quick victory, Bizet plainly saw the disaster that lay ahead: "To have suffered so much, learned so much, taught so much, experimented so much for so many thousands of years, and to have arrived at this! It's heartbreaking."[46] "Our poor philosophy, our dreams of universal peace, of international brotherhood, of human fellowship! Instead of that we have tears, blood, piles of bodies, and crimes without number and without end!"[47]

---

46. Curtiss (1950), p. 379.
47. Galabert (1909), p. 192.

CHAPTER SEVEN

1870–1872: Djamileh

NEVER HAVE SUCH CONFIDENT EXPECTATIONS OF VICTORY AS THOSE SHOUTED in the streets of Paris in July 1870 ("à Berlin! à Berlin!") been so swiftly overturned as in the six weeks that followed the declaration of war. Unlike the Prussian armies under von Moltke, the French armies were ill-equipped and ill-organised, yet convinced that victories would be as easily gained as they had been sixty-five years earlier. The revelation of their weakness was painful and immediate. A series of defeats along the German border east of Metz cost the lives of over 12,000 French soldiers, and the army was soon surrounded in the town of Sedan, a name forever associated with national humiliation since the French had no choice but to surrender; the Emperor himself was taken prisoner. Two days later, on 4 September, the government was replaced and the Third Republic proclaimed in Paris, a moment of reassurance, even joy, to those who had always hated the Empire—chief among them Victor Hugo, who arrived back after years of self-imposed exile to acclamation as a national hero. Bizet felt a great stirring of emotion at the new republic.

Remnants of the defeated army poured into Paris, and two new corps were rapidly put together: the Gardes Mobiles for younger and unmarried men, and the Gardes Sédentaires, or Garde Nationale, a militia composed of all male citizens between the ages of twenty-five and thirty-five. Bizet, now thirty-one, joined the Sixth Battalion and became one of over 100,000 men newly in uniform who paraded on 13 September before General Trochu, charged with the defence of Paris, lining the boulevards all the way from the Place de la Bastille to the Arc de Triomphe. He was supplied with a rifle that weighed fourteen pounds. "These weapons recoil, spit, do everything possible to be more disagreeable to those who use them than to the enemy."[1] As a winner of the Prix de Rome, Bizet was entitled to avoid military service, but he, Guiraud and Massenet nonetheless all signed on; Parisian patriotism was so intense that they probably had little choice. Fauré and Duparc were enlisted, so was Saint-Saëns, still just under thirty-five. He took part in skirmishes around Arcueil and Cachan in the southern suburbs. Thomas was nearly sixty, but as a citizen of Metz he felt a passionate desire to serve and was said to have wielded a rifle on the ramparts.[2]

A German attack on Paris was expected, but instead Bismarck chose to set up his headquarters in Versailles, surround the city, and wait for Paris's volatile politics to create enough chaos to force a surrender. Canny politician though he was, and despite an attempt by communards to take over the government at the end of October, Bismarck misjudged the tenacity of the Parisians, for the siege, which began on 19 September with the cutting of the last telegraph lines, continued for nineteen weeks through unimaginable hardship, cold, starvation and despair. In addition to the physical deprivation and suffering inflicted on the people of Paris, there was the uncertainty created by the flood of rumours (often intensified by the press) since reliable news from outside was reduced to a trickle. Balloons were able to leave Paris and cross the German lines with some regularity (but without any notion of where the wind would take them), but the homing pigeons they carried seldom found their way safely back into the city. Tales of French armies coming to the relief of the capital were no sooner circulated than contradicted, and the inability of the provinces to come to Paris's aid or of the city's armies to break out of confinement simply underlined the incompetence of the French military command. Three notable attempts to break the German cordon were made, all failures: on 27 November a sortie east of Paris (in which both Fauré and Guiraud fought) was beaten back. Another attempt in the direction of Le Bourget on 20 December was equally fruitless since the Germans were forewarned of the attempt and daylight hours were so short. The last attempt, on 19 January 1871, directed to the west of the city in the direction of Versailles, was even more disastrous, many half-starved soldiers being cut down by their own men by mistake. Guiraud again saw action here. This battle took the life of the painter Henri Regnault, aged twenty-seven, a close friend of Saint-Saëns, Fauré, Duparc, and d'Indy. Regnault had won the Prix de Rome and only recently returned from Italy.

Bizet's duties included sentry duty, patrols, and working in dressing-stations. He had his personal notehead: Ambulances de la Presse Française—M. Georges Bizet, Membre Protecteur.[3] He had a "rampart-mate" named Delacour, an aspiring actor.[4]

Paris was ringed by fifteen defensive forts; most were in need of repair and all had to be manned day and night in case the Germans attacked. Sometimes Bizet

---

1. Curtiss (1950), p. 380.
2. Rogeboz-Malfroy (1994), p. 54
3. US-NHb.
4. US-NHb Koch 914, letter to Ludovic Halévy of December 1871.

had to be out all night. Among a series of little notes to his wife we read: "Mon amour chéri, I can't see you this morning. I am on sentry duty at 11 o'clock—and I haven't even time to grab a bite to eat on the run, but I shall come back for dinner—I just don't know what time. In any case have dinner ready at six o'clock."[5] Geneviève had insisted on staying in Paris while her mother, who would certainly have been a colossal liability in the circumstances, was able to get away in time with her brother to the family home in Bordeaux. Geneviève remained remarkably stoical: "We are not yet dying of hunger," she wrote at the end of November, "and I must admit that I have not yet eaten cat or dog or rat or mouse, as is being done in the *best* society; I shall taste donkey for the first time today."[6]

★ ★ ★ ★ ★

Museums were boarded up and musical life came to a standstill. Except for the occasional patriotic concert the theatres were closed, although the indefatigable Pasdeloup managed to resume a concert or two in October. It is hard to imagine that Bizet had either the time or the inclination to compose, yet a letter to Guiraud of 13 December reports that Choudens had recently paid a visit to "collect the songs I was writing for him."[7] These must be the four songs Choudens published the following year, one of which, "La Fuite", a fine song for two voices, is dated 29 November 1870 (at the height of the first sortie) on the autograph.[8] Taken from an 1845 collection by Théophile Gautier, the poem is a small drama for two lovers set in the desert. Kadidja (soprano) begs Ahmed (tenor) to flee with her in the darkness, but he is frightened of her family, of the desert, and of the night. Yet in Bizet's fascinating setting there is more passion and tension in Ahmed's replies while Kadidja more confidently urges him "Fuyons! fuyons!" at the end of each verse. In Bizet, but not in Gautier, Ahmed yields, and at the end they both sing her first verse together and both, we may assume, run off into the night. It is curious that Duparc, who was twenty-two and therefore serving in the Garde Mobile, composed a setting of the same poem just a month earlier, although we have no evidence of any contact between them. Duparc also has both singers sing the first verse again at the end.

The other songs submitted to Choudens will have been "Chant d'amour", "Chanson d'avril" and "Absence", all published at the end of 1871 or early in 1872. Bizet told Guiraud that it was his habit to tell Choudens in advance what texts he was setting, so it is possible that these were composed before the ordeal of that winter. On the other hand if he had the urge to compose at all he would be more likely to distract himself with songs than with opera. The "Chant d'amour" sets three out

---

5. Curtiss (1950), p. 381
6. Curtiss (1958), p. 266.
7. Gallet (1891), p. 55.
8. US-Wc ML96.B584(Case).

of four verses of a poem by Lamartine, full of images of flowers and nature. The melody is attractive, very typical of the salon style, but the accompaniment is formulaic and the melody of each verse is the same, with an extra flourish for the third verse. "Chanson d'avril" is also a romantic poem about nature and love, this one from an 1859 collection by Louis Bouilhet. The harmony and structure are more elaborate than in "Chant d'amour", the piano part is more responsive, and we hear more of what we may reasonably identify as the new style of the previous two years. This is a beautiful song that has rightly proved one of his most popular. Gautier's poem "Absence" is better known in its setting by Berlioz in his collection *Nuits d'été*. Bizet takes a different, more dramatic approach, well illustrated by the singer's first bar (Example 7.1). The vocal line is impulsive and irregular, full of a desperate longing for the far distant beloved, although a trace of resignation creeps in at the end.

Example 7.1

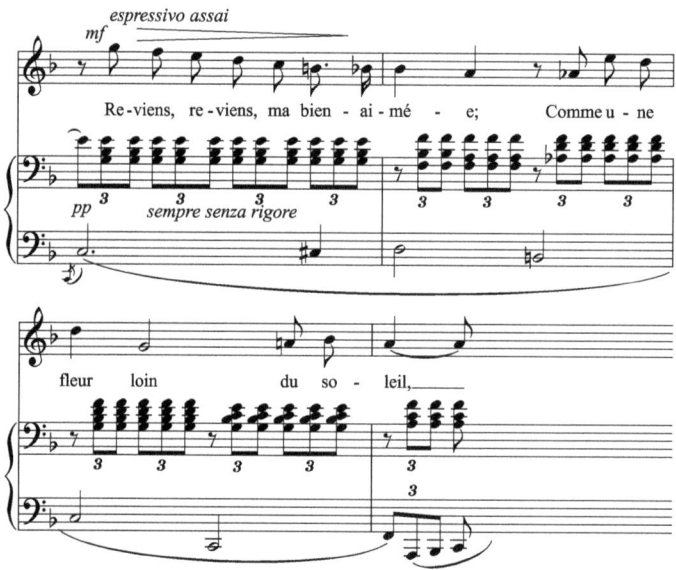

Bizet also offered Choudens a setting of Hugo's patriotic poem "Hymne", suggesting the title "Morts pour la France", but no such song has come down to us. Choudens was not enthusiastic, and once the moment had passed there was no need for it. Perhaps this got no further than a discussion.

★ ★ ★ ★ ★

Death stalked the streets in the heart of that very cold winter, and what was left of life, already at the lowest level of sustenance, became even worse in January when

Bismarck gave up his strategy of hoping Paris would collapse from within and started to bombard the city itself, not just the fortifications. Deliberate attacks on civilians, all too familiar in the twentieth century, were still regarded as outside the proper conduct of warfare, so it was done with a certain restraint. It would not have seemed so to the residents of the southern part of the city where most of the shells fell. Bizet and the musicians in the northern *quartiers* were relatively unscathed, but we have to imagine César Franck in the Boulevard Saint-Michel desperately anxious for himself, his family and his church, Sainte-Clotilde, not far away. The horror and uncertainty of where the next shell would fall undoubtedly hastened the end of the siege.

Already faced with the prospect of famine on an unimaginable scale, the government decided to negotiate an armistice, and Jules Favre, the Foreign Minister, was sent to Versailles to get the best terms he could. The guns went silent on 26 January; in the treaty that followed France had to pay Prussia a huge indemnity (eventually a fateful element in the Versailles Treaty in 1919); Alsace and most of Lorraine would remain in German hands; the forts were to be disarmed; and the Garde Nationale was allowed to keep their arms, an unfortunate detail in the weeks that ensued.

Food returned to the capital as the trains and the post began to work again. A certain torpor lasted for a week or two, and then elections on 8 February produced a government sitting in Bordeaux made up largely of monarchists of various kinds, to the disgust of Parisians who felt they had borne the brunt of the country's troubles. There was another humiliation to suffer on 1 March when German troops marched down the Champs-Élysées to a resounding silence from the city's population. The government's move from Bordeaux to Versailles was then seen as weakness in the face of rumbling insurrection in Paris, and it was not long before revolt broke out into the open. On 18 March an attempt to contain the problem failed, and the agitators were able to set up the Paris Commune at the Hôtel de Ville, bringing yet more agony to Paris's weary citizens who found themselves once again in a state of siege. Two chaotic and destructive months ended in May when Adolphe Thiers, head of the government, ordered his Versailles army to attack the city, leading to the worst bloodshed and destruction of the whole *année terrible*. When the firing ended, the dead were piled up too many to be counted, and much of Paris lay in ruins, including the Tuileries palace and the Hôtel de Ville; the Théâtre-Lyrique at the Châtelet was badly damaged. But the Third Republic was restored. Few at that moment could have imagined that what was about to begin would ever be called the *belle époque*.

At the sight of Prussian jackboots on 1 March the citizens were naturally not disposed to cheer, but in any case those who could leave had left. Fauré abandoned his uniform and joined his brother in Rambouillet, while Bizet and Geneviève went to join her mother in Bordeaux. Some musicians had escaped the siege entirely. Gounod and his family were on holiday in Normandy when the war started and then left from there to England, where Gounod was in fact to remain for four years. Lalo went to Bruges in August 1870 and stayed there until it was safe to return. Chabrier, being a civil servant, left Paris with the government at the start of the war and followed it to Tours, then Bordeaux, then Versailles. Offenbach, whose German origins would have made him unwelcome in Paris, had actually been in the spa Ems, where he was in charge of the music, when the diplomatic row between Ems and Paris erupted in July 1870, and he went directly from there to Étretat in Normandy where he had a home, feeling, as he insisted, much more French than German. One of his regular librettists, Ludovic Halévy, was in Étretat at the same time, so he too escaped the siege, while his partner Meilhac was another member of the Garde Nationale in Paris.

Massenet eventually left for Biarritz and Saint-Saëns for England, but not before solidifying, in February 1871, a plan that had been in his mind for some time: a concert organisation entitled the Société Nationale de Musique to be devoted to the propagation of music by living French composers. Franck, Guiraud, Massenet, Fauré, Dubois and Duparc were among the first adherents. This was an extraordinarily prompt symptom of the cultural regeneration that France was going to need, put in place almost immediately after the relief of the city.

For the year 1871 we are fortunate to have an extensive series of letters, many of them long, addressed by Bizet to his mother-in-law and her brother Rodrigues, which Mina Curtiss published in 1950.[9] Bizet's wordy commentary on the sanguinary struggles between left and right in those turbulent months show him by turns passionate, indifferent, patriotic, angry, ambitious, anxious, and in many other impressionable states, as one might expect in such unsettled times. He was equally hostile to the monarchists and imperialists on the Catholic right wing and to the "scoundrels" on the left, having profound admiration for Thiers and longing for the honest republic that should have replaced the corrupt Second Empire.

Bizet was at first reluctant to leave Paris, thinking it would be cowardice to do so. His troublesome throat was also acting up again. But early in February he was persuaded by Rodrigues to make the attempt, even though travel was still difficult and expensive, even dangerous. Being absent from Paris, Bizet was unable to attend the founding meeting of Saint-Saëns's Société Nationale de Musique, and the visit to Bordeaux was a disaster, for Geneviève, who had seen her mother only once since her marriage, reacted violently to their meeting and had to be taken back to Paris in a state of nervous collapse. The cause of it is a mystery, but no doubt the delicate nerves of both mother and daughter were unable to take the strain, and some hideous falling-out ensued. They returned to Paris, Bizet blaming himself for what happened since he had been advised that Geneviève should be kept away

---

9. Curtiss (1950). There is also an extensive and fascinating study of Bizet's relations with the Halévy family in Curtiss (1958), chapters 17 and 21.

from her mother. "Where we thought we had one invalid," he wrote to Rodrigues, "we now have two."[10] The happiness of his marriage, which he had enjoyed for eighteen months, was now darkened by the uncertainty of Geneviève's recovery and the haunting thought that her family's troubles would devolve willy-nilly upon him.

They returned before the Prussians paraded through Paris, for Bizet reported that the National Guard was on duty on that day. The Prussians then moved out, leaving him acutely conscious of the turbulence and instability of political affairs. He could foresee trouble ahead and spoke defiantly of the need for Thiers to move to Paris and crush the agitators. Instead, on 18 March, the insurrection routed an inadequate force on the Butte de Montmartre (Bizet was in uniform that day but was left idle without orders) and on 29 March the Commune was declared. Anxious to get back to work and to be ready for the eventual reopening of the theatres, Bizet and his wife left Paris in a hurry at that point to escape the second encirclement of Paris; they caught a train to Compiègne, north of the city, which was still full of Prussians who struck Bizet as a good deal more civilised than the murderous gang then in charge in Paris.

Somehow they reached Le Vésinet where a German garrison provided security from any spillover of violence from Paris. In the middle of April Bizet's spirits were at their lowest point: "Music will have no future here. We will have to become expatriates. Shall I go to Italy, England, or America?... I am completely discouraged and have no hope for anything more here. Life had started so well for us."[11] On 13 May, just as the assault on Paris was about to begin, old Auber, head of the Conservatoire, died aged eighty-nine, his spirit broken by the tumult all around his house in the Rue St-Georges. Of his two beloved horses named Almaviva and Figaro one had been slaughtered for meat during the siege and the other had escaped by being signed up by Pleyel for carting pianos.[12] Only a few days earlier Bizet had been grumbling about the corrupt way the Conservatoire was being run under Auber's feeble leadership. The successor immediately appointed by the Commune, Salvadore Daniel, lasted no longer than a week, being shot in the Rue Jacob by the regular army on 24 May. Once normal conditions were restored, it was Ambroise Thomas who took over the Conservatoire, after Gounod declined the offer from his London refuge. Bizet described Thomas as "that kind and honourable man".[13]

By the end of May the fighting was over and the Republic could now begin the urgent task of rebuilding the city and the country. Bizet was now most alarmed at the thought of a Catholic reaction, but Thiers miraculously staved off threats from monarchists and Bonapartists and remained President for a crucial two years, helping

10. Curtiss (1950), p. 384.
11. Curtiss (1950), p. 392.
12. Mordey (2007).
13. Curtiss (1950), p. 395.

the Third Republic to establish itself and the economy to revive, which it did in a surprisingly short time. Cultural affairs were also quick to come back to life, with a sense of relief when the autumn season of 1871 offered concerts, operas, plays, books and exhibitions, which Parisians have always craved as much as food and drink. The Bizets went into Paris to check their apartment in the Rue de Douai and to their relief found everything intact.

★ ★ ★ ★ ★

In the week following Auber's poorly attended obsequies in the Trinité church, which were held over until 15 July by his friends determined to spare the old man a godless funeral under the Commune, Bizet's uncle, François Delsarte, died at the age of fifty-nine. Bizet had seen much less of him in the ten years since his mother's death, so much so that a notice of Delsarte's illness was sent to Adolphe Bizet's address and not forwarded to Le Vésinet. Both the letter reporting his illness and a second letter reporting his death reached the Bizets too late. Georges had reason to regret his uncle's passing since he had certainly played a leading part in his nephew's musical development as a child.

Bizet's preoccupations in the summer of 1871 were his two operas, *Grisélidis* and *Clarisse Harlowe*, both *Calendal* and *Rama* having been tacitly set aside for the time being. Sardou, the librettist of *Grisélidis*, who lived just across the Seine from Le Vésinet in Port-Marly, had still not written the last of the four acts, being constantly preoccupied with other projects. The proximity was little help. When Bizet called on him, he found an elegant carriage outside the door and was told that M. Sardou could not see him, "being engaged with a collaborator". Bizet must have guessed that the collaborator was Offenbach, who was then working with Sardou on a new work *Le Roi Carotte* for the Gaîté Theatre. In July du Locle told Bizet that the four acts of *Grisélidis* were beyond the resources of the Opéra-Comique, offering as compensation the possibility of a one-act opera instead. *Grisélidis* was thus abandoned, with sketches for the first two acts already done. The story of the Marquis of Saluzzo who submits his wife Griselda to almost unendurable trials was taken from Boccaccio's *Decameron*, but Sardou's incomplete libretto has not survived, so we have no idea of how the story was treated. Massenet later wrote a *Grisélidis, conte lyrique* in three acts to a libretto, no doubt entirely different from Sardou's, by Armand Silvestre and Eugène Morand, first performed at the Opéra-Comique in 1901.

Some twenty pages of Bizet's sketches survive, some showing over fifty continuous bars of music, so although there is often only a vocal line and hints of the accompaniment in a handwriting never easy to read, it is possible to get a partial idea of certain scenes in the first two acts. The sketches reveal two pieces now well known from later works. The Innocent's theme in *L'Arlésienne* is found as the introduction and play-out of no. 4 in Act I, and Don José's famous Flower Song from

Carmen is sketched in the key of C major for baritone to the words "Quand le pâtre rêveur admire". This seems to have been no. 4 in Act II tableau 1. In addition *Grisélidis* was the source of three songs which Bizet adapted with new words, but which were not published until after his death: "Conte," with new words supplied by Paul Ferrier (original words "Et le conte finit"), "Le Gascon", with new words by Catulle Mendès, and "L'Abandonnée", with new words by either Mendès or Philippe Gille (the printed edition is confused). These are all agreeable short songs wholly in the style of opéra-comique, "Le Gascon" standing out for its forthright character.

The one-act opera offered by du Locle was to be *Djamileh*, with a libretto by Louis Gallet, whose words Bizet had recently set (without any personal contact with the author) in *La Coupe du Roi de Thulé*. Unlike most librettists of the time Gallet preferred to work on his own. For the opera to be ready for the winter the music had to be composed at once. Du Locle had originally assigned the libretto to the composer Jules Duprato, winner of the Prix de Rome in 1848, whose lethargy was such, according to Gallet, that he could not get beyond setting one number from the opera. In despair du Locle invited Gallet and Bizet to dinner with an offer that made up for the disappointment over *Grisélidis*. Bizet threw himself into the task with great energy. Gallet spent a day in Le Vésinet with Bizet and his wife and his father, and describes the composer in fully relaxed mode. Their discussion was all conducted walking around, whether indoors or out, and the conversation never stopped for a moment, continuing while Bizet and Geneviève walked Gallet back to the station, taking a ferry to reach it since the bridge had been blown up and not yet repaired.[14]

Djamileh was soon finished, but Offenbach stood in the way of its scheduled production since another new work of his, *Fantasio*, a three-act opéra-comique, had been written for du Locle, absorbing some of the cast that Bizet had in mind for his own piece, namely Mmes Galli-Marié and Priola, either of whom he would have liked for the title role. Bizet's language to describe Offenbach's works was close to unprintable. He was very particular about getting the right singers, as we saw with *Noé*, and could not let *Djamileh* be done until they were available and booked. In this case it meant a wait until May 1872.

Madame Halévy planned to move back from Bordeaux to Versailles, close enough to Le Vésinet to alarm Geneviève and to remind Bizet that whatever happiness his wife brought him, he would never escape from family problems that required his firm response and active mediation. He could do nothing to alleviate his mother-in-law's financial problems. He always wrote affectionately to her, even though she could be an interfering nuisance. He was annoyed when she wrote a letter to Thomas, at the Conservatoire, suggesting her son-in-law as professor of harmony, and equally piqued when she wrote directly on his behalf to the wife of

---

14. Recounted in Gallet (1891).

Émile Perrin, an old friend of hers, when an opening came up at the Opéra. The directorship was to pass from Perrin to Olivier Halanzier, an experienced theatre director whom Bizet had known as a child, and there were vacancies in the music staff owing to Gevaert's return to his native Belgium and the death in April of Vauthrot. Halanzier was encouraging, and soon Bizet was able to announce that on 1 October he would take over the job of *chef du chant* at a salary of five or six thousand francs a year. The rest is, inexplicably, silence, for the appointment evaporated into thin air, never mentioned again by Bizet or in the official records. It is possible, as Mina Curtiss has suggested, that he threw an angry fit at the treatment of his friend Reyer, a revival of whose *Érostrate* was chosen to reopen the Opéra in October. This is the work whose birth Bizet had attended in Baden-Baden in 1862 and whose revival he was therefore perfectly equipped to oversee now. Perhaps in response to Halanzier's interfering methods or to the mocking attitude of the press (Reyer was himself the music critic for the *Journal des débats*), Bizet's departure was as immediate as the termination of the opera after only two performances, an unprecedented failure in the history of the Opéra. On 1 November it was announced that Bizet's friend Hector Salomon was to be *chef du chant*.

★ ★ ★ ★ ★

Bizet then composed a work that betrays nothing of the tensions that had dogged him for months. It was quite unlike anything he had done before: a group of piano duets, written for the daughters of two of Geneviève's friends, Marguerite de Beaulieu (actually a cousin) and Fanny Gouin. *Jeux d'enfants* is not music for children, since it is not at all easy for the players, but it is about children and certainly evocative of the children's world. It may have been prompted by the appearance of a suite for piano by Massenet entitled *Le Roman d'Arlequin*, with the subtitle "Children's pantomimes". Published by Hartmann in July 1871, this work (later orchestrated) is written, unlike Bizet's, in a simple idiom, intended for children to play. Bizet's games are these:

1	L'Escarpolette - Reverie	The Swing
2	La Toupie - Impromptu	The Top
3	La Poupée - Berceuse	The Doll
4	Les Chevaux de bois - Scherzo	Wooden Horses
5	Le Volant - Fantaisie	The Shuttlecock
6	Trompette et Tambour - Marche	Trumpet and Drum
7	Les Bulles de Savon - Rondino	Soap Bubbles
8	Les Quatre Coins - Esquisse	Puss in the Corner
9	Colin-Maillard - Nocturne	Blind Man's Bluff
10	Saute-Mouton - Caprice	Leapfrog

| 11 | Petit mari, Petite femme - Duo | Playing Houses |
| 12 | Le Bal - Galop | The Ball |

At the same time, Bizet orchestrated at least six of the twelve pieces and put five of them into a *Petite Suite d'orchestre*, dropping the reference to children. In September he sold the work in both forms—piano duets and orchestral suite—to a new publishing house that had set up in business soon after Hartmann and just across the street from his shop. This was Durand, Schoenewerk et Cie; they issued the duets and the suite in April 1872.

With *Djamileh*, this music reveals a new mastery in Bizet's music; the rough-hewn harmonic style of 1868–69 has now been left behind and he displays an effortless ingenuity of invention and style. It can reasonably be argued that the trauma of 1870–71 and the experience of death and suffering on a large scale, not to mention the very different experience of marriage, released in Bizet a fluency and individuality that had been missing up to this point. The four years 1871 to 1875 were to see the production of the four works that truly define Bizet's place among the great composers: *Djamileh*, *Jeux d'enfants*, *L'Arlésienne* and *Carmen*. What should have been his central maturity turned out to be in fact his late period.

The suite as an orchestral form had an ancient pedigree, but it was being enthusiastically revived at this time both in France and in Germany. Massenet's *Première Suite d'orchestre* was played by Pasdeloup in 1867, and he followed it with six more orchestral suites in the next fifteen years entitled *Scènes hongroises*, *Scènes dramatiques*, *Scènes pittoresques*, *Scènes napolitaines*, *Scènes de féerie*, and *Scènes alsaciennes*. These, not opera, were the basis of his celebrity and success in his early years. Guiraud's *Suite d'orchestre* was another contemporary piece premiered by Pasdeloup in January 1872, and Bizet's two suites, *L'Arlésienne* and *Scènes bohémiennes* were to follow in the same niche.

Some of the pieces in *Jeux d'enfants* seem tailor-made for the orchestra: "La Toupie", with its endless spinning in the violas, for example; "Trompette et tambour", too, most of which came from Act IV of *Ivan IV* and was already orchestrated. In the duet version he wrote a new middle section and retained the key of B minor moved up in the new orchestral suite to C minor. "Petit mari, petite femme", which really portrays a passion too grown-up for children, profits greatly when the dialogue is played on violins and cellos in sweet counterpoint. "Le Bal" works equally well as finale to one set as to the other. There is perhaps some special humour in having the double basses lead off and a bassoon respond in the quasi-fugal passage in the middle, but its cheerful vigour in either version is without a rival in French music of the period. Of the unorchestrated pieces "L'Escarpolette" is pianistic, rather like an étude for two players; "Les Bulles de savon" is whimsically dissonant, perhaps deriving from Schumann's "Vogel als Prophet" with almost nothing for Prima's left hand to do. Of "Saute-mouton" one can well imagine a Bizet orchestration even though it is peculiarly satisfying for pianists to play. Of "Les Quatre Coins" there exists a Bizet orchestration, but he left it out of the *Petite Suite*. He copied out the string parts himself, suggesting that it was at least played somewhere.[15] This piece has the curious feature of a silent bar at the beginning (as in Liszt's "Mephisto Waltz" no. 1). Bizet also planned at some point to orchestrate "Les Chevaux de bois", but if he did, it has not survived.

Bizet must have been thinking of Schumann, the other master painter of the child's world, when he composed *Jeux d'enfants*. No other work by him carries such a smile or gives off such joy. We may attribute his new level of invention and polish to the upheaval in his (and everyone's) life at that time, but there is no reason to think he had particularly nostalgic memories of his own childhood, or even that the autumn of 1871 was a particularly happy period of his life—in fact he was under the same stresses as before—but the fluency and precision of these pieces are features he had never yet displayed so perfectly. It is almost as if he was deliberately challenging his critics to throw the Wagnerian label at him, so inappropriate in all his music and especially out of place here.

Schumann was in his mind, in any case, since Durand, Schoenewerk et Cie also published Bizet's arrangement of the six *Studien* for pedal-piano, op. 56. Since this instrument had never caught on (Alkan's enthusiasm was exceptional), it made sense to arrange them for piano duet. Again we wonder if this publisher employed him for any more arrangements of this kind.

On 19 November 1871 we should imagine Bizet and Massenet as duettists playing *Jeux d'enfants* to a gathering that included its dedicatees and their mothers. They then went on to compose a piano duet together entitled "Simplicité—waltz not for dancing" in which Massenet wrote the prima part and Bizet the seconda.[16] They then presented it to Madame de Beaulieu, Geneviève's cousin, Bizet writing "convinced manifestation of my musical hopes!" and Massenet writing "antimanifestation without conviction". A languorous waltz in G flat major with a sudden outburst in 2/4 time toward the end betrays the consummate skill of both composers, clearly now friends if once there had been some bitterness on Bizet's part over *La Coupe du Roi de Thulé* when he let slip a remark about Massenet's "intrigues".

Piano duet was Bizet's medium for the season, for he was engaged by Choudens to arrange Gounod's latest choral work, *Gallia*, for duet. It was a lament for the sufferings of France and first performed in the Royal Albert Hall, London, in May followed by the first performance in Paris, in Gounod's absence, given by the Société des Concerts on 29 October and then followed by eight staged perfor-

---

15. It is included in the recording of the *Petite suite* by the Orchestre National du Capitole de Toulouse under Michel Plasson, 1992.
16. GB-Lbl (O.W. Neighbour deposit).

mances at the Opéra-Comique. The words, in biblical style in both Latin and French, are by Gounod himself. The first concert of Saint-Saëns's Société Nationale de Musique was given in the Salle Pleyel, Rue Richelieu, on 17 November, and on 9 January they introduced Saint-Saëns's own symphonic poem *Le Rouet d'Omphale*.

Suddenly Bizet was being repeatedly featured as a concert artist in the Société's concerts. On 9 December, with Massenet again, he performed the latter's *Scènes hongroises*. In its orchestral form it had just been premiered by Pasdeloup, and Bizet later arranged it for solo piano, to be published by Hartmann around 1875. Two weeks later he played the finale of his Second Symphony arranged for eight hands, also the "Variations chromatiques" as a solo item. He then accompanied Julie Lalo, the composer's wife, in her song "Ma vie a son secret" and the Sérénade from *Les Pêcheurs de perles*. On 23 March 1872 he and Guiraud performed Guiraud's new suite as a piano duet.

The year 1872 opened with the need to break the news to Mme Halévy that Geneviève was expecting their first child. Knowing that a confrontation between mother and daughter was potentially explosive he begged his mother-in-law to let him know "on a separate sheet of paper which I shan't show her" if she planned to come to Paris, "as you give us reason to hope," he added, surely between his teeth. As far as we know the visit did not take place. The failure of the Opéra position and impending fatherhood compelled him to teach more and more lessons and to accept any arrangements he could secure. Hartmann had him arrange Massenet's *Scènes hongroises*, as we have seen, and in addition he gave him Massenet's *Six danses* for piano duet to be arranged for piano solo. Both in the duet and solo versions these were eventually published as *Scènes de bal*. Choudens gave him an Entr'acte from Gounod's *La Colombe* to arrange for the then fashionable combination of violin (or cello), piano and harmonium. He arranged one of three works by Gounod entitled "Prière du soir", also a piece entitled "Temple ouvre-toi", a chorus from Gounod's incidental music for *Les Deux Reines*, a drama in four acts by Ernest Legouvé staged in 1872. None of these Choudens publications give the name of the arranger on the printed copy. We only know of them from mentions in his correspondence or, in the case of *La Colombe*, by the survival of Bizet's autograph, so the likelihood that there were many more such arrangements of which we know nothing is considerable.

He continued for a while to work on *Clarisse Harlowe*, although he had no more reason to expect a future for it than for *Grisélidis*. The last we hear of it is in a letter to Lacombe from the winter of 1871–72. It survives, like *Grisélidis* but a little fuller in extent, in the form of sketches and some songs later included in the *Seize Mélodies*. The libretto was by Philippe Gille, with whom he had worked on *La Prêtresse* in 1864, and Adolphe Jaime, an immensely prolific writer for the theatre who had contributed to some of Offenbach's librettos and collaborated with Gille in 1869 for *La Cour du roi Pétaud*, an opéra-bouffe by Delibes. Richardson's novel

Clarissa, or the History of a Young Lady, published in 1748, is a very long epistolary novel concerning a young lady of good family who is wooed by the unscrupulous Robert Lovelace. She eventually yields to him, and later dies of shame. If it was intended for the Opéra-Comique Bizet would have had to confront the problem of its tragic ending. He sketched the whole of the first two acts and the opening number of the third (of three) acts, although in the absence of the libretto it is hard to follow the action of Bizet's sketches.

Bizet later rescued four pieces from *Clarisse Harlowe* and arranged them as songs or duets with new words. The solo songs "Aubade", "La Nuit", "Voyage" and "Si vous aimez", all published after Bizet's death, have their origins here. The first, Lovelace's Air (no. 2) "Qu'un fou sanglotte et pleure" is a light-hearted song in which Lovelace (whose name is pronounced as four syllables) sets out his belief that there are plenty of fish in the sea and that a man should never weep over one lost love. He is a standard opéra-comique type, like Haroun in *Djamileh*. It was later transformed into a love song with a poem by Paul Ferrier as "Aubade", a song that clearly calls for orchestral accompaniment. The last two numbers in Act I survive complete with piano accompaniment. They make a powerful finale in which Clarisse attempts to dissuade Lovelace from pursuing her sister Arabelle, only to enflame his passion for herself instead. It builds to a tremendous duet at the end of which she exclaims "Je veux partir!" and rushes from the stage.

From the second act we have a beautiful duet for Clarisse and Arabelle, "Ah! reste dans mes bras", offering mutual comfort in the face of Clarisse's unwanted marriage. This has an impassioned melodic line and a rich accompaniment whose persistent tonic pedal would no doubt have been softened by Bizet's orchestration. This appeared in two posthumous versions: as the duettino for two voices "Les Nymphes des bois", with words by Jules Barbier, and in a shorter version in a lower key as the song "La Nuit" with words by Paul Ferrier. Later in the second act comes a scene later converted into another duet, "Le Retour", part of which Bizet also adapted as a song, "Voyage".

In sum, the surviving material for *Clarisse Harlowe* is extensive enough to suggest that Bizet could have had it ready for the Opéra-Comique within a few months if the management had wanted it. After *Djamileh*, however, they wanted something *gai*, which this clearly could never have been.

Fantasio was a failure (by Offenbach's standards) at the Opéra-Comique in January 1872, but *Le nozze di Figaro*, commandeered from the now silent Théâtre-Lyrique, was an immense success, with Mme Carvalho an enchanting Cherubino. Four young composers were to be featured in the repertoire for the year: Paladilhe, Bizet, Saint-Saëns and Massenet. First up was Paladilhe, whose *Le Passant* opened on 24 April. His song "La Mandolinata" was breaking all sales records, but the opera was disappointing, especially since Galli-Marié and Priola, the two singers Bizet would have been happy to cast as Djamileh, were taking part. It survived only three performances, gunned down in the press by the usual charges of Wagnerism, of which Paladilhe was certainly innocent.

★ ★ ★ ★ ★

So *Djamileh* went into rehearsal. Du Locle's co-director at the Opéra-Comique was the older Adolphe de Leuven, of Swedish extraction, who had been writing countless librettos and vaudevilles for over thirty-five years. One of his librettos was the evergreen *Postillon de Longjumeau*, set by Adam in 1836. By the time he came to be director of the Opéra-Comique his tastes were firmly set in an earlier era and he thus had little patience with anything he thought was disruptively modern. Bizet certainly came into that category. But du Locle acted as a healthy counterpoise, teasing his colleague and deliberately provoking Victor, the elderly régisseur who shared de Leuven's disgust at modernisms of any kind. Du Locle had a sharp eye for décor and saw to it that the characters had sufficiently authentic and exotic costumes. Gallet described the set as "hispano-moorish" with a multicoloured lantern that was moved around the stage and lit up the interior when night fell.

The singers who were eventually cast were not Bizet's ideal, despite his efforts to secure the best. His Djamileh was the very beautiful Aline Prelly, with an alluring figure and big brown eyes. She had been a society beauty during the Second Empire and was now looking for success on the stage. Unfortunately she had little training or experience as a singer or actor. She sang a secondary role in a revival of Auber's *Fra diavolo* that February, so Bizet knew that he would have to work hard to get her up to scratch. In the end he described her as "less than mediocre".[17] The Haroun was the tenor Adolphe Duchesne, who had sung briefly at the Théâtre-Lyrique and served gallantly in the siege, being wounded and awarded a military medal. He then sang Faust in Bordeaux with his arm in a sling before joining the Opéra-Comique.

The opera opened on 22 May 1872 on a triple bill with Deffès's opéra-comique *Le Café du roi* and Gounod's *Le Médecin malgré lui*. Bizet stationed himself in the prompter's box, which allowed him to give the singers leads and instructions as required. Gallet was sitting near, beneath the stage. All went well until Mme Prelly's important solo, the "Ghazel", from which she inadvertently cut a whole verse. Deloffre, the conductor, "spurred on the orchestra" to catch up with her while Bizet was tearing his hair out below. At the end Bizet leaned over to Gallet and said "Well then, a complete flop!" He was not quite right, happily, since the opera went well and received eleven performances. But it was certainly not a success either.

The action is loosely based on the brief Chant III of the long poem *Namouna* by Alfred de Musset.[18] So slight is its debt to the poem that du Locle proposed

---

17. Imbert (1894), p. 192.
18. For a discussion of the libretto's debt to de Musset, see Charlton (2010).

changing the name Hassan to Haroun and the heroine's name to Djamileh, a name he had heard in Egypt when working on *Aida*. Gallet claimed that some elements of the story were taken from an eighteenth-century collection of tales, and the character Splendiano is Gallet's creation. There are three sung roles, one speaking role and one dancing role. The nine numbers in the score are linked by dialogue, some of it quite extensive. In view of the similarity of the opera's setting and characters to those of *La Guzla de l'Émir*, Bizet might well have drawn upon his unheard score for the new work.

The Ouverture is built in a basic sonata form partly on material from the opera and partly on fresh music. It opens with part of the March to which the slave merchant leads in his parade of slaves, with an added middle section of soaring scales in the wind. The second main theme is new, with a toytown character as if it had strayed in from *Jeux d'enfants*, and it reappears speeded up and much reduced at the end.

The curtain opens on Haroun's palace in Cairo. At the back between columns of pink marble and behind a bubbling fountain elegant lattice windows reveal glimpses of blue sky. The sun is setting. The first few lines of a poem by Gallet printed at the front of the libretto and addressed to du Locle further describe the scene:

> Beneath a Byzantine arch the pale moon glides,
> Its opal glow softly caressing
> Tall ebony tripods encrusted with lapis-lazuli.
> Water spills into the basin in a silver cascade,
> And the golden tulips in Chinese vases
> Mingle, shedding petals, with the carpet's roses.
> Intoxicating aromas rise in the clear evening light.

Haroun (tenor) is reclining on some cushions smoking, while Splendiano (also tenor) is squatting at a low table, writing. In the distance female voices greet the twilight over a wordless men's chorus, supported by an oboe, a tambourine and a piano, the instrument Bizet had also used off-stage in *La Coupe du Roi de Thulé*. The effect is certainly oriental without literally adopting any oriental scale. The second verse is to sound less distant than the first. The orchestra slithers in with some idly waving figures that exactly set the tone for Haroun's indistinct fantasy of "exquisite forms" taking shape before his half-open eyes. His melody imposes few intervals on his sleepy voice, and before it reaches its end, both he and Splendiano have drifted into sleep.

The strings give out a new melody over throbbing wind chords which we may label Djamileh's motif even though it is heard only twice more. Its rich harmony, with plenty of sevenths of various kinds, was one of the main targets for the critics who found Bizet's music too advanced. But it admirably meets the requirement of presenting the beautiful Djamileh to the audience for the first time (and to Haroun in his dreams). During this music she enters and glides silently across the stage, leans adoringly over the sleeping Haroun, and then vanishes. In the original production this vision sent a ripple of sensual delight around the audience at the sight of la Prelly's undulating curves. Her singing came later. One more verse from the off-stage chorus closes the number.

A lengthy dialogue follows in which Haroun comes to himself and wakes the dozing Splendiano. We learn that Splendiano was once Haroun's teacher and is now the keeper of his accounts, also that Haroun loves wine, horses, gambling and women. Every month he needs a new slave-girl. Djamileh's month as his mistress is now up, so she is to be given a necklace that evening and dismissed. Splendiano then confesses that he himself is in love—with Djamileh. Haroun has no objection since she has served her time with him. Splendiano is not so sure that that is true.

The Duo (no. 2) explores this delicate situation in a number of keys and a number of tempos, more than would be expected in an opéra-comique of the time. Splendiano warns his master that love can take hold unexpectedly, tracing an elegant line somewhat belied by the marking *prétentieusement*. In a stream of triplets Haroun mocks Splendiano's image of seedlings and flowers, convinced that no such thing could happen to him; Djamileh will be replaced by some unknown lovely, a thought that convinces Splendiano to join in a swift, sunny duet on the theme of the "inconnue". So Haroun is happy for Splendiano to choose his next slave-girl for him and to enjoy Djamileh for himself.

Haroun here sings his *couplets*, the heart of the duet, in which he declares he is indifferent as to whether a girl is Moorish, Jewish or Greek, blonde or brunette, he loves not women, but love itself. Bizet astutely took Splendiano's response ("All the better for me!"), which Gallet had put after the second verse, and inserted it earlier between the two. Each verse turns deliciously from minor to major at the refrain "Que l'esclave soit brune ou blonde" in the key of G flat major, the key of love *par excellence*. A reprise of the speedy ensemble about the "inconnue" rounds off the duet.

Djamileh appears, so Splendiano leaves to order the supper. The Trio that follows, no. 3, like the Duo, consists of several sections at different speeds and in different keys, with a set piece in the middle. As Djamileh's motive is heard in the orchestra, Haroun asks her why she is so pale, so she describes a dream she has had: over an inner pedal similar to the one in the Prélude to *Les Pêcheurs de perles* (and to the Trio in Beethoven's Seventh Symphony), except that it is too low for violas and is therefore carried by a horn, she describes the frightening sensation of drowning in the desert, such as only a dream could create. The sombre melody is spread over a three-octave unison. Haroun's response—that she is losing her wits, which she suspects herself—moves the melody to unison pizzicato strings, and its cadence in the major key represents her thought that the dream, by vanishing, tells her that Haroun truly loves her.

The rest of the Trio is entertainment, first supper, then song. Splendiano and some slaves bring in the meal and serve it while the three of them express their thoughts independently, as singers in opera can, unconcerned with what the other two are saying. Djamileh is hopeful that love shines in Haroun's eyes, Haroun cares only for the pleasure of the moment, and Splendiano looks forward to when he can confess all to a Djamileh softened up by wine. The music is pure operetta, in a light 6/8. Haroun then asks her if she longs for her liberty. In a more serious tone she responds that she has fully recovered and asks for nothing more than to remain in his house. Splendiano is getting drunk, and since Djamileh refuses to drink, Haroun begs her to sing to them instead. Muttering his lascivious expectations, Splendiano goes off to fetch a lute on which he plays a comic prelude before handing it to her.

There follows the "Ghazel", a mock-Arabic song in two verses about Noureddin, King of Lahore, for whom a young girl yearns, only to be disappointed by his indifference. The accompanying rhythm on alternating clarinets and flutes is that of "Adieux de l'hôtesse arabe" from five years before, while the lute (imitated by pizzicato violins), and perhaps the song itself, may be a relic from *La Guzla de l'Émir* from 1862. The melody is strangely vagrant, with an eerily scored diminished seventh at the cadence on "La naïve enfant!" The closing bars of each verse bring a superb example of Bizet's taste for a phrase descending chromatically while the bass holds an open fifth on the tonic, now borrowing the Arabic rhythm from the woodwinds. The song tests the singer's powers of expression and narrative without requiring any traditional vocal display. It also tests Haroun's patience since he knows how the story ends and is anxious to change the mood. So he introduces a bland waltz rhythm and a witless tune to remind everyone that this is the Salle Favart, not the deserts of Araby. Splendiano and Djamileh, returning to the world of operetta, join in and close the Trio.

In dialogue Haroun apologises for interrupting her song, but she is not offended. He then produces a pearl necklace, while flute and muted strings are heard behind the dialogue (Scène et Chœur, no. 4). She says she prefers the hand that gives it to the necklace itself. He is carrying out his regular procedure and expecting Splendiano to dismiss her. At this point Gallet wrote some lines for an off-stage chorus calling the faithful to prayer, but Bizet did not set them, having Splendiano simply tell Haroun that his gambling friends have arrived. They enter and burst into song, expecting a night of pleasure at the tables. Djamileh stands apart, but she has not put on her veil, so the men inevitably notice her and voice their admiration in the most perfectly woven comic men's chorus imaginable. Bizet's craft is at its superb best here, compact and clever in every detail.

As the oboe recalls the "Ghazel", she looks reproachfully at Haroun, who nonchalantly introduces her, then returns to entertaining his guests and ignoring the call from the minaret in a relaxed ensemble over which Splendiano, in comic patter style, looks forward to his eagerly awaited conquest. Gallet wrote a part for Djamileh in the ensemble, full of anxiety about Haroun's behaviour, but Bizet left her out, making Splendiano's part in it a great deal easier to convey. The men all leave.

There follows a long stretch of dialogue. Djamileh, alone, worries why Haroun seems to be saying goodbye. Splendiano comes back in, causing Djamileh to fear that he brings news of her dismissal. At length he explains Haroun's habit of replacing his slave-girls every month and that her month is now over. The "inconnue" is awaited. Djamileh cannot believe that he does not love her. Splendiano's hints that she need not look far for another lover go unheeded; she is in despair.

From the next room comes the sound of Haroun and his friends singing vigorously to invoke Lady Luck (Chanson, no. 5). Convinced that Haroun has forgotten her, Djamileh tests Splendiano's assertion that he loves her by asking him to introduce her to Haroun as the next slave-girl. If Haroun rejects her, she will agree to be Splendiano's slave instead. Splendiano is called out to speak with the slave merchant, who has just arrived.

Djamileh's solo Lamento (no. 6) "Sans doute l'heure est prochaine", is brief and touching, full of that quasi-modal colour of which Bizet was a master. Even on the second verse the harmony can catch the listener by surprise. The vocal demands are slight, but the expressive potential enormous.

She hides, as instructed, as Splendiano returns with Haroun and his friends, annoyed at being called away from the tables. The slave merchant is brought in along with a group of slave-girls and musicians while a strange march is heard on *pianissimo* strings. As the girls are paraded, the strings turn to more voluptuous phrases. Haroun is unconcerned and threatens to leave, so to hold his attention the merchant introduces an *almée* who is instructed to dance on a special carpet laid in the centre of the stage while the musicians sing and play in the background. The key, A minor, had been the standard choice for Middle-Eastern music from Mozart to David.[19] Against a syncopated rhythm on cellos and drum the cor anglais and flutes exchange exotically charged chromatic phrases. This Danse et chœur (no. 7) is the furthest that Bizet went in evoking a Middle-Eastern music, more angular and outlandish than anything in, for example, Saint-Saëns's *Samson et Dalila* (Example 7.2). Haroun's friends comment in subdued rhyming phrases, while the female singers articulate the single syllable *lou* in unexpected rhythms. The dancing *almée* eventually collapses in delirious exhaustion.

During the dance Djamileh creeps out of hiding for a jealous look at the dancer and then leaves on a sign from Splendiano. Haroun tells the merchant that Splendiano will decide the choice of slave and returns with his friends to the adjoining room. They exit to a snatch of their opening comic chorus, now on bassoons, violas and cellos.

19. See Locke (1998).

Example 7.2

Splendiano offers the merchant two hundred sequins, not for the *almée*, but to go out and take instruction from Djamileh. Alone on stage, Splendiano is confident that he can win Djamileh by betraying her: he will explain the whole plot to Haroun, who will thereupon reject her. In his Couplets (no. 8) that follow, those sentiments are joyfully expressed in a two-verse song, opéra-comique style. The faulty declamation of the words sends a hint that this music was originally intended for different words in a different work. That work may have been *Les Templiers* of 1868 since a letter to Gallet of 1871 gives the words of an earlier scene in which one of the characters is called Renaud, suggesting that the same music would do for a "personnage léger" in *Djamileh*.[20] The original first two lines then would have been

> Jardins où l'ombre est descendue,
> Calme charmant des nuits d'été,

here replaced by:

> Il faut éteindre ma fièvre,
> Une douce réalité,

Is it possible that the mention of "nuits d'été" in the earlier text caused Bizet to recall Berlioz's "Villanelle" (and its progenitor in Beethoven's Eighth Symphony, second movement) in the gently repeated wind chords of the accompaniment?

Splendiano brings in Djamileh now dressed in the *almée*'s costume and half veiled. Haroun enters asking Splendiano to find him more gold coins since he is losing at the table, and as he turns to leave he spots what he takes to be the dancer. In the Mélodrame violins outline the dancer's angular theme (Example 7.2).

---

20. See Lacombe (2000), pp. 523–524, where he comes to the conclusion that the music for the earlier text was not used in *Djamileh*.

Djamileh runs off pursued by Haroun, who is much struck by her curious behaviour and so takes no notice of Splendiano, who is given the gold pieces and ordered to take Haroun's place at the gaming table, which he reluctantly does, confident that Haroun will dismiss Djamileh.

The Duo final (no. 9) now begins, with Haroun observing Djamileh's obvious nervousness and deciding to put her response to the test. To warm, unmistakably amorous music he courts her, begging her to unveil, while she pleads the need to cover her recent tears. Their voices blend snugly as if already foretelling the outcome. In recitative Haroun tells her that the previous girl was less diffident, "and I loved her". Djamileh immediately asks him why then did he dismiss her? His reply is a simple cantilena in Massenet's manner explaining that their bond ended with their final embrace and that he preserves only the memory of their mutual affection. He makes no commitments in love, a fact underlined by the violas spelling out the shallow tune that followed the "Ghazel" in which he proclaimed his hedonistic philosophy.

She reacts strongly with tears and an attempt to run away. When her features are suddenly outlined by the moonlight, he recognises her and draws her back. All is clear to him: she loves him, while she remains convinced that his heart is dead. Thinking all is lost, she launches into the third verse of the "Ghazel" which he had earlier refused to hear, recounting the young girl's death from unrequited passion. Haroun's heart is hardened and he violently tells her to leave. Cellos divided into four parts give us a laser-like view of Djamileh's emotional state (Example 7.3).

Example 7.3

For once the critics who cried "Wagner!" had the trace of an excuse. But Bizet's chromaticism, though more persistent in *Djamileh* than in any other work, is rarely of this type (sustained sliding part-writing), much more often inflected by juxtaposing unrelated harmonies and by modal colouring, and in any case Wagner's music was of little interest to him. This whole scene, concluding the opera, has a passionate intensity not seen before in his music, for Djamileh declares solemnly that love means more to her than liberty, and therefore she must go. Her motif as it had accompanied her first silent appearance at the start of the opera is heard once again. She staggers to the door and is about to fall when Haroun catches her, at the same time picking up the second half of her theme. It was a test, he tells her. "In understanding your heart, I have recovered my own." His conversion is swift, and for the remainder of their duet he is in love not any more with love, but with Djamileh herself. As the singing comes to an end, Splendiano is seen making "a comic gesture of despair" (Gallet even proposed that he should say "Eh bien!…et moi?", which Bizet wisely omitted) while Haroun replaces Djamileh's veil to hide her from the prying eyes of his friends.

★ ★ ★ ★ ★

As opéra-comique, *Djamileh* required a happy ending and an element of comedy. The latter was supplied by Splendiano, who was clearly intended by Gallet to be absurd in his aspiration to the love of Djamileh and amusing in his gestures and manner of speech. Haroun's friends are to be interpreted in that way too. The happy ending is supplied by Haroun's conversion, firmly discounted throughout the opera until the final scene when the sight of Djamileh dressed as the *almée* begins to work its magic. The real force that wins Haroun is Djamileh's deep emotional distress at being passed over; he is as much sorry for her as in love with her. This puts the main responsibility for conveying the force of her distress on the shoulders of the singer playing Djamileh, and it was perhaps Prelly's inadequacy in this regard that prevented the opera from winning over the public and enjoying a longer run in 1872.

Within the terms of the genre it was sufficient for the hero to change his spots by rejecting his taste for a succession of different partners and showing, at least for the while, the promise of fidelity. Audiences were not shocked by Haroun since he is oriental and different, but they still expected this to be corrected at the final curtain in favour of normal Christian modes of conduct. Set the issue the other way round by having the woman be the philanderer and the man the soul of constancy, and bring the setting a little nearer home, to Spain, and we have *Carmen*, with its much higher dramatic tension and its much more disturbing message for audiences of the day.

Linking the nine separate numbers of the opera are dialogues, usually short but on two occasions, between nos. 1 and 2 and between nos. 4 and 6 (with the short no. 5 heard off-stage during the conversation), much longer than is tolerated today in the opera house or in recordings. Opéra-Comique audiences at that time were used to extensive dialogue, and singers were trained in declamation, so it distressed no one. Dialogue helps to set out details of the plot and normally declines in extent as the opera proceeds. Another standard element of opéra-comique was *mélodrame*, the provision of music under spoken dialogue, widely adopted in French opera of the nineteenth century and rich in dramatic potential, as we know from film scores of the 1940s. In *Djamileh* there are four passages of *mélodrame*. Since the librettist would not normally determine where *mélodrame* was to fall, the composer's judgment must be credited for the effectiveness of this device. Two of the *mélodrames* are decorative, serving in turn to introduce the parade of new slaves on offer and the following exit of Haroun and his friends. The first *mélodrame* underlines the presentation of the necklace to Djamileh, and the fourth *mélodrame* is crucial since it supports Haroun's change of heart before the final duet.

Bizet's score is consistently impressive. It has provoked studies and interpretations that credit what was intended as a simple one-act opéra-comique with surprisingly complex implications.[21] When the music seems to fall to a lower level of sophistication, it is usually a deliberate move to convey hollowness or shallowness of sentiment. Splendiano's solo, for example, is plain, in keeping with his simple character. Elsewhere Bizet is clearly comfortable with a richly chromatic idiom, rarely providing music free of surprising melodic and harmonic inflexions. Chromatics are well suited to an exotic setting, too. It was a style he owed entirely to himself, since neither Gounod nor David nor Thomas nor Saint-Saëns had chosen to go in that direction; although almost everyone assumed it came from Wagner, or at least from Verdi, no one would mistake Bizet's music for anything by those two masters. It is also free of the awkwardness that his earlier attempts at an advanced harmony, in the period 1867–69, had displayed.

A sure sign of Bizet's determination to transcend the genre of opéra-comique is the extension of musical movements, especially nos. 2 and 3, each of which contains a sequence of scenes in a variety of different keys and tempos. This was traditional in the opening Introduction and in the finale to an act, but the other numbers were generally set in a single tempo and a single key. At no point, however, was Bizet pursuing the goal of a seamless, numberless opera.

Djamileh ran for eleven performances, ending on 29 June 1872. Choudens brought out the vocal score, arranged for piano by Bizet himself, and Lévy published the libretto. Bizet was very satisfied with the production (if not with the singers) in a work that he declared at the start to be difficult to bring off. Saint-Saëns wrote him a sonnet, suggesting that playing the opera at the Opéra-Comique was casting pearls before swine. Massenet wrote him a glowing letter. The press was generally favourable, with strong support from serious critics whom Bizet respected and a few mean-spirited attacks from the lower breed.[22] But he came through the experience of presenting his first work at the Opéra-Comique with confidence in himself and his future: "What pleases me more than the opinion of all those gentlemen is the absolute certainty that I have found my way. I know what I'm doing."[23]

---

21. Lacombe (2000) and Charlton (2010), for example.

22. For selections from the reviews see Gallet (1891), pp. 26–40, and Lacombe (2000), pp. 543–586.

23. Galabert (1909), p. 199.

CHAPTER EIGHT

1872–1873: Don Rodrigue

BEFORE *DJAMILEH* HAD FINISHED ITS SHORT RUN AT THE OPÉRA-COMIQUE, ANOTHER work in the series of presentations by younger composers was heard there. This was *La Princesse jaune* by Saint-Saëns, whose one-act libretto was also by Gallet. The first performance was on 12 June 1872, on the same bill as *Djamileh*, and although its five performances made a better score than that of Paladilhe's *Le Passant*, it was less than *Djamileh*'s eleven. The three operas were bundled together in the same dismissal: "one was just the second act of the other, and the music of one could equally serve to illustrate the other."[1] With this new work Gallet suggested a different shade of exoticism, for his libretto concerns a Dutch couple who are obsessed with all things Japanese, allowing Saint-Saëns to include some pentatonic scales to suggest the Far East. Like Bizet, Saint-Saëns found Gallet very congenial to work with, but the latter's memoirs, written while Saint-Saëns was still alive, are relatively silent about him compared to the generous portrait he painted of Bizet. Like Bizet, Saint-Saëns was absurdly accused of writing "music of the future" (as a term of abuse). But at least the opera was performed, unlike his two earlier operas *Le Timbre d'argent* and *Samson et Dalila*, both of which had to wait another five years to be seen on the stage.

For Bizet the best outcome from *Djamileh* was reported in letters to Galabert and Lacombe: "De Leuven and du Locle have commissioned an opera in three acts from me. Meilhac and Halévy will be my librettists. They'll write something *gai* which I'll treat in as compact a manner as I can. The Opéra has apparently decided to ask me to write something. Doors are opening. It's taken ten years to get here. I have plans for oratorios, symphonies, etc., etc. And you? Are you working? One

---

1. Bonnerot (1922), p. 67.

must produce; time hurries on; we must not peg out before giving what we have within ourselves."[2] The two directors had clearly given Bizet the go-ahead to work with two librettists whose main recent works had been written for Offenbach, and who specialised in operetta of the lighter kind. They certainly understood *gai*, and that is probably what Bizet expected to compose. He was given three scenarios to look at, including one called *L'Oiseau bleu,* which may be the same as an opéra-comique later composed by his fellow-prizewinner from 1856, Lecocq.[3] On 27 June, while these discussions were proceeding, Barbier's long-standing partner and Bizet's collaborator in *Les Pêcheurs de perles,* Michel Carré, died at the age of forty-nine.

On 10 July Geneviève gave birth to their son Jacques at home in the Rue de Douai. Despite all apprehensions about the mother's delicate nerves the pregnancy and delivery went well, and no doubt for the next several weeks Bizet's preoccupations were domestic rather than musical, leaving aside projects for operas, oratorios and symphonies for the time being. At least they would have been, had not a proposal come at that moment from his earlier benefactor, Léon Carvalho, who had risen again from his collapse at the Théâtre-Lyrique and taken over the artistic management of a new theatre, the Théâtre du Vaudeville, at the foot of the Rue de la Chaussée d'Antin. Carvalho had in hand a new play by Alphonse Daudet which provided important opportunities for music, and the day after the baby's birth Bizet attended a reading at the theatre. The press announced that Bizet was to compose incidental music for the production and he set to work at once. A little younger than Bizet, Daudet was brought up in Provence but had spent his adult life in Paris working as a journalist and writer. His successful *Lettres de mon moulin* in 1866 made his name as a leading Provençal voice in French literature. His new play, *L'Arlésienne,* written in 1869, drew upon some characters and a story from the earlier book. Set in the Camargue, the story was based on a real incident, the suicide of a young relative of the poet Mistral, frustrated in his passion for a woman from Béziers. It provided Bizet with an opening for exotic music of a different kind from that of *Djamileh*. He may have already explored Provençal melodies when he was thinking about *Calendal* in 1869 and then encountered François Vidal's collection *Lou Tambourin, Istori de l'Estrumen Prouvençau* published in Avignon in 1864. Three melodies from this collection found their way into the new score.

The incidental music that accompanied the performance of all plays in the nineteenth century is a vast lost continent, since it had no function outside the theatre for which it was composed and cannot easily be transferred to the concert hall. Little of it was ever published and manuscript material used in theatres was always at risk of casual collection, damage, and loss. Certain scores by well-known composers

2. Imbert (1894), pp. 192–193.
3. US-NHb, Koch 914.

have risen to the surface, such as Beethoven's *Egmont* and Mendelssohn's *A Midsummer Night's Dream*, but they can rarely be performed with the plays to which they belong. Only the richest theatres, furthermore, supported a full orchestra, although they all employed at least a few musicians forming small ensembles of different constitutions for different purposes. Some specimens of incidental music, such as Grieg's *Peer Gynt*, have been kneaded into orchestral suites, and this was to be the means by which Bizet's *L'Arlésienne* has been best known, leaving in obscurity the short connecting links and *mélodrames* that give life to particular moments in the drama. Carvalho undoubtedly had in mind a more carefully fashioned contribution in this case than was normal in the theatre at the time.

Composing the score was made especially difficult by Mme Halévy, who, no doubt debarred from visiting her grandson at home, lay in wait for him when he was being taken to the park by his nurse. She was, at all events, making "outrageous demands" and railing against the baby's father.[4] At the same time Bizet had to escort her brother-in-law Léon Halévy to Dr Blanche's famous clinic for mental disorders in Passy, where Gounod had also from time to time required treatment. In spite of this Bizet finished the score quite quickly, having it ready for rehearsal by the end of August. Bizet struck up a close friendship with Daudet at this time despite the latter's strong monarchist beliefs. They worked well together and felt that their collaboration had produced something unusually powerful in the theatre. Both inscribed copies of the work—Daudet the printed play, Bizet the vocal score—to the other with touchingly sincere expressions of admiration.

The play opened on 30 September 1872 and ran for nineteen performances, the last on 18 October. By common consent this was a failure. Plays expected to run for many more performances than operas, but the press was not good. Incidental music in any case tended to attract little attention from that quarter. Pierre Berton was unable to see the play until the run was nearly over, and when he did there were fewer than thirty people in the stalls. The first-night audience could see little appeal in the story or in all that regional speech, and found the music to be intrusive. The play simply failed to catch on with Paris's chattering classes, so attendance quickly dropped off. Good reviews by Bizet's friends in the press, Reyer and Johannès Weber (the only two music critics he trusted), and compliments about the music from Massenet and Pasdeloup were small consolation. At least Choudens issued a vocal score, which was dedicated to Hippolyte Rodrigues.

Daudet was more cast down by the play's failure than Bizet, who snatched success from the embers by rapidly turning five extracts from his score into a suite for full orchestra in four movements. This was scored, copied and rehearsed in time to be played by Pasdeloup in one of his Concerts Populaires on 10 November. For the

---

4. Curtiss (1958), p. 331.

first time in his life Bizet found himself the composer of a popular success, for the suite was played several times again by Pasdeloup and taken up by other orchestras. It was heard some fifteen times in the thirty months he still had to live.

★ ★ ★ ★ ★

The play, divided into five tableaux, is set in the Castelets' farm in a Provençal village on the banks of the Rhône. The drama centres on the young man Frédéri, who is in love with a girl from Arles. She is never named nor seen. His widowed mother Rose Mamaï and his grandfather Francet Mamaï are concerned that such girls have a flighty reputation, which is confirmed when a visitor, Mitifio, claims to be the girl's lover and has letters to prove it. In despair Frédéri goes along with his mother's plan to take his mind off the Arlésienne by agreeing to marry the shy and blameless Vivette, who has loved him from afar. But the return of Mitifio enflames his furious passion and he takes his own life by jumping from the top of the farm building. Parallel interest derives from L'Innocent, Fréderi's simpleton young brother, whose mind becomes clearer as Frédéri's becomes more deranged, and from the old shepherd Balthazar, reunited with his own lost love Renaude, Vivette's grandmother, after fifty years.

Bizet scored the music for a reduced orchestra, perhaps limited by space in the pit. There are no trumpets or trombones, but an alto saxophone is required. This instrument was familiar at that time from its important solo in the Comedians' mime scene in Thomas's *Hamlet* still playing regularly at the Opéra. There is also a chorus who sing in the wings, supported by a harmonium and piano.

The full-length Prélude opens with a sixteen-bar march in a forceful unison, the tune being the "Marcho dei Rèi", also known as the "Marche de Turenne" once attributed to Lully. It is subjected to a series of four variations ranging widely from smooth and delicate to strong and noisy. We then hear the theme associated with L'Innocent (drawn from the sketches of *Grisélidis*). Giving this beautiful theme to the saxophone makes a powerful, indeed shocking, impression, stronger in fact than the character himself warrants. The third section introduces Frédéri's theme played by violins in octaves with piano accompaniment. It conveys a strong sense of desperation and tragedy. Its repetition on full strings against throbbing wind triplets anticipates the kind of scoring more familiar from uninhibited moments in Tchaikovsky and Puccini, although with a small orchestra, as here, it remains tastefully understated.

Music is heard twenty-five times in the course of the play, always at the beginning and end of the five tableaux, and using a chorus in the wings on six occasions. Most of the interventions during the action are *mélodrames*, heard behind spoken dialogue and intended to heighten the dramatic or emotional moment. Most of these are short, as little as six bars long. The first three all offer differently harmonised and differently scored versions of L'Innocent's theme. Later on it is subjected to two different time-signatures also. Frédéri's theme is similarly varied when it occurs in *mélodrame*, and at the end of the first and last tableaux it drives home the tragedy *con tutta forza*. For Frédéri's entrance in the final scene Bizet's imaginative ear led him to score the double-bass line to move upward from a unison with the cellos while leaving the cellos to sustain the bottom note, an effect he had already put to good use in the slow movement of the Second Symphony. The longest *mélodrame* is in the fourth tableau: it starts and ends as a gentle sicilienne for two flutes to accompany the entry of Mère Renaude, and while she and Balthazar reaffirm their long suppressed love, Bizet supports the dialogue with a sublime Adagio for muted string quartet, one of the most beautiful and most perfectly crafted passages in all his music. Throughout *L'Arlésienne* we are forced to regret that Bizet never wrote an independent string quartet, nor indeed any chamber music at all.

One of the *mélodrames* in the second tableau is heard while L'Innocent falls asleep. Here Bizet inserts a Provençal theme, "Èr dou Guet", scored for muted string quartet. A third folk theme is the "Danso dei chivau-frus", a lively farandole to be danced and sung by peasants against the constant beat of the *tambourin*, a long hand-beaten drum. The Parisian Bizet had no difficulty in recreating this rustic opéra-comique cliché with delicate skill. In the final Entr'acte the chorus sing the "Marcho dei Rèi", already heard in the Prélude, first in unison, then in canon between men and women half a bar apart, then in harmony, and finally in counterpoint with the Farandole as a crowning tour de force.

When it came to composing longer independent interludes he supplied a Pastorale, an Entr'acte, an Intermezzo and a Carillon, all better known from their places in the two *Arlésienne* suites. The Pastorale suggests heavy-booted peasants more than Arcadian shepherds, then it merges with a delicious chorus from the wings recalling the Boléro from *Vasco de Gama* (and *Ivan IV*). A high descant on piccolo and harmonium makes charming play with accented wrong notes. The Entr'acte introducing the second tableau opens with a ponderous unison and then presents a long theme of great nobility scored at first for saxophone and horn in octaves gradually accruing other wind. This is sometimes referred to as Vivette's theme, since she is on stage (or about to be) when it is heard, but really it is far above her social station, and its harmonisation is broad and grand.

The Intermezzo (also labelled "Valse-Menuet" by Bizet) sounds strangely tepid on the small orchestra for which it was written, at least for its loud beginning. But when it returns after a long middle section on a drone, it is infinitely soft and most delicately scored. This is followed immediately by the Carillon, the constant three-note ostinato on horns and piano supplying Sunday bells and a technical challenge for the composer.

It cannot be denied that although the original version of *L'Arlésienne* has its strong admirers, three of the five pieces that Bizet selected for his orchestral suite sound marvellously effective in their full orchestral dress. The Prélude was otherwise unaltered; the Minuetto (= the Intermezzo) benefits from a full string section for its loud opening statement and from a six-bar prolongation of the *pianissimo* ending. The Adagio section from the *mélodrame* in the fourth tableau, renamed Adagietto, is now to be played by full strings, not by a quartet, and loses a few degrees of intimacy thereby. Carillon is an extended version of the Carillon in the play with a bridge into the sicilienne music that earlier encircled the Adagio and a full reprise of the carillon music to close.

★ ★ ★ ★ ★

Within a week of the *Arlésienne* suite's success in Pasdeloup's concert, a new work by Bizet was performed at the Théâtre du Château-d'Eau, one of many new theatrical enterprises that sprang up in the wake of the restoration of civilisation a year earlier. This was *Sol-si-ré-pif-pan*, a *bouffonnerie musicale* in one act, of which we know almost nothing. The author was Geneviève's cousin, William Busnach, earlier Bizet's collaborator in *Malbrough s'en va-t-en guerre*, but we have only the word of Bizet's biographer Pigot that the music was by Bizet since the libretto submitted to the censorship names no composer and the newspapers seem to have overlooked it. The music is in any case lost. A silly story about two sea-captains and their mistresses is resolved with the aid of Sol-si-ré-pif-pan, a one-man band. It is tantalising to wonder how Bizet would have composed for such a character, but we should not take too censorious a view of his attempts to find success in the theatre at any level; he saw himself as a creature of the theatre, and rightly or wrongly he made no attempt to contribute to the revival of French chamber music at that time (as did Saint-Saëns and Lalo) and little to the repertoire of orchestral music. His Second Symphony and his *Petite Suite* aroused little interest while, again, Saint-Saëns and Lalo, even Guiraud, were doing better in this sphere. There may have been other farces and operettas he contributed to without telling anyone.

He contributed a song, for example, to a play by another of Geneviève's cousins, Ludovic Halévy, with his usual partner Meilhac. This was *Le Roi Candaule*, played at the Théâtre du Palais Royal on 9 April 1873. The song, "De ce gaillard entretien", which is in fact a light-hearted dialogue between two characters, has survived, although it was not published. Again, no one save the authors probably knew that it was his.

Bizet's overriding occupation in the winter of 1872–73 was to supervise a revival of Gounod's *Roméo et Juliette* at the Opéra-Comique, which he undertook as a favour to the composer, still in England. An exchange of letters between the two men precisely reflects the sensitivites of their mutual regard. In reply to Gounod's invitation Bizet wrote:

The ties that unite us are such that neither absence nor silence can undo them. You were the beginning of my career as an artist. I am a product of you. You are the cause and I am the consequence. I was afraid of being absorbed, I can now tell you, and you must have observed the effects of this anxiety. Today I believe I am more master of my craft, and I feel only the benefit of your salutary and decisive influence. I don't think I am being ungrateful to our dear Halévy in crediting you with what is so legitimately your due.

Gounod replied: "Yours is a nature too musical not to have your own musical nature. You are now *named*, that is to say *distinct*, separate from the mass, untouched by the confusion, and your fame will have the right to be yours just as you will have the right to belong to it."[5]

Since its successful run at the Théâtre-Lyrique in 1867–68, *Roméo et Juliette* had been heard in a dozen foreign cities. Now du Locle wanted it for his own theatre and he secured the participation of Mme Carvalho, who had sung the role of Juliet over a hundred times already. At the Opéra-Comique, where it was to be played nearly three hundred times before transferring yet again to the Opéra in 1888, Mme Carvalho stayed with the production for at least two years. Deloffre, as before, was the conductor. Gounod had made a number of revisions which had to be implemented in the scores and parts, so it fell to Bizet as repetiteur to oversee these and to rehearse the singers.[6] Twelve pages of full score survive in Bizet's hand, showing an alteration in the finale to Act III which he orchestrated and may even have composed. There were many other passages that required his attention. The theatre's records show Bizet attending rehearsals almost every day from 8 October until opening night on 20 January 1873. Duchesne, Bizet's Haroun, was Roméo, and Ismaël, his Nadir, was Frère Laurent. Contrary to the theatre's traditions there was no spoken dialogue. Gounod's gratitude was sincere:

> I would be betraying the friendship that I have for you as much as that which you have shown toward me if I did not thank you for the essential part you have played in this revival, a part which will no doubt be rewarded with the great success of the work and of the performance. I do not like ingratitude; I know many ungrateful people and I would be horrified to add to that grievous list. I know that whatever qualities a work may have are unlikely to impress the public unless they are revealed by those responsible for preparing and interpreting the work.[7]

---

5. Curtiss (1958), pp. 342–343; Gounod (1899), pp. 700–701.

6. The versions of *Roméo et Juliette* are set out by Joël-Marie Fauquet in *Avant-scène opéra* (1982), pp. 66–72. Gounod's instructions to Bizet were given in two letters from October 1872 published by Poupet (1982), p. 71.

7. Gounod (1899), pp. 702–703.

Faust also needed Bizet's attention during Gounod's absence. Playing regularly now at the Opéra, the opera's last act had acquired a ballet in 1869. Reducing the seven ballets to two and changing their order required new modulations to lead out of and into the surrounding scenes, and these Bizet was called in to supply.

Bizet was not entirely devoid of envy, but he can only have been impressed by the success of his generation of composers, some younger than himself, as opera and concert life in Paris steadily expanded throughout the 1870s. French music in the remaining years of the century could boast a wealth and variety of composers unequalled elsewhere, at least in terms of numbers, among whom Bizet would surely have been a leader, had he lived. Guiraud was his closest friend in this group. Guiraud's two-act opéra-comique *Madame Turlupin* opened at the Théâtre de L'Athénée on 23 November 1872 and enjoyed a modest success. It was his fourth opera to be staged in Paris since he returned from Italy. Next to be heard was Massenet, still something of a novice in the field of opera, with his comedy *Don César de Bazan* premiered at the Opéra-Comique a week later on 30 November. The boy Lazarille was played by Galli-Marié, Charles II by Lhérie, and Don César by Bouhy, all three to be cast in leading parts in *Carmen* three years later. On 8 December Pasdeloup introduced Lalo's *Divertissement*, one of his best orchestral works. On 6 January of the new year Leconte de Lisle's play *Les Érinnyes* opened at the Odéon with incidental music by Massenet scored for an ensemble larger but even more unusual than Bizet's for *L'Arlésienne*: thirty-six strings, three trombones, and timpani. One of the *mélodrames* took on a life of its own as a beautifully affecting cello solo with a melody to which the ever inventive Gallet wrote some words. Four days later the Opéra gave *La Coupe du Roi de Thulé* as composed by Eugène Diaz, winner of the competition of 1869. We might imagine Massenet, Guiraud and Bizet (if he had time off from *Roméo et Juliette* across the street), all of whom had set the same libretto themselves, eagerly listening to their friend's score. The role of Paddock was played by Faure, now the Opéra's most luminous star and one of Bizet's friends. If he could bear the further humiliation of hearing someone else's setting of another text he had set himself, Bizet might have gone to *La Guzla de L'Émir*, as set by Théodore Dubois and performed at the Théâtre de L'Athénée on 30 April. Dubois, eventually to be appointed Director of the Conservatoire, was evidently not part of Bizet's close circle.

Parisians were astonished at this time by the emergence of the legendary pianist Charles-Valentin Alkan, now over sixty, who had not performed in public for twenty years. In Erard's salon he gave a series of six "Petits Concerts" at fortnightly intervals featuring, besides his own music, his transcriptions of the classics and some works for the pedal-piano of which he was a vigorous exponent. Unfortunately he skirted around the performance of his most formidably difficult works, which were left for later generations to confront.

Like Bizet, Massenet was not above composing farce. His operetta *L'Adorable Bel-Boul* was played at the aristocratic Cercle des Mirlitons on 17 April. The music was thought to be destroyed, but a manuscript turned up at auction in 2013. Much more important in the promotion of Massenet's career was a concert promoted by his publisher Hartmann and given by a new organisation, the Concert National, in the Odéon theatre on Good Friday, 11 April 1873, conducted by Édouard Colonne, a conductor with an important future. The single work on the programme was Massenet's oratorio *Marie-Magdeleine*, with a text (one might call it a libretto) by Gallet. With Pauline Viardot singing the part of Méryem, the work created a sensation.

Bizet's music did not go entirely unheard in this torrent of new works. The first concert of the Concert National took place on 2 March 1873. Despite the title "Concert National" the programme included works by Mendelssohn, Schubert and Schumann, balanced by some new French works. These were Saint-Saëns's Piano Concerto no. 2, Bizet's *Petite Suite*, and Guiraud's "Carnaval" (the last movement of his *Suite d'orchestre*). This was not the first performance of Bizet's suite, for it was rehearsed by Pasdeloup for the Concerts Populaires a year earlier, but withdrawn by Bizet when he decided that it was being given too little rehearsal. A more careful conductor, Jules Danbé, with yet another new concert body, the Concerts du Grand Hôtel, came to the rescue and gave the work its first performance in May 1872.

★ ★ ★ ★ ★

A further distraction from composition was Choudens's plan to issue a volume of Bizet's songs. He had already published two sets of twenty songs by Gounod and was preparing a third. Bizet's correspondence from the closing months of 1872 mentions two series, which may represent a plan to publish two sets of ten or twelve songs each, even perhaps two sets of twenty. In the end it was a single volume of twenty songs, in conformity with the Gounod volumes and contributing to a distinctive tradition for French composers which embraced *Vingt Mélodies* also from Fauré, Massenet, Lalo, Godard, Chausson, Saint-Saëns, Hahn and others. Bizet's *Vingt Mélodies* was published late in 1873 or early in 1874 in two forms, for high or low voice. The collection included one extract from each of his four stage works: "Sérénade" from *Les Pêcheurs de perles*, Mab's couplets from *La Jolie Fille de Perth*, Haroun's "J'aime l'amour" from *Djamileh*, and the "la-la-la" chorus from *L'Arlésienne* arranged as a solo song under the title "Le Matin". The author of the words is given as ★★★, which might indicate Bizet himself; at least that is what the publisher Hamelle thought in 1879 when that house published a setting of the same verses composed by Ferenc Korbay.

Seven of the songs in the collection had been ceded to Choudens by Hartmann, their original publisher: "Rêve de la bien-aimée", " Ma Vie a son secret", "Pastorale", "Berceuse", "La Chanson du fou", "La Coccinelle" and "Tarentelle" (with a new

French text by Édouard Pailleron to replace the original Italian folk song). Eight songs had been published earlier by Choudens himself: "Vieille Chanson", "Chanson d'avril", "Adieux de l'hôtesse arabe", "Absence", "Douce Mer", "Après l'hiver", "Chant d'amour" and "L'Esprit saint". Just a single song was published for the first time, a setting of a poem by Casimir Delavigne entitled "L'Âme en purgatoire", which Bizet called "Vous ne priez pas !," this being the recurrent last line of the three (out of eight) stanzas he set. To compensate for the persistent figuration retained unchanged in the accompaniment throughout its ninety-six bars, tempo and dynamics are adjusted for each of the three verses and the climax of each is passionate and strong. The sense of despair in the last verse is overwhelming, caused largely by the very persistence of the piano's obsessive figuration. Bizet's control of the major-minor alternation is superb.

Three songs that survive in manuscript may have been intended for this collection. Since they came to the Bibliothèque du Conservatoire as a single set from the collection of Charles Malherbe, a common purpose is likely.[8] One of them is no earlier than 1868, but otherwise they give no clue as to when they were composed. "Vœu" is a slight but charming setting of one of Hugo's oriental fantasies about a leaf blown across the sea to settle on a young girl's brow. Another Hugo setting, "Sérénade", is a delightfully cheerful song whose carefree tunefulness may be seen from its opening phrase (Example 8.1). The poem was also set by Liszt and by Lalo.

Example 8.1

8. F-Pn MS 463–465.

If Lalo's version is a good deal more ponderous than Bizet's, Liszt's song is a masterpiece of feeling and expression, to which Bizet's song does not pretend to aspire. The third song, "Le Colibri" (the Humming-Bird), took a poem by Alexandre Flan from the same 1868 collection where Bizet found "Rêve de la bien-aimée" by Louis de Courmont. Like "Sérénade" it is light and vaporous, all over in the twinkling of an eye, less than a minute in fact, an ideal encore piece. All three songs may have struck Bizet (or Choudens) as too insubstantial for an important collection such as this.

After the publication of the *Vingt Mélodies* in 1873 it seems that Bizet planned a second collection, perhaps to include these three songs. It was more probably a plan to compile a collection of songs based on material from three operas which he regarded as having no future: *La Coupe du Roi de Thulé*, *Clarisse Harlowe* and *Grisélidis*. All these pieces required new words, since the original words would make little sense out of context. A set of unusual manuscripts[9] shows that Bizet wrote out the piano parts leaving the words to be filled in later by Paul Ferrier, Philippe Gille, Jules Barbier or Catulle Mendès.

One song, "Pastel", was composed as a song, but to different words. It was originally "Le Portrait", with words by Eugène Manuel. The melody is long and beautifully crafted, falling easily into two strophes. The remaining songs came from the abandoned operas. Three pieces were duets for two voices and piano, all with new words by Jules Barbier. "Le Retour" and "Les Nymphes des bois" were scenes from *Clarisse Harlowe*, and "Rêvons" was from *La Coupe du Roi de Thulé*. These duets were published in the 1880s but have remained cloaked in the darkest obscurity, never having been recorded and rating barely a mention in any of Bizet's biographies. Coming from operas, they have a clear dramatic character. The poem of "Le Retour" imagines a soldier returning from war who tells a young girl that her fiancé has fallen in battle. Her display of grief convinces him of her love. He then reveals that he is himself her fiancé, and they sing joyously of reunion. Bizet made solo versions, or extracts, from these duets: "Voyage" from "Le Retour" (yet new words from Gille), and "Aimons, Rêvons" from "Rêvons".

He prepared a further seven songs from these operas, two from *La Coupe du Roi de Thulé*, three from *Clarisse Harlowe*, and three from *Grisélidis*. None of these were published at this time, although they formed the bulk of the collection *Seize Mélodies* published by Choudens in the mid-1880s.

★ ★ ★ ★ ★

As the spring of 1873 arrived Bizet could at last look forward to a return to composition and the chance to retreat to Le Vésinet, with or without wife and baby.

---

9. Private collection.

There is no indication that in the rush of the winter season he had given any thought to the opera he was supposed to compose with Halévy and Meilhac for the Opéra-Comique. The librettists were themselves busy. Ludovic Halévy had already written twenty-one librettos for Offenbach, the last ten of them, starting with *Le Brésilien* in 1863, in collaboration with Henri Meilhac, whose special gifts were for parody and humorous dialogue. Offenbach showed no sign of slowing down. At this moment Halévy was working with his cousin William Busnach on *Pomme d'Api* for Offenbach, at the same time putting together *La Vie parisienne*, also for Offenbach, with Meilhac.

In thrusting Bizet into this collaboration and suggesting something *gai*, du Locle and de Leuven could only have expected to acquire a comic, even farcical, work. The moment that put Mérimée's *Carmen* into Bizet's mind cannot be pinpointed, but it is to be celebrated not only because it led to the creation of one of the world's great operas but also because it shows Bizet's extraordinary courage, recklessness even, in thinking that the subject would be acceptable either to his collaborators or to the management of the theatre. As far as we know, there was no fight, little debate even. Many years later (and with plenty of hindsight) Halévy recalled that he and Meilhac were immediately enthusiastic about Mérimée's story, and that only de Leuven showed any resistance, stubborn though it was. "I beg you, try to avoid her dying," de Leuven told him. "Death at the Opéra-Comique! Such a thing has never happened, do you hear? Never! Don't make her die, I beg you, my dear child."[10] In fact, as we have seen, heroines had died on the stage of the Opéra-Comique before, but not violently murdered by their lovers. Even though Bizet's proposal took the raw edge off Mérimée's novella, there was much else in the story besides Carmen's death that caused de Leuven to be anxious for the *bien-être* of his traditional audience. All must have been decided by March or April 1873. The first reference to *Carmen* is found in a letter dated 7 May 1873 from Léon Halévy to the publisher Heugel: "Ludovic and Meilhac are at work finishing a libretto which will give Bizet the chance to apply his talent,"[11] while a letter from Bizet to Lacombe written before 8 June reports that he had finished the first act of *Carmen* and that he was pleased with it.[12]

Meanwhile he was approached by the baritone Faure who had been struck, while singing *La Coupe du Roi de Thulé* at the Opéra, by the skill of the librettists Gallet and Blau and who suggested that they should write a libretto for Bizet in which he, Faure, could be featured in a leading role. He was no doubt hoping for a successor to Thomas's *Hamlet*, in which he sang the title role. The librettists conferred over possible subjects, suggesting de Musset's play *Lorenzaccio* since it somewhat

---

10. Rose (2013), p. 216.
11. Archives Heugel, Vente Ader, 26 May 2011.
12. Imbert (1894), p. 197.

resembled *Hamlet*. This was not to Faure's liking. "He wants everything," suggested Bizet. "Not only must his character be tall and handsome, generous and strong, people must also speak highly of him when he's not on stage." Bizet himself then came up with the suggestion of using *Las Mocedades del Cid* by Guillén de Castro y Bellvis (1569–1631) which he had read in translation. This was the source for Pierre Corneille's well-known play *Le Cid* (which was revived at the Comédie Française on 3 October 1872). "Le Cid the lover, the devoted son, Christian, heroic, and triumphant: what more could he want?"[13] Bizet was especially attracted to a scene with a beggar, which Corneille had excluded.

It is possible that with two librettos on his desk Bizet spent the summer of 1873 working on both operas simultaneously, but his real enthusiasm for *Don Rodrigue* (his chosen title for the Cid opera), which he displays in his correspondence with Gallet, suggests strongly that *Carmen* was made to wait while the other opera took precedence; the Opéra after all carried far more prestige than the Opéra-Comique. This correspondence, like the equivalent exchanges with Galabert over *La Coupe du Roi de Thulé*, tells us much about Bizet's approach to the shaping of the drama. We have no equivalent record of his work on *Carmen*, so the chronology of its genesis is largely obscure. Gallet records that *Don Rodrigue* was finished by the end of the summer. In the last week of October Bizet played it through to Gallet, Blau and Faure, singing all the parts "in the feeblest voice in the world" and accompanying himself from a score in which he had written all the vocal lines but left the orchestral part largely blank. Faure was delighted with it, undertaking to approach Halanzier, the director, and giving librettists and composer real hope that the opera would be accepted. A few days later, on the night of 28–29 October, the opera house in the Rue Le Peletier, which had housed the great era of French Grand Opera since its opening in 1821, burned to the ground. It is always argued that the loss of the building sealed the fate of *Don Rodrigue*, but the company moved temporarily to the Salle Ventadour to await the opening of the grand new opera house, the Palais Garnier, on 5 January 1875. Halanzier remained its director throughout this period, so he could easily have staged the opera if he had wished to. Faure, after all, was a trump card. But Halanzier had little interest in promoting new works and he doubtless remembered Bizet's petulant behaviour in October 1871 when he refused the position of *chef du chant*. One more Bizet opera fell into limbo.

The manuscript of the opera[14] remains to this day in the condition that Gallet described: 686 pages of 32-stave music paper set out ready for orchestration with the vocal line and words written in throughout. The surviving sketches of *Grisélidis* and *Clarisse Harlowe* show Bizet entering the vocal line with a few bass notes and a

---

13. Gallet (1891), pp. 62–63.
14. F-Pn MS 477.

few figures (to represent the harmony) on two staves filling cramped pages. *Don Rodrigue* reached the next stage, ready for the filling out and completion on pages already laid out to show the full orchestration. The vocal parts are complete in ink throughout. There is almost no orchestration, but there are many pencilled suggestions for harmony and accompaniment. The last fifty-four bars of no. 22, whose music is also part of the overture *Patrie*, are fully scored. The manuscript lacks an overture and the ballet. Hervé Lacombe suggests that at least certain scenes could be reconstructed and performed,[15] but there is really too little on which to build such a reconstruction. Bizet's surprising harmony and inventive interludes cannot be recreated with any claim to plausibility.

Like *Ivan IV* this was to be a five-act grand opera in the Meyerbeer tradition.[16] The libretto provided opportunities for Spanish local colour and spectacular scenes, such as the royal ceremony at the beginning and Rodrigue's triumph at the end, and it included a drinking chorus for the troops as well as strong solo scenes for the main characters. The Opéra's lavish off-stage brass would have been busy. The essential drama is set up by a quarrel between the fathers of the lovers Don Rodrigue and Chimène. Rodrigue avenges an insult to his father by killing Chimène's father in a duel, for which Chimène cannot forgive him. Their long duet in Act III is full of tension since he begs Chimène to kill him, and although she cannot do so, her desire for vengeance is only satisfied when Rodrigue agrees to go to the King for justice. He will accept his fate by leading the army against the Moors. Returning victorious, he is forgiven by Chimène and applauded by all.

The scene that appealed so much to Bizet occurs in Act IV when on the eve of battle a beggar appears in the Spanish camp. Rodrigue dismisses the soldiers and takes pity on the beggar, who falls asleep. Rodrigue prays for his soul and soon falls asleep himself. He sees a vision in which the beggar appears as Lazarus in heaven while celestial voices proclaim the end of Rodrigue's torment and his victory in battle. Such a scene fell into a tradition of other-worldly scenes in French opera, usually supported by mystic voices, organ, and harps and most recently illustrated by Ophelia's mad scene in *Hamlet*. In Massenet's version of the story, Rodrigue has a vision of St-Jacques.

The curious thing is that there is no prominent part for a baritone; the leading role is for tenor. The king is a baritone and the two fathers are basses, all secondary roles. It is hard to imagine Bizet rewriting the role of Rodrigue as Thomas had done with Hamlet, and consequently Faure might have expended less than his full energy persuading Halanzier to mount the opera if his own part in it was not as prominent as he liked.

15. Lacombe (2000), pp. 629–630.
16. For a survey of the Cid theme in opera see Yon (1994).

The bare vocal lines reveal how much Bizet's musical character resided in harmony and orchestration, which in this case he carried in his head. A comprehensive critique of the work as it stands or any attempt to imagine what the opera might have been is impossible on the basis of vocal setting only. With little sign of local Spanish colour its style is inevitably different from that of *Carmen*, a fact that has convinced his admirers that grand opera was not his proper sphere and that *Ivan IV* is therefore also deficient in theatrical merit. At the age of thirty-five Bizet had no reason to see himself confined to one genre at the expense of all the others, for he knew well that composers blessed with long careers had no difficulty in encompassing operas of extreme types from farce to tragedy. Gounod, Thomas, and Massenet all ranged successfully across the whole spectrum. Given another score of years, or even just a dozen, Bizet might have produced a serious five-act opera and proved that he could rival Massenet in all fields.

If the opera had been completed and performed, Massenet would not have been free to compose his own opera on the subject, *Le Cid*, performed to great applause at the Opéra in 1885, although that success did not discourage Debussy from attempting a *Rodrigue et Chimène* of his own, left unfinished, like Bizet's. Massenet's libretto is credited to Adolphe d'Ennery in addition to Gallet and Blau, and it shares some of the same lines as Bizet's.

★ ★ ★ ★ ★

With *Carmen* on hold and *Don Rodrigue* in progress Bizet was once more called upon to stand in for his old mentor Gounod. On 1 June 1873 Offenbach, always the entrepreneur as well as the leading composer of operetta, took over the Théâtre de la Gaîté, traditionally a home for melodrama and pantomime, and refurbished it at great expense. He planned a double company, one troupe for plays and one for opera. Even before taking control he agreed to stage a patriotically inspired play, *Jeanne d'Arc*, by Jules Barbier, who went to London to persuade Gounod to write the incidental music. The score was almost as substantial as an opéra-comique. Offenbach vetoed Gounod's plan to use a "pyrophone" to represent the voices that speak to Joan of Arc. This was an instrument in which glass pipes, set in vibration by burning hydrogen, produced a sound close to that of the human voice. Unable to attend in person, Gounod engaged Bizet to supervise the rehearsals, which began in October. A vivid glimpse of Bizet at this point was provided by Armand Gouzien in a memoir written on Bizet's death:

> We were present one day at Offenbach's when he he'd just been sent Gounod's score for Jules Barbier's *Jeanne d'Arc* from London. Bizet sat down at the piano and put up the still unopened orchestral score. He didn't even glance through it to get used to the master's fine handwriting, to look out for trouble spots which might be lurking, or to get a rapid

idea of the work and its surprises. No, he attacked the opening chord. Then when he got to the chorus he sang along with us as we read the manuscript, all the time reproducing all the orchestration as far as the rebellious piano would allow. Here a horn entry, which he was careful not to miss, there a phrase for violin or for flute, then a tutti where the bass notes on the piano growled like timpani under his fingers or rang out like triangles.[17]

Rehearsals kept him busy while he was also preparing to present *Don Rodrigue* at the Opéra. Opening night was on 8 November, and the play's successful run prompted the publisher Gérard to commission both a vocal score and a piano solo version of the music from the ever-obliging Bizet, amounting to two hundred pages in print. Bizet's opinion of the music (or the play) may be inferred from a note to Guiraud: "We'll go for dinner in the Rue de Médicis, then afterwards to *Jeanne d'Arc*. We'll have a laugh!"[18] After Sarah Bernhardt took up the play (and the title role) in 1890 the vocal score was reissued in great numbers by Choudens without any mention of Bizet's name.

On 29 November 1873 Bizet accompanied the great Spanish violinist Sarasate in a performance of Lalo's violin sonata at a concert of the Société Nationale, and a few months later in the same series he accompanied Julie Lalo, the composer's wife, in the Sérénade from *Les Pêcheurs de perles* and the song "Vous ne priez pas", which was dedicated to her.[19]

The only section of *Don Rodrigue* that Bizet orchestrated is the last fifty-four bars of the opening scene in Act V. This is the scene where the triumphant Spanish armies process on stage with the captured enemy standards and the traditional spoils of war. It is a vigorous march in the key of C minor and it reappears as the main theme of an orchestral work that he was invited to compose by Pasdeloup for his thriving Concerts Populaires for the winter season 1873–74. Pasdeloup asked three composers each to write an "Ouverture dramatique". Bizet's overture named *Patrie* was completed in December 1873 and first performed on 15 February 1874, followed a week later by Massenet's overture *Phèdre*, and a week after that by Guiraud's *Ouverture de concert*. *Patrie* was published the same year in full score and in his own arrangement for piano duet. On the first page of the duet version appears the heading: "Episode from the Polish War (Battle of Racławice won against the Russians by Kosciuszko in 1792)". (The correct date of the battle is 1794.) Pigot asserted that Bizet's true purpose was to evoke the sufferings of Paris in 1870–71, like a number of patriotic pieces produced by French composers in those years. Joseph Bennett said the title was Pasdeloup's choice.[20] Pasdeloup

---

17. Armand Gouzien, *L'Événement*, 6 June 1875.
18. *Avant-scène opéra* (1982), p. 116.
19. Lacombe (2000), p. 536.
20. *The Musical Times*, 1 December 1886, p. 709.

repeated it a number of times in subsequent seasons, and after Bizet's death it enjoyed frequent performances in Paris and elsewhere along with the Second Symphony, both works now almost invisible in the concert hall. Bizet dedicated the overture to Massenet and inscribed copies of both score and piano duet arrangement to him.

The overture is sectional, with robust martial music at the beginning and end. Brass fanfares interrupt the flow from time to time. The second section introduces a stirring low tune on clarinets, bassoons and violas accompanied by gruff cellos and basses. In the manner of the Prélude to *L'Arlésienne* this is treated to variations, the first soft and suavely harmonised, the second heroic, with plenty of percussion. The third section is a lament for the fallen in the manner of a funeral march, and this leads into a fourth section, a picture of paradise in the major key, the most strikingly personal section of the work. For the reprise the march is heard as if from a distance over a long grumbling ostinato similar to those in Beethoven's Seventh and Ninth Symphonies (Example 8.2). The overture closes with a crude 6/8 variation of the second section, *tutta forza*, and a final reminiscence of the fourth section, now triumphant.

Example 8.2

Patriotic music is by its very nature inclined to bombast, since it is addressed to the masses, and representations of victory can be short on sensitivity. *Patrie* does not escape these criticisms, but it is redeemed by the impressive third and fourth sections, by its skillful orchestration throughout, and by Bizet's fondness for slipping deftly from key to key, as if nothing had happened (Example 8.3).

Example 8.3

* * * * *

During these months when Bizet was preoccupied with *Jeanne d'Arc*, with *Don Rodrigue* and with *Patrie*, he was in discussion with du Locle and his librettists about who was to sing the crucial role of Carmen, with a view to a production in the early part of 1874. One of Offenbach's stars (also his mistress) Zulma Bouffar was first considered but rejected. More seriously considered was Marie Roze, already known at the Opéra-Comique, but she declined out of distaste for Carmen's dubious morality. Next in line was Célestine Galli-Marié, destined to be immortalised as the first Carmen but already well known in Paris for a series of roles at the Opéra-Comique and elsewhere, often playing boyish roles rather than the traditional soubrette young girl in love. The triumphant success of *Mignon* was largely due to her impersonation of the title role. She was two years younger than Bizet and already an experienced singing actress with a string of engagements both in Paris and on tour in Belgium. When she first appeared in Paris in 1862 a critic wrote of her: "She is small and delicate, moves like a cat, has an impish, pert face, and her whole personality seems unruly and mischievous. She acts as though she had been trained in the sound tradition of Molière; she sings in a full fresh voice, piquant and mellow."[21] Her correspondence shows her to have possessed a strong personality and a lively spirit of adventure. By September 1873 Bizet felt she was right for the part, but her celebrity created problems of both finance and availability. He had played her part to her, which suggests that he had completed more than Act I. The rest of the opera was probably sketched or at least in his head, for he can hardly have finished a complete draft until the early months of 1874. By the end of 1873

---

21. Paul de Saint-Victor in *La Presse*, cited in Soubies (1893), p. 44 and Curtiss (1958), p. 358.

Galli-Marié had agreed to be available for the four months October to December 1874. Shortly after that de Leuven resigned as co-director of the Opéra-Comique, largely, it is said, out of distaste at the prospect of Bizet's opera being staged; at seventy-two he felt it was time to go. Du Locle, now in sole charge, was more receptive, but not without misgivings of his own.

After the performance of *Patrie* on 15 February, Bizet had the completion of *Carmen* as his main priority. Despite the overture's success at Pasdeloup's concert he was in low spirits, plagued as ever by recurrences of the angina he'd suffered since childhood. He sometimes referred to it as a throat ailment. It was severe enough in either form to depress him. Relations with Geneviève since the birth of the baby, furthermore, were strained to the point where they spent two or three months apart. Galabert kept none of Bizet's letters from this period since they revealed facts about the marriage that he felt his friend would not want to be known. Geneviève went to stay with her cousin Ludovic in Port-Marly, just across the river from Le Vésinet. The cottage in Le Vésinet was not big enough for a family of three with a maid and her thirteen-year-old son, so Bizet found a summer retreat that year in Bougival, in a handsome villa a short distance up the Seine from Port-Marly and close to the river where he loved to swim.

He also had two more suites to prepare for Choudens. One was *Scènes bohémiennes*, a group of four movements from *La Jolie Fille de Perth* for full orchestra, perhaps modelled on Massenet's *Scènes hongroises*, which he had recently transcribed. The new suite required little arranging since the main difference with the opera version is in the omission of the voices. He nevertheless wrote out new full scores of all four movements. It was perhaps at this time too that he helped Gounod once again by preparing a four-movement suite of music from the 1860 opera *Philémon et Baucis*. Gounod had already made one suite, but he now suggested another. The overture and the Danse des Bacchantes were already orchestrated, but the two middle movements, the Chœur des Bacchantes and the Chœur de l'ivresse, both involving choir, required reorchestration. Bizet scored the first of these (which he had already arranged for piano solo as one of the *Six Chœurs célèbres*), but suggested the Mélodrame as an alternative to the Chœur de l'ivresse and orchestrated that instead. In the end neither of these movements was published.

Although never a teacher at the Conservatoire, Bizet contributed from time to time to the academic processes of that institution. In 1869 he wrote a fugue subject for the preliminary round of the Prix de Rome, and in 1873 he served as an external member of the jury that heard the six finalists' cantatas of that year. He set fugue subjects for various organ competitions too. In 1874 he composed two short pieces as sight-reading exercises, one for bassoon (with cello accompaniment) and one for oboe (with piano accompaniment). Once again we are reminded how fresh and rewarding his chamber music might have been, had he written any.

CHAPTER NINE

1873–1875: Carmen

WHILE BIZET WAS WRITING WIND PIECES AND ORCHESTRATING ALL 1200 PAGES of *Carmen*, Geneviève was with him in Bougival during the summer of 1874; at least that seems to have been the arrangement they came to, however precarious. There is strong evidence to suggest that Geneviève was more than usually friendly with one of her husband's friends, Élie-Miriam Delaborde, a virtuoso pianist whose talent he inherited from his father, the equally remarkable Alkan, and who spent the summer nearby in Bougival. Bizet was aware of her warm feelings for Delaborde, which she did not hide.[1] The manner in which members of the Halévy family destroyed or concealed crucial evidence suggests that something was amiss. The appearance, however, is of a threesome who got on well enough. Delaborde, like Bizet, enjoyed swimming. He was a vigorous athlete, an advocate of the pedal-piano, an experienced traveller, and the possessor of innumerable apes and parrots as pets—congenial and interesting company, in other words. The most significant pointer to Geneviève's interest in Delaborde is the marriage contract they both signed in August 1876, scarcely a year after Bizet's death.[2] The marriage did not take place; both parties eventually married other spouses. But this is a matter in which gossip passed down through the years seems for once to have been right. Geneviève nevertheless told Gounod later that there was not a moment of her six years with Bizet she would not want to live again.[3]

We have at the same time to contend with the parallel gossip that linked Bizet to Galli-Marié. Bizet, as we know, was susceptible to female charm, especially if he

1. Malherbe (1951), p. 13.
2. Wright (1981), p. 14.
3. Malherbe (1951), p. 55.

was feeling sour about his marriage; Galli-Marié also had a history, since she was married at fifteen, widowed at twenty-one, and had for some while been the lover of Émile Paladilhe, a composer no less successful than Bizet at this point in his life. It has many times been pointed out that her free-spirited attitudes were not unlike those of the doomed gypsy she so famously played. Set two such individuals in the milieu of the theatre where hours are unpredictable and long, where tensions are easily stirred and personal emotions are never far from the surface, and the likelihood of such a liaison is inescapable. These were also the circumstances in 1863 when Léontine de Maësen sang Léïla in *Les Pêcheurs de perles*. In the case of *Carmen* there is more than guesswork to go on, for the two other leading singers in the production, Lhérie as Don José and Bouhy as Escamillo, lived well into the twentieth century and passed on backstage gossip about the affair which they would have had little reason to invent.[4]

A new work at the Opéra-Comique would normally require a rehearsal period of about a month. Since the performance schedule was not announced more than a few days in advance there was great flexibility in the process, which could be held up by illness, cancellations, technical problems on stage, diva behaviour, directorial whim, or any other reason. *Carmen*'s four acts with four different sets would require extra time to prepare. In the end, the rehearsal period was extended over six months, for part of the extraordinary story of the opera's birth derives from the resistance and obstacles the opera inevitably faced.

Rehearsals were already under way by 1 September 1874. The chorus had first to learn their music while copyists prepared the orchestral parts. Galli-Marié reported for duty in October, as required in her contract. On certain evenings she was appearing as Mignon in the same theatre, which may account for the gap in rehearsals that month. She was also singing in revivals of Maillart's *Les Dragons de Villars*. Serious rehearsals did not begin until 12 November, continuing almost daily until the end of the following February. The reason for such an extended rehearsal period lay not in the principal singers, who were all sufficiently skilled to sing their parts and also devoted to the work and its composer, but in the chorus, who were required to sing music of a complexity they had not encountered before. The opera may be thoroughly familiar today, but it remains very difficult to sing and act convincingly. One can well imagine a weary Bizet making the women in the chorus sing this (Example 9.1) over and over again until it was up to speed and the notes were right.

One problem was that there were too few women in the chorus. Bizet had to badger du Locle to get him to engage a few more, with consequent delays. At the same time they were singing tricky music, the female chorus were required to

---

4. See Curtiss (1958), pp. 358–359.

Example 9.1

Qu'elle a-chè-te-rait sans fau - te un â - ne qui lui plai- sait

squabble, fight and—horror of horrors—smoke. They declared the music to be unperformable and threatened to go on strike. As Ludovic Halévy recalled, they were accustomed to "standing still in neat lines, their arms dangling loosely at their side, their eyes fixed on the conductor and their thoughts elsewhere."[5] The Opéra-Comique's stage director, Charles Ponchard, embodied the older way of doing things, so that Bizet had to contend with him on a daily basis. Getting the chorus to enter one by one, for example, rather than in a block, met with resistance or refusal. Du Locle, who had set the whole thing in motion and had shown prophetic faith in Bizet's talent, was inclined to be cautious, being desperate to avoid a failure or a scandal. He famously told Saint-Saëns that the music was "Cochin-Chinese", which is explained only by du Locle's true preference for scenic, rather than musical, extravagance. Bizet was sorely fatigued and tested by the whole process, and his short fuse burned dangerously low at times. With a troublesome throat in addition, he must have been difficult to live with.

The conductor was once again the fifty-eight-year-old Jules Deloffre, who had been on the podium for all of Bizet's three previous operas, a man in whom almost no one was closely interested. He was experienced and competent, but probably no more. Fétis said his beat was unclear and Berlioz said he stamped noisily while beating.[6] A position we would now regard as crucial was then no more significant in the public eye than that of the stage manager. Bizet himself would have been in charge of all the rehearsals, including those for orchestra alone, which would not have started until the opera was getting close to readiness.

How far Meilhac and Halévy were involved is hard to say. A gossip who followed every operatic event with sharp ears reported that they were particularly assiduous in getting the ladies to act their parts convincingly from the very first rehearsals.[7] But both were, as before, in great demand at other theatres, not just in opera but as playwrights also. Three of their plays and a libretto set by Offenbach were all staged in the last four months of 1874. In January they were able to attend some rehearsals, causing Halévy at least to lose his habitual sang-froid. As he later

---

5. Halévy (1905) cited in Rose (2013), p. 226.
6. Walsh (1981), p. 40.
7. Mortier (1876), p. 88.

claimed, it was no great matter to him or to Meilhac if *Carmen* was a failure, but they both sincerely cared about Bizet's career and knew that this was a work on which his future hinged. With this in mind they were anxious to soften any outrageous elements of the subject by stopping Escamillo from patting the cheeks of the gypsies in the chorus and by attempting to tone down Galli-Marié's realistic acting. Du Locle wanted to change the ending so that *Carmen* is not brutally knifed on stage, but both Galli-Marié and Lhérie, the Don José, threatened to walk out if this was done. Bizet, it is clear, was ready to adjust his score for musical and dramatic reasons, but not to sugar the essential pill of the story.

There were a few distractions. On 5 January 1875 the new home for the Opéra, the Palais Garnier, opened at the head of the grand new Avenue de l'Opéra, a location that still reminds Parisians and tourists of the centrality of opera in French culture. Although the auditorium was not unusually capacious, the building itself was the largest home of opera in the world, and the ornamental luxury of its public spaces and exterior surfaces represented the most extravagant taste of the age. The leading diva, Christine Nilsson, withdrew from the opening gala at short notice, so that the extracts from *Faust* and *Hamlet* were dropped and a Meyerbeer scene substituted. With some ballet music from *La Source*, Delibes was the only living composer represented.

Early in February Bizet heard that he was to be awarded the cross of the Légion d'Honneur. The public announcement of this award was not made until Wednesday 3 March 1875, the day that *Carmen* finally opened at the Opéra-Comique, on which occasion someone was heard to say: "They announced it this morning because they knew that by tonight it would no longer be possible to give him the decoration."[8]

★ ★ ★ ★ ★

Carmen is an opéra-comique. It has separate musical numbers connected by dialogue and occasional *mélodrame* (speech over music). It is not comic, although elements of a comic tradition are included. Bizet composed each number separately, paginating each one in his manuscript with a start at page 1. Some motifs and passages recur, but there is little sense of a through-composed or organically connected work. It was written with the modest resources of the Opéra-Comique in mind: a medium-sized mixed chorus; dancing, but no corps de ballet; off-stage instruments, but no off-stage band (which means that when the cornets and trombones are off-stage in the final scene, they are unable to reinforce the final confrontation). Four acts was long for an opéra-comique but by no means unprecedented.

---

8. Curtiss (1958), p. 387.

In all of these respects (except being written for a different theatre) it is closely parallel to *Les Pêcheurs de perles*.

The music has been described and analysed countless times, and its relationship to Mérimée's novella scrutinised in depth.[9] Mérimée's own debt to an earlier story by Pushkin, "Tsygany" (The Gypsies), is not so well recognised.[10] A. D. P. Briggs has shown convincingly that Meilhac and Halévy worked not only from Mérimée's *Carmen* but also from Mérimée's translation of Pushkin's poem, from which his own story drew. Some elements of the libretto come directly from Pushkin, not from Mérimée. Briggs sums it up thus:

> The basic story, when stripped of its exaggerations and excessive derring-do, is that of *Tsygany*. A gypsy girl is stabbed to death by a jealous non-gypsy who loves her passionately, refuses to share her with a rival, or indeed anyone else, and fails to impose upon her the standards of constancy which are alien to her wilful character. He himself is no paragon, having had to flee from the law.[11]

Some lines in the opera, such as "Coupe-moi, brûle-moi!" at the beginning of no. 9, come from Pushkin, not from Mérimée. Mérimée's *Carmen* is a dark story about passion and death amid Spanish tribal conflicts (José is Basque) and gypsy morality. José is a ruffian and a bandit even before he meets Carmen, so the librettists had to apply a great deal of sugar-coating to make the story socially acceptable and to give it some variety and balance. José thus becomes a young soldier untainted by the world's wiles. Inventing the innocent Micaëla was a brilliant stroke, since it created a sharp contrast with Carmen and made José's passion for Carmen all the more destructive. Lillas Pastia, Le Dancaïre and Le Remendado all make brief appearances in the book, and a bullfighter named Lucas is a shadowy prototype of Escamillo. Mercédès and Frasquita are new creations. With Le Dancaïre and Le Remendado they make two pairs of characters, each pair serving the purpose of one individual, a comic convention that went back to Beppo and Giacomo in Auber's *Fra Diavolo* of 1830. There is a light-hearted spirit in these four characters that fits well with the comic genre.

The Prélude combines three extracts from the opera in the traditional way except that the third theme, with its stark augmented second and scored on clarinets, bassoons and low cornets, is disturbing and full of menace, sufficient to inject a strong hint of tense drama to come, whether it is labelled a "fate" theme or not (Example 9.2).

9. Recent examples include Wright (1982), de Solliers (1989), McClary (1992), Stricker (1999), Lacombe (2000), etc.

10. It is curious to recall that Turgenev proposed this story to Brahms as the basis for an opera. Rachmaninov's first opera, *Aleko*, is based on it.

11. Briggs (1995).

Example 9.2

It reaches an abrupt end and a silence. The effect of the curtain then rising on an open-air scene in Seville and a completely conventional orchestral warm-up to the opening chorus is disconcerting, to say the least, and the chorus of soldiers, when they sing "Sur la place, chacun passe", exactly captures the casual laziness of the scene. Micaëla comes in and asks for Don José, a sergeant. Moralès, also a sergeant, is rather taken with her and invites her to stay with his company while she waits. She very properly prefers to return later. When Moralès explains to her that José will be there with his own company when the guard changes, Bizet inserts a tune with a military clip that the soldiers irresistibly echo. Even Micaëla picks up its attractive allure. Bizet is already displaying the prodigal abundance of good tunes that has contributed so much to the opera's success. Once she leaves the stage the soldiers return to their casual opening chorus, as the convention for such pieces required.

There follows a Pantomime for Moralès which is almost invariably cut in performance and is missing from most recordings. It appears to have been cut during the 1875 run, although it is found in the original vocal scores. It has no bearing on the main plot of the opera and offers merely a diverting scene; such scenes were not uncommon in opéra-comique and the librettists surely liked it. An elderly gentleman (identified in an early production manual as an Englishman) enters with his young wife on his arm. She is looking around anxiously and soon her lover appears. He speaks to the gentleman and distracts his attention by pointing to something while slipping a note to the wife. Moralès and his men describe and enact what is happening and are much amused by it. One might regard such a scene as typically Parisian, but it hardly reinforces the standards of morality the Opéra-Comique was supposed to uphold, and the style of the music verges on operetta (Example 9.3). It is hard to argue for including this delightful scene in any interpretation of the opera as realist tragedy, so it will remain forever a rarity on the stage.

Example 9.3

A bugle-call off-stage and two piccolos introduce the new guard for duty, followed by a group of small boys. Lieutenant Zuniga leads in the new company with José as the sergeant. The boys imitate the soldiers' drill, a charming unforgettable scene. Moralès tells José in dialogue (originally *mélodrame*) that a young girl is looking for him. He guesses it is Micaëla. The relieved guard marches off with the exuberant boys close behind and disappears from sight to a miraculously neat orchestral diminuendo.

In dialogue José explains to Zuniga, who is new in town, that the building near the square is where four or five hundred girls work, rolling cigarettes. They will be back soon after their break. "Are some of them pretty?" he asks. José hasn't noticed because, as Zuniga realises, he is thinking of the girl Moralès said was looking for him. José explains that Micaëla is her name; she is seventeen, and an orphan very close to José's mother.

A busy orchestral build-up, based on the tune the girls are about to sing, brings in the young men who gather to watch the girls going back to work. Their song is utterly innocent and gentle, not the least suggestive of predatory Mediterranean types. When the girls appear, all smoking, the older men comment on the girls' impudent manner, but their song, in E major 6/8, is relaxed and charming, as they quietly enjoy the pleasures of smoking.

The character of the music changes sharply when some of the onlookers ask why Carmencita has not appeared. She does so immediately, to a speeded up version of Example 9.2, full of menace. She is the centre of all attention, so she has to introduce herself with a song. Her Habanera is framed as conventional couplets, a two-verse song, with the singer joined in the refrain by the chorus. Another traditional aspect is the switch from minor to major in each verse. The tune is adapted from the song "El Areglito" by the Spanish composer Sebastián Yradier published by Heugel in the collection *Fleurs d'Espagne* in 1864, but a good part of its bewitching effect comes from the repetitive figure in the cellos heard throughout, replacing

Areglito's conventional harmonisation.[12] The words were drafted by Bizet himself after rejecting what may be an earlier idea for this song in a different document:[13]

> Nous allons chanter la ronde
> des Gitanes que voilà
> Est-il rien en ce bas monde
> de tel que ces oiseaux-là.

This is in Bizet's hand with the annotations "D minor" and "gypsies walking around", both of which apply to the eventual Habanera, as does the image of a bird, which is also found in the Pushkin story.

The young men crowd around Carmen, but she has her eye on Don José, who is concentrating on making a brass priming-wire for his rifle. Over Example 9.2 she draws a cassia flower from her bosom and throws it in his face. She runs off, and as the factory bell rings the girls all go into work, the people drift off, and the soldiers leave José alone. He muses quietly on her effrontery and smells the flower. When Micaëla enters he hurriedly hides the flower. His mother has sent her, she says.

Their Duo begins at this point, a movement rich in melody and sentiment and beautifully scored. To start with, the music follows the suggestions of the words (effectively churchy when she refers to his mother's chapel) and then she launches into her main strain at "Et tu lui diras que sa mère", one of Bizet's greatest melodies, over exquisite harmony. José replies with a tune in a different key and a different meter, "Ma mère, je la vois!", with the same inner pedal we first observed in the Prélude to *Les Pêcheurs de perles*, this time on the horn. Before they return to the main melody there is a frightening moment when José worries that some "démon" may trap him (Example 9.2 again). He manages to deflect Micaëla's alarm and the bulk of the duet is reprised with a perfectly shaped coda.

In dialogue José reads his mother's letter, which speaks so affectionately and purposefully of Micaëla's suitability to be his bride that the young girl leaves in some embarrassment, promising to return. He *will* marry her, he promises once he is alone, and is about to throw Carmen's flower away when an orchestral tumult is heard announcing a disturbance in the cigarette factory. This is one of the scenes that caused such trouble in rehearsal since the girls, who had seemed so well-behaved at their first entrance, have to split into two quarrelling groups and sing and jostle one another at a swift tempo. The notes are not easy either (see Example 9.1). Carmen and Manuelita are reported to have turned an argument into a fight, so Zuniga orders José to take two soldiers into the factory and sort it

---

12. Areglito's song is shown in Stricker (1999), pp. 312–314.
13. US-CAh bMS Mus 232(67) (Pauline Viardot papers).

out. The music has the quality of a brilliant symphonic scherzo, and at the end, as the girls retreat and José brings on Carmen, the violins softly give out a tune we heard just after she threw the flower in his face.

Don José explains to Zuniga in dialogue how he found three hundred women in uproar. One girl had cuts on her face and Carmen was responsible. She protested that she was simply defending herself, and José was obviously inclined to make light of her guilt. To Zuniga's question "What do you say for yourself?" she breaks into song and a series of impudent tra-la-las to a haunting Spanish rhythm, thinly accompanied. While Carmen nonchalantly carries on her song, the rest of the scene is *mélodrame* with Zuniga giving orders for Carmen to be tied and led off to prison by José. "You can sing your gypsy songs there," he tells her and leaves.

José and Carmen are left to find out a good deal about each other in dialogue. At first she claims to be from Navarre, like him, but then admits to being a gypsy. She persuades him to loosen her cords and reminds him that he will do whatever she wants because she knows that the flower has done its work. He has little to say in response, and he still contributes few words when she breaks into her Séguedille, an irresistible Spanish number with a spring in the rhythm. The modulations here are kaleidoscopic and the scoring particularly imaginative, with the flute flirtatiously duetting with Carmen. Here appear the first signs of the tension that will lead to tragedy, for she makes it clear that her affections are easily bought from one day to the next. If I love you, he asks, will you love me back? Yes, she replies, meaning something quite different from what José would like it to mean. The song is at the same time a joyous invitation to her friend Lillas Pastia's tavern just outside the town, where Manzanilla is drunk and a good time is had by all. Her final top B is invariably thrilling.

For the brief finale to the first act the strings bustle with figures from the fight scene while Zuniga gives orders to José to lead Carmen away. She whispers her plan to push him over; he is to fall and let her get away. She parts from Zuniga with a brief reprise of her Habanera, but as soon as they move away she pushes José over and runs off with a shriek of laughter.

The first act is largely based on the action in Mérimée's story, but the rest of the opera relies more heavily on the librettists' invention. Before Act II the orchestra gives out an Entr'acte which rather strangely allies two bassoons with a military drum. The piece is a skillful meditation on José's unaccompanied Chanson later in the act, passing the tune to the clarinet, then flute, with a brief but pretty section of pure ballet music in the middle.

Set in Lillas Pastia's tavern, the second act opens with the Chanson bohème. A group of gypsies are dancing to the accompaniment of guitars and tambourines. Carmen is with her friends Mercédès and Frasquita. Spanish music is typically coloured by the familiar harmonies that lie comfortably on the guitar, but here Bizet pushes the idiom to an extreme by shifting the harmony abruptly, yet always mindful of the way the upper chord can move freely over a fixed bass, in this case the note E, the bottom string of a guitar, even though no guitar is actually heard. She sings three verses, each a little faster than the last and each with different orchestration, and the two girls join in the refrain each time. The whole piece is carefully marked to speed up from 100 beats a minute (Andantino) to 152 beats a minute (Presto) at the end, although most performances exceed those speeds.

Zuniga, Moralès and some other soldiers are there. In dialogue Lillas Pastia politely suggests that it is time for the soldiers to leave, although Zuniga is aware that the tavern is a haunt for smugglers. The soldiers invite the girls to go with them into the city, but one by one they refuse. Zuniga thinks Carmen holds a grudge because of what happened in the first act, but she shrugs that off as ancient history. She is surprised to learn that Don José was punished for his failure to bring her in by being reduced to the ranks and condemned to a month in prison. He was released only yesterday, Zuniga tells her.

Before the soldiers have time to go, a group of men are heard singing outside. Frasquita reports that this is Escamillo, the famous toreador from Grenada. Moralès is excited to meet him and urges them to come in despite Lillas Pastia's protests.

Escamillo immediately breaks into song, as new characters in opéra-comique often do. Like the Habanera, the toreador's Couplets are set in two verses, each with a refrain for the chorus and each moving from minor to major in each verse. The refrain, with a brazen vigour that exactly matches the character of the bullfighter, supported by strong orchestration and a rousing march beat, is one of the most familiar tunes in all classical music. The minor-key sections display some awkward word-setting as if the melody might originally have been intended for something else. The text here contrives to compare the toreador's life to a soldier's (for Zuniga's benefit) and then exults in the thrill of the arena.

Escamillo finds himself next to Carmen and asks her with a celebrity's arrogance if she would be disposed to love him. Not for the moment, she replies, with a hint that the future might be different. Moralès again tries to get the girls to go with them, and Zuniga promises Carmen that he will be back later. Everyone leaves except the three girls and the innkeeper, who explains that he had to get rid of the soldiers since the smugglers Le Dancaïre and Le Remendado are expected. Pastia calls them in and shuts all the doors. They have just come back from Gibraltar ("lots of Englishmen there, good-looking men, a little cold but distinguished") and they need the girls to help them hide contraband in the mountains.

Here follows the miraculous Quintette, reminiscent of Mozart in its swift exchanges and natural flow. The way that Mercédès is from time to time allowed to soar above the other voices and the extraordinary precision in the orchestration are beyond praise, especially since the effect of the whole is of effortless sleight of hand. The dramatic middle section spells out some of the details, whereupon Carmen declares that she won't go with them and confesses that she is in love.

In the dialogue Carmen tells them that she is expecting the soldier who did her the service of letting her escape and went to prison for it. She sent him money and a file, but he did not use the file to escape from prison. They don't believe he will come this evening, but they immediately hear him outside singing a Chanson about the "Dragons d'Alcala". Le Dancaïre suggests that if Carmen is to follow them a day later, she should bring her soldier with her. The four of them leave while José is reunited with Carmen.

José explains that he did not dare escape from prison using the file since desertion is a crime. He has the money still, so they call Lillas Pastia to order whatever food he can find. Carmen promises José that on a gypsy's honour she will repay him for what he suffered on her behalf. Food arrives. She tells him Zuniga made a move on her, and José admits he's jealous. Since she danced for the officers she will now dance for José, just for him. She breaks a plate in two to serve as castanets (a trick that probably proved too difficult on stage: the printed libretto has her finding the real castanets).

The long Duo that follows reveals Bizet developing the relationship of Carmen and Don José with masterly skill and moving inexorably into the territory of high drama. His inspiration is at its peak. At first Carmen dances to the simple accompaniment of her castanets and pizzicato strings. It is a seductive performance and she does not notice the distant bugle-call that tells José he must return to barracks. When he tells her so, she goes wild, mocking him for claiming to love her and mocking the bugles, hurling abuse and telling him to go. He makes little headway protesting, finally insisting that she listen to him.

The cor anglais brings back Example 9.2 as an ominous warning, and this leads into the centrepiece of the duet, his love song "La fleur que tu m'avais jetée". Salvaged from the *Grisélidis* sketches and made to fit the new words, however awkwardly, the melody is one of Bizet's most perfect creations. It does not go back on itself but reaches further and further into the depths of José's heart, spreading onward with marvellously varied and apt orchestration until the phrase "Et j'étais une chose à toi!" settles on a soft high B flat, after which the simple statement "Carmen, je t'aime" lays his feelings bare.

Her hushed response "Non, tu ne m'aimes pas!" is shocking after such a piece, for she taunts him by saying that if he really loved her he would go away with her to the mountains. A happy diatonic tune over a chromatic bass (one of Bizet's signature textures) paints an alluring picture of a freedom that is second nature to the gypsy but unknown to the soldier. Suddenly he bursts out with a straight refusal. The orchestra boils with verismo tension as they shout "Adieu!" to one another.

A knock on the door heralds the finale. Zuniga arrives for what he thinks is an assignation with Carmen. He breaks down the door and finds Don José. How could you prefer a soldier to an officer, he asks Carmen with a sneer and drags José away. José draws his sword and Carmen calls for her gypsy friends (who are conveniently nearby) to disarm Zuniga. The ensemble brings back a lighter tone, especially since Le Dancaïre and Le Remendado are there. Zuniga is sent home and José has no choice but to join the gang of smugglers and gypsies with a happy cry of "liberté!"

The Entr'acte before Act III is an exquisite movement whose gentle beginning for flute and harp suggests a world far away in time and place (as it did in *Les Pêcheurs de perles*), but surely not Spain. The piece has a perfection of idea and craftsmanship shared by very few such short pieces (Saint-Saëns's "Le Cygne" is perhaps a rival). Whether intended or not, it takes our minds away from José's troubles and the disaster looming behind the curtain, which, when it rises, reveals a wild spot in the mountains where the smugglers gather. Bizet had opened the fifth act of *Ivan IV* and the second act of *La Jolie Fille de Perth* with quiet marches full of atmosphere and expectation, so here he achieves the same effect with a Sextuor et Chœur in march tempo and a striking tune that keeps returning to the same note, G. Gypsies and smugglers sing of the perils and joys of their life. One striking oft-quoted passage illustrates well the alarm felt by everyone at the Opéra-Comique at a style Du Locle called Cochin-Chinese (Example 9.4). The six principals (Mercédès, Frasquita, Carmen, Don José, Le Remendado and Le Dancaïre) are put on the spot by an extended ensemble passage opera singers are notoriously liable to garble, "Notre métier".

Example 9.4

While the gypsies light a fire, Le Remendado and Le Dancaïre go off to reconnoitre the gap in the city walls where they plan to take in their merchandise. The conversation between Carmen and Don José is already strained. Her love is much less sure so long as he makes demands on her freedom. He utters veiled threats and asks if she is the devil. Yes, she says. He wanders off.

The three girls come together in a Trio which begins as a duet for Mercédès and Frasquita playing cards and reading their fortunes. The game and the music are playful, for Frasquita sees in her future a passionate lover, a leader of men, while Mercédès's beau is old and rich. He showers her with diamonds and gifts and conveniently dies, leaving her the inheritance. Carmen takes the cards in her turn and immediately turns up the cards that signify the death of both herself and Don José. Over dark string chords she spells out the sombre verses in even syllables:

> Mais si tu dois mourir, si le mot redoutable
> Est écrit par le sort,
> Recommence vingt fois, la carte impitoyable
> Répétera : la mort !

> But if you are to die, if the dreaded word
> Is written by destiny,
> Try it even twenty times, the pitiless cards
> Will say: death!

She turns more cards, but they all say the same thing. The others dream blindly on about love and wealth, but the last word is whispered by the cellos and basses (Example 9.2), the motif now clearly signifying a fateful destiny.

The smugglers return with the names of three customs agents guarding the city gate. The three girls are designated to "take care of" them, which enrages José, who is left behind to guard the merchandise that remains. An ensemble in which José pointedly takes no part sends the party on its way with another irresistible tune. The happy prospect of outwitting the city guards is set to music very easy on the ear but very difficult to sing, especially in the middle section. The fade-out as they all leave the camp is expertly executed by the orchestra alone.

With José somewhere out of sight Micaëla appears. She has somehow learned that José is with the smugglers and somehow found a guide who knows where the smugglers' hideout is. On the way there they passed Escamillo leading a herd of bulls, which did not alarm her, so the guide feels able to leave her there alone and wait for her at an inn.

Having told the guide that she was not frightened, her solo Air "Je dis que rien ne m'épouvante" confesses that she is. But she puts her faith in the Lord. In the middle section of her ternary aria (originally intended for *Grisélidis*) she is determined to confront Carmen, of whom she has apparently heard something, without fear. The main section then returns with its beautiful scoring for horns, flowing cellos and divided violins. The coda introduces the kind of harmony that impressed Tchaikovsky and passed into Russian music (Example 9.5).

Example 9.5

She espies Don José at a distance and calls out to him. He responds by firing his gun, which sends her diving for cover. Operatic coincidence then brings Escamillo, of all people, on to the scene, he too having somehow learned where the smugglers and gypsies hide. Don José challenges him, which launches them into their dramatic Duo. Escamillo explains that he has come to find Carmen, with whom he is in love, nonchalantly adding that she no longer loves the soldier who deserted for her. Enraged, José identifies himself and forces Escamillo into a fight, drawing his *navaja*. Escamillo merely defends himself, refusing to attack out of pity for his opponent. José charges him again but is overpowered. My job is fighting bulls, Escamillo says, not slaughtering men. This first phase of their fight was evidently cut in 1875 and is cut in most performances today, although like Moralès's pantomime in Act I it is found in the original vocal score.

José is not ready to give up, so the challenge and fight are repeated, but this time Escamillo's knife breaks. José is about to strike when, again with perfect operatic timing, Carmen appears with the whole party of smugglers and gypsies. The city guards having presumably been "taken care of" they have returned for the contraband. In a complicated finale which Bizet revised several times, Carmen is clearly keen to protect Escamillo and get rid of Don José. Escamillo is willing to fight José again later. He invites them all to the bullfight in Seville. He then departs to a reprise of his Couplets elegantly scored for lower strings and lower woodwind, each divided into four parts, first cellos and clarinet holding the tune. Everyone is ready to leave when Le Remendado spots Micaëla in her hiding place. She launches immediately into the ravishing melody of her plea to Don José in Act I. Carmen urges José to go with Micaëla, which brings from him a defiant oath not to leave Carmen even if it costs him his life, to a powerful phrase derived from a similar moment in *La Coupe du Roi de Thulé* (see Figure 6.6). The passage comes twice, but then Micaëla steps forward with more to say: his mother is dying. This finally decides him to leave with Micaëla, promising Carmen that they will meet again. As Escamillo is heard singing in the distance, Carmen would rush to join him, but her way is barred by José. The last music of the act is an echo of the smugglers' march from its opening scene.

Act IV's Entr'acte is a vigorously Spanish piece for the full orchestra, making strong play with the D harmonic minor scale and again suggesting the guitars that are not actually playing. It was based on a tune from Manuel Garcia's opera *El criado fingido* printed in *Échos d'Espagne* in 1872. It locates us securely in Spain, then the view zooms in to the specific public square in Seville where the action is to take place. Street traders are selling their wares while the people amble about. The close is another deft diminuendo.

In conversation Frasquita tells Zuniga that Carmen is now with Escamillo and madly in love, and learns in exchange that Don José went to visit his mother and slipped past the soldiers sent to arrest him. Frasquita is alarmed to think of him on the loose.

From here to the end the music is continuous. Any staging of the procession that brings in the bullfighters and city dignitaries has to be colourful indeed to match the splendour of the music, which Bizet rightly selected to serve also as the brilliant opening of the Prélude. Groups of bystanders and children wave and cheer, sometimes all together and sometimes in separate entries, which must have given more trouble to the Opéra-Comique chorus in 1875. Example 9.6 is a brief example of the second soprano line in the middle of the texture.

Example 9.6

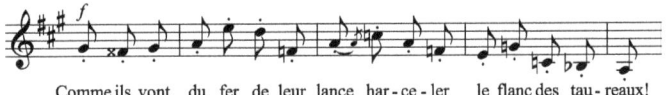

Escamillo makes a grand entrance in torero's costume with Carmen at his side while the crowd sings his tune in full-blooded unison. When the hubbub dies down, Escamillo turns to Carmen and addresses her with distinct nobility, reinforced by the rich scoring for divided violas and cellos. Their confession of love is a private moment in a very public scene. While more dignitaries follow, Frasquita urges Carmen to be careful; she has seen Don José in the crowd, but Carmen scorns her warning.

The whole crowd moves into the arena, whose gates are seen at the back of the stage, leaving Carmen and Don José alone. Their final scene is cruelly tense since the end is never in doubt. Carmen rigidly affirms her love for Escamillo and her refusal to love Don José, yet it is the principle of her liberty for which she is willing to die. Gypsy fatalism compels her to cling to this sacred principle. Don José, meanwhile, is firm only in his now inexplicable love for Carmen; he is ready to go with her wherever she wants, to join the bandits and live outside the law. He simply cannot accept her refusal to love him, and the impact of two immovable objects ends inevitably in the death of both of them: hers on stage while the crowd acclaim Escamillo's triumph in the bullring, his as the inevitable consequence of the law.

The painful drama enacted before our eyes is also fed into our ears by the resourceful chromatics and tense harmonies of Bizet's orchestra, often invoking the motive of doom, Example 9.2. This is all the while counterpointed by the shouts and cheers from the bullring and the innocent vitality of the toreador's song. The power of the scene comes from Bizet, while the compactness of the action comes from Pushkin, not Mérimée, in whose story the murder of Carmen takes place in a remote gorge, after which José has to bury the body and ride to Cordoba to give himself up. Even then he escapes the death penalty.

In *Carmen* Bizet reached the height of his creative powers. He had never before had such a strong libretto to work on, and never before did he have such a consistent stream of inspiration at his command. He is fully at home in popular Spanish idioms, encouraging yet more French composers to explore them. The influence of the opera was to be felt far and wide, especially in Italy where demonstrations of jealous passion as violent as Don José's became a commonplace of the verismo school. The vitality of Bizet's melodies will alone keep the music of *Carmen* alive in perpetuity, and the title role will always be a challenge for great singing actresses. No other French opera has ever achieved the same status as a popular classic.

★ ★ ★ ★ ★

The first night of *Carmen* is etched in history as one of those famous moments when a great new work failed under the onslaught of hostility and incomprehension. As usual with such legends, the truth is a little more complicated. The response of the audience was immediate, that of the press took a few days, and the memories of those who were there became gradually coloured by the opera's ascent to becoming, as Tchaikovsky predicted, the most popular opera in the world. Many individuals in the audience can be identified, representing a fair cross-section of the Parisian musical world. Seasonal colds at the Opéra closed that theatre for a week allowing a number of singers and staff to attend the Opéra-Comique. Many of Offenbach's stars were there. The press was there en masse, especially since hints of scandal and failure, some of them circulated by du Locle himself, had already surfaced. It is not clear if Geneviève or Mme Halévy were there; the former never spoke about it. Adolphe Bizet, we trust, was there. Certainly we can name Gounod (now back from England), Thomas, Delibes, Offenbach, Massenet, d'Indy, Lecocq, Guiraud, Godard, Reyer, Duprato, Delaborde, Daudet, Dumas *fils*, Faure, Choudens, Hartmann, Heugel, Pasdeloup, and of course Meilhac and Halévy. No sign of Alkan, Franck, Fauré, or Lalo. Pierre Berton was not able to go until the second performance, Saint-Saëns not until a week later; Tchaikovsky was there on 15 March, overwhelmed.

With so many professionals in the first-night audience one might have expected a clamour at least of admiration if not of acclamation, but they were outnumbered by the *boulevardiers* and socialites who never missed an important first night, and by opera-goers of many years' standing who clung to the routine formulae they expected but did not get. It was a *froid*, as Berton discovered before seeing it himself. "The most upsetting thing for an artist is not a colleague's success, whatever anyone says; it's the success of a work you despise, and, even more, the rejection of a masterpiece you admire."[14] There was no riot, nor any organised booing, but the words "immoral" and "scandalous" were heard being muttered in the three intervals, with fewer and fewer people going backstage (as was the custom) to congratulate the composer. Although certain numbers, such as the Habanera and the Quintette in Act II, were applauded, a sense of bewilderment intensified as the evening went on, as the opera moved inexorably away from the comforting certainties of opéra-comique, as it was widely understood. Despite the congratulations and earnest efforts of his friends, Bizet's spirits sank to the point where he was convinced it was a failure. He walked the streets afterwards, totally silent and downcast, and indifferent to comforting words from Guiraud and others.

Reviews began appearing in the papers the very next day and continued throughout the month. The critics' response, often reported to be universally negative, has been summed up by Lesley Wright: "A few critics were thoroughly vitriolic and dismissive, but overall *Carmen* was damned with faint praise. Some did applaud the work, but many more were tepid, mixed or disapproving."[15] No one, it is fair to say, spotted a major masterpiece. Joncières was perhaps the most enthusiastic, speaking of Bizet's "enormous talent" and refuting the absurd charges that the

---

14. Berton (1913), p. 243.

15. Wright (2001), p. vi. This book mentions about a hundred entries in the Paris press and quotes from thirty-three of them.

music lacked melody and was indebted to Wagner. Reyer too wrote warmly but cautiously on Bizet's behalf. Most of the critics referred to the young ladies whose morals would most certainly be affected by such a wanton display, as if they would all rush out and risk their lives by throwing themselves at soldiers and bullfighters. In their concern for public morality they had little to say about the music except to commend the leading singers for fine performances and to rebuke Bizet for making the chorus's music too difficult.

The finest of the singers was happily Carmen herself, Galli-Marié, equally at home with speech as with singing and an experienced, versatile performer. Her performance was outstanding, shockingly realistic in the opinion of some, and perhaps definitive for the next generation. This was a role she made her own, performing it in many cities for many years. The tenor, Lhérie, was good but his pitch was so fallible that Bizet had to get d'Indy to provide a discreet harmonium accompaniment during his unaccompanied Chanson. Bouhy was a fine Escamillo and Marguerite Chapuy good as Micaëla. Joncières described the chorus as execrable, for neither they nor the orchestra were ever going to be up to the standard the piece required, although as the run went on things settled down considerably. For *Carmen* was not a failure. There were forty-five performances before the end of 1875 and three more in 1876; whether attracted by the strength of the work or by the whiff of scandal, the box office held up reasonably well. After the thirty-third performance the fact of Bizet's death added a macabre curiosity to the work's attraction.

The second night, which Berton attended, was a solid success. But Bizet himself was not there; in fact, according to Lhérie, he never returned to the theatre after the opening. As far as he was concerned, *Carmen* was a failure, and his spirits sank to a low point. Berton then met him in the street outside the burned-out shell of the old Opéra and attempted to convey to him that the second night was a success. The usually ebullient Bizet remained silent, and when Berton spoke of the press, Bizet's pain was all too obvious. He was deeply wounded by the press reception of his opera. It is fair to say that he never got over it, whatever comfort his friends may have tried to offer.

Having compromised the success of the opera by his unconcealed reservations about its suitability when he should have been promoting it to the hilt, du Locle displayed either folly or vision, as he had after *Djamileh*, by inviting the composer and his librettists to write another opera for his theatre.[16] It is doubtful if Bizet made the slightest move in that direction, for although he had mentioned his desire to write a piano concerto,[17] the only composition in the immediate future was an

---

16. See Dean (1965-1), p. 122.
17. Imbert (1894), p. 199.

oratorio, *Geneviève de Paris*, in emulation of the success of Massenet's *Marie-Madeleine* and its successor *Ève*, first performed on 18 March. The public was displaying a growing taste for this kind of work. The texts of both Massenet's works were by Gallet, to whom Bizet turned in 1874 suggesting the story of the patron saint of Paris whose prayers had saved the city from being overrun by Attila the Hun. The plan that Bizet agreed to was as follows: Geneviève as a child being blessed by the bishop of Auxerre; Geneviève comforting refugees from the approach of Attila; Geneviève invoking a storm and miraculously bringing a cargo of wheat to the besieged city; Geneviève exhorting the Parisians and triumphing over Attila with the power of prayer.[18]

It is hard to imagine Bizet being drawn to such a religious subject unless he particularly wanted to honour the saint who shared his wife's name. But the text has plenty of opportunities for choral writing in which he had progressed enormously since the ill-fated *Te Deum* of 1858, and he would no doubt have relished the depiction of Satan. Furthermore the subject would have evoked sympathetic memories of the city's torment under siege five years earlier.

Conscious of his unfamiliarity with the world of sacred choral music he attended César Franck's organ class at the Conservatoire in the first months of 1875. Franck's pupils in fact studied composition rather than the organ in that class, which is where d'Indy became close enough to Bizet to attend rehearsals of *Carmen*. Gallet delivered the final text of *Geneviève de Paris* in May 1875 just as Bizet and his family were leaving for Bougival, and he paid a visit to him before he left. He found him downcast and melancholy but full of enthusiasm for the collaboration they were about to engage in. He was struck by the fact that Bizet had never before received him sitting down but otherwise noticed nothing untoward. Guiraud had already received a note that said: "Colossal angina. Don't come on Sunday. Imagine a double-pedal A flat-E flat going through your head from the left ear to the right. I can't do any more."[19] Visiting Bizet to play some of his recent music Guiraud found him deaf in one ear. "The shrill, shaky tone of his voice made me wince. The man I saw was no longer Bizet, the friend full of youth and vigour I had always known. The peaked, sickly look he had at that moment made a profound impression on me."[20]

References to angina, quinsy and illnesses affecting his throat had recurred regularly since his time in Italy. Bizet was clearly accustomed to these complaints and had learned to live with them, perhaps paying them too little attention. According

---

18. The plan of the oratorio is set out in Gallet (1891), p. 88, and the text is given in Stricker (1999), pp. 294–309. No sketches or music survive.
19. Gallet (1891), p. 92.
20. Curtiss (1958), p. 416.

to Curtiss he suffered an abscess at the root of his tongue at this time, although the inflammation soon disappeared, and according to Guiraud and Geneviève he had a tumour in his left ear that caused deafness.[21] In May he was attacked by muscular rheumatism which may also have been a chronic condition since childhood. Toward the end of the month he complained of difficulty breathing and fell one morning when getting out of bed.

On Saturday 29 May the air at Bougival revived him and the rheumatic pains seemed to vanish. He went for a walk along the river bank with his wife and Delaborde, and the two men then went for a swim in the river. The next day the rheumatism came back with a high temperature and severe immobility in his arms and legs. On the Monday night he had a heart attack, followed by another a day later. The doctor's visits were of little help, and he died in the early hours of Thursday 3 June. He was thirty-six years old. His wife, their maid and his two sons were there, and both Delaborde and Ludovic Halévy called regularly. Ludovic immediately took Geneviève away to his house after telegraphing the tragic news to their closest friends. Adolphe Bizet, who taught in Beauvais every Monday and Tuesday, arrived from Paris on Thursday morning, too late.[22] Galli-Marié was quite overcome, and the performance of *Carmen* that evening was cancelled.

Suicide was suspected by many but never seriously entertained. The cause of death was later studied by Dr Eugène Gelma, whose conclusion was that Bizet died, not, as romanticised legend might wish, from disappointment over *Carmen*, but of "a cardiac complication of acute articular rheumatism. Without the febrile polyarthritis following a chill, he would not have died during a convalescence from a recurrent throat angina."[23]

The funeral took place that Saturday, 5 June 1875, at the church of the Sainte-Trinité whose construction he had daily observed ten years before. Geneviève was at Ludovic's house and did not attend. The church was packed with mourners, chief among them Adolphe Bizet on Ludovic's arm and many members of the Halévy family. The pall-bearers were Gounod, Thomas, Doucet and Du Locle. The entire company of the Opéra-Comique, including the cast and crew of *Carmen*, were there, and Pasdeloup brought his orchestra for the Concerts Populaires. Bizet's young friends shared their appalling loss: Guiraud, Massenet, Delaborde, Paladilhe. That year's Prix de Rome candidates, sequestered at the Institute, sent a wreath. This, the funeral of a man in the flower of life, was a very different occasion from the reverential funerals of Rossini and Berlioz in the same church a few years before.

21. Malherbe (1951), p. 97.
22. Lacombe (2000), p. 804.
23. Gelma (1949), cited in Curtiss (1958), p. 419.

The orchestra played parts of the *Arlésienne* suite and *Patrie*, which was in their repertoire, and Chopin's Funeral March. The rest of the music, as a harbinger of things to come, presented Bizet's music in some form of adaptation: the organist improvised on themes from *Les Pêcheurs de perles* and played a grand fantasy on themes from *Carmen*. The famous duet from *Les Pêcheurs de perles* was sung to the words of "Pie Jesu", arranged by Guiraud. Funeral orations were delivered by Jules Barbier, Du Locle and Gounod. *Carmen* was performed that night at the Opéra-Comique. "All the singers wept on stage. The evening was too devastating to discuss. Only a great painter could reproduce so moving a sight."[24] The next two performances were cancelled and the last performance before the summer break took place on 13 June.

Bizet was buried in the Cimetière Père Lachaise where his monument, unveiled in 1876, was designed by Charles Garnier and crowned by a bust by his friend from their time in Italy together, the sculptor Paul Dubois. Geneviève gave Dubois the autograph manuscript of *Djamileh* as a token of thanks.

★ ★ ★ ★ ★

Bizet's friends were truly devastated by his death, not simply because his gifts as a composer were clearly exceptional; they loved him as a friend. He could be moody, of course, but he was normally gregarious, gossipy, opinionated, not taken in by the flim-flam that surrounded theatrical politics and determined to rise above the mediocrity he could see all around him. We have the reminiscences of Saint-Saëns, Reyer, Galabert, Gallet, Marmontel, Berton and others, all of whom enjoyed his company and prized his special position in Parisian music. Everyone was dazzled by his extraordinary musicianship and facile piano playing. He had a sharp ear and nimble fingers; he could take in an orchestral score at a glance. He was impatient with lazy and incompetent musicians, and he could have made a fine conductor or a successful pianist if he had chosen to. Unlike Saint-Saëns, equally gifted, who maintained his skill in every branch of music, something in Bizet's temperament steered him away from these activities. He had a vast knowledge and prodigious memory of music, represented by his extensive library.[25]

Portraits and photographs show him heavily bearded with thick, curly, dark hair, usually wearing a pince-nez. People must have thought him older than he was. He was always at least a little overweight. He was fastidious about his clothes, but no dandy. His concern for orderliness in his living quarters (in Italy, for example) is at odds with his wretched handwriting and his casual habit of rarely dating letters, as if he were in a permanent hurry, which he probably was. Wine and women he

---

24. *Le Ménestrel*, 13 June 1875.
25. See Curtiss (1958), pp. 472–474.

assuredly admired and enjoyed, and he liked to play cards. Mortier reports that he played écarté with Meilhac and Halévy every Wednesday, and always won.[26] Reyer remembered:

> On his return from Italy he passed through a period of wild energy, irritated by the slightest little incident. He would take up the challenge in defence of something or someone without the slightest provocation. He could be teased and disarmed with a few calming words, which he always listened to. Later he would laugh about those fits of temper and confess that in those violent jabs, which—fortunately—were usually wide of the mark, there was nothing but youthful exuberance and hot air.[27]

And Marmontel:

> Bizet was kind, generous, devoted, faithful to all his beliefs. His friendship was sincere and unchanging, as firm as his convictions.... Faithful friend and loyal comrade, Bizet was free of envy and trivial jealousy, with a warmth that was always genuine. He rejoiced in the success of yesterday's competitors and tomorrow's rivals. His fine mind and delicate feeling caused him to encourage the least fortunate and console those brought down by misfortune. It was with real sincerity that he applauded his rivals' triumphs.[28]

And Gallet:

> Looking very gentle and refined behind the invariable pince-nez, his lips always arched in an imperceptibly mocking smile, he spoke clearly in a slightly wheezy voice with a detached manner which was very characteristic. He discussed whatever was in his mind with real, noble modesty which did not consist of seeming to doubt his own achievement, but rather letting you see that while being fully aware of his own worth he always regretted not having done better whatever it was he was required to do.[29]

And Saint-Saëns:

> His love of openness, unsubtle though it was, was there for all to see. Loyal and sincere, he concealed neither his likes nor his dislikes. This was a characteristic he shared with me. Otherwise we were completely different and in pursuit of different ideals. He was above all in search of passion and life; I chased after the chimera of stylistic purity and formal perfection. Our conversations never ended; our arguments were friendly and lively, with a charming quality I have never found in anyone else.[30]

26. Mortier (1876), p. 86.
27. Reyer (1909), p. 304.
28. Marmontel (1881), pp. 255–256.
29. Gallet (1891), p. 8.
30. Saint-Saëns (1899), p. 176.

His views on religion were addressed to Galabert in 1866:

> Religion is for the strong a means of exploitation of the weak; religion is the disguise of ambition, injustice and vice. The progress you speak of does move forward, slowly but surely. It is gradually destroying all superstition. Truth stands out, science spreads, religion is weakened. It will soon fall, in a few centuries, that's to say tomorrow. That will be good, but let's not forget that the religion you do without—you, me and a few others—has been an admirable instrument of progress. It's religion, especially the Catholic religion, that taught us the principles which allow us to do without it now. Ungrateful children, we kill the breast that nourished us because the nourishment it gives us today is no longer worthy of us. We despise that false clarity that has gradually accustomed our eyes to the light. Without it we would be blind from birth, for ever![31]

When it came to assessing Bizet's standing as a composer, his contemporaries were at a loss. At the time of his death it was far from clear that *Carmen* would have much of a future, however much they may have admired the work itself. Pasdeloup gave a handful of his orchestral pieces an occasional hearing, but none of his other stage works showed any prospect of revival. His friends resented the fact that he had never been heard at the Opéra, even though it was rare for young composers to achieve that status; most were treated exactly as he was. He had a few friends in high places but he lacked the diplomatic skills and personal charm with officials that might have twisted the system in his favour. It is ironic to imagine the fawning treatment he would have received even twenty years later, had he lived, as the composer of one of France's national treasures.

He had the misfortune to live at a time when the practice of music criticism in France was at a low ebb, staffed for the most part by a characteristically French type, the cultured *belle-lettriste* who lives by the pen, reads every new novel and every new book of poetry, goes to every play and ballet and opera, mixes easily in literary salons, and writes fluently and elegantly on all of these. Critics with training in music, such as Berlioz, Reyer or Joncières, were too rare to sway the critical body as a whole in favour of young talent. Furthermore the less well-informed critics were obsessed with the question of Wagner, whose music they barely knew. No issue could be less relevant to the assessment of Bizet's music, since although he knew perfectly well what Wagnerian style was, he simply showed no inclination and no need either to imitate or to avoid it. When Pougin called Bizet a "farouche Wagnérien", he was not simply wrong, he did untold damage to a reputation that was to suffer for over a century from misrepresentation and falsehood.

Bizet has been compared to Mozart, who died at thirty-five, for his exceptional facility, untidy domestic arrangements and dramatic flair, but Mozart reached maturity in his early twenties and left a huge body of music of outstanding quality

---

31. Galabert (1909), pp. 80–81.

whereas Bizet's full maturity arrived in his early thirties despite some marvels composed much earlier, such as the First Symphony and *Les Pêcheurs de perles*. It is easier to posit a great post-1875 achievement for Bizet than to imagine works that Mozart might have written after 1791. A fairer comparison might be with Gershwin, another musician of dazzling talent, who composed one operatic masterpiece and died at thirty-eight with a brilliant future visible to all but seen by none.

From a longer perspective Bizet is best seen as perhaps the most talented, if not the most strongly represented, of the galaxy of French composers who came to maturity with the Third Republic and adorned the belle époque with a rich and varied repertoire in all genres: Lalo, Saint-Saëns, Reyer, Delibes, Paladilhe, Holmès, Godard, Guiraud, Massenet, Fauré, Duparc, d'Indy, Chausson, Bruneau and many others, in turn ushering in the next constellation whose brightest stars were Charpentier, Pierné, Debussy, Roussel and Ravel. Neither Germany nor Italy could boast such an array, and it invites comparison with the profusion of fine French painters in the same period. In writing about the Italian Renaissance Jacques Barzun has asked: "What conditions bring about great artistic periods, seemingly at random, here or there, and for a relatively short time?" His reply was, "It is not, as some have thought, prosperity, or wise government support, or a spell of peace and quiet—Florence at its height was in perpetual conflict inside and outside. The first requisite is surely the clustering of eager minds in one place....It takes hundreds of the gifted to make half a dozen of the great."[32]

Bizet was certainly one of the many "eager minds" who contributed more than his share to the rich flowering of French music in the Third Republic. He was poised to play a major part in the effulgence that followed his death and to prove himself one of the half-dozen greats, not one of the gifted hundreds. His style, inherited largely from Halévy, David, Gounod and Thomas, was the lingua franca of his generation of French composers, to which each added his own seasoning. Despite his overflowing enthusiasm for Italy while he was in that country, it left no mark on his later works except perhaps when he approached the world of operetta. His voluminous reading, too, is somehow unrepresented in his work. He had read the poetry and philosophy of the ancients, he knew Dante, Shakespeare and Montaigne, yet these great figures do not feature in his music. If he had not read Mérimée there would be no *Carmen*, it is true, but he had no burning literary attachments, as Berlioz had to Shakespeare and Virgil. The Bizet spice that most later composers wanted to imitate was his unsurpassed evocation of Spanish music in *Carmen*, although he himself would consider that merely professionalism. Given the opportunity, he would have composed operas that suggested a variety of epochs and nations, as Massenet and Ravel did, and done them all in the same brilliantly accomplished manner.

32. Barzun (2000), p. 67.

A complete appreciation of his music cannot be readily attempted while such works as *Ivan IV* and *La Jolie Fille de Perth* are so poorly represented on stage and in the recording catalogues. Both operas deserve, but have never had, good editions and thoughtful staging. Without those his œuvre will seem spotty and lacking in direction, since a familiarity with the First Symphony, *Les Pêcheurs de perles*, the *L'Arlésienne* suites and *Carmen* shows a less than complete picture of his achievement. Even if all his surviving music is studied in depth and enjoyed, the might-have-been of his early death casts a sorry shadow. He would surely have extended the list of masterpieces had he lived. Verdi, after all, found his true voice at about the same age and lived into his eighties. Wagner, at thirty-six, had still to write his seven greatest operas. Massenet, whose early career was similar to Bizet's in every respect, had to wait, like Bizet, until his mid-thirties for his first operatic success, and he lived to be seventy. No matter how satisfying we find *Carmen* and all the music that preceded it, the hint of yet finer unwritten works to follow is inescapably dispiriting.

CHAPTER TEN

1875–2014: Life after Death

HE FATE OF BIZET'S MUSIC IN THE 139 YEARS SINCE HIS DEATH HAS BEEN A SAD chronicle of neglect and misrepresentation. At the same time he is among the most familiar of great composers, for *Carmen* has been performed constantly all over the world; certain of his melodies, particularly the Toreador's Song, the duet from *Les Pêcheurs de perles*, and one or two other melodies from *Carmen*, are well known to people who know little or nothing about music. They are heard as ring-tones or on television commercials with few giving a thought as to their origin or purpose. Bizet's name is far from forgotten, yet his work as a whole is still unevenly and incorrectly circulated. There has never been either a systematic catalogue or a scholarly edition of his works, two working tools enjoyed by many composers far less deserving than Bizet. There is no collected edition of his letters. A good number of pieces are unpublished and many more have long been out of print. Certain works—notably *Don Procopio*, *Ivan IV* and *La Jolie Fille de Perth*—are to be found easily enough on library shelves but in editions that reveal nothing about the falsifications, omissions and substitutions that have been inflicted on them. The dialogues in *Carmen* are still often rejected in favour of Guiraud's recitatives, and when they are preserved they are invariably cut. No recording of *Carmen* is complete, since most versions omit the second number of the opera and all versions replace or shorten the dialogue. Of the seven orchestral suites that bear Bizet's name, only two, the *Petite Suite* and the first *L'Arlésienne* suite, are now heard in a form that Bizet intended. Of the remainder *Roma* is a symphony, not a suite; the two *Carmen* suites were arranged by other hands; the second *L'Arlésienne* suite was arranged by Guiraud who inserted a movement from *La Jolie Fille de Perth*

· 234 ·

without a word of explanation; in the *Scènes bohémiennes* one of the four standard movements is a replacement for the movement Bizet intended.

In 1951 Jean Chantavoine wrote an article, "Les inédits de Bizet ou le culte des maîtres en France", lamenting the imperfect recognition of Bizet in his own country. This was taken up by Winton Dean, who added an appendix to the 1965 edition of his biography of Bizet similarly, and ironically, entitled "The Cult of the Masters in France", rebuking French publishers and scholars with some heat for the shameful treatment of one of their national treasures.[1] Michel Poupet also took up the cause.[2] The situation has changed little in the last half-century, although there are now scholarly editions of *Jeux d'enfants*, *L'Arlésienne* and *Carmen,* and penetrating studies of Bizet's life and music from Rémy Stricker and Hervé Lacombe.

Responsibility for the imperfect transmission of his music rests partly with Bizet's family and partly with the publisher Choudens. After his son's death Adolphe Bizet stayed on in Le Vésinet and the apartment in the Rue de Douai until his death in 1886, but he seems to have played no part in the promotion of his music. Bizet's widow, Geneviève, held a great number of the composer's manuscripts, including *Carmen*, but she made no attempt to put them in order or to get unpublished works published or performed. In 1886 she married Émile Straus, a wealthy lawyer, and she became a prominent society hostess in the Rue de Miromesnil at the turn of the century. She was courted by Maupassant and was close to Proust, who modelled the character of the Duchesse de Guermantès on her. Reynaldo Hahn was a close friend. Forever anxious about the state of her health, she died aged seventy-seven in 1926, bequeathing to the Bibliothèque du Conservatoire the autograph manuscripts of *Carmen* and *L'Arlésienne*. After the death of her husband in 1928 his nephew René Sibilat offered the Conservatoire many more manuscripts including some early piano music, *Don Rodrigue*, *Ivan IV* and some "practice" Prix de Rome cantatas. In 1933 Hahn passed to the Conservatoire a further set of manuscripts he had himself received from Geneviève Straus. These included the First Symphony and *La Jolie Fille de Perth*.

Bizet's son Jacques, who looked like his father, inherited one or both of the cottages at Le Vésinet. He worked in the automobile business in its infancy, was twice married, once divorced, and his life ended in 1922 at age fifty in suicide over an unhappy love affair.[3] Bizet's illegitimate son Jean Reiter was trained in the printing business, worked on *Le Temps* for many years, and died aged seventy-seven in 1939.

Bizet's music was published by Choudens, Heugel, Hartmann, Durand and others, but as publishers of his operas none had greater influence on his posthumous

---

1. Chantavoine (1951); Dean (1965–1).
2. Poupet (1965).
3. See Klein (1968).

standing than Choudens. Besides the five main stage works, Choudens also published the overture *Patrie* and the *Vingt Mélodies*, and at the time of Bizet's death had printed, but not published, the Second Symphony. The rapid spread of *Carmen* around the world persuaded Choudens to publish more of Bizet's music and later to persuade theatres to revive the other operas. In the ten years preceding his death in 1888 Antoine Choudens presided over a remarkable diffusion of Bizet's name and music by his firm, executed always in the spirit of commercial enterprise rather than textual correctness. Before we look at the strange and varied versions in which the music was presented to the public, it has to be recognised that a music publisher's primary responsibility is to his customers, not to his composers—at least that is the way the trade was conducted in the later nineteenth century. Since there was no control over theatre managements who chose to make alterations in the operas they staged—substituting one voice for another, or one singer for another, and making cuts or insertions to suit the resources of the theatre—composers could not expect to apply a restraining hand unless they were at least present to oversee rehearsals. A dead composer was especially vulnerable. Theatre-goers who wished to buy the vocal score of an opera they had just seen would prefer to purchase the version they had heard, an element of demand to which Choudens seems to have been especially alert, adjusting his publications to match current productions wherever they might be. Thus a wide variety of versions of a single work, although customarily blamed on the publisher's recklessness, may more fairly be attributed to the directors and singers who devised different productions in different places.

For five years or so following his death, Bizet's music was represented by *Patrie* and the *Arlésienne* suite in the concert hall and by the remarkable success of *Carmen* abroad. Performances of the opera continued at the Opéra-Comique in the autumn of 1875, with twelve more beginning on 15 November and the last for seven years on 2 February 1876. Its worldwide spread was initiated in Vienna on 23 October 1875 with a performance in German at the city's Hofoper, for which the dialogue had been set as recitative by Guiraud, but apparently not in fact used then. The next foreign theatre was La Monnaie in Brussels, starting a long run on 3 February 1876. Within four years *Carmen* was played in Antwerp, Budapest (in Hungarian), St Petersburg (in Italian), Stockholm (in Swedish), London, Dublin, New York, Philadelphia, Baltimore, Chicago, Boston, Melbourne, Naples and San Francisco. There were productions even in the French provinces, in Boulogne and Marseille. Choudens's investment in Bizet was now paying off, but with no benefit to the composer. Vocal scores were needed with Italian and German translations and with Guiraud's recitatives, and the full score was printed in 1877 also. Like the new vocal scores the full score included the recitatives, confirmed certain cuts, and also provided three ballet movements for those theatres where a ballet was expected.

For this purpose two movements were taken from *L'Arlésienne* and one from *La Jolie Fille de Perth*, and printed in the body of the score.

Around 1879 Choudens began to exploit the success of *Carmen* by looking at Bizet's other works. In this endeavour he was assisted by Guiraud, who has ever after had to suffer the contempt often meted out to those who cherish and promote a deceased friend's work. Rimsky-Korsakov has always been derided for disfiguring his friend Mussorgsky's music, although his purpose, in which he was completely successful, was simply to get it better known. Guiraud, similarly, was Bizet's closest friend for nearly twenty years; he was an excellent pianist and good composer, and no one was better placed to edit and arrange Bizet's music. An unwritten code of *fraternité* among French composers allowed and encouraged the completion of unfinished works by others. Bizet, as we have seen, completed Halévy's *Noé*; Guiraud and Massenet completed Delibes's *Kassya* (1893); Arthur Coquard completed Lalo's *La Jacquerie* (1894); Saint-Saëns and Dukas completed Guiraud's *Frédégonde* (1895), and no less than five different hands orchestrated Franck's *Ghiselle*—all operas left unfinished at the composer's death.

Choudens started with a second suite from the music of *L'Arlésienne*. With the first *L'Arlésienne* suite doing well in the concert hall, he had Guiraud prepare a second suite. Like the first, this suite contains four movements, but only three sections from the original score were suitable for the purpose: the Pastorale, from which the chorus was omitted; the Intermezzo; and the Farandole, which he extended into a substantial movement. In third place he inserted the Menuet from *La Jolie Fille de Perth*, or rather from the suite *Scènes bohémiennes* as arranged by Bizet but not yet published (except in a piano arrangement). Since this second *L'Arlésienne* suite has been much more frequently played than the opera on which this movement drew, it, with its graceful flute melody, is often assumed to belong to the original *L'Arlésienne* incidental music.

Within the group heading *Collection des Œuvres posthumes de Georges Bizet* Choudens then published the Second Symphony under the false title *Roma: 3ème suite de concert* as a successor to the two *L'Arlésienne* suites. It was engraved and prepared for press in 1869, soon after the first performance, but not issued at that time. Its publication in 1880 supported a performance by Pasdeloup on 31 October, actually the first complete performance of all four movements, and a series of performances abroad, in London, New York, Boston and St Petersburg. Edouard Colonne, Pasdeloup's long-standing rival, gave it twice in his series at the Châtelet in January 1885. It was taken up by conductors such as Theodore Thomas, Felix Mottl, and George Henschel and frequently heard in the last decades of the century. In 1898 it was heard in Vienna under the baton of Mahler. Breitkopf & Härtel published the score and parts in 1902, and Eulenburg issued it in Leipzig in 1924, an edition that was reissued by Eulenburg, London, in 1957. It has been recorded by Beecham, Frémaux, Gardelli, Casadesus, Plasson and others, always under the title *Roma*. Yet performances are now very rare; it falls far behind Bizet's best-known works in popularity, and certainly far behind the First Symphony. Winton Dean's vehement denigration of the work in his 1948 biography has not helped. Hans von Bülow regarded the work as a "große Schweinerei", but Nietzsche and Hanslick both had good things to say about it, and Lacombe, more recently, has written of the symphony's "séduction incontestable".[4] The musical world might perhaps take it more seriously if it knew it was really a symphony, not a programmatic suite.

Choudens then issued a full score and a piano reduction of the Prélude to *La Coupe du Roi de Thulé* under the misleading title Marche funèbre, an unfortunate choice since Bizet had already composed a Marche funèbre as the original slow movement of his Second Symphony. Again, no mention was made of its origin or correct identity. Still offering suites, Choudens next brought out the *Scènes bohémiennes* which Bizet himself prepared, drawing on four pieces from *La Jolie Fille de Perth*. Bizet intended the suite to include the Prélude, Smith's Sérénade, the Menuet and Danse bohémienne, all arranged for orchestra alone. In piano arrangements the suite had appeared just after Bizet's death in Choudens's *Collection de ballets et fragments célèbres*, and the Danse bohémienne had already been inserted as a ballet in the full score of *Carmen*. But because the Menuet had been stolen for the second *L'Arlésienne* suite, Guiraud had to arrange the Marche from the beginning of Act II of the opera to replace it in the orchestral suite. In this incorrect form the *Scènes bohémiennes* has been published, performed and recorded ever since. At least all the music comes from the one opera, *La Jolie Fille de Perth*.

Two suites from *Carmen* were published in the mid-1880s, each containing five movements. The arranger's name is not given. Breitkopf & Härtel later published these suites, each with an extra movement, and it is the latter version available today in a Kalmus reprint.

There then appeared from Choudens a group of three choral works, all published for the first time: a vocal score of the "ode-symphonie" *Vasco de Gama*, composed in Italy in 1860 and performed once only in 1863. There is no record of any performances at the time of publication, however, nor since, and the full score was not published, a remarkable instance of the total neglect of a perfectly viable work. Next were the two choral works written for the preliminary rounds of the Prix de Rome in 1856 and 1857, respectively *Le Golfe de Baïa* and *La Chanson du rouet*, the latter provided with new words by Edouard Blau. It would be charitable to suppose that this was done in response to Leconte de Lisle's refusal to allow publication of his verse, but it may have been easier for Choudens to commission new poems

---

4. See Macdonald (2012).

from one of the librettists in his circle than go to the trouble of approaching the original author.

*****

The next publication from Choudens also offered new words attached to old music, but this time it seems that Bizet was himself behind the substitutions. A second volume of songs, mostly planned by Bizet himself, came out as the *Seize Mélodies* in about 1883. Despite generous prefatory matter, the volume nowhere indicates the source of these pieces. According to Pigot, Guiraud edited the collection, drawing on remnants of *Clarisse Harlowe, Grisélidis, Geneviève de Paris* and *Les Templiers*, filling out incomplete fragments where necessary.[5] In fact the origin of only one of the songs, "La Chanson de la rose", remains unexplained, and there is no evidence that any music was ever composed for *Geneviève de Paris. Les Templiers* may have supplied one number in *Djamileh*, as we have seen, but probably nothing for the *Seize Mélodies*. Three songs came from *La Coupe du Roi de Thulé*, four from *Clarisse Harlowe*, and three from *Grisélidis*. "Pastel" (words by Philippe Gille) was originally a setting of a different poem by a different poet, "Le Portrait" (words by Eugène Manuel). Whether Bizet left any instructions for the remaining four songs in the collection, they fit the pattern of salvaging good music from works that seemed to be beyond hope of revival. "Ouvre ton cœur" was originally in *Vasco de Gama*, later transferred to *Ivan IV*; "Pourquoi pleurer" and "Qui donc t'aimera mieux" came from the music Bizet supplied for Halévy's *Noé*. "Le Doute" is an arrangement of the slow movement of the Second Symphony, words courtesy of Paul Ferrier.

The collection has never received as much attention as the earlier *Vingt Mélodies*, but there are some fine songs here, some of them betraying their origins with, or intended for, orchestral accompaniment. All sixteen songs were issued separately by Choudens with illustrated title pages, each in two keys. If the publisher's plate numbers can be trusted, the full collection was printed first in about 1883, with the separate songs appearing in the following two or three years. Last, by quite a margin, was "La Chanson de la rose", the orphan of the set, whose original purpose must therefore remain obscure, even if its authenticity is not in doubt. It is one of Bizet's liveliest and most charming songs.

The three duets Bizet arranged from *La Coupe du Roi de Thulé* and *Clarisse Harlowe* were also published in the later 1880s separately, but not in any collection. Choudens even unearthed the two early songs from 1854, "Petite Marguerite" and "La Rose et l'abeille", and had Armand Silvestre write now words for them. These were issued with new titles: "En avril" and "Rive d'amour".

---

5. Pigot (1886), p. 323.

A number of songs were published in English by Metzler in London, and in Italian by Sonzogno in Milan. In New York in 1888 Schirmer brought out all thirty-six songs with English translations, and in 1898 Hansen of Copenhagen published the entire collection with the texts in French, Swedish and Danish. Curiously there were no German editions of the songs. The fine set of six songs published by Heugel under the title *Feuilles d'album* was forgotten.

★ ★ ★ ★ ★

The resurgence of Bizet's music really began in 1883. *Carmen* continued to conquer the world's opera houses and on 21 April of that year it finally returned to the Opéra-Comique, its original home, for a protracted run. Galli-Marié joined the revival a few months later, sealing its success. Even more remarkable was the burst of interest in *La Jolie Fille de Perth*, which was played in Rouen (27 February) and in Lille (a shared production), in Weimar and Vienna in Julius Hopp's German translation, and in Rome and Milan in Zanardini's Italian translation, all within the year. Pigot reports that it was played in Antwerp and Ghent also. It was heard all over Italy in the 1890s. Choudens issued a variety of vocal scores and piano arrangements to meet this demand, none of them matching the original version. The Milan publisher Sonzogno, anxious to promote French music in his rivalry with Ricordi, negotiated with Choudens to bring out vocal scores of the operas and a selection of songs with Italian words. Bizet's operas, like Massenet's, were extremely popular in Italy in the last years of the nineteenth century. Already in 1888 an Italian critic named Mastrigli brought out a book on Bizet's life and his operas. It was through Sonzogno that *Les Pêcheurs de perles* was awakened from its twenty-three-year slumber, with a production in Milan on 23 March 1886, followed by performances in Rome and Turin. Before the end of the decade it had been heard in twenty cities including Buenos Aires and St Petersburg, finally returning to Paris for a performance on 20 April 1889 at the Théâtre-Italien, in Italian! In that year it opened two days apart in St Petersburg, Prague and Rome's Costanzi Theatre. It was in these posthumous performances that both *La Jolie Fille de Perth* and *Les Pêcheurs de perles* were subjected to changes and substitutions, countless and inextricable in the former case,[6] almost so in the latter, whose ending has been the subject of debate even though Bizet himself only ever contemplated one ending, as far as we know.[7]

Choudens's "Édition nouvelle" of *La Jolie Fille de Perth* contained no less than twenty-one substantial changes in the order and sequence of the opera. The chief alterations include the cuts Bizet himself introduced for the Brussels performances of 1868. All posthumous vocal scores replaced Catherine's Air "Vive l'hiver" with a

---

6. See Westrup (1966), Dean (1975), pp. 291–293, and Macdonald (2010-2).
7. See Lacombe (2001).

Rêverie. This is a version with new words of the song "Rêve de la bien-aimée", composed and published in 1868 to words by Louis de Courmont. A document in private hands suggests that this piece was orchestrated by Guiraud. Another is apparently paginated in Bizet's hand, aligning it with the pagination of the autograph full score of the opera. If this is correct, the decision to replace Catherine's Air with the Rêverie would have been made by Bizet himself or with his approval, almost certainly to spare the singer the extravagant demands of the original Air, either in Paris or in Brussels.

The opening number of Act III, Chœur et scène, was modified in all the posthumous scores in various different ways, and the Chœur de la St-Valentin in the last act was transposed up a semitone to A major, for no clear reason, with an alteration to the beginning of the following scene to assist the modulation back. One published version even included in Act IV a Quintette fashioned from a scene in *La Coupe du Roi de Thulé* with new words. Smaller changes were inflicted on almost every scene. The full score was not engraved, but circulated as a lithographed copy of a very poor handwritten score.

La Jolie Fille de Perth returned to Paris for the first time on 3 November 1890, when it was staged at the Opéra-Comique. By that time the confusion displayed by all the different vocal scores in circulation and their remoteness from Bizet's original would be enough to discourage theatre directors from staging it, for revivals have been scarce in the twentieth century, usually in theatres prepared to step outside the well-beaten operatic repertory. The last major house to stage it was London's Covent Garden in 1920. The standard scores available today from Kalmus, Belwyn Mills and Eroica Publications reproduce one or other of the corrupt Choudens editions. The recording made by EMI in 1985 with June Anderson and Alfredo Kraus, nevertheless, is the complete 1867 version with excellent singing that makes a fine case for the opera, although Prêtre's conducting is careless and often too fast.

Les Pêcheurs de perles was treated only marginally better in Choudens's new scores than *La Jolie Fille de Perth*, being subjected to only nine structural alterations. The first substantial change was to replace the close of the Nadir-Zurga duet at the end of the first scene with a reprise of the main tune "Ah! c'est elle!", which, as we observed earlier, misses the point that the tune, heard once, reflects the fact that Leïla was glimpsed but once and remained for both men an obsessive memory. Presumably the tune was thought to be too good not to be heard one more time. Large cuts were made in Leïla's duet with Zurga in Act III and in the Chœur dansé at the start of the final scene. An eighty-three-bar Trio was introduced in the last scene, traditionally supposed to have been composed by Benjamin Godard, and the close was rewritten to show Zurga put to death by the natives on the flaming pyre prepared for Leïla. The forest also goes up in flames. A third version has a shorter ending in which Zurga is knifed in the back by an Indian chief (or in the full score by Nourabad) and the lovers are heard singing the melody of the duet, as in the original.

Even in corrupt versions *Les Pêcheurs de perles* has steadily climbed in popularity so that it is now a repertoire work appearing in both large and small theatres worldwide. Its currency is undoubtedly underpinned by the popularity of the men's duet, which has been listed in classical music Top Fifty charts. The widely circulated reprints from Kalmus and Belwyn Mills reproduce one of the corrupt editions of the vocal score, but at least for this opera there have been new editions based on Bizet's 1863 score. In 1975, to mark the centenary of Bizet's death, Michel Poupet persuaded Choudens to issue such a version, although even then the correct ending of the duet in Act I was placed in a supplement, with the corrupt ending in the main text. In 1983 Henschel, of Berlin, brought out a version in German based on the 1863 score, edited by Joachim-Dietrich Link.

It was due to the popularity of the *L'Arlésienne* suites in the concert hall that Daudet's play was revived in 1885 at the Théâtre de l'Odéon, with Edouard Colonne conducting an orchestra larger than what Bizet originally had in mind. Needless to say, the score was substantially altered, and it now mixed original sections of incidental music, including *mélodrame*, with longer movements drawn from the two orchestral suites. It was enormously successful this time, being revived regularly in later years. The five-hundredth performance was in 1905 and the thousandth in 1951.[8] Choudens brought out a new vocal score and a full score which matched the new version, including two movements in Bizet's full orchestration and three in Guiraud's. Around 1890 two pieces from *L'Arlésienne* achieved incredible popularity in false garb: the Prélude was transformed into an Ave Maria, and the Entr'acte (no. 15) became an Agnus Dei, both appearing in a vast variety of arrangements for different choirs and instruments. The original 1872 score of the *L'Arlésienne* incidental music was not published until 1989, when Clifford Bartlett issued a version based on the autograph, followed by a critical edition for Choudens by Hervé Lacombe, published in 2010.

Halévy's *Noé* eventually received its first performance in 1885 in Karlsruhe, billed as "by F. Halévy and G. Bizet". It was conducted by Felix Mottl and sung in German; a performance followed soon after in Cologne and another, in Polish, in Warsaw. Choudens promoted these performances and printed both a vocal score and a full score, although no later performances have come to light until 2004 when it was revived in Compiègne. In preparing the opera for Karlsruhe no ballet music and no finale to the last act could be found. The missing last act was replaced by a second tableau to Act III comprising an intermezzo, L'Arc-en-ciel, evidently not Bizet's work, and a finale which Choudens adapted from Bizet's song "Chant

---

8. See Lamothe (2008), pp. 68–90, 267.

d'amour", a setting of Lamartine first published by Choudens in 1872. Six ballets were created by adapting the song "La Coccinelle" and five sections of *Djamileh*.

Djamileh itself was next to be revived, but not in France. Bizet's biographers all repeat the information that it was never revived until 1938, but that is true only for France. It was widely popular outside France in the 1890s, starting with the first revival in Stockholm in Swedish on 25 February 1889, followed by a performance in Rome, engineered by Sonzogno, in October 1890. In September 1892 it was heard in Manchester and Dublin under the title *The Slave in Love*, and a month later it was a huge success in German in Berlin and Hamburg, the latter performance conducted by Mahler. Sonzogno issued an Italian version, Simrock a German version, and Ascherberg an English version. In 1893 an Italian impresario took the opera on tour in the United States. When he heard the news of Gounod's death, he announced the opera as being by Gounod as homage to Gounod![9] In modern times revivals are scarce but regular, affected by the difficulties opera houses have with one-act operas, but always surprising audiences and critics with the richness of its music. *Djamileh* never suffered any depredations at the hands of Choudens, so alone of Bizet's operas the published scores represent what Bizet actually wrote.

The immense catalogue of Choudens's Bizet publications printed at the front of the *Seize Mélodies* is evidence of the astonishing circulation of his music in the later 1880s. Within fifteen years of his death he had become one of the most widely played of French composers, both on the stage and in domestic settings.

At his death in 1871 Auber, Director of the Conservatoire, left his music manuscripts to two nieces. In 1894 Jean-Baptiste Weckerlin, librarian of the Conservatoire, examined the collection and claimed for his library many *envois* from Rome that Auber had "inadvertently" retained among his own manuscripts, including the manuscript of Bizet's Italian opera *Don Procopio*. Charles Malherbe, assistant archivist at the Paris Opéra, described the discovery in *Le Figaro* in February 1895 and set about attempting to have the opera performed for the first time. This eventually took place on 10 March 1906 at the Opéra de Monte Carlo, sung in French. It was billed as an "opéra bouffe" with a libretto by Paul Collin and Paul Bérel, the latter being a pseudonym of Paul de Choudens. An obvious problem was the lack of an original libretto, since the musical numbers require linking recitative, which Bizet did not write. Nor did he provide an overture. So a new libretto was written and eight recitatives were composed by Malherbe, along with some new linking material and an Entr'acte of 112 bars, also by Malherbe, although the vocal score published by Choudens does not say so. A second edition was quickly issued that expanded the work even further by introducing two extra numbers adapted from the posthumous collection *Seize Mélodies*, neither of them the least bit Italian: "Le

---

9. Unidentified cutting in US-Bp.

Gascon" and "Aubade", whose origins, ironically, were in other discarded Bizet operas, *Grisélidis* and *Clarisse Harlowe* respectively. The full score matches this enlarged version. The music Bizet wrote for this opera constitutes only a fraction of what the printed score provides.

This revival of *Don Procopio* seems to have failed miserably. Apart from performances in Barcelona and Rome no further performances are recorded until the 1950s. Since that time performances have taken place steadily in different parts of the world, although there is no correct edition to work from and many hurdles have to be crossed in putting it on the stage. Recordings, too, have been rare.

The next works to emerge were those that had remained in the possession of Bizet's widow and Reynaldo Hahn. Once they arrived at the Bibliothèque du Conservatoire they were surveyed in detail by Jean Chantavoine in a series of articles in *Le Ménestrel* in August and September 1933.[10] Chantavoine was particularly interested in the First Symphony of 1856, the early *Ouverture* and *Ivan IV*, none of which had been seen since Bizet's lifetime, and his detailed account of these works led eventually to performances. Bizet's first biographer in English, D. C. Parker, read Chantavoine's article and persuaded Felix Weingartner to perform the Symphony. The first performance took place under Weingartner in Basel on 26 February 1935 and caused a sensation. Within a year of its première the Symphony was played in Vienna, London, Amsterdam, Madrid, Brno, Copenhagen, Prague, Stuttgart, Königsberg, Riga, Capetown, Frankfurt, Cincinnati and Rochester. The Paris première was given by Charles Münch and the Société des Concerts on 29 May 1936.

It was published by Universal Edition, Vienna, in 1935 under the title "1. Symphonie" (Bizet had labelled it "1ère Symphonie"), but since the Second Symphony was then known only as *Roma*, the First Symphony became known as the "Symphony in C". Apart from its frequency in the concert hall and its many recordings, this work is also well known as a ballet created by Balanchine in 1947, originally called *Le Palais de crystal* but later entitled *Symphony in C*.

In 1938 the early *Ouverture* received its first performance at the Opéra-Comique. It was not until 1972 that it was published, by Universal Edition. Both Dutoit and Plasson have recorded this work.

Bringing *Ivan IV* to life took a little longer. In 1943, during the German Occupation, a read-through of the opera took place in the Théâtre des Capucines, Paris, although no details have come to light as to who was responsible or who sang. It was presumably with a piano accompaniment. It may have been arranged by Ernst Hartmann, a German musicologist, since it was he who organised a performance

---

10. Chantavoine (1933), pp. 316–373. All the Conservatoire's Bizet manuscripts were transferred to the Département de la Musique of the Bibliothèque Nationale (now Bibliothèque nationale de France) in 1964.

of excerpts from the opera with just two singers and piano accompaniment in Schloss Hohenmühringen, near Tübingen, on 13 September 1946.[11] Plans to have the opera published by Schotts Söhne of Mainz and edited by Hartmann were halted when Choudens successfully claimed the right of first publication.

The true première of the opera took place in Bordeaux on 12 October 1951 in a version prepared by Henri Busser. It will come as no surprise to learn that Busser's version made cuts and alterations in almost every number of the opera. The five acts were realigned as four. No. 3 Air et chœur was omitted. A Prélude dramatique not by Bizet was inserted after Act I. A version of the song "Rêve de la bien-aimée" (already playing truant in some versions of *La Jolie Fille de Perth*) was inserted as a Duo for Marie and Ivan in the new Act III with new words; and so on. The only task that Busser was correct to undertake was to supply the orchestration of the last two numbers, of which Bizet left only the vocal lines complete. Choudens issued a vocal score and a full score, in the latter of which there is no mention of Busser's contribution. The opera has been heard since that date mostly in concert performances, including some in which an effort to restore Bizet's text has been made, notably by Winton Dean for the BBC in 1975 and by Howard Williams in performances in London, Montpellier and Paris. The recording by Michael Schønwandt adopts Williams's version. The opera still awaits a faithful edition in print and a worthy production on stage.

In 1962, in response to a number of performances in England, the first of which seems to have been a broadcast by the BBC in 1953, a vocal score of the early operetta *Le Docteur Miracle* was published by Éditions Françaises de Musique, Paris. Since that time it has become almost popular, more popular than *Don Procopio* certainly, and there have been a few recordings. The full score is still not published.

In 1955 Winton Dean prepared the Prélude and three surviving extracts from *La Coupe du Roi de Thulé* to be broadcast by the BBC in a performance by the Philharmonia Orchestra under Stanford Robinson. Unfortunately no recording was made. More unknown Bizet was excavated in May 1971 when the Berlin Singakademie under Matthieu Lange gave the world première of Bizet's *Te Deum* from 1858. This was one of the pieces recovered from Auber's collection, but the manuscript had been at the Conservatoire since 1894, observed only by Chantavoine and performed by no one. The vocal score appeared from Simrock in 1971 and the full score from À Cœur Joie in 1995. A further enhancement of general access to Bizet's music was provided by Michel Poupet's edition of fourteen early piano pieces, published by Éditions Mario Bois in 1984 under the title *Œuvres pour piano*. These pieces all date from Bizet's childhood and student years. A curious Bizet première took place at the University of Texas, Austin, in 1989, when William E.

11. See Schwandt (1991).

Girard staged *La Maison du docteur*, Bizet's first opera, having translated and orchestrated the work himself. Girard conducted four performances and published the score as his DMA dissertation.

★ ★ ★ ★ ★

The study of Bizet's life and work began at his death, at which moment no one expected to be asked to summarise his achievement at such short notice. Among many obituaries the most informative was that by Victor Wilder in *Le Ménestrel*.[12] Galabert wrote a short memoir of his friend in 1877, and in 1886, at the height of Bizet's posthumous success, a biography appeared from Charles Pigot, a writer unknown for any other contribution to musical or literary studies and who had not known Bizet personally. But he admired his work and had help from Guiraud, who never wrote about Bizet himself. Pigot narrated the main events in Bizet's life with the recognition that his genius is not only to be found in *Carmen* but in the earlier operas too, to which he devotes much attention. Marmontel's reminiscences appeared in 1881, Gallet's in 1891, Saint-Saëns's in 1899, Maréchal's in 1907, Reyer's in 1909 and Berton's in 1913. In 1894 Hugues Imbert published Bizet's correspondence with—actually only to—Paul Lacombe,[13] an edition that strangely exists in two forms, one in which ungenerous references to living persons (for example, the remark that Gounod is "too Catholic") have been removed, and another that contains the full uncensored text and also a series of letters to Guiraud. These revisions may have been made possible by Gounod's death in October 1893 and Guiraud's a year earlier.

A substantial correspondence with Gounod appeared in the *Revue de Paris* in 1899, and in 1907 Louis Ganderax edited the extensive letters Bizet wrote to his parents from Italy in 1858–60, along with some letters written during the siege of Paris in 1870–71. Edmond Galabert's invaluable *Lettres à un ami* appeared in 1909, although he felt it necessary to suppress much of their correspondence from the period of Bizet's marriage. French biographers display an undertow of hostility in this period. Although a certain resentment (at what? not being Wagnerian enough? not being successful enough?) can be felt in Arthur Pougin's notice in the supplement to Fétis's *Biographie universelle de musiciens*, published in 1878, and outright hostility in a "biographie critique" credited to Henry Gauthier-Villars but actually written by Vuillermoz, published in 1912, there were more serious efforts to assess Bizet's achievement by Bellaigue (1892), Rolland (1908), Séré (1911), Brancour (1913), Landormy (1929) and Delmas (1930). All these writers were unknowingly

12. Victor Wilder, "Georges Bizet: Esquisse biographique", *Le Ménestrel*, 41 (July 1875), pp. 241–259.
13. Imbert (1894).

hampered by ignorance of the treasures held by Bizet's widow, and by the confusion displayed by published scores. Abroad there were brief studies in Italian (Mastrigli, 1888) and German (Voss, 1899), and the first biography in English came from D. C. Parker in 1926. In England a long series of articles on Bizet by John W. Klein appeared between 1924 and 1974.

The centenary of Bizet's birth in 1938 was marked by an exhibition at the Paris Opéra in which many manuscripts, letters, photographs and other items were displayed. Some little-known songs and piano pieces were performed there too. The *Revue de musicologie* devoted a whole issue to Bizet. The Opéra-Comique staged *Les Pêcheurs de perles* and *Djamileh*. *Carmen* of course was performed everywhere.

After the war Bizet studies advanced forcefully, thanks first to Winton Dean's powerful advocacy on behalf of Bizet's dramatic genius in his book first published in 1948 and later considerably expanded. The portrayal of Bizet's character is penetrating and vivid, although his opinions of individual pieces have an air of unarguable finality that may deter the reader from venturing to differ. At the same time the American scholar Mina Curtiss, sister of the great ballet impresario Lincoln Kirstein, while pursuing the papers of the Halévy family in connection with her work on Proust, traced a treasure-house of documents to Émile Straus's nephew, René Sibilat, who had died in 1945. From his widow she acquired the whole collection, which included hundreds of letters between Bizet and the Halévys as well as some musical manuscripts and sketches. There were letters addressed to Bizet by others too, including many from Galli-Marié. This remarkable story was told in her book *Bizet and His World*, which came out in 1958. The book was a revelation concerning Bizet's private world, especially his relations with his wife and mother-in-law and other members of the Halévy family. It also painted vivid portraits of the many figures who played a part in his career as theatre managers, librettists, critics and friends. Curtiss was not concerned with the nature and quality of the music (for which she relied on Dean's judgments), although the history of its performance and reception were generously covered. All later writers on Bizet have been inescapably indebted to her work and to the arrangement by which, since her death in 1985, the documents from Sibilat have been housed at the Bibliothèque nationale. Her working papers are held by the New York Public Library.

In the 1960s Michel Poupet emerged as a scholar with a clear idea of what needed to be done to correct the falsehoods surrounding the transmission of Bizet's music. He published a number of articles on this theme and also edited the volume of early piano music mentioned earlier, but his early death sadly cut short his important contribution to Bizet studies. The American scholar Lesley A. Wright has been writing a long series of highly scholarly articles on many different aspects of Bizet's works, including her Princeton dissertation *Bizet before Carmen*, issued by University Microfilms in 1981. This looked closely for the first time at Bizet's methods of work, his manuscripts and sketches, with detailed tracing of the genesis of both *Ivan IV* and *La Jolie Fille de Perth*. She has also written extensively on the Prix de Rome and on Parisian music criticism during and after Bizet's time. In 1988 she published the series of more than a hundred Bizet letters in the Stiftelsen Musikkulturens Främjande, Stockholm. These were part of the large collection assembled between the wars by Rudolf Nydahl, a Swedish collector with a particular taste for French music. The collection also includes Bizet's desk, and the autograph manuscript of *Djamileh* has since been added to their holdings.

Two important studies of Bizet in French appeared in 1999 and 2000, by Rémy Stricker and Hervé Lacombe respectively. Both take full account of the work of Curtiss and Wright, and while Stricker explores certain aspects without attempting a comprehensive exegesis of Bizet's life and work, Lacombe is voluminously thorough in covering Bizet's life and his relationship to the musical conventions of his time. He is particularly sensitive to questions of genre and he treats the major works with great penetration. Many of the smaller works are overlooked, however. Lacombe and Thierry Bodin are preparing an edition of Bizet's complete correspondence, a formidable task not only because of Bizet's dreadful handwriting but also because the letters are widely scattered and are often very difficult to date.

At least the better-known works are finally getting published with discernment and care. The *Jeux d'enfants* for piano duet has had plenty of attention from editors, including a scholarly version edited by Noël Lee for Éditions Musicales du Marais, published in the series "Patrimoine" in 1990. In 1995 Garland reprinted a selection of songs, including the forgotten set of *Feuilles d'album*. As for *Carmen*, it filled the opera houses of the world with delighted listeners for nearly a hundred years before anyone looked more closely at its origins. In Paris it passed from the Opéra-Comique to the big stage of the Opéra in 1907 and became an all-sung, all-danced spectacular, often with a famous soprano taking the title role with plenty of transposition to fit the higher voice. The first of countless recordings was made in 1908 in Berlin with Emmy Destin, and it has been seen in over seventy film versions.[14] It is not clear who can claim the distinction of first restoring dialogue in place of Guiraud's recitatives, but after the war a few brave conductors (and eventually Covent Garden and the Met) introduced at least some of the dialogue, although many listeners regarded this as a regressive step.[15] Controversy erupted in 1964 when Fritz Oeser published an edition of *Carmen* with Alkor Edition which included a great deal of music no one had seen before. Oeser examined the original performance parts from the Opéra-Comique and included in his edition every trace of music he found there. This might have been a valuable exercise had he not

---

14. See Wlaschin (2004).
15. Klein (1959), for example.

ignored the evidence of the 1875 Choudens vocal score, which Bizet had supervised himself. Oeser reinstated many cuts made in rehearsal in 1874–75, and although both the dialogues and Guiraud's recitatives were included, Oeser's tendentious claim to be presenting the correct version was strongly criticised. Three new editions of *Carmen* have recently appeared, all seeking to right not just the wrongs of a long performance tradition but also to settle this controversy by presenting the opera in the same sequence as the 1875 vocal score, albeit showing alternatives for those who need to see what other versions passed through Bizet's mind at one time or another.[16]

It will be a long and hard road to win for Bizet's music the respect it was not accorded in his lifetime and was denied even more gratuitously after his death. A popular composer, which Bizet is, ought to be a fully served composer, provided with reliable editions of all his music, with performance materials available, with good recordings, with a thorough documentation of his life, and with a tradition of performance that understands the original functions of his music even when it is reconfigured in the taste of the moment. His is a story of struggle, not martyrdom, with a mixed legacy of music that sometimes ambles casually along the upper levels of Parisian Second Empire culture and sometimes rises to heights of great beauty and timeless significance. He deserves to be given our full critical attention and to be known as much more than just the composer of *Carmen*.

16. These editions are edited, respectively, by Robert Didion for Schott (Mainz, 2000), by Michael Rot for Hermann (Vienna, 2009), and by Richard Langham Smith for Peters (London, 2013).

APPENDIX A

Calendar

Year	Age	Life	Contemporary Musicians and Events
1838		Bizet born, Paris, 25 Oct.	Auber (56), Paganini (55), Meyerbeer (47), Rossini (46), Donizetti (40), Halévy (39), Berlioz (34), Glinka (34), Mendelssohn (29), Chopin (28), Schumann (28), David (28), Liszt (27), Thomas (27), Verdi (25), Wagner (25), Alkan (24), Gounod (20), Offenbach (19), Bruckner (15), Lalo (15), Franck (15), Smetana (14), Brahms (5), Borodin (4), Saint-Saëns (3), Delibes (2), Balakirev (1), Guiraud (1).
1839	0		Mussorgsky born.
1840	1	Baptised Georges Bizet, 16 March.	Paganini dies. Tchaikovsky born.
1841	2		Dvořák born.
1842	3		Massenet, Sullivan born.
1843	4		
1844	5		Rimsky-Korsakov born.
1845	6		Fauré born.
1846	7		
1847	8	Attends Marmontel's class at the Conservatoire.	Mendelssohn dies.
1848	9	Full enrolment at the Conservatoire.	Donizetti dies.
1849	10	Wins 2ème 1er Prix for solfège.	Chopin dies.

· 251 ·

Year	Age	Life	Contemporary Musicians and Events
1850	11		
1851	12	First compositions. Wins 2ème Prix for piano.	Verdi's *Rigoletto*.
1852	13	Wins 1er Prix for piano. Joins organ class of Benoist. Writes piano music.	
1853	14	Wins 1er Accessit in organ. First attempt at the Prix de Rome. Meets Gounod. Joins Halévy's composition class.	Liszt's B minor Sonata. Verdi's *Il trovatore* and *La traviata*. Wagner begins *The Ring*.
1854	15	Wins 2ème Prix in organ. Transcribes Gounod's *La Nonne sanglante*.	Berlioz's *L'Enfance du Christ*.
1855	16	Wins 1er Prix in organ. Transcribes Gounod's First Symphony. Perhaps composes *La Maison du docteur*. First Symphony, Nov.	
1856	17	Second attempt at the Prix de Rome, May. Composes *Dr Miracle*.	Schumann dies.
1857	18	*Dr Miracle* staged at the Bouffes-Parisiens, April. Third attempt at the Prix de Rome. Wins 1er Prix. Leaves for Rome, Dec.	Glinka dies. Elgar born.
1858	19	Reaches Rome via Florence and Siena, 27 Jan. *Te Deum*, May. Summer hike with Heim. Composes *Don Procopio*.	Puccini born. Berlioz's *Les Troyens* completed.
1859	20	Visits Naples and Pompeii, Sept. Begins Second Symphony.	Verdi's *Un ballo in maschera*. Wagner's *Tristan und Isolde* completed.
1860	21	Composes *Vasco de Gama*. Leaves the Villa Medicis with Guiraud, July. Travels north to Venice. Cuts short his trip on hearing of his mother's illness. Reaches Paris, September.	Wolf, Mahler born.
1861	22	Mother dies, 8 Sept. Moves to 32, Rue Fontaine-St-Georges.	Wagner's *Tannhäuser*, March. Reyer's *La Statue*, April. Liszt in Paris, May.

Year	Age	Life	Contemporary Musicians and Events
1862	23	Halévy dies, 17 March. Composes *La Guzla de l'Émir*. Birth of Jean, Bizet's illegitimate son. Works on Reyer's *Erostrate*. Visit to Baden-Baden, August.	Debussy born.
1863	24	*Vasco de Gama* performed, 8 Feb. Composes *Les Pêcheurs de perles* for the Théâtre-Lyrique. Opens 30 Sep.	Berlioz's *Les Troyens à Carthage* opens 4 Nov.
1864	25	Composes *Ivan IV*. Assists Gounod with *Mireille*. Begins summer stays in Le Vésinet. Plans *La Prêtresse* with Gille.	Meyerbeer dies. Strauss born.
1865	26	*L'Africaine* opens, 28 April. Galabert becomes Bizet's pupil. *St-Jean de Pathmos* composed. Begins working as arranger for Heugel.	Brahms's *Requiem*. Sibelius born.
1866	27	Piano pieces and *Feuilles d'album* published by Heugel. Liszt in Paris, March. Friendship with Céleste Mogador. Returns to the Second Symphony. Composes *La Jolie Fille de Perth*.	Clapisson dies. *Mignon* opens 17 Nov. Smetana's *Bartered Bride*.
1867	28	Makes two arrangments of *Mignon*. Exposition Universelle in Paris. Composes a *Hymne* and a cantata for the Exposition competitions. Paul Lacombe becomes his pupil. Serious relationship with Geneviève Halévy. *Malbrough s'en va-t-en guerre* opens 12 Dec. *La Jolie Fille de Perth* opens 26 Dec.	Verdi's *Don Carlos* opens, 11 March. *Roméo et Juliette* opens 27 April. Wagner's *Die Meistersinger* completed.
1868	29	*La Jolie Fille de Perth* played in Brussels, March. Makes two arrangements of *Hamlet*. More songs composed. *Variations chromatiques* for piano.	Thomas's *Hamlet* opens 9 March. Rossini dies.
1869	30	Three movements of the Second Symphony performed, 28 Feb. Composes *La Coupe du Roi de Thulé*. Marries Geneviève Halévy, 3 June. Completes Halévy's *Noé*.	Berlioz dies.

Year	Age	Life	Contemporary Musicians and Events
1870	31	Starts work on three operas: *Calendal, Grisélidis* and *Clarisse Harlowe*. Summer stay at Barbizon. War with Prussia declared July. Third Republic proclaimed September. Siege of Paris begins. Bizet joins the Garde Nationale. More songs composed.	
1871	32	Siege ends, Jan. Bizet and Geneviève visit Bordeaux, Feb. Société Nationale de Musique founded, Feb. The Commune seizes power March–May. *Djamileh* commissioned. *Jeux d'enfants* composed.	Verdi's *Aida*. Auber dies.
1872	33	*Djamileh* opens, 22 May. Another opera commissioned by the Opéra-Comique. Bizet's son Jacques born, 10 July. *L'Arlésienne* opens 30 Sep.	
1873	34	Prepares revival of *Roméo et Juliette*, Jan. Publication of *Vingt Mélodies*. Composes first act of *Carmen*. Drafts *Don Rodrigue*. Fire destroys the Opéra, 28 Oct. *Patrie* composed, Dec.	
1874	35	*Carmen* completed. Rehearsals begin, Sep.	Schoenberg born.
1875	36	The Palais Garnier opens 5 Jan. *Carmen* opens, 3 March. Begins the oratorio *Geneviève de Paris*. Bizet dies, 3 June.	David (65), Thomas (63), Liszt (63), Wagner (62), Alkan (61), Verdi (61), Gounod (56), Offenbach (55), Lalo (52), Franck (52), Smetana (51), Bruckner (50), Brahms (42), Borodin (41), Saint-Saëns (39), Delibes (39), Balakirev (38), Mussorgsky (35), Tchaikovsky (35), Dvořák (33), Massenet (33), Sullivan (33), Rimsky-Korsakov (31), Fauré (30), Elgar (18), Puccini (16), Wolf (15), Mahler (14), Debussy (12), Strauss (10), Sibelius (9), Schoenberg (0), Ravel born.

APPENDIX B

List of Works

1. Operas (performable)

Cat. No.		
1	*La Maison du docteur*	opéra-comique in one act, composed?1854–55 libretto: Henry Boisseaux first performance: 23 Feb. 1989, Austin, TX. first published: 1990 note: exists in vocal score only
2	*Le Dr Miracle*	opéra-comique in one act, composed 1856 libretto: Léon Battu and Ludovic Halévy, after Sheridan first performance: 9 April 1857, Bouffes-Parisiens, Paris first published: 1962
3	*Don Procopio*	opera buffa in two acts libretto: after Carlo Cambiaggio first performance: 10 March 1906, Monte Carlo first published: 1905 note: in Italian
4	*Les Pêcheurs de perles*	opéra in three acts libretto: Michel Carré and Eugène Cormon first performance: 30 September 1863, Théâtre-Lyrique, Paris first published: 1863
5	*Ivan IV*	opéra in five acts libretto: François-Hippolyte Leroy and Henri Trianon first performance: 12 October 1951, Bordeaux first published: 1951

Cat. No.		
6	*La Jolie Fille de Perth*	opéra in four acts libretto: Jules-Henry de St-Georges and Jules Adenis, after Scott first performance: 26 December 1867, Théâtre-Lyrique, Paris first published: 1868
7	*Noé*	grand opéra in three acts libretto: Jules-Henry de St-Georges first performance: 5 April 1885, Karlsruhe first published: 1886 note: completion of Halévy's opera
8	*Djamileh*	opéra-comique in one act libretto: Louis Gallet, after de Musset first performance: 22 May 1872, Opéra-Comique, Paris first published: 1872
9	*Carmen*	opéra-comique in four acts libretto: Ludovic Halévy and Henri Meilhac, after Mérimée first performance: 3 March 1875, Opéra-Comique, Paris first published: 1875

2. **Operas (fragmentary)**

Cat. No.	Date of Composition	Title	Genre and Acts	Librettist(s)	First performance, in Paris unless otherwise stated	Published	Remarks
10	1864	*La Prêtresse*	opérette, 1	Philippe Gille			a sketch survives
11	1867	*Malbrough s'en va-t-en guerre*	opéra-bouffe, 4	Paul Siraudin and William Busnach	13 Dec. 1867, Théâtre de l'Athénée		Bizet wrote Act I only. One song survives
12	1868–69	*La Coupe du Roi de Thulé*	opéra, 3	Louis Gallet	12 Dec. 1880, Concerts du Châtelet (Prélude), 12 July 1955 (fragments)	1880 (Prélude only)	only fragments survive
13	1870–71	*Grisélidis*	opéra-comique, 4	Victorien Sardou, after Boccaccio			sketches and some songs survive
14	1869–72	*Clarisse Harlowe*	opéra-comique, 3	Philippe Gille and Adolphe Jaime, after Richardson			sketches and some songs survive
15	1873	*Don Rodrigue*	opéra, 5	Louis Gallet and Edouard Blau, after Guillén de Castro y Bellvis			complete draft of the vocal lines

3. Operas (projected or lost)

Cat. No.	Year	Title	Genre, Acts	Librettist	Remarks
16	1858	?	opéra-comique	Edmond About	projected
17	1858	*Parisina*	opéra, 3	Felice Romani, after Byron	in Italian, projected
18	1858–59	*Esmeralda*	opéra, 4	Victor Hugo	projected
19	1859	*Don Quichotte*	opéra	after Cervantes	projected
20	1859	*Le Tonnelier de Nuremberg*	opéra, 3	after E.T.A. Hoffmann's *Meister Martin der Küfner und seine Gesellen*	projected
21	1859–60	*L'Amour-peintre*	opéra-comique	after Molière, *Le Sicilien ou L'Amour peintre*	perhaps started
22	1862	*La Guzla de l'Émir*	opéra-comique, 1	Jules Barbier and Michel Carré	completed, lost
23	1865	*Nicolas Flamel*	opéra	Ernest Dubreuil	projected
24	1868	*Les Templiers*	opéra, 5	Léon Halévy and Jules-Henry de St-Georges	projected
25	1868–69	?	opéra	François-Hippolyte Leroy and Thomas Sauvage	projected
26	1869–70	*Vercingétorix*	opéra	Emile Delerot	projected
27	1869–70	*Calendal*	opéra, 4	Paul Ferrier, after Mistral	projected
28	1869–71	*Rama*	opéra, 4	Eugène Crépet, after the *Ramayana*	Projected
29	1872	*Sol-si-ré-pif-pan*	bouffonnerie, 1	William Busnach	16 Nov 1872, Théâtre du Château-d'Eau, lost

4. Incidental Music

Cat. No.	Year	Title	Playwright	First performance	Published
30	1872	*L'Arlésienne*	Alphonse Daudet	30 September 1872, Théâtre du Vaudeville	1872

5. Choral Works with Orchestra

Cat. No.	Year	Title	Text	Forces	First performance	Published	Remarks
31	1853	*La Brigantine*	Casimir Delavigne	?			Prix de Rome, lost
32	1855	*Valse avec chœur*	Eugène Scribe	SSTB		1978	
33	c. 1855	*Chœur d'étudiants*	Eugène Scribe	TTBB			
34	1856	*Le Golfe de Baïa*	Alphonse de Lamartine	SSTB, ST solo		1880	Prix de Rome
35	1857	*La Chanson du Rouet*	Leconte de Lisle	SSTB, S solo		1880	Prix de Rome
36	1858	*Te Deum*		SSTTBB, ST solo	1971	1971	
37	1859	*Ulysse et Circé, ode-symphonie*	Victor Fournel, after Homer				projected
38	1860	*Vasco de Gama, ode-symphonie*	Louis Lacour-Delâtre, after Camões	SSTTBB, SSTB solo, récitant	1863	1880	
39	1867	*Hymne de la paix*	Gustave Chouquet	SSTB, brass			
40	1867	*Les Noces de Prométhée*	Romain Cornut	?			lost
41	1869	*La Mort s'avance, cantique*	Abbé Pellegrin	SSTTBB		1869	based on Chopin *Études*
42	1870	*Morts pour la France*	Victor Hugo	?			lost
43	1875	*Geneviève de Paris, légende dramatique*	Louis Gallet	?			projected

6. Choral Works with Keyboard

Cat. No.	Year	Title	Text	Forces	First performance	Published	Remarks
44	1867	Notre Rosa	Auguste-Nicolas Cain	unison chorus, piano			
45	?	Ecce sacerdos	Graduale romanum	women's chorus, organ		1885	

7. Choral Works Unaccompanied

Cat. No.	Year	Title	Text	Forces	First performance	Published	Remarks
46	1860	Carmen saeculare	Horace	double chorus			unfinished, lost
47	1865	St-Jean de Pathmos	Victor Hugo	men's chorus	1865	1874	

8. Prix de Rome Cantatas

Cat. No.	Year	Title	Text	Forces	Remarks	First performance	Published
48	1850	[cantata]	None	piano reduction	fragment		
49	1853–57?	Ange et Tobie	Léon Halévy	tenor, orchestra	fragment		
50	1853–57?	Le Chevalier enchanté	Amédée-David de Pastoret	soprano, tenor, orchestra	fragment		
51	1853–57?	Herminie	J.-A.Vinaty	soprano, orchestra			
52	1853–57?	Loyse de Montfort	Emile Deschamps	soloists, chorus, orchestra	fragments		
53	1853–57?	Le Retour de Virginie	Auguste Rollet	soloists, orchestra	fragments		
54	1856	David	Gaston d'Albano	soloists, orchestra	1856 concours	1856	
55	1857	Clovis et Clotilde	Amédée Burion	soloists, orchestra	1857 concours	1857	

9. Songs with Orchestra

Cat. No.	Year	Title	Poem	First performance	Published
56	1867–69	*Tarentelle*	Édouard Pailleron	1881	

10. Two Voices and Piano

Cat. No.	Year	Title	Poem	Voices	First performance	Published	Remarks
57	1850	*Barcarolle*	no words	SS			
58	1870	*La Fuite*	Théophile Gautier	ST		1872	
59	1873	*De ce gaillard entretien*	Meilhac and Halévy	SS	1873		
60	1873–75	*Le Retour*	Jules Barbier	ST		1885	derived from *Clarisse Harlowe*
61	1873–75	*Rêvons*	Jules Barbier	M-S, B		1887	derived from *La Coupe du Roi de Thulé*
62	1873–75	*Les Nymphes des bois*	Jules Barbier	S, M-S		1887	derived from *Clarisse Harlowe*

11. Songs for Voice and Piano

Cat. No.	Composed	Title	Poem	Published	Remarks
63	1850	*Vocalise*			
64	1851–52	*Romance*	Alphonse de Lamartine		
65	by 1854	*Petite Marguerite*	Olivier Rolland	1854	later issued as *En avril* with words by Armand Silvestre
66	by 1854	*La Rose et l'abeille*	Olivier Rolland	1854	later issued as *Rive d'amour* with words by Armand Silvestre
67	by 1854	*La Foi, l'espérance et la charité*	Théophile Rousseau-Lagrave	1854	
68	1860	*Ouvre ton cœur*	Henri Trianon	1869	*Seize Mélodies*, no. 2, from *Vasco de Gama* and *Ivan IV*
69	1863	*Sérénade*	Michel Carré and Eugène Cormon	1863	*Vingt Mélodies*, no. 10, from *Les Pêcheurs de perles*
70	by 1865	*Vieille Chanson*	Charles-Hubert Millevoye	1865	*Vingt Mélodies*, no. 3
71	1866	*A une Fleur*	Alfred de Musset	1867	*Feuilles d'album*, no. 1
72	1866	*Adieux à Suzon*	Alfred de Musset	1867	*Feuilles d'album*, no. 2
73	1866	*Sonnet*	Pierre de Ronsard	1867	*Feuilles d'album*, no. 3
74	1866	*Guitare*	Victor Hugo	1867	*Feuilles d'album*, no. 4
75	1866	*Rose d'amour*	Charles-Hubert Millevoye	1867	*Feuilles d'album*, no. 5
76	1866	*Le Grillon*	Alphonse de Lamartine	1867	*Feuilles d'album*, no. 6
77	1866	*Adieux de l'hôtesse arabe*	Victor Hugo	1867	*Vingt Mélodies*, no. 4
78	1866	*Je n'en dirai rien*	Jules Adenis and Jules-Henry de St-Georges	1868	*Vingt Mélodies*, no. 18, from *La Jolie Fille de Perth*
79	1866–67	*Après l'Hiver*	Victor Hugo	1867	*Vingt Mélodies*, no. 15
80	1866–67	*Douce Mer*	Alphonse de Lamartine	1867	*Vingt Mélodies*, no. 14
81	1868	*Ma Vie a son secret*	Félix Arvers	1868	*Vingt Mélodies*, no. 8
82	1868	*La Coccinelle*	Victor Hugo	1868	*Vingt Mélodies*, no. 16

83	1868	Pastorale	Jean-François Regnard	1868	Vingt Mélodies, no. 9
84	1868	Berceuse	Marceline Desbordes-Valmore	1868	Vingt Mélodies, no. 11
85	1868	Rêve de la bien-aimée	Louis de Courmont	1868	Vingt Mélodies, no. 5
86	1868	La Chanson du fou	Victor Hugo	1868	Vingt Mélodies, no. 12
87	by 1869	Tarantelle (1)	Italian folksong	1869	in Italian
88	by 1869	L'Esprit saint	Cantiques de Saint-Sulpice	1869	Vingt Mélodies, no. 19
89	1869	Pourquoi pleurer?	Jules-Henry de St-Georges	1883	Seize Mélodies, no. 3, from Noé
90	1869	Qui donc t'aimera mieux?	Jules-Henry de St-Georges	1883	Seize Mélodies, no. 11, from Noé.
91	by 1871	Chant d'amour	Alphonse de Lamartine	1872	Vingt Mélodies, no. 17
92	by 1871	Chanson d'avril	Louis-Hyacinthe Bouilhet	1871	Vingt Mélodies, no. 1
93	by 1872	Absence	Théophile Gautier	1871	Vingt Mélodies, no. 13
94	by 1872	Tarantelle (2)	Édouard Pailleron	1873	Vingt Mélodies, no. 20. Also with orchestra.
95	by 1872	Vous ne priez pas	Casimir Delavigne	1873	Vingt Mélodies, no. 7
96	1872	Le Matin	? Bizet	1873	Vingt Mélodies, no. 2, from L'Arlésienne
97	by 1872	Le Colibri	Marie-Alexandre Flan		
98	by 1872	Vœu	Victor Hugo		
99	by 1872	Sérénade	Victor Hugo		
100	1872	J'aime l'amour	Louis Gallet	1872	Vingt Mélodies, no. 6, from Djamileh arranged from L'Arlésienne
101	1872	Lamento	?		
102	1873–75	La Sirène	Catulle Mendès	1883	Seize Mélodies, no. 1, adapted from La Coupe du Roi de Thulé
103	1873–75	Voyage	Philippe Gille	1883	Seize Mélodies, no. 4, adapted from Clarisse Harlowe
104	1873–75	Aubade	Paul Ferrier	1883	Seize Mélodies, no. 5, adapted from Clarisse Harlowe

(continued)

Cat. No.	Composed	Title	Poem	Published	Remarks
105	1873–75	La Nuit	Paul Ferrier	1883	Seize Mélodies, no. 6, adapted from Clarisse Harlowe. The same music as Les Nymphes des bois.
106	1873–75	Le Doute!	Paul Ferrier	1883	Seize Mélodies, no. 7, adapted from Symphony no. 2.
107	1873–75	Conte	Paul Ferrier	1883	Seize Mélodies, no. 8, adapted from Grisélidis.
108	1873–75	Aimons, rêvons!	Paul Ferrier	1883	Seize Mélodies, no. 9, adapted from La Coupe du Roi de Thulé. Partly the same music as Rêvons.
109	1873–75	La Chanson de la rose	Jules Barbier	1883	Seize Mélodies, no. 10
110	1873–75	Le Gascon	Catulle Mendès	1883	Seize Mélodies, no. 12, adapted from Grisélidis.
111	1873–75	N'oublions pas!	Jules Barbier	1883	Seize Mélodies, no. 13, adapted from La Coupe du Roi de Thulé
112	1873–75	Si vous aimez	Philippe Gille	1883	Seize Mélodies, no. 14, adapted from Clarisse Harlowe.
113	1873–75	Le Portrait	Eugène Manuel	1883	Seize Mélodies, no. 15, as Pastel, words by Philippe Gille.
114	1873–75	L'Abandonnée	Philippe Gille or Catulle Mendès	1883	Seize Mélodies, no. 16, adapted from Grisélidis

12. Orchestral Works

Cat. No.	Composed	Title	First performance	Published	Remarks
115	1855	Symphony no. 1 in C	26 Feb 1935, Basel	1935	
116	1855–57?	Ouverture	26 Oct 1938, Opéra-Comique		
117	1860	La Chasse d'Ossian		1972	lost, but probably the original first movement of Symphony no. 2
118	1859–68	Symphony no. 2 in C	12 Oct 1860, Institut (Andante and Scherzo); 28 Feb 1869 (all but the Scherzo); 31 Oct 1880 (complete work)	1880	Original slow movement, *Marche funèbre*, unpublished.
119	1871	Petite suite d'orchestre Marche Berceuse Impromptu Duo Galop	15 May 1872, Concerts Danbé	1872	5 movements of *Jeux d'enfants*
120	1871	Les Quatre Coins	1992, Toulouse		Movement 8 of *Jeux d'enfants*
121	1872	L'Arlésienne Suite Prélude Minuetto Adagietto Carillon	10 Nov 1872, Concerts populaires	1873	Four movements from the *L'Arlésienne* incidental music
122	1873	Patrie, ouverture dramatique	15 Feb 1874, Concerts populaires	1874	
123	1874	Scènes bohémiennes Prélude Sérénade Menuet Danse bohémienne	23 Dec 1883, Angers	1882	Four movements from *La Jolie Fille de Perth* usually replaced by *Marche*

13. **Piano Solo**

Cat. No.	Composed	Title	Published	Remarks
124	1851	1er Caprice original	1984	2 versions
125	1851	2ème Caprice original	1984	3 versions
126	1851–52	4 Préludes	1984	
127	1851–52	Thème	1984	
128	1851–52	Valse	1984	
129	1851–52	Romance sans paroles	1984	in C in 4/4
130	1852	Étude		
131	1854	Grande valse de concert	1984	
132	1854	1er Nocturne	1984	in F
133	1856	Romance sans paroles	1856	in C in 9/8
134	1856	Casilda	1856	
135	1858	L'Enterrement de Clapisson		never written down
136	1865	Chants du Rhin	1866	on poems by Méry
		L'Aurore		
		Le Départ		
		Les Rêves		
		La Bohémienne		
		Les Confidences		
		Le Retour		
137	1865	Chasse fantastique	1866	
138	1868	Marine	1868	
139	1868	1er Nocturne	1868	in D
140	1868	Variations chromatiques	1868	
141	1874	Souvenirs de l'Auvergne	1875	lost, doubtful

14. Piano Duet

Cat. No.	Composed	Title	Published	Remarks
142	1871	*Jeux d'enfants* *L'Escarpolette* *La Toupie* *La Poupée* *Les Chevaux de bois* *Le Volant* *Trompette et tambour* *Les Bulles de savon* *Les Quatre Coins* *Colin-maillard* *Saute-mouton* *Petit mari, petite femme!* *Le Bal*	1872	12 pieces for piano duet, five orchestrated as *Petite Suite d'orchestre*
143	1871	*Simplicité*		piano duet, co-composed with Massenet

15. Piano, Harmonium or Organ

Cat. No.	Composed	Title	Published
144	1856	*Méditation religieuse*	1853–56

16. Harmonium

Cat. No.	Composed	Title	Published
145	1857	*Trois Esquisses musicales*	1858

17. Chamber Music

Cat. No.	Composed	Title	Published
146	1874	[*Duo*] for bassoon and cello	1970
147	1874	[*Duo*] for oboe and piano	

18. Miscellaneous

Cat. No.	Composed	Title	
148	1853	*Fugue*	lost
149	1854	*Fugue* in A minor	
150	1855	*Fugue* in D major	incomplete
151	1855	*Fugue* in F minor	
152	1856	*Fugue* in G major	
153	1857	*Fugue* in E minor	
154	1849–54	*Fugues, exercices*	
155	1869–74	*Sujets de fugue*	
156	1869	[Albumleaf]	

19. List of Transcriptions

	Composer	Work	Transcribed for	Date
T1	various	*100 Fragments*	piano-scandé	1853–54
T2	Gounod	*La Nonne sanglante*	vocal score	1855
T3	Gounod	Symphony no. 1	piano duet	1855
T4	various	*Trois Duos*	harmonium and piano	1858
T5	Reyer	*La Statue*	vocal score	1861
T6	Gounod	*Faust*	piano duet	1861–62
T7	Gounod	*La Reine de Saba*	vocal score	1862
T8	Nicolai	*Les Joyeuses Commères de Windsor*	orchestration	1862
T9	Reyer	*Érostrate*	vocal score	1862
T10	Pascal	*Le Cabaret des amours*	vocal score	1862
T11	Gounod	*Mireille*	vocal score	1864
T12	Gounod	*Mireille*, "Heureux petit berger"	piano solo	1864
T13	Gounod	*Ave Maria*	piano solo	1865
T14	Wagner	*L'Ange*	piano solo	1865
T15	Gounod	Symphony no. 2	piano solo	1865
T16	Gounod	Symphony no. 2	piano duet	1865
T17	various	*Le Pianiste chanteur*	piano solo	1865–66
T18	Mozart	*Don Giovanni*	piano solo	1866
T19	Mozart	*Don Giovanni*, overture	piano duet	1866
T20	Gounod	*Tobie*	vocal score	1866
T21	Gounod	*Six Chœurs célèbres*	piano solo	1866
T22	Handel	*L'Harmonieux Forgeron*	piano solo	1866
T23	Gounod	*Noël*	women's voices, orchestra	1866
T24	Massé	*Le Fils du brigadier*	vocal score	1867
T25	Saint-Saëns	*Le Timbre d'argent*	vocal score	1867
T26	Thomas	*Mignon*	piano solo	1867

	Composer	Work	Transcribed for	Date
T27	Mozart	L'oca del Cairo	piano solo	1867
T28	–	Chants des Pyrénées	voice and piano	1867
T29	Thomas	Mignon	piano duet	1868
T30	Thomas	Hamlet	piano solo	1868
T31	Thalberg	L'Art du chant	piano solo	1868
T32	Thalberg	L'Art du chant	piano duet	1868
T33	Saint-Saëns	Piano Concerto no. 2	two pianos	1868
T34	Thomas	Hamlet	piano duet	1869
T35	Gounod	Méditation	piano duet	1869
T36	Ritter	Les Courriers	piano duet	1869
T37	Saint-Saëns	Introduction et rondo capriccioso	violin and piano	1870
T38	Gounod	Gallia	piano duet	1871
T39	Saint-Saëns	Piano Concerto no. 2	piano solo	1871
T40	Gounod	Seconde Méditation	violin and piano or harmonium	1872
T41	Gounod	La Colombe, Entr'acte	violin or cello, harmonium and piano	1872
T42	Gounod	Roméo et Juliette	orchestration	1872
T43	Gounod	"Temple ouvre-toi"	piano solo	1872
T44	Ascher	Mazurka des traîneaux	orchestra	1873
T45	Schumann	Six Études en forme de canon	piano duet	1873
T46	Gounod	Jeanne d'Arc	vocal score	1873
T47	Gounod	Jeanne d'Arc	piano solo	1873
T48	Gounod	Philémon et Baucis, suite	orchestra	1874
T49	Gounod	Chanson du printemps	unknown	1874
T50	Massenet	Scènes hongroises	piano solo	1875
T51	Massenet	Scènes de bal	piano solo	1875
T52	Massenet	Sarabande espagnole	piano solo	1875
T53	Gounod	La Nuit	piano solo	?
T54	Gounod	Prière du soir	?	?
T55		La Madeleine	voice	?

APPENDIX C

Personalia

About, Edmond (1828–1885). Writer and journalist. He met Bizet through Offenbach and again in Rome in 1858 when he was assigned by the French government to report on Italian affairs.

Adenis, Jules (1823–1900). Prolific writer of plays and librettos who contributed to *La Jolie Fille de Perth*, and also wrote librettos for Guiraud and Massenet.

Auber, Daniel-François-Esprit (1782–1871). Successful composer of opéra-comique who was Director of the Paris Conservatoire from 1842 until his death. His *La Muette de Portici* (1828) was his most successful grand opera. Bizet was no admirer of his music.

Barbier, Jules (1825–1901). Playwright and librettist whose greatest successes were achieved in collaboration with Michel Carré. Bizet's setting of their *La Guzla de l'Émir* is lost. Barbier provided verse for some of Bizet's posthumously published songs, some of which appeared in *Seize Mélodies*.

Barthe, Gratien-Norbert, *dit* Adrien (1828–1898). Composer who won the Prix de Rome in 1854 and despite winning the Prix Rodrigues in competition with Bizet remained his friend. He later taught at the Conservatoire.

Benoist, François-Joseph (1794–1878). Organist and composer, teacher of Saint-Saëns, Bizet and Franck. He won the Prix de Rome in 1815.

Berlioz, Hector (1803–1869). Composer and conductor whose later works greatly impressed Bizet, especially *L'Enfance du Christ* and *Les Troyens*. Bizet acted as rehearsal pianist for the former work in 1863.

Berton, Pierre (1842–1912). Actor and playwright whose posthumous memoir includes a record of his friendship with Bizet from 1860 on.

Bizet, Adolphe-Amand (1810–1886). Composer and singing teacher, Bizet's father. He was trained as a *coiffeur* but moved to music on marrying into a musical family. His presence in Bizet's life was without any marked influence upon his son's career.

Bizet, Aimée (1815–1861). Bizet's mother. A talented pianist who took on most of her son's early education, she played an important part in his adolescence and followed his studies closely. Her early death created a definite void in her son's life.

Blau, Édouard (1836–1906). Librettist of *La Coupe du Roi de Thulé,* who later wrote librettos, usually with partners, for Lalo, Franck and Massenet.

Busnach, William (1832–1907). A cousin of Geneviève Bizet through the Rodrigues family, he was a journalist and theatre manager who wrote the librettos of operettas by Lecocq, Offenbach and others, including two for Bizet.

Capoul, Victor (1839–1924). Lyric tenor to whom Bizet dedicated *Douce Mer.* He sang at the Opéra-Comique throughout the 1860s and was best known for his impersonation of Wilhelm Meister in *Mignon.*

Carafa, Michel (1787–1872). Composer of Neapolitan origin who came to Paris in 1827 as a friend of Rossini. His success in opéra-comique led to his election to the Institut, in which office he was much scorned by Bizet and his friends.

Carré, Michel (1822–1872). Prolific librettist often in collaboration with Jules Barbier, especially for Gounod and Thomas. With Cormon he wrote *Les Pêcheurs de perles* for Bizet.

Carvalho, Léon (1825–1897). One of the most active opera directors in Paris, who ran the Théâtre-Lyrique and later the Opéra-Comique with a mixture of bold enterprise and blatant crowd-pleasing. He was responsible for getting Bizet to write three operas (*Les Pêcheurs de perles, Ivan I,* and *La Jolie Fille de Perth*) and the incidental music to Daudet's *L'Arlésienne.*

Carvalho, Caroline (1827–1895). Soprano. Born Caroline Miolan, she had a highly successful career in the 1850s and 1860s as a coloratura soprano whom Bizet greatly admired. She married Léon Carvalho in 1853. She never sang in any Bizet opera, but created some of Gounod's leading roles.

Choudens, Antoine de (1825–1888). Music publisher who set up in business in 1844 but was not prominent until he secured Gounod's *Faust* in 1859. Thereafter he published much of Gounod and all Bizet's stage works. He strongly promoted Bizet's music in the 1880s. His son Antony was Bizet's pupil.

Clapisson, Louis (1808–1866). Composer ridiculed by Bizet and his friends for the feebleness of his music, especially since he was a Member of the Institut. One or two of his comic operas enjoyed prolonged success. His notable collection of early instruments was sold to the Conservatoire in 1861.

Cohen, Jules (1835–1901). Fellow-student with Bizet at the Conservatoire, he had some success in opéra-comique and was favoured by Napoléon III. Bizet was uncharitable about his connections with bankers and aristocrats.

Colin, Charles-Joseph (1832–1881). Composer and oboist, winner with Bizet of the Prix de Rome in 1857. Bizet tired of his company in Rome. He later taught the oboe at the Conservatoire.

Colonne, Edouard (1838–1910). Violinist and conductor who established the Concert National in 1873, later known as the Concerts Colonne. He twice conducted Bizet's Second Symphony and also conducted the revivals of *L'Arlésienne* in 1885.

Cormon, Eugène (1810–1903). Playwright and librettist who wrote the libretto of *Les Pêcheurs de perles* with Michel Carré and innumerable works for other composers.

Crépet, Etienne-Eugène (1827–1892). Editor of various journals, including the *Revue nationale et étrangère,* which published Bizet's only article in 1867. He discussed writing an opera with Bizet named *Rama,* but it came to nothing. His wife was a singer and a member of the Garcia family.

Daudet, Alphonse (1840–1897). Provençal writer and journalist for whose play *L'Arlésienne* Bizet provided incidental music in 1872. His novel *Sapho* was the basis of Massenet's opera of that name.

David, Félicien (1810–1876). Composer whose participation in the Saint-Simonian movement led to his voyages in the Middle East, which in turn led to his success as the purveyor of exotic music, of which the most successful was *Le Désert* (1844). Bizet was considerably drawn to his style and modelled *Vasco de Gama* on his *Christophe Colomb*.

David, Samuel (1836–1895). Organist and composer who won the Prix de Rome in 1858. Bizet found his company irksome, but he went on to have a successful career as composer and teacher.

Delaborde, Eraïm-Miriam (1839–1913). Virtuoso pianist, supposedly the natural son of Valentin Alkan. Bizet was impressed by his playing, especially of the pedal-piano. In 1873 he became a professor at the Conservatoire and was close to both Bizet and his wife, to whom he was briefly engaged after Bizet's death.

De Leuven, Adolphe (1800–1884). Of Swedish birth, he was a prolific librettist who became Director of the Opéra-Comique in 1862. He was more conservative than his colleague Du Locle and is said to have resigned in 1874 in protest at the approaching staging of *Carmen*.

Delibes, Léo (1836–1891). Composer who studied at the Conservatoire with Bizet but never competed for the Prix de Rome. His early career was successful in operetta, but his chief success was in ballet (*Coppélia* and *Sylvia*). He was chorus master at the Théâtre-Lyrique for the production of *Les Pêcheurs de perles*.

Deloffre, Louis-Michel-Adolphe (1817–1876). He conducted more of Bizet's music in the composer's lifetime than anyone else, being the main staff conductor first at the Théâtre-Lyrique and then at the Opéra-Comique at the time of four opera premières, including *Carmen*.

Delsarte, François (1811–1871). Bizet's uncle. As a singer he was led by certain theories about voice production to attach himself to older styles and to the revival of French music of the eighteenth century and earlier. He was also devoted to the music of the Catholic Church.

Diaz, Eugène (1837–1901). Son of the famous painter Narcisse Diaz, he was a friend of Bizet's at the Conservatoire. His main successes were *Le Roi Candaule* in 1865 and as winner of the competition for settings of *La Coupe du Roi de Thulé*.

Didier, Jules (1831–1914). Landscape painter, winner of the Prix de Rome in 1857. He was Bizet's travelling companion on trips around Rome and Naples in the summer of 1859. One of his best-known paintings showed the departure of Gambetta by balloon from besieged Paris in 1870.

Dubois, Paul (1829–1905). He won the Prix de Rome for sculpture and was Bizet's travelling companion on their trip to Naples in 1859. He carved the bust on Bizet's tomb.

Du Locle, Camille (1832–1903). Nephew of Émile Perrin and the theatre director responsible for commissioning both *Djamileh* and *Carmen* for the Opéra-Comique. He collaborated on the libretto of Verdi's *Aida*.

Galabert, Edmond (?1838–?). Son of a wine-grower from Montauban, Galabert came to Paris each year from 1865 to about 1869 to study with Bizet. They became close friends. Galabert published an important record of their correspondence and friendship.

Gallet, Louis (1835–1898). Librettist of *La Coupe du Roi de Thulé*, *Djamileh* and *Geneviève de Paris*. He worked also with Saint-Saëns, Massenet and Bruneau and wrote an affectionate memoir of visits to Bizet at Le Vésinet.

Galli-Marié, Célestine (1840–1905). Mezzo-soprano whose career in Paris began in 1862. She was wholly associated with two of the most successful roles of the period: Thomas's Mignon and Bizet's Carmen, both of which she performed all over Europe.

Gounod, Charles-François (1818–1893). The first major musician in Bizet's life, he encouraged and probably taught Bizet during his Conservatoire years and arranged many transcription engagements through the publisher Choudens. Their relationship cooled in later years but was never completely severed.

Guiraud, Ernest (1837–1892). Both he and his father won the Prix de Rome, Ernest joining Bizet in Rome in 1859. He was probably Bizet's closest friend; he was a good composer and a devoted promoter of Bizet's music after his death. He had a number of operas performed in Paris but is now remembered mostly for his recitatives for *Carmen* and *Les Contes d'Hoffmann*.

Halévy, Fromental (1799–1862). Bizet's composition teacher at the Conservatoire and a major figure in French intellectual circles as Permanent Secretary of the Institut. He also taught Gounod and Saint-Saëns. He was a prolific composer, with a string of successes at the both the Opéra and the Opéra-Comique.

Halévy, Geneviève (1849–1926), younger daughter of Fromental Halévy who married Bizet in 1869. She later married Émile Straus and became a notable society hostess.

Halévy, Ludovic (1834–1908), nephew of Fromental Halévy and collaborator with Bizet as librettist of *Dr Miracle* and *Carmen*. He was a fertile playwright and librettist, working frequently with Offenbach.

Hartmann, Georges (1843–1900). As impresario and publisher he was a major force in the regeneration of French music after the chaos of 1870–71. His main composer was Massenet, but he also published most young French composers, including Bizet and Debussy. His shop in the Boulevard de la Madeleine was a major meeting-place for musicians.

Heim, Eugène (1830– ?). Architect, son of the painter François-Joseph Heim, he won the Prix de Rome in 1857 and travelled to Italy with Bizet. They took a holiday trip together in 1858, but illness and discouragement eventually caused him to abandon architecture and return to Paris earlier than intended.

Heller, Stephen (1813–1888). Pianist and composer of Hungarian birth who studied in Vienna and moved to Paris in 1838. His piano music in the smaller forms was very successful and he was admired and befriended by Berlioz, Bizet and most other French musicians.

Heugel, Jacques-Léopold (1815–1883). Music publisher who set up in business in 1839. He published a number of Bizet's works in the mid-1860s and also employed him extensively as an arranger, especially of the operas of Thomas.

Hugo, Victor (1802–1885). Leading French poet and novelist of his time. He was in self-imposed exile throughout the Second Empire. Bizet set six of his poems to music and at one time contemplated writing an opera on his *Notre-Dame de Paris*.

Joncières, Victorin de (1839–1903). Painter, composer and critic. As a supporter of new music, including that of Wagner, he was a leading voice as critic for *La Liberté*. He and Bizet were friends, but his operas never enjoyed much success.

Lacombe, Paul (1837–1927). Composer who studied by correspondence with Bizet and achieved considerable success with piano and orchestral music. He remained in Carcassonne throughout his life.

Lalo, Édouard (1823–1892). Violinist and composer from Lille whose early career was devoted to chamber music. His orchestral music and concertos were popular in the 1870s and his opera *Le Roi d'Ys* was a success at the Opéra-Comique in 1888.

Lecocq, Charles (1832–1918). Composer of operettas who shared the prize with Bizet for his setting of *Le Docteur Miracle* in 1857, he enjoyed steady success for fifty years without ever aspiring to any higher achievements.

Liszt, Franz (1811–1886). Perhaps the greatest pianist of the age. Born in Hungary, he studied in Vienna and came to Paris in 1823. In Bizet's time his visits to Paris were rare, but he heard Bizet play in 1861 and was astonished at his ability.

Maësen, Léontine de (1835–1906). Belgian soprano who sang Leïla in *Les Pêcheurs de perles* in 1863. She also sang well-known roles such as Marguerite, Gilda and Donna Anna. She gave up her career on her marriage in 1865. Bizet's *Berceuse* was dedicated to her.

Marmontel, Antoine-François (1816–1898). Bizet's piano teacher at the Conservatoire and an important mentor in his early years. His memoirs include an affectionate section on Bizet. He also taught d'Indy and Albeniz.

Massenet, Jules (1842–1912). His career ran closely parallel to Bizet's in the early 1870s when both were producing orchestral suites and both aiming for success in the theatre. After Bizet's death he embarked on a long string of successes in opera, starting with *Le Roi de Lahore* at the Opéra in 1877.

Meilhac, Henri (1831–1897). Prolific librettist for Offenbach and others who collaborated with Ludovic Halévy on the libretto of *Carmen*. One of his librettos is the basis for Strauss's *Fledermaus*.

Musset, Alfred de (1810–1857). Popular poet and author of *Namouna*, from which *Djamileh* was derived. Bizet set two of his poems for his collection *Feuilles d'Album* in 1866.

Nilsson, Christine (1843–1921). Swedish soprano whose debut in Paris was in *La traviata* in 1864. The role of Catherine in *La Jolie Fille de Perth* was intended for her, but she did not sing it. Bizet wrote the song "Tarantelle" for her.

Offenbach, Jacques (1819–1880). Prolific composer of operettas who promoted the prize shared by Bizet and Lecocq in 1857. He embodied the pleasure-loving spirit of the Second Empire. Bizet seems to have had no further contact with him after returning from Rome.

Paladilhe, Emile (1844–1926). He won the Prix de Rome at the age of sixteen and enjoyed immense success on his return to Paris. He was certainly in competition with Bizet, but they were friends. His later career faded and he composed little music over his great span of years.

Pasdeloup, Jules-Etienne (1819–1887). An energetic and enterprising conductor who expanded the public for serious concerts with his series of Concerts Populaires. As a conductor he lacked outstanding gifts, but as an entrepreneur he was unrivalled. *Carmen* was dedicated to him in thanks for the concerts in which Bizet's music had been featured.

Perrin, Emile (1814–1885). Painter and theatre director who managed almost all the important Paris opera houses at one time or another. His rejection of Bizet's *Ivan IV* showed him to be little concerned with younger talent, but he always remained in good odour with the government and had a clear grasp of what the public would pay for.

Reyer, Ernest (1823–1909). Composer and critic who wrote the *feuilleton* in the *Journal des débats* for many years. Bizet was closely involved with the production of his operas *La Statue* and *Erostrate* and was affectionately remembered in his memoirs. His later operas *Sigurd* and *Salammbô* were successful in the later part of his life.

Rodrigues, Jacques-Hippolyte (1812–1898). Brother-in-law of the composer Halévy, he was helpful to Bizet as his niece's husband. He was a financier by profession, but he wrote plays and essays and even music.

Rossini, Gioacchino (1792–1868). Italian composer who lived most of his life in Paris, following his worldwide successes in the 1820s. Bizet met him while still a student at the Conservatoire and occasionally attended his soirées.

Saint-Georges, Jules Henry de (1799–1875). Librettist to almost all the composers of the period, including Bizet. He was a well-known dandy of aristocratic birth and a prolific producer of doggerel rhyme.

Saint-Saëns, Camille (1835–1921). Although not always well disposed to his fellow-musicians, he liked Bizet and enjoyed a close friendship in the last years of the latter's life. Possessing prodigious gifts as a musician, he played an important part in almost all branches of French music for more than fifty years.

Schnetz, Victor (1787–1870). Painter, student of David, who was director of the French Academy in Rome from 1841 to 1846 and again from 1853 to 1866.

Thomas, Ambroise (1811–1896). He never taught Bizet but he fostered his talent and followed his career with interest. After becoming director of the Conservatoire in 1871 he had less time for composition. Bizet arranged both of his successful operas *Mignon* and *Hamlet* for two hands and for four hands.

Trélat, Marie (1837–1914). Soprano who preferred the salon to the stage. With her surgeon husband, she held a salon in which Bizet often appeared as accompanist. He dedicated a number of songs to her.

Verdi, Giuseppe (1813–1901). Although never very happy there, Verdi spent a good deal of time in Paris, where his operas were always popular. Bizet never had a very high opinion of his music, yet he has been accused of imitating him, especially in *Ivan IV*.

Wagner, Richard (1813–1883). The most talked-about composer of the age, hence the common accusation that Bizet was a Wagnerian, which he never was. There is no record that Bizet met Wagner, but he possessed a number of Wagner's scores and understood clearly what Wagnerism was.

Zimmerman, Pierre (1785–1853). Although right at the end of his career as piano teacher at the Conservatoire when Bizet appeared as a student, he appreciated the boy's talent and encouraged him as pianist and composer. Gounod was his son-in-law.

Select Bibliography

For more extensive bibliographies, see Stricker (1999), Lacombe (2000), and *Oxford Bibliographies On Line*.

Bizet Letters

Curtiss (1950) — "Unpublished Letters by Georges Bizet", *Musical Quarterly*, 26 (1950), 375–409. Thirty letters to his wife and her family between 1869 and 1875.

Galabert (1877) — Galabert, E. *Georges Bizet: Souvenirs et Correspondance.* Paris, 1877.

Galabert (1909) — *Lettres à un ami, 1865–1872.* Edited by Edmond Galabert. Paris, 1909. Letters to Edmond Galabert written between 1865 and 1872, with a 51-page memoir by Galabert, discreetly censored.

Ganderax (1907) — *Lettres de Georges Bizet: Impressions de Rome (1857–1860): La Commune (1871).* Preface by Louis Ganderax. Paris, 1907. Seventy-six letters to his family from his time in Rome 1858–60, with ten letters to members of the Halévy family written from Paris during the siege and Commune. Some of the letters have suffered omissions.

Glayman (1989) — Bizet, G. *Lettres (1850–1875).* Edited by Claude Glayman. Paris, 1989. A selection of letters reprinted from earlier collections (1907, 1909, and 1988).

Gounod (1899) — "Lettres à Georges Bizet", *Revue de Paris*, 6 (1899), 677–703. Nineteen letters written by Gounod to Bizet between 1856 and 1873, and one letter from Bizet to Gounod from 1858.

Imbert (1894) — Imbert, H. "Lettres à Paul Lacombe", in *Portraits et études.* Paris, 1894. Contains twenty-two letters from Bizet to Paul Lacombe. There are two editions, one of 213 pages including some letters to Guiraud, one of 197, the latter without some sensitive passages. Page references are to the longer edition.

Wright (1988) — Bizet, G. *Letters in the Nydahl Collection.* Edited by Lesley A. Wright. Stockholm, Sweden, Royal Swedish Academy of Music, 1988. About a hundred letters from all periods of Bizet's life from the collections held by the Stiftelsen Musikkulturens främjande, Stockholm.

Biography and General

Agenda (1836)	*Agenda musical ou indicateur des amateurs, artistes et commerçans en musique pour 1836* (Paris, 1836; repr. Geneva, 1981)
Avant-scène (1980)	*L'avant-scène opéra*, 26 (1989) [*Carmen* issue]
Avant-scène (1982)	*L'avant-scène opéra*, 41 (1982) [*Roméo et Juliette* issue]
Avant-scène (1989)	*L'avant-scène opéra*, 124 (1989) [*Les Pêcheurs de perles* issue]
Baker (1990)	Evan Baker, "The Scene Designs for the First Performance of Bizet's *Carmen*", *19th Century Music*, 13 (1990), 230–242
Baldick (1964)	Robert Baldick, *The Siege of Paris* (London, 1964)
Barzun (2000)	Jacques Barzun, *From Dawn to Decadence* (New York, 2000)
Bellaigue (1890)	Camille Bellaigue, *Georges Bizet, sa vie et ses œuvres* (Paris, 1890)
Berlioz (1972)	Hector Berlioz, *Correspondance générale*, t. i–viii (Paris, 1972–2003)
Berton (1913)	Pierre Berton, *Souvenirs de la vie de théâtre* (Paris, 1913)
Blaze de Bury (1865)	Henri Blaze de Bury, *Meyerbeer: sa vie, ses œuvres et son temps* (Paris, 1865)
Bonnerot (1922)	Jean Bonnerot, *C. Saint-Saëns* (Paris, 1922)
Boschot (1912)	Adolphe Boschot, *La Crépuscule d'un Romantique: Hector Berlioz 1842–1869* (Paris, 1912)
Brancour (1913)	René Brancour, *La Vie et l'œuvre de Georges Bizet* (Paris, 1913)
Briggs (1995)	A. D. P. Briggs, "Did *Carmen* Come from Russia?", English National Opera programme (1995–96)
Champavier (1890)	Maurice Champavier, "L'Âme d'Hérold", *Revue illustrée*, 5/10 (June–December 1890), 355
Changeur (1951)	J.-P. Changeur, "Ivan IV", *La Vie bordelaise* (October–November 1951)
Chantavoine (1933)	Jean Chantavoine, "Quelques Inédits de Georges Bizet", *Le Ménestrel*, 95 (4 August–22 September 1933)
Chantavoine (1951)	Jean Chantavoine, "Les inédits de Bizet ou le culte des maîtres en France", *La Vie musicale*, 2:11–12 (December 1951–January 1952)
Charlton (2010)	David Charlton, "Opera as Poetry: *Djamileh* and the Ironies of Orientalism", in *Art and Ideology in European Opera: Essays in Honour of Julian Rushton*, ed. Cowgill, Cooper and Brown (Woodbridge, 2010), 303–326
Christiansen (1984)	Rupert Christiansen, *Tales of the New Babylon* (London, 1984)
Clamon (1938)	J. Clamon, "Bizet et le folklore provençal", *Revue de musicologie*, 22/68 (1938), 150–153
Clément (1877)	Félix Clément and Pierre Larousse, *Dictionnaire lyrique*, 3rd supplement (Paris, 1877)
Cooper (1938)	Martin Cooper, *Georges Bizet* (London, 1938)
Comettant (1869)	Oscar Commettant, *La Musique, les Musiciens et les Instruments de Musique à l'Exposition Internationale de 1867* (Paris, 1869)
Condé (2009)	Gérard Condé, *Charles Gounod* (Paris, 2009)
Curtiss (1954)	Mina Curtiss, "Bizet, Offenbach and Rossini", *Musical Quarterly*, 40 (1954), 350–359
Curtiss (1958)	Mina Curtiss, *Bizet and His World* (New York, 1958)

Dean (1947)	Winton Dean, "An Unfinished Opera by Bizet", *Music & Letters*, 28 (October 1947), 347–363
Dean (1948)	Winton Dean, *Bizet* (London, 1948)
Dean (1955)	Winton Dean, "Bizet's *Ivan IV*", *Fanfare for Ernest Newman*, ed. van Thal (London, 1955), 58–85, reprinted in Winton Dean, *Essays on Opera* (Oxford, 1990), 262–280
Dean (1960)	Winton Dean, "Bizet's Self-Borrowings", *Music & Letters*, 41 (July 1960), 238–244
Dean (1965-1)	Winton Dean, *Bizet*, 2nd ed. (London, 1965)
Dean (1965-2)	Winton Dean, "The True *Carmen*?", *Musical Times*, 106 (November 1965), 846–855
Dean (1973)	Winton Dean, "The Corruption of *Carmen*: The Perils of Pseudomusicology", *Musical Newsletter*, 3/4 (1973)
Dean (1975)	Winton Dean, *Bizet*, 3rd ed. (London, 1975)
Delmas (1930)	Marc Delmas, *Georges Bizet* (Paris, 1930)
del Sarte (1938)	Maxime Réal del Sarte, "Souvenirs sur Georges Bizet", *Revue de musicologie*, 22 (November 1938), 132-134
de Solliers (1989)	Jean de Solliers, "Commentaire littéraire et musical", *Bizet Carmen*, *L'Avant-Scène Opéra*, 26 (1989), 23–94
Dratwicki (2005)	Alexandre Dratwicki, "Les 'Envois de Rome' des compositeurs pensionnaires de la Villa Médicis (1804–1914)", *Revue de musicologie*, 91/1 (2005), 108
Exposition (1938)	*Exposition Georges Bizet (1838–1875) au Théâtre National de l'Opéra* (Paris, 1938)
Galabert (1877)	Edmond Galabert, *Georges Bizet: Souvenirs et Correspondance* (Paris, 1877)
Gallet (1891)	Louis Gallet, *Notes d'un librettiste* (Paris, 1891)
Gauthier-Villars (1912)	Henry Gauthier-Villars [recte Emile Vuillermoz], *Bizet: biographie critique* (Paris, 1912)
Gelma (1949)	Eugène Gelma, "La Mort du musicien Georges Bizet", *Cahiers de Psychiatrie*, 2 (Strasbourg, 1949)
Girard (1990)	William Eugene Girard, *A Performing Version of Georges Bizet's "La Maison du Docteur"* (Ann Arbor, 1990)
Hahn (1946)	Reynaldo Hahn, *Thèmes variés* (Paris, 1946)
Halévy (1905)	Ludovic Halévy, "La Millième Représentation de *Carmen*", *Le Théâtre*, 1 (1905), 5–14
Halévy (1938)	Daniel Halévy, "Souvenirs de famille", *Revue de musicologie*, 22 (November 1938), 129–132
Holoman (2004)	D. Kern Holoman, *The Société des Concerts du Conservatoire* (Berkeley, 2004)
Huebner (1993)	Steven Huebner, "Carmen as *corrida de toros*", *Journal of Musicological Research*, 13/1–2 (1993), 3–29
Imbert (1894)	Hugues Imbert, *Portraits et Études* (Paris, 1894)
Imbert (1902)	Hugues Imbert, *Médaillons contemporains* (Paris, 1902)
Irvine (1994)	Demar Irvine, *Massenet: A Chronicle of His Life and Times* (Portland, 1994)

John (1982)	*Georges Bizet: Carmen*, English National Opera Guide, ed. Nicholas John (London, 1982)
Jordan (1996)	Ruth Jordan, *Fromental Halévy: His Life & Music 1799–1862* (New York, 1996)
Jullien (1892)	Adolphe Jullien, *Musiciens d'aujourd'hui* (Paris, 1892)
Klein (1937)	J.W. Klein, "Bizet's Early Operas", *Music and Letters*, 18 (1937), 169–175
Klein (1940)	J.W. Klein, "Bizet's *L'Arlésienne*", *Musical Opinion*, 12 (1940), 53–54
Klein (1957)	J.W. Klein, "Bizet's *Ivan IV*", *Chesterian*, 32/191 (1957), 1–7
Klein (1959)	J.W. Klein, "The Spoken Dialogue in *Carmen*", *Chesterian*, 33 (Spring 1959), 109–113
Klein (1960)	J.W. Klein, "Nietzsche's Attitude to Bizet", *Music Review*, 21 (1960), 220
Klein (1964)	J.W. Klein, "The Centenary of Bizet's *The Pearl Fishers*", *Music Review*, 26/4 (1964)
Klein (1968)	J.W. Klein, "Bizet's Tragic Son", *Music & Letters*, 49 (1968), 357–366
Klein (1974)	J.W. Klein, "Reflections on Bizet's *Djamileh*", *Music Review*, 35 (1974), 293–300
Lacombe (1996)	Hervé Lacombe, *Georges Bizet: Les Pêcheurs de perles: Dossier de presse parisienne* (Heilbronn, 1996)
Lacombe (1997)	Hervé Lacombe, *Les Voies de l'opéra français au XIXe siècle* (Paris, 1997)
Lacombe (2000)	Hervé Lacombe, *Georges Bizet: Naissance d'une identité créatrice* (Paris, 2000)
Lacombe (2001)	Hervé Lacombe, *The Keys to French Opera in the Nineteenth Century* (Berkeley, 2001)
Lamothe (2008)	Peter Lamothe, *Theater Music in France, 1864–1914*, Ph.D. diss., University of North Carolina, 2008
Landormy (1924)	Paul Landormy, *Bizet* (Paris, 1924)
Laparra (1935)	Raoul Laparra, *Bizet et l'Espagne* (Paris, 1935)
Laudon (2012)	Robert Tallant Laudon, *The Dramatic Symphony: Issues and Explorations from Berlioz to Liszt* (Hillsdale, 2012)
Lionnet (1888)	A. et H. Lionnet, *Souvenirs et anecdotes* (Paris, 1888)
Locke (1998)	Ralph P. Locke, "Cutthroats and Casbah Dancers, Muezzins and Timeless Sands", *19th Century Music*, 22 (1998), 37–38
Locke (2009-1)	Ralph P. Locke, *Musical Exoticism: Images and Reflections* (Cambridge, 2009)
Locke (2009-2)	Ralph Locke, "Spanish Local Color in Bizet's *Carmen*", in *Stage Music and Cultural Transfer: Paris 1830 to 1914*, ed. Everist and Fauser (Chicago, 2009), 316–360
Lu and Dratwicki (2011)	Julia Lu and Alexandre Dratwicki, ed., *Le Concours du prix de Rome de musique (1803–1968)* (Lyon, 2011)
Macdonald (2008)	Hugh Macdonald, "The Musicians' Arrondissement", in *Beethoven's Century: Essays on Composers and Themes* (Rochester, 2008), 183–192

Macdonald (2009)	Hugh Macdonald, "Georges Hartmann: The Ideal Publisher", *Journal of Musicological Research* (October 2009), 295–311
Macdonald (2010-1)	Hugh Macdonald, "Bizet's Aspirations to the Opéra", in *Le Répertoire de l'Opéra de Paris (1871–2009)*, ed. M. Noiray and S. Serre (Paris, 2010), 85–90
Macdonald (2010-2)	Hugh Macdonald, "Bizet's *La Jolie Fille de Perth* in Print and in Performance", *John Ward and His Magnificent Collection*, ed. Hollis (Beverly Hills, 2010), 93–105
Macdonald (2012)	Hugh Macdonald, "Bizet's Second Symphony", *Noter, annoter, éditer la musique: mélanges offerts à Catherine Massip*, ed. Reynaud and Schneider (Paris, 2012), 539–550
Malherbe (1895)	Charles Malherbe, "Une trouvaille musicale", *Le Figaro* (17 February 1895)
Malherbe (1951)	Henry Malherbe, *Carmen* (Paris, 1951)
Maréchal (1907)	Henri Maréchal, *Paris, souvenirs d'un musicien* (Paris, 1907)
Marix (1938)	Thérèse Marix, "Séjour de Bizet au Vésinet", *Revue de musicologie*, 22 (November 1938), 142–150
Marmontel (1881)	Antoine Marmontel, *Symphonistes et virtuoses* (Paris, 1881)
Massenet (1992)	Jules Massenet, *Mes Souvenirs*, ed. Gérard Condé (Paris, 1992)
Mastrigli (1888)	Leopoldo Mastrigli, *Giorgio Bizet: la sua vita e le sue opere* (Rome, 1888)
McClary (1992)	Susan McClary, *Georges Bizet: Carmen* (Cambridge, 1992)
Mordey (2007)	Delphine Mordey, "Auber's Horses: *L'Année terrible* and Apocalyptic Narratives", *19th Century Music*, 30/3 (Spring 2007), 213–229
Mortier (1876)	Arnold Mortier, *Les Soirées parisiennes de 1875 par un Monsieur de l'orchestre* (Paris, 1876)
Moser (1935)	Françoise Moser, *Vie et Aventures de Céleste Mogador* (Paris, 1935)
Muller (1976)	Monique Muller, *L'Œuvre pianistique originale de Georges Bizet* (Yverdon, 1976)
Noske (1970)	Frits Noske, *French Song from Berlioz to Duparc* (New York, 1970)
Parker (1926)	D. C. Parker, *George Bizet: His Life and Works* (London, 1926)
Pigot (1886)	Charles Pigot, *Georges Bizet et son œuvre* (Paris, 1886)
Pigot (1911)	Charles Pigot, *Georges Bizet et son œuvre*, 2nd ed. (Paris, 1911)
Poupet (1965)	Michel Poupet, "Les Infidélités posthumes de partitions lyriques de Georges Bizet", *Revue de musicologie*, 51 (1965), 170–200
Poupet (1976)	Michel Poupet, "A propos de deux fragments de la partition originale de *Carmen*", *Revue de musicologie*, 62 (1976), 139–143
Poupet (1977)	Michel Poupet, "A propos de la mort de Bizet: une lettre inédite de Célestine Galli-Marié", *Revue de musicologie*, 63 (1977), 148–153
Poupet (1982)	Michel Poupet, "Gounod et Bizet", *Avant-Scène Opéra*, 41 (May–June 1982), 106–117
Revue (1938)	*Revue de musicologie*, 22 (November 1938) [Bizet issue]
Reyer (1875)	Ernest Reyer, *Notes de musique* (Paris, 1875)
Reyer (1909)	Ernest Reyer, *Quarante ans de musique* (Paris, 1909)
Robert (1965)	Frédéric Robert, *Georges Bizet* (Paris, 1965)

Rogeboz-Malfroy (1994)	Elisabeth Rogeboz-Malfroy, *Ambroise Thomas ou la tentation du lyrique* (Besançon, 1994)
Rose (2013)	Michael Rose, *The Birth of an Opera* (New York, 2013)
Roy (1983)	Jean Roy, *Bizet* (Paris, 1983)
Sainte-Beuve (1864)	C.-A. Sainte-Beuve, *Nouveaux Lundis*, ii (Paris, 1864)
Saint-Saëns (1899)	Camille Saint-Saëns, *Portraits et souvenirs* (Paris, 1899)
Saint-Saëns (1913)	Camille Saint-Saëns, *Ecole Buissonnière* (Paris, 1913)
Schwandt (1991)	Christoph Schwandt, *Georges Bizet* (Reinbek, 1991)
Séré (1921)	Octave Séré [Jean Poueigh], *Musiciens français d'aujourd'hui* (Paris, 1921)
Shanet (1958)	Howard Shanet, "Bizet's Suppressed Symphony", *Musical Quarterly*, 44 (1958), 461–476
Sonzogno (1995)	*Casa Musicale Sonzogno: Cronologie, saggi, testimonianze* (2 vols), ed. Morini and Ostali (Milan, 1995)
Soubies (1893)	Albert Soubies and Charles Malherbe, *Histoire de l'Opéra-Comique, La Seconde Salle Favart 1860–1887* (Paris, 1893)
Stricker (1999)	Rémy Stricker, *Georges Bizet* (Paris, 1999)
Tiersot (1927)	Julien Tiersot, "Bizet and Spanish Music", *Musical Quarterly*, 13 (1927), 566–581
Vallas (1938)	Léon Vallas, "Georges Bizet et Vincent d'Indy", *Revue de musicologie*, 22 (November 1938), 134–137
Vittu (2005)	Mathilde Vittu, *Études de composition sous la direction de Georges Bizet* (Wavre, 2005)
Voss (1899)	Paul Voss, *Georges Bizet* (Leipzig, 1899)
Walsh (1981)	T. J. Walsh, *Second Empire Opera: the Théâtre Lyrique, Paris, 1851–1870* (London, 1981)
Westrup (1966)	Jack Westrup, "Bizet's *La Jolie Fille de Perth*", *Essays Presented to Egon Wellesz*, ed. Westrup (Oxford, 1966), 157–170
Wilder (1875)	Victor Wilder, "Georges Bizet : esquisse biographique", *Le Ménestrel*, 41 (July 1875)
Wlaschin (2004)	Ken Wlaschin, *Encyclopedia of Opera on Screen* (New Haven, 2004)
Wright (1978)	Lesley A. Wright, "A New Source for *Carmen*", *19th Century Music*, 2 (July 1978), 61–71
Wright (1981)	Lesley Alison Wright, *Bizet before Carmen*, Ph. D. diss., University of Michigan, 1981
Wright (1982)	Lesley A. Wright, "A Musical Commentary", *Carmen*, English National Opera Guide (London, 1982), 19–36
Wright (1986)	Lesley A. Wright, "*Les Pêcheurs de perles*: Before the Première", *Studies in Music*, 20 (1986), 27–45
Wright (1992)	Lesley A. Wright, "Bias, Influence, and Bizet's *Prix de Rome*", *19th Century Music*, 15/3 (1992), 215–228
Wright (1993)	Lesley A. Wright, "Gounod and Bizet: A Study in Musical Paternity", *Journal of Musicological Research*, 13 (1993), 49–66
Wright (2001)	Lesley A. Wright, *Carmen: Dossier de presse parisienne (1875)* (Weinsberg, 2001)

Wright (2007)   Lesley A. Wright, "Une critique revisitée : réflexions sur l'accueil de *Carmen* à Paris en 1883", in *Musique, Esthétique et Société au XIXe siècle*, ed. Colas, Gétreau and Haine (Wavre, 2007), 187–197

Wright (2011)   Lesley A. Wright, "Bizet et la Prix de Rome : de l'initiation à l'accomplissement", *Le Concours du prix de Rome de musique (1803–1968)*, ed. Lu and Dratwicki (Lyon, 2011), 529–548

Yon (1994)   Jean-Claude Yon, "Les avatars du Cid", *L'Avant-Scène Opéra*, 161 (September–October 1994), 112–119

Library Sigla

F-Pan   Archives nationales, Paris
F-Pmlm   Musée de lettres et de manuscrits, Paris
F-Pn   Bibliothèque nationale de France, Département de la Musique, Paris
F-Po   Bibliothèque-Musée de l'Opéra, Paris
GB-Lbl   British Library, London
S-Ssm   Stiftelsen Musikkulturens Främjande, Stockholm
US-Bp   Boston Public Library
US-CAh   Houghton Library, Harvard University
US-NHb   Beinecke Library, Yale University
US-NYp   New York Public Library
US-STu   Stanford University Library
US-Wc   Library of Congress, Washington

Works Index

Entries followed by **(T)** in **bold** denote transcriptions.

100 morceaux for piano-scandé **(T)**, 19, 268
À une fleur, 107, 262
Abandonnée, L', 175, 264
Absence, 169–70, 199, 263
Adieux à Suzon, 107, 262
Adieux de l'hôtesse arabe, 33, 116–19, 199, 262
Aimons, rêvons, 163, 200, 264
Amour-peintre, L', 48, 258
Ange et Tobie, L', 31, 260
Après l'hiver, 116–118, 199, 262
Arlésienne, L', 36, 86, 153, 174, 177, 191–95, 197–98, 206, 235, 242, 259
Arlésienne, L', suite no. 1, 72, 177, 192–93, 195, 229, 233–34, 236–38, 242, 265
Arlésienne, L', suite no. 2, 193, 233–34, 237, 242
Ascher, *Mazurka des traîneaux* **(T)**, 109, 269
Aubade, 180, 244, 263

Barcarolle, 14, 261
Berceuse sur un vieil air, 144, 198, 263
Brigantine, La, 30, 259

Calendal, 156, 164–65, 174, 191, 258
Caprice original, 1ᵉʳ, 16, 266
Caprice original, 2ᵐᵉ, 16, 266
Carmen, 8, 17, 24, 27, 49, 58, 70, 87, 97, 102, 128, 161, 163, 174–75, 177, 188, 190, 197, 201–202, 204, 207–29, 231–38, 240, 246–49, 256
Carmen saeculare, 51–52, 260
Casilda, 25, 266
Chanson d'avril, 169–70, 199, 263
Chanson de la rose, 239, 264
Chanson du fou, 145, 198, 263
Chanson du rouet, 33, 238, 259
Chant d'amour, 169–70, 199, 242–43, 263
Chants des Pyrénées **(T)**, 126, 269
Chants du Rhin, 13, 105–106, 108, 266
Chasse d'Ossian, La, 60, 152, 265
Chasse fantastique, 105, 266
Chevalier enchanté, Le, 31, 260
Chœur d'étudiants, 30, 259

Clarisse Harlowe, 89, 164–165, 174, 179–180, 200, 202, 239, 244, 257
Clovis et Clotilde, 33, 50, 75, 260
Coccinelle, La, 143, 145, 198, 243, 262
Colibri, Le, 200, 263
Conte, 175, 264
Coupe du Roi de Thulé, La, 147, 149, 154–55, 157–63, 175, 178, 182, 200, 202, 223, 238–39, 241, 245, 257

David, 32–33, 75, 260
De ce gaillard entretien, 195, 261
Djamileh, 33, 57, 68, 114, 163, 174–75, 177, 180–91, 198, 226, 229, 239, 243, 247–48, 256
Don Procopio, 40, 42–46, 48–50, 54, 75–76, 95, 131, 234, 243–45, 255
Don Quichotte, 46, 258
Don Rodrigue, 202–205, 207, 235, 257
Docteur Miracle, Le, 20, 24–25, 33, 42–43, 73, 245, 255
Douce Mer, 116–18, 199, 262
Doute, Le, 239, 264
Duo for bassoon and cello, 208–209, 267
Duo for oboe and piano, 208–209, 267

Ecce sacerdos, 260
Enterrement de Clapisson, L', 112, 266
Esmeralda, 45–46, 258
Esprit saint, 151, 199, 263
Étude, 17, 266

Feuilles d'album, 107, 145, 240, 248
Foi, l'Espérance et la Charité, La, 20, 262
Fuite, La, 169, 261

Gascon, Le, 175, 244, 264
Geneviève de Paris, 227, 239, 259
Golfe de Baïa, Le, 32, 98, 238, 259
Gounod, *Ave Maria* **(T)**, 93, 268
Gounod, *Chanson du printemps* **(T)**, 269
Gounod, *Colombe, La* **(T)**, 269
Gounod, *Faust* **(T)**, 58, 69, 268

· 285 ·

Gounod, *Gallia* **(T)**, 178–79, 269
Gounod, *Jeanne d'Arc* **(T)**, 205, 207, 269
Gounod, *Méditation* **(T)**, 269
Gounod, *Mireille* **(T)**, 86, 268
Gounod, *Noël* **(T)**, 109, 268
Gounod, *Nonne sanglante, La* **(T)**, 19, 58, 268
Gounod, *Nuit, La* **(T)**, 269
Gounod, *Philémon et Baucis* **(T)**, 69, 208, 269
Gounod, *Prière du soir* **(T)**, 179, 269
Gounod, *Reine de Saba, La* **(T)**, 58, 64, 268
Gounod, *Roméo et Juliette* **(T)**, 196–97, 269
Gounod, *Seconde Méditation* **(T)**, 269
Gounod, *Six Chœurs célèbres* **(T)**, 108, 208, 268
Gounod, Symphony no. 1 **(T)**, 19, 21, 268
Gounod, Symphony no. 2 **(T)**, 20, 69–70, 108, 268
Gounod, *Temple, ouvre-toi* **(T)**, 179, 269
Gounod, *Tobie* **(T)**, 19, 108, 268
Grande Valse de concert, 20, 266
Grillon, Le, 107–108, 117, 262
Grisélidis, 154, 156, 164–65, 174–75, 179, 193, 200, 202, 219, 221, 239, 244, 257
Guitare, 107–108, 262
Guzla de l'émir, La, 64, 66–68, 70, 72, 75–76, 81, 138, 182, 184, 258

Handel, *Harmonious Blacksmith* **(T)**, 108–09, 268
Herminie, 31, 260
Hymne de la paix, 123, 259

Ivan IV, 32, 49, 68, 85–91, 93–102, 104, 108–109, 111, 116, 128, 138, 148, 157, 177, 194, 203–204, 220, 233–35, 239, 244–45, 248, 255

J'aime l'amour, 263
Je n'en dirai rien, 262
Jeux d'enfants, 100, 176–78, 182, 235, 248, 267
Jolie Fille de Perth, La, 27, 44, 57, 96, 116–17, 120, 124–36, 138–40, 148, 156, 163, 198, 208, 220, 233–35, 237–38, 240–42, 245, 248, 256

Lamento, 263
Loyse de Montfort, 31, 260

Maison du docteur, La, 20–21, 24, 42, 245, 255
Malbrough s'en va-t-en guerre, 127–28, 140, 195, 257
Marine, 145, 266
Matin, Le, 198, 263
Massé, *Le Fils du brigadier* **(T)**, 119, 268
Massenet, *Sarabande espagnole* **(T)**, 269
Massenet, *Scènes de bal* **(T)**, 179, 269
Massenet, *Scènes hongroises* **(T)**, 179, 269
Ma vie a son secret, 143, 179, 198, 262
Méditation religieuse, 25, 267
Mort s'avance, La, 147, 150, 259
Morts pour la France, 170, 259
Mozart, *Don Giovanni* **(T)**, 105, 268
Mozart, *Oca del Cairo, L'* **(T)**, 269

Nicolai, *Joyeuses Commères de Windsor, Les* **(T)**, 69–70, 114, 268
Nicolas Flamel, 91, 258
Noces de Prométhée, Les, 123–24, 154, 259
Nocturne, 1ère [in D], 20, 145–46, 266
Nocturne, 1ère [in F], 20, 145, 266
Noé, 65, 70, 157, 164, 175, 239, 242–43, 256
Notre Rosa, 125, 260
N'oublions pas, 160–61, 264
Nuit, La, 180, 264
Nymphes des bois, Les, 180, 200, 261

Ouverture, 20, 22–23, 244, 265
Ouvre ton cœur, 97, 108, 262

Parisina, 40, 258
Pascal, *Cabaret des amours, Les* **(T)**, 69–70, 268
Pastel, 200, 239
Pastorale, 143–144, 198, 263
Patrie, 203, 205–208, 229, 236, 265
Pêcheurs de perles, Les, 27, 32, 39, 42, 57, 60, 68, 72–83, 85, 88, 90, 95–96, 101, 114, 120, 126, 135, 138, 179, 183, 198, 205, 210, 213, 216, 220, 229, 232–34, 240–42, 247, 255
Petite Marguerite, 21, 239, 262
Petite Suite, 177–178, 195, 198, 234, 265
Pianiste chanteur, Le **(T)**, 92–93, 105, 268
Portrait, Le, 200, 239, 264
Pourquoi pleurer?, 157, 239, 263
Préludes, 14, 266
Prêtresse, La, 89, 179, 257

Quatre Coins, Les, 265
Qui donc t'aimera mieux?, 157, 239, 263

Rama, 164, 174, 258
Retour, Le, 180, 200, 261
Retour de Virginie, Le, 31, 75, 260
Rêve de la bien-aimée, 144–45, 198, 200, 241, 245, 263
Rêvons, 163, 200, 261
Reyer, *Érostrate* **(T)**, 66–67, 69–70, 268
Reyer, *La Statue* **(T)**, 58, 268
Ritter, *Courriers, Les* **(T)**, 269
Roma, see Symphonie no. 2
Romance, 14, 21, 262
Romance sans paroles, 14, 25, 266
Rose d'amour, 107–108, 262
Rose et l'abeille, La, 21, 239, 262

Saint-Jean de Pathmos, 91–92, 260
Saint-Saëns, *Introduction et rondo capriccioso* **(T)**, 151, 269
Saint-Saëns, Piano Concerto no. 2 **(T)**, 151, 269
Saint-Saëns, *Le Timbre d'argent* **(T)**, 119, 268
Scènes bohémiennes, 177, 208, 235, 237–38, 265
Schumann, *Six Études* **(T)**, 178, 269

Seize Mélodies, 157–58, 160–61, 179, 200, 239, 243
Sérénade, 199–200, 262, 263
Simplicité, 178, 267
Sirène, La, 161–63, 263
Si vous aimez, 180, 264
Sol-si-ré-pif-pan, 195, 258
Sonnet, 107, 262
Souvenirs de l'Auvergne, 266
Symphony no. 1, 20–23, 25, 44, 60, 115, 152–53, 232–33, 235, 238, 244, 265
Symphony no. 2, 21, 45, 48, 52, 60–61, 71, 80, 115–17, 142, 147, 149, 151–54, 156, 179, 194–95, 205, 234, 236–39, 244, 265

Tarentelle, 147, 150–51, 198, 261, 263
Te Deum, 38–40, 42, 44, 54, 76, 104, 227, 245, 259
Templiers, Les, 148, 186, 239, 258
Thalberg, L'Art du chant **(T)**, 93, 269
Thème, 14–16, 266
Thomas, Hamlet **(T)**, 138–39, 269
Thomas, Mignon **(T)**, 119, 138–39, 268–69

Tonnelier de Nuremberg, Le, 46–47, 258
Trois duos **(T)**, 26
Trois Esquisses musicales, 25, 267

Ulysse et Circe, 46, 259

Valse, 266
Valse avec chœur, 15, 259
Variations chromatiques, 146–47, 179, 266
Vasco de Gama, 17, 47–51, 59–60, 71–72, 90, 97, 114, 157, 194, 238–39, 259
Vercingétorix, 156, 258
Vieille Chanson, 92, 199, 262
Vingt Mélodies, 151, 198, 200, 236, 239
Vocalise, 14, 262
Vœu, 199, 263
Vous ne priez pas!, 199, 205, 263
Voyage, 180, 200, 263

Wagner, L'Ange **(T)**, 63, 268

Index

About, Edmond, 25, 40–41, 270
À Cœur joie, 245
Adam, Adolphe, 17, 19, 24, 31–32, 34, 62, 148
   Giralda, 17
   Orfa, 85
   Postillon de Longjumeau, Le, 181
   Toréador, Le, 17
Adenis, Jules, 116, 122, 124, 149, 270
Aeschylus, 88
Agoult, Marie d', 12n
Alatri, 46
Albano, 40
Albano, Gaston d', 32
Alboni, Marietta, 149
Alexander II, Tsar, 121
Alexander the Great, 156
Alizard, Louis, 10
Alkan, Charles-Valentin, 12–13, 123, 178, 197, 209, 225
Alkan, Napoléon, 12–13
Amalfi, 47
Ambérieu-en-Bugey, 53
Amsterdam, 244
Anagni, 46
Anderson, June, 241
Antwerp, 91, 139, 236, 240
Anzio, 46
Ariosto
   Orlando furioso, 123
Arles, 36
Arvers, Félix, 143
Ascher, Joseph
   Mazurka des traîneaux, 109, 269
Ascherberg, 243
Assisi, 52
Attila the Hun, 227
Auber, Daniel-François-Esprit, 4, 9–10, 17, 19, 23, 26, 29–32, 48, 51, 87, 112, 123, 173–74, 243, 245, 270
   Fra diavolo, 181, 213
   Lac des fées, Le, 30
   Muette de Portici, La, 4
   Manon Lescaut, 27, 117
Augier, Émile, 18
Augustus, Emperor, 51

Austin, 245
Avignon, 35, 191
Azevedo, Alexis-Jacob, 125

Bach, Johann Sebastian, 29
   Wohltemperirte Clavier, Das, 93
Baden-Baden, 3, 61, 66–67, 70, 85, 89, 176
Balanchine, George, 244
Baltimore, 236
Balzac, Honoré de, 3, 10
Barbier, Jules, 61, 63–64, 67–68, 70, 72, 111, 114, 117, 122, 138, 160, 163, 180, 191, 200, 229, 270
   Cora, 63
   Jeanne d'Arc, 204
Barbizon, 125, 165
Barcelona, 244
Barthe, Adrien, 42, 104, 157, 270
   Fiancée d'Abydos, La, 104
   Judith, 42
Bartlett, Clifford, 242
Barzun, Jacques, 232
Basel, 244
Battu, Léon, 24
Bazille, Auguste, 119
Bazin, François-Emmanuel-Joseph, 10, 23, 34, 65, 157
Beaulieu, Marguerite de, 176, 178
Beaumarchais, Caron de, 41
Beaumont, Alfred, 60, 70
Beauvais, 3, 106, 138, 228
Beecham, Sir Thomas, 238
Beethoven, Ludwig van, 5, 9, 19, 22, 31, 36, 42, 72, 75, 79, 88, 112–13
   Egmont, 192
   Piano Sonata, op. 26, 149
   Symphony no. 5, 112–13
   Symphony no. 6, 31
   Symphony no. 7, 183, 206
   Symphony no. 8, 186
   Symphony no. 9, 206
   Thirty-Two Variations in C minor, 146
Bellaigue, Camille, 246
Bellini, Vincenzo, 5, 93, 149
   Norma, 74, 88
Belwyn-Mills, 241–42

Bénazet, Édouard, 66
Bennett, Joseph, 205
Benoist, François, 13, 270
Benoît-Champy, Adrien-Théodore, 93–94, 155
Bériot, Charles de, 13
Berlin, 88, 167, 241, 243, 248
Berlioz, Hector, x, 3, 5, 9–10, 12, 17–19, 22,
    26–29, 32, 51, 53–54, 61, 64, 66–67, 73,
    82–83, 95, 102, 112–13, 123, 149–50, 211, 228,
    231–32, 270
  Béatrice et Bénédict, 67, 69, 71–72, 113
  Damnation de Faust, La, 10, 27, 50, 72
  Enfance du Christ, L', 27, 73, 75, 81, 100, 139
  Fuite en Égypte, La, 112
  Grande Messe des morts, 17
  Grand Traité d'instrumentation, 77
  Nonne sanglante, La, 19
  Nuits d'été, Les, 170, 186
  Symphonie fantastique, 27
  Symphonie funèbre et triomphale, 150
  Te Deum, 12, 27
  Troyens, Les, 27, 66, 72–73, 83, 90, 94–95, 101,
    112–13, 120, 161
  Zaïde, 49
Bernardin de St-Pierre, 31
  Paul et Virginie, 31
Bernhardt, Sarah, 205
Bertin, Louise,
  Esmeralda, 45
Berton, Pierre, 65, 136, 192, 225–26, 229,
    246, 270
Bertrand, Mme Ernest, 114
Bismarck, Otto von, 121, 168, 171
Bizet, Adolphe-Amand, 6–8, 10–11, 15, 25, 28, 35,
    38, 40, 45, 53–56, 63–64, 70, 88–89, 91,
    103–104, 108, 114–15, 155, 174–75, 225, 228,
    235, 246, 270
Bizet, Aimée, 7–8, 11, 20, 28, 35, 38–42, 45, 48,
    52–53, 56, 63–64, 91, 103, 174, 246, 270
Bizet, Georges
  Birth, 6
  Childhood, 6–10,
  Description, 28, 65, 229
  Christian names, 7
  Conservatoire studies, 10–14, 20, 28–34, 65
  Critic, 125
  Domiciles, 7, 7n, 28, 56, 64, 155, 174, 208
    (*see also* Vésinet, Le)
  Illness, 39, 46, 48, 65, 147, 208, 227–28
  Piano playing, 8, 12–13, 32, 39, 57, 105–106, 113,
    179, 205, 229
  Piano teaching, 18–19, 58
  Reading, 8, 11, 28, 38–39, 41, 43, 140, 147, 232
  Religion, 9, 20, 39, 151, 227, 231
  Women, 40–41, 52–53, 63–64, 82, 115, 140–41,
    209–10
Bizet, Geneviève (née Halévy), x, 64–65, 140–42,
    147, 155, 158, 165, 169, 171–73, 175–76, 179,
    191, 195, 200, 208–09, 225, 227–29, 235, 244,
    247, 273
Bizet, Jacques, 191–92, 200, 208, 228, 235
Blanche, Antoine-Émile, Dr, 82, 192
Blau, Édouard, 149, 159, 201–02, 204, 238, 271
Blois, 7
Boccaccio, 154, 174
Bodin, Thierry, 248
Boieldieu, François-Adrien,
  Dame blanche, La, 70
Bois, Mario, 245
Boisseaux, Henry, 21
Bologna, 45, 53
Bonaparte, Princess Mathilde, 13
Bonaparte, Napoléon, 3, 6, 11, 122, 156
Bonheur, Rosa, 125
Bonnet, Paul-Émile, 47
Bordeaux, 3, 70, 135, 169, 171–72, 175, 181, 245
Boston, 236–37
Botte, Adolphe, 60
Bouchet, Fanny, 118, 126
Bouffar, Zulma, 207
Bougival, 208–209, 227–28
Bouhy, Joseph, 197, 210, 226
Bouilhet, Louis, 170
Boulanger, Ernest, 88, 157
  Docteur Magnus, Le, 88
Boulanger, Lili, 88
Boulanger, Nadia, 88
Boulogne, 236
Brahms, Johannes, 213n
Brancour, René, 246
Brandus & Dufour, 19, 58, 69
Breitkopf & Härtel, 237–38
Briggs, A.D.P., 213
Brno, 244
Bruneau, Alfred, 232
Brussels, 3, 91, 139–40, 236, 240–41
Budapest, 236
Buenos Aires, 240
Bülow, Hans von, 63, 238
Burion, Amédée, 33
Busnach, William, 127, 140, 195, 201, 271
Busser, Henri, 245
Byron, George, Lord, 40, 88

Caesar, Julius, 156
Cain, Auguste-Nicolas, 125
Cain, Henri, 125
Cambiaggio, Carlo, 40
Cambrai, 7, 91
Camões, Luiz Vaz de
  Lusiad, 47
Campra, André, 8
Camus, Albert
  Étranger, L', 53

Capetown, 244
Capoul, Victor, 118, 271
Capua, 142
Carafa, Michele, 10, 31–32, 51, 271
Carré, Michel, 59, 61, 64, 67, 70, 72–73,
    77–78, 81–83, 86, 88, 111, 114, 117, 122,
    138, 191, 271
Carvalho, Caroline Miolan-, 9, 17, 71–73, 78, 86,
    92, 108, 111, 113, 117, 122, 124, 138, 140, 180,
    196, 271
Carvalho, Léon, 71–73, 81, 85–86, 88–91, 93, 95,
    104–105, 109, 111, 113, 116–17, 120, 124, 127,
    138–40, 154, 156, 191–92, 271
Casadesus, Robert, 238
Caspers, Émile, 59
Castro y Bellvis, Guillén de
    Mocedades del Cid, Les, 202
Cavour, Camillo Benso, Count, 38, 51, 53
Cendrier, Mme, 20, 25
Cervantes, Miguel de,
    Don Quixote, 46
Chabrier, Emmanuel, 82, 172
Chambéry, 53
Chantavoine, Jean, 235, 244–45
Chapuy, Marguerite, 226
Charlemagne, 156
Charles X, King of France, 11
Charles XV, King of Sweden, 122
Charlot, Auguste, 116
Charpentier, Gervais, 125
Charpentier, Gustave, 29, 232
Charton-Demeur, Anne, 113
Chateaubriand, François-René, 41
Chausson, Ernest, 232
    Vingt Mélodies, 198
Chéri, Victor, 83
Chérouvrier, Edmond-Marie, 91
    Nicolas Flamel, 91
    Roi des mines, Les, 91
Cherubini, Luigi, 5, 14, 29–30, 149
    Cours de contrepoint et de fugue, 30
Chicago, 236
Chiusi, 52
Chopin, Frédéric, 5, 10, 14, 19–20, 25, 36, 105–06,
    149–50
    Études, 150
    Marche funèbre, 229
    Nocturnes, 146
Choudens, Éditions, x, 58, 142, 235–43, 245
Choudens, Antoine de, 19, 58, 67, 70, 72, 83,
    86, 92, 108–11, 116–17, 119, 122, 139,
    151, 154, 156, 163, 169–70, 178–79, 189,
    192, 198, 200, 205, 208, 225, 236–41,
    243, 271
Choudens, Antony, 58, 122
Choudens, Paul de, 243
Chouquet, Gustave, 123

Cimarosa, Domenico, 93
Cincinnati, 244
Città della Pieve, 52
Cività Castellana, 47
Civitavecchia, 52
Clapisson, Antoine-Louis, 31–32, 51, 59, 112–13,
    117, 271
    Fanchonnette, La, 112–13
Clément, Félix, 88, 158
Cohen, Jules, 13, 65, 124, 271
    Bleuets, Les, 124–25
Colin, Charles-Joseph, 34–35, 38, 43, 271
Colin, Marie, 13
Colle-Pardo, 46
Collin, Paul, 243
Cologne, 242
Colombier, 19, 58
Colonne, Édouard, 198, 237, 242, 271
Compiègne, 242
Comte, Auguste, 147
Coninck, Pierre-Louis-Joseph de, 47
Conte, Jean, 38
Copenhagen, 240, 244
Coquard, Arthur, 237
Cormon, Eugène, 72–73, 77–78, 81, 88, 271
Corneille, Pierre
    Cid, Le, 202
Cornut, Romain, 123
Corot, Jean-Baptiste-Camille, 165
Courmont, Louis de, 144, 200, 241
Crépet, Etienne-Eugène, 125, 164, 271
Crépet-Garcia, Maria, 107, 125
Crosnier, François-Louis, 85
Curtiss, Mina, ix–x, 64, 144, 172, 176, 228,
    247–48
Czerny, Carl, 16, 93

Dalayrac, Nicolas, 93
Danbé, Jules, 198
Daniel, Salvadore, 173
Danieli, Mme, 139
Dante Alighieri, 88, 232
Daudet, Alphonse, 191–92, 225, 271
    Lettres de mon moulin, 191
    Arlésienne, L', 191–95, 242
David, Félicien, 10, 17, 22, 44, 49, 61, 71, 81, 185,
    189, 232, 272
    Christophe Colomb, 49, 71
    Désert, Le, 10, 17, 25, 46, 49
    Esclave, L', 88
    Lalla Roukh, 70, 73, 77
    Herculanum, 54, 148
    Perle de Brésil, La, 27
David, Samuel, 43, 45, 48
Dean, Winton, ix–x, 85, 98, 101–02, 157–58, 161,
    235, 238, 245, 247
Debillement, Jean-Jacques, 59

Debussy, Claude, 5, 29, 75, 232
   Jardins sous la pluie, 144
   Roderigue et Chimène, 204
Deffès, Pierre-Louis, 59
   Le Café du roi, 181
Delaborde, Élie-Miriam, 105, 209, 225, 228, 272
Delacour, 168
Delavigne, Casimire, 30, 199
Delerot, Émile, 156
De Leuven, Adolphe, 70, 181, 190–91, 201, 208, 272
Delibes, Léo, 13, 25, 59, 89, 103, 127, 143, 164–65, 212, 225, 232, 272
   Coppélia, 164
   Cour du roi Pétaud, Le, 179
   Kassya, 237
   Source, La, 212
Delioux de Savignac, Charles, 13
Delmas, Marc, 246
Deloffre, Louis-Michel-Adolphe, 71, 82, 122, 135, 181, 196, 211, 272
Delsarte, François, 7–10, 18, 20, 28, 72, 91, 103, 113, 155, 174, 272
Delsarte, Rosine, 7–9, 18, 20, 103, 155
Del Sarto, 39
D'Ennery, Adolphe, 204
Desbordes-Valmore, Marceline, 144
Deschamps, 13
Destin, Emmy, 248
Devriès, Jeanne, 124, 135
Diaz, Eugène, 40, 157–58, 165, 272
   La Coupe du Roi de Thulé, 157–58, 197, 201
   Le Roi Candaule, 157
Diaz, Narcisse-Virgilio, 165
Didier, Jules, 35, 45–47, 103–04, 272
Didion, Robert, 249n
Dijon, 21
Donizetti, Gaetano, 5, 10, 43
   Don Pasquale, 43–44, 88, 90
   Fille du régiment, La, 116
   Lucia di Lammermoor, 134
   Parisina, 39
Doucet, Camille, 73, 94, 228
Dublin, 236, 243
Dubois, Paul, 47, 229, 272
Dubois, Théodore, 68, 172, 197
   Guzla de l'Émir, La, 197
Dubreuil, Ernest, 91
Duchâtel, 126
Duchesne, Adolphe, 181, 196
Dufresne, Alfred, 59
Dukas, Paul, 237
Du Locle, Camille, 154, 156, 174–75, 181–82, 190–91, 196, 201, 207–08, 210–12, 220, 225–26, 228–29, 272
Dumas, *fils*, Alexandre, 225
Dumas, *père*, Alexandre, 10
Duparc, Henri, 168–69, 172, 232

Duprato, Jules-Laurent, 157, 175, 225
Duprez, Gilbert, 10, 85
Durand, Schœnewerk & Cie, 151, 177–78, 235
Dussek, Jan Ladislav,
   Piano sonata op. 9, 16
Dutoit, Charles, 244

Éditions françaises de musique, 245
Edward, Prince of Wales, 121
Eiffel, Gustave, 120
Elwart, Antoine, 150
Elizabeth I, Queen, 17
Erard pianos, 5, 105
Eroica Publications, 241
Ernst, Heinrich, 5
Eugénie, Empress, 26, 125, 137
Eulenburg, 237

Favre, Jules, 171
Fauré, Gabriel, 146, 168, 171–72, 225, 232
   Dolly Suite, 144
   Vingt Mélodies, 198
Faure, Jean-Baptiste, 9, 121, 138, 149, 158, 197, 201–02, 225
Ferentino, 46
Ferrara, 40, 53
Ferrier, Paul, 156, 175, 180, 200, 239
Fétis, François-Joseph, 211
Fiorentino, Pier Angelo, 34
Fissot, Alexis-Henri, 153
Flamel, Nicolas, 91
Flan, Alexandre, 200
Florence, 36–37, 45, 53, 149, 232
Flotow, Friedrich, 22, 246
   Martha, 93, 116
Fontaine-de-Vaucluse, 35
Fossanova, 46
Fournel, Victor, 46–47
Fournier, Édouard, 34
Franck, Adolphe, 155
Franck, César, 13, 143, 171–72, 225, 227
   Ghiselle, 237
Frankfurt, 244
Franz Josef, Emperor, 84, 121
Frascati, 40
Frémaux, Louis, 238
Frosinone, 46

Gade, Niels
   Symphony in B flat, 152
Galabert, Edmond, 91–92, 105, 107, 115, 120, 123, 126, 140–41, 146–47, 149, 152, 154, 158, 160, 163, 190, 202, 208, 229, 231, 246, 272
Gallet, Louis, 6–7, 82, 114, 149, 158–59, 175, 181–88, 190, 197–98, 201–02, 204, 227, 230, 246, 272
Galli-Marié, Marie-Célestine, 70, 88, 117,

175, 180, 197, 207–10, 212, 226, 228, 240, 247, 273
Ganderax, Louis, 246
Ganne, François, 165
Garcia, Eugénie, 107
Garcia, Manuel, 107
  El criado fingido, 223
Gardelli, Lamberto, 238
Garibaldi, Giuseppe, 46, 51, 53
Garnier, Charles, 62, 229
Gastinel, Léon-Gustave-Cyprien, 59
Gautier, Théophile, 169–70
Gaveaux-Sabatier, Mme, 106
Gelma, Dr Eugène, 228
Genoa, 36, 40
Genzano, 40
Gérard, E., 205
Gershwin, George, 232
Gevaert, François-Augustus, 23, 71, 157, 176
  Quentin Durward, 54
Ghent, 240
Giacomotti, Félix, 64
Giambologna, 53
Gille, Philippe, 89, 175, 179
Giotto, 52–53
Girard, Caroline, 114
Girard, Narcisse, 22
Girard, William E., 245–46
Gluck, Christoph Willibald, 8–9, 28, 113
  Armide, 113
  Orphée, 54, 58, 113
Godard, Benjamin, 225, 232, 241
  Vingt Mélodies, 198
Goethe, Johann Wolfgang von, 138
  Faust, 117, 158
  Wilhelm Meisters Lehrjahre, 117
Gouin, Fanny, 176, 178
Gould, Glenn, 146
Gounod, Charles, x, 18–23, 26, 29, 31, 33–34, 36, 46, 49, 51, 53–54, 58–59, 61, 64–65, 67, 70, 72–73, 80–81, 85–87, 89–90, 94–95, 103, 112–13, 118, 122, 150, 171, 173, 179, 189, 192, 195–98, 204, 208–209, 225, 228–29, 232, 243, 246, 273
  Ave Maria, 93, 268
  Ange et Tobie, L', 19, 108, 114, 268
  Chanson du printemps, 269
  Cinq-Mars, 58
  Colombe, La, 58, 61, 114, 118, 179, 269
  Deux reines, Les, 179
  Deux vieux amis, 18
  Faust, 18, 54, 58–59, 61, 69–71, 83, 85–86, 97, 108, 117, 139, 181, 197, 212, 268
  Gallia, 178–79, 269
  Iwan le terrible, 85–86, 98
  Jeanne d'Arc, 204–205, 207, 269
  Médecin malgré lui, Le, 54, 58, 85, 181

  Mireille, 67, 82, 85–87, 95, 97, 108, 156, 268
  Noël, 109, 268
  Nonne sanglante, La, 19, 22, 28, 58, 268
  Philémon et Baucis, 54, 58, 69–70, 74, 89, 96, 108, 161, 208, 269
  Polyeucte, 58
  Prière du soir, 179, 269
  Reine de Saba, La, 58, 64, 67, 85, 108, 268
  Roméo et Juliette, 110–11, 116, 118, 120, 122–24, 139–40, 146, 195–97, 269
  Sapho, 18–19, 22, 75
  Seconde Méditation, 269
  Symphony no. 1, 19, 21, 268
  Symphony no. 2, 20, 69–70, 108, 268
  Ulysse, 108
  Vingt Mélodies, 198
Gouvy, Louis-Théodore, 22
Gouzien, Armand, 204
Grandval, Marie Vicomtesse de, 103
Grétry, André-Ernest-Modeste, 26, 93
  Richard-Cœur-de-lion, 26
  Épreuve villageoise, L', 82
Grieg, Edvard, 25
  Peer Gynt, 192
Grisar, Albert, 59
Gruyer, Hector, 54
Guiraud, Ernest, 48–49, 51–53, 83, 88, 91, 103, 123, 141, 143, 153–54, 157–58, 168–69, 172, 179, 195, 197, 205, 225, 227–29, 232, 234, 236–39, 241, 246, 248–49, 273
  En Prison, 154
  Frédégonde, 237
  Kobold, Le, 165
  Madame Turlupin, 197
  Ouverture de concert, 205
  Suite d'orchestre, 177, 179, 198
  Sylvie, 88, 116

Habeneck, François-Antoine, 6
Hahn, Reynaldo, 235, 244
  Vingt Mélodies, 198
Halanzier, Olivier, 176, 202–203
Halévy, Esther, 65, 140–41
Halévy, Fromental, 4, 9–10, 13, 19–20, 23–26, 28–32, 34, 49, 63, 65, 70–71, 81, 89, 91, 94–95, 107, 112, 140, 156–57, 232, 273
  Charles VI, 164
  Éclair, L', 116
  Guido et Ginevra, 156
  Juive, La, 4, 28, 61, 65
  Juif errant, Le, 26
  Magicienne, La, 54
  Noé, 65, 70, 157, 164, 175, 237, 239, 242–43, 256
  Reine de Chypre, La, 156
  Val d'Andorre, Le, 59

Halévy, Geneviève, *see* Bizet, Geneviève
Halévy, Léon, 141, 148, 155, 165, 192, 201
Halévy, Léonie, 28, 38, 65, 71, 140, 155, 169, 171–72, 175, 179, 192, 225, 247
Halévy, Ludovic, 24–25, 121, 141, 155–56, 165, 172, 190–91, 195, 201, 207–208, 211–13, 225–26, 228, 230, 273
  Roi Candaule, Le, 195
Hamburg, 243
Hamelle, Julien, 198
Hansen, Wilhelm, 240
Halle, Karl, 5,
Handel, George Frederic, 38
  Ariodante, 128
  Harmonious Blacksmith, 108–109, 268
Hanslick, Eduard, 238
Hanssens, Charles-Louis, 139
Hartmann, Ernst, 244–45
Hartmann, Georges, 142–45, 150–51, 154, 176–77, 179, 198, 225, 235, 273
Haussmann, Georges-Eugène, Baron, 3, 56, 62, 120, 137
Haydn, Joseph, 22, 72
Hébert, Ernest, 40, 89
Heim, Eugène, 35, 40–41, 45, 53, 273
Heller, Stephen, 5, 14, 106, 146, 273
Henschel, 241
Henschel, George, 237
Henrion, Mlle, 34
Hermann-Léon, 107, 138
Hérold, Ferdinand, 36
Herz, Henri, 10–11, 13, 16
  Piano Concerto no. 3, 13
Heu, 127
Heugel, Jacques-Léopold, 92–93, 105, 107–08, 116–17, 119, 126, 138, 142, 145, 151, 201, 215, 225, 235, 240, 273
Hignard, Jean-Louis-Aristide, 59
Hiller, Ferdinand, 5,
Hoffmann, E.T.A., 46
Holmès, Augusta, 232
Homer, 46
  Odyssey, 47
Hopp, Julius, 240
Horace
  Carmen saeculare, 51
Hugo, Victor, 10, 45, 107–08, 117–18, 143, 145, 167, 170, 199, 273
  Contemplations, 92
  Cromwell, 145
Hünten, Franz, 14,

Ibert, Jacques, 29
Imbert, Hugues, 246
Indy, Vincent d', 168, 225–27, 232
Ingres, Jean-Auguste-Dominique, 9, 85
Isabey, Eugène, 103

Ismaël, Jean-Vital, 81–83, 90, 114, 196
Ischia, 41, 47, 118, 145
Ivan the Terrible, Tsar, 85, 95

Jadin, Emmanuel, 145
Jaime, Adolphe, 179
Janin, Jules, 143
Joan of Arc, 41, 84, 204
John of Patmos, St, 92
Jonas, Émile, 65, 127
Joncières, Victorin de, 103, 143, 225–26, 231, 273
  L'Amour-peintre, 48
  Sardanapale, 120
Jourdan, Pierre-Marius, 139
Jouvin, Benoit, 67

Kalmus, 241–42
Karlsruhe, 242
Kirstein, Lincoln, 247
Kiselyov, Count, 39
Klein, John W., 247
Königsberg, 244
Korbay, Ferenc, 198
Kraus, Alfredo, 241
Krauss, Marie-Gabrielle, 151
Krupp, Alfred, 121

Lacheurié, Eugène, 32–33
Lacombe, Hervé, x, 85, 102, 144, 203, 235, 238, 242, 248
Lacombe, Louis Trouillon-, 59
Lacombe, Paul, 126, 139, 141, 149, 154, 179, 190, 201, 246, 273
  Violin Sonata, op. 8, 126
Lacour-Delâtre, Louis-Michel-James, 48
La Fontaine, Jean de, 9, 114
Lagrave, Rousseau de, 20
Lajarte, Théodore, 59
Lalo, Édouard, 107–08, 143, 172, 195, 199, 225, 232, 273
  Divertissement, 197
  Jacquerie, La, 237
  Oh ! quand je dors, 200
  Vingt Mélodies, 198
  Violin Sonata, 205
Lalo, Julie, 179, 205
Lamartine, Alphonse-Marie-Louis, 10, 12, 15, 32, 41, 107–08, 118, 170, 243
  Nouvelles Méditations poétiques, 118
Lambert, F., 109
Landormy, Paul, 246
Lange, Matthieu, 245
Leblicq, Charles-Théodore, 59
Leborne, 23
Lecocq, Charles, 24, 89, 225, 274
  Dr Miracle, Le, 24
  Oiseau bleu, 191

Leconte de Lisle, Charles, 33, 238
   Érinnyes, Les, 197
   Dr Miracle, Le, 24
Le Couppey, Félix, 13
Lécuyer, 91
Lee, Noël, 248
Lefébure-Wély, Louis, 25–26
Legouix, 127
Legouvé, Ernest, 179
Leipzig, 164, 237
Lemoine, Achille-Philibert, 109, 156
Lentz & Houdart, 19
Leopold II, King, 121
Leroy, André, 248
Leroy, François-Hippolyte, 85–86, 94, 148–49
Lestoquoy, 13
Lesueur, Jean-François, 38
Lévy, Michel, 189
Lewis, Matthew, 19
   The Monk, 19
Lhérie, Paul, 197, 210, 212, 226
Liège, 91
Lille, 240
Lind, Jenny, 9
Link, Joachim-Dietrich, 241
Liszt, Blandine, 63
Liszt, Franz, 5, 10, 14, 63, 105–06, 111–12, 164, 199, 274
   "Gran" Mass, 111–12
   Mephisto Waltz no. 1, 178
   Oh ! quand je dors, 200
Litolff, Henry Charles, 66, 149, 156
Littré, Émile, 147
Livorno, 36
London, 21, 24, 120, 124, 138, 178, 204, 236–37, 240–41, 244–45
Louis XIV, King, 4
Louis-Philippe, King, 8, 10–11
Lucretia, 41
Ludwig II, King, 121
Lully, Jean-Baptiste, 8, 93, 193
Lyon, 35

Mâcon, 53
Madrid, 244
Maësen, Léontine de, 81–83, 86, 88, 114, 144, 154, 210, 274
Magenta, Battle of, 45
Mahler, Gustav, 237, 243
Maillart, Aimé, 59, 67–68, 157
   Dragons de Villars, Les, 59, 210
   Lara, 88
   Pêcheurs de Catane, Les, 59
Malherbe, Charles, 199, 243
Malibran, Maria, 13, 107, 124
Manchester, 243
Maniglier, Henri-Charles, 47

Manuel, Eugène, 200, 239
Maréchal, Henri, 246
Marmontel, Antoine-François, 10–14, 20, 57, 146, 229–30, 246, 274
   24 Grandes études, 105
Marseille, 36, 164, 236
Massé, Victor, 17, 19, 23, 26, 28n, 59, 65, 157
   Fils du brigadier, Le, 119, 268
Massenet, Jules, 27, 29, 75, 123–25, 143, 157–58, 168, 172, 174, 178–80, 189, 192, 197–98, 204–205, 225, 228, 232–33, 237, 240, 274
   Adorable Bel-Boul, L', 198
   Cid, Le, 203–204
   Coupe du Roi de Thulé, La, 157–58, 178
   Don César de Bazan, 197
   Érinnyes, Les, 197
   Ève, 227
   Grand'Tante, La, 124
   Grisélidis, 174
   Marie-Magdeleine, 198, 227
   Mes Souvenirs, 47
   Phèdre, 205
   Première Suite, 124, 177
   Roman d'Arlequin, Le, 176
   Sarabande espagnole, 269
   Scènes alsaciennes, 177
   Scènes de bal, 179, 269
   Scènes de féerie, 177
   Scènes dramatiques, 177
   Scènes hongroises, 177, 179, 208, 269
   Scènes napolitaines, 177
   Scènes pittoresques, 177
   Simplicité, 178
   Templiers, Les, 148
Massy, 135
Mastrigli, Leopoldo, 240, 247
Mathilde, Princesse, 93
Maupassant, Guy de, 235
Maxmilian I, Emperor, 84, 121
Mayrargues, Nephtali, 83, 103
Méhul, Etienne, 22
Meifred, Pierre-Joseph-Emile, 10
Meilhac, Henri, 121, 172, 190–91, 195, 201, 207, 211–13, 225–26, 230, 274
   Roi Candaule, Le, 195
Melbourne, 236
Melleville, 23
Membrée, Edmond, 148
Mendelssohn, Felix, 5, 22, 38, 72, 198
   Lieder ohne Worte, 106
   Midsummer Night's Dream, A, 192
   Reformation Symphony, 152
Mendès, Catulle, 175, 200
Mérimée, Prosper, 232
   Carmen, 201, 213, 217, 224

Méry, Joseph, 66, 105
Metz, 167–68
Metzler & Co., 240
Meyerbeer, Giacomo, 4, 27, 42, 47, 82, 87–88,
    95–96, 102, 121, 202, 212
  Africaine, L', 47, 87, 90, 93, 121, 164
  Étoile du nord, L', 27
  Huguenots, Les, 4, 61
  Pardon de Ploërmel, Le, 54, 61
  Prophète, Le, 10, 17–18, 61, 87
  Robert le diable, 4, 61
Michelangelo Buonarroti, 39, 42, 88
Michot, Pierre-Jules, 118, 122
Milan, 53, 240
Millevoye, Charles-Hubert, 92, 107–108
Miolan, Caroline, *see* Carvalho,
    Caroline Miolan-
Mistral, Frédéri, 86, 191
  Calendal, 156
  Mirèio, 86
Mogador, Céleste, 115, 141
Molière,
  Sicilien, Le, 48
Moltke, Helmuth von, 167
Montaigne, Michel de, 232
Monte Carlo, 243
Monte Circeo, 46
Montijo, Eugénie de, *see* Eugénie,
    Empress
Montjauze, Jules, 71
Montpellier, 245
Morand, Eugène, 174
Moreau, Gustave, 40
Morini, François, 81–83, 86
Morio, Irma, 73
Mortier, Arnold, 230
Mottl, Felix, 237, 242
Mozart, Wolfgang Amadeus, 12, 27, 36, 42–43, 45,
    72, 93, 102, 185, 218, 231–32
  Ave verum, 39
  Don Giovanni, 26, 105, 113, 128, 154, 164, 268
  Nozze di Figaro, Le, 86, 180
  Oca del Cairo, L', 126, 269
  Requiem, 16
  Zauberflöte, Die, 90
Münch, Charles, 244
Musset, Alfred de, 107, 115, 274
  Lorenzaccio, 201
  Namouna, 181
Mussorgsky, Modest, 237

Nadar, 120
Naples, 45, 47–48, 53, 142, 152, 236
Napoléon I, *see* Bonaparte, Napoléon
Napoléon III, 8, 12–13, 26, 32, 37–38, 45,
    52, 54, 62, 84, 120–22, 137, 156,
    164–65, 167

Nerval, Gérard de, 64
New York, 236–37, 240
Nice, 36, 53, 65
Nicolai, Otto, 69
  Lustige Weiber von Windsor, Die, 69–70,
    114, 268
Niedermeyer, Louis
  Robert le Bruce, 95
Nietzsche, Friedrich, 238
Nieuwerkerke, Count Emilien de, 13, 92, 106, 118
Nilsson, Christine, 90, 93, 113, 120, 124–25, 135,
    138, 149, 151, 212, 274
Nîmes, 36
Norma, 40
Nuremberg, 46
Nydahl, Rudolf, 248

Oeser, Fritz, 248–49
Offenbach, Jacques, 17, 23–25, 27, 40, 82, 85,
    121–22, 172, 174–75, 179, 191, 201, 204, 207,
    211, 225, 274
  Barbe-bleue, 121
  Belle Hélène, La, 121
  Brésilien, Le, 201
  Contes d'Hoffmann, Les, 58
  Fantasio, 175, 180
  Grande Duchesse de Gérolstein, La, 121–22
  Orphée aux enfers, 27
  Pomme d'Api, La, 201
  Roi Carotte, Le, 174
  Vie parisienne, La, 121, 201
Ollivier, Émile, 164–65
Onslow, Georges, 30
Orange, 36
Orsini, Félix, 37, 85
Orvieto, 52
Ossian, 152
Ostia, 41
Otis Brothers, 120

Pacini, Émilien, 66–67
Padua, 53
Paestum, 47
Paganini, Nicolo, 5
Pailleron, Édouard, 199
  Amours et haines, 151
Paisiello, Giovanni, 93
Paladilhe, Émile, 25, 103, 140, 143, 155, 157,
    180–81, 210, 228, 232, 274
  Mandolinata, La, 180
  Passant, Le, 180–81, 190
Paliard, Léon, 59
Paradol, Lucinde, 165
Paris
  Ambigu-Français, 63
  Bouffes-Parisiens, 23, 27, 33, 59, 73,
    84–85, 115

Cercle de l'Union Artistique, 71
Concert National, 198
Concerts du Grand Hôtel, 198
Concerts populaires, 71, 112, 115, 151, 164, 192, 205, 228
Conservatoire, 5–13, 18, 20, 28–34, 61, 112–13, 155–56, 165, 173, 175, 197, 208
Exposition universelle of 1855, 26, 120
Exposition universelle of 1867, 116, 120–24, 137, 149
Folies-Nouvelles, 59
Grand Théâtre Parisien, 84
Opéra, 4–6, 9–10, 12, 17–20, 26, 28, 38–39, 45, 56, 61–62, 64, 70, 83–87, 90, 93–95, 104–105, 109, 117, 120–21, 125, 148–49, 156, 158, 164, 176, 179, 190, 193, 196–97, 201–203, 205, 212, 224, 231, 248
Opéra-Comique, 6, 8, 10, 17, 21, 26–28, 39, 52, 59–60, 70, 72, 84, 88, 114, 117–19, 123–24, 138, 149, 154, 156, 165, 174, 179–81, 188–90, 195–97, 202, 207–208, 210–12, 220, 225, 228, 236, 240–41, 244, 247–48
Orphéon, 18
Société des Concerts du Conservatoire, 6, 10, 22, 72, 112, 116, 152, 178, 244
Société des Jeunes Artistes du Conservatoire, 19, 63
Société Nationale de Beaux-Arts, 60, 71
Société Nationale de Musique, 147, 153, 172, 179, 205
Théâtre de la Gaîté, 204
Théâtre de l'Athénée, 127, 140, 197
Théâtre du Vaudeville, 191
Théâtre-Italien, 6, 26, 90, 105, 113, 139, 148, 151, 156, 164, 240
Théâtre-Lyrique, 27, 54, 58–59, 61–62, 67–68, 70–73, 77, 81, 83–84, 86, 89–91, 93–95, 104–05, 109, 113, 118, 120, 122, 124, 126–28, 139, 148–49, 154, 156–57, 164, 171, 180–81, 191, 196
Pâris, Claude, 46
Pâris, fils, 46–47
Parker, D. C., 244, 247
Parma, 45
Pascal, Prosper, 59
 Cabaret des amours, 69–70, 268
 Templiers, Les, 148
Pasdeloup, Jules, 19, 23, 63, 71, 112, 115, 124, 148, 151–52, 154, 156–57, 164, 169, 177, 179, 192–93, 195, 197–98, 205–206, 208, 225, 228, 231, 237, 274
Patti, Adelina, 90, 113, 149
Paul, St, 20
Pellegrin, Abbé
 Cantiques spirituels, 150

Péreire, Émile, 140, 155
Pergolesi, Giovanni Battista,
 Serva padrona, La, 70
Périer, Émile, 114
Perrin, Émile, 70, 94, 148–49, 154, 157, 176, 274
Perugia, 52
Philadelphia, 236
Pierné, Gabriel, 232
Pigot, Charles, 30, 63–64, 70, 112, 158, 195, 205, 239–40, 246
Pillet-Will, Comtesse, 87
Piperno, 46
Pisa, 36
Planté, Francis, 13
Planté, Gaston, 53
Plasson, Michel, 75, 178n, 238, 244
Pleyel pianos, 5, 173
Pleyel, Marie, 10
Pompeii, 47
Ponchard, Charles, 211
Poniatowski, Joseph, Prince, 59, 90, 157
 Aventurier, L', 90
 Pierre de Médicis, 90
Ponsard, Francois, 19
 Ulysse, 19
Pont du Gard, 36
Pougin, Arthur, 142, 231, 246
Poupet, Michel, 14, 235, 241, 245, 247
Prague, 240, 244
Prelly, Aline, 181, 183, 188
Prêtre, Georges, 241
Prévost-Paradol, Anatole, 165
Priola, Margaret-Marie-Sophie, 175, 180
Prokofiev, Sergei, 22
 Symphonie classique, 22
Proust, Marcel, 235, 247
Puccini, Giacomo, 193
Pushkin, Alexander
 Tsygany, 213, 224

Rachmaninov, Sergei
 Aleko, 213n
Racine, Jean-Baptiste, 9
Rameau, Jean-Philippe, 8
 Hippolyte et Aricie, 150
Raphael, 39, 42, 52
Ravel, Maurice, 29, 232
Ravenna, 53
Reber, Henri, 9–10, 22, 30–32, 51
 Nuit de Noël, La, 30
Regnard, Jean-François, 143
Regnault, Henri, 168
Régnier-Canaux, 25–26
Reiter, Jean, 64, 208, 228, 235
Reiter, Marie, 63–64, 208, 228

Reyer, Ernest, x, 17, 27, 57, 59, 61, 63, 66–67, 70, 72–73, 83, 164, 176, 192, 225–26, 229–32, 246, 274
  Érostrate, 66–67, 69–70, 88–90, 176, 268
  Maître Wolfram, 27
  Sélam, Le, 17, 49
  Statue, La, 58, 61–62, 68, 82, 269
Richard d'Ivry, Paul de, 21
  Maison du docteur, La, 21
Richardson, Samuel
  Clarissa, 156, 179–80
Ricordi, 240
Ries, Ferdinand, 17
Rieti, 46
Riga, 244
Rimini, 52–53
Rimsky-Korsakov, Nicolay, 237
Ritter, Théodore
  Courriers, Les, 269
Rivay, Mlle, 59
Rivoli, 41
Robert, Frédéric, 85
Robinson, Stanford, 245
Rochefort, Henri, 137
Rochester, 244
Rodrigues, Édouard, 38, 42
Rodrigues family, 127, 140
Rodrigues, Hippolyte, 140–41, 155, 165, 172–73, 192, 274
Roger, Gustave, 17
Rolland, Olivier, 20
Rolland, Romain, 246
Rollet, Auguste, 31
Romani, Felice, 40
Rome, 29, 34, 36–43, 45–48, 52–54, 64, 67, 152, 240, 243–44
Ronsard, Pierre de, 107
Roqueplan, Nestor, 19
Rossini, Gioacchino, 4–5, 25–27, 36, 42, 82, 87, 90, 93, 123–24, 149, 228, 275
  Barbiere di Siviglia, Il, 26, 164
  Guillaume Tell, 4
  Hymne, 124
  Petite Messe solennelle, 26, 87
Rossini, Olympe, 87, 149
Rot, Michael, 249n
Rothschild family, 140
Rouen, 6, 240
Rousseau, Théodore, 165
Roussel, Albert, 232
Royer, Alphonse, 85, 94
Roze, Marie, 207
Rubens, Peter Paul, 139
Rubinstein, Anton
  Ocean Symphony, 152
Ruelle, Jules, 126

Sachot, Octave, 73
Sadowa, Battle of, 104, 121
St Petersburg, 236–37, 240
Sainte-Beuve, Charles, 29, 143
Saint-Georges, Vernoy, Marquis de, 23, 65, 116–17, 124, 148–49, 275
Saint-Saëns, Camille, 9, 13, 22–23, 25, 27, 29, 31, 57, 59, 71, 75, 86, 103, 106, 111–14, 123–24, 126, 138, 143, 153–54, 157, 164, 168, 172, 179–80, 189–90, 195, 211, 225, 229–30, 232, 237, 246, 275
  Cygne, Le, 220
  Introduction et Rondo capriccioso, 151, 269
  Noces de Prométhée, Les, 123–24
  Piano Concerto no. 2, 151, 198, 269
  Piano Concerto no. 3, 164
  Princesse jaune, La, 190
  Rouet d'Omphale, Le, 179
  Samson et Dalila, 138, 185, 190
  Symphony no. 1, 22
  Symphony no. 3, 153
  Timbre d'argent, Le, 111, 119, 138, 140, 190, 268
  Vingt Mélodies, 198
Salerno, 47
Salomon, Hector, 110–11, 122, 139, 176
Sand, George, 10
San Felice, 46
San Francisco, 236
Sarasate, Pablo de, 205
Sardou, Victorien, 154, 156, 174
Sasse, Marie, 66, 90, 121, 156
Sauvage, Thomas, 148–49
Savary, Edmond, 13
Sax, Adolphe, 10, 95
Scarlatti, Domenico
  Cat's Fugue, 16
Schiller, Friedrich
  Don Carlos, 121
Schimon, Adolphe, 122
Schirmer & Co., 240
Schotts Söhne, 245
Schneider, Hortense, 122
Schnetz, Victor, 36, 39, 41–42, 47, 275
Schønwandt, Michael, 245
Schubert, Franz, 22, 75, 93, 198
Schumann, Robert, 25, 178, 198
  Studien, op. 56, 178, 269
  Vogel als Prophet, 177
Scott, Sir Walter
  The Fair Maid of Perth, 116, 128
Scribe, Eugène, 4, 19, 23, 30, 90
Scudo, Paul, 71
Sedan, Battle of, 167
Seghers, François, 23
Sellenick, Adolphe-Valentin, 59
Sellier, Charles-François, 35

Semet, Théophile, 59, 157
  Gil Blas, 86
Séré, Octave, 152, 246
Shakespeare, William, 17, 90, 122, 138, 232
  As You Like It, 141
  Hamlet, 138, 201
  Macbeth, 163
  Much Ado About Nothing, 128
Sheba, Queen of, 64
Sheridan, Richard Brinsley, 24
  St Patrick's Day, 24
Sibilat, René, 235, 247
Sicily, 45
Siena, 36, 53
Silvestre, Armand, 174, 239
Simrock, 243, 245
Siraudin, Paul, 127
Smithson, Harriet, 5
Solesmes, 91
Solferino, Battle of, 45
Solomon, King, 64
Sonnino, 46
Sonzogno, Edoardo, 240, 243
Sorrento, 47
Spontini, Gasparo, 4
  Vestale, La, 74
Stendhal, Henri Beyle, *dit*
  Vanina, 148
Stockholm, 236, 243, 248
Strasbourg, 73, 81
Straus, Émile, 235, 247
Strauss, Johann, *fils*, 121
  Blue Danube, The, 121
Stricker, Rémy, x, 85, 235, 248
Stuttgart, 244
Subiaco, 41, 46
Suppé, Franz von, 22

Taldoni, 126
Tamburini, Antonio, 149
Taylor, Baron, 112
Tchaikovsky, Pyotr Ilyich, 193, 222, 224–25
Temryukova, Maria, 85, 95
Terni, 46
Terracina, 46
Thalberg, Sigismund, 10, 13, 106
  Art du chant appliqué au piano, L', 92–93, 269
  Grand Duo sur les motifs de Norma, 13
Thiers, Adolphe, 171–73
Thomas, Ambroise, 10, 17, 19, 23, 31–33, 51, 70–71, 87, 112, 116–17, 123, 138, 148, 168, 173, 175, 189, 204, 225, 228, 232, 275
  Caïd, Le, 17
  Hamlet, 117, 138, 164, 193, 201, 203, 212, 269
  Mignon, 116–17, 119, 138, 207, 210, 268–69
  Psyché, 61
  Songe d'une nuit d'été, Le, 17

Thomas, Theodore, 237
Tivoli, 40
Toulon, 36
Tournois, Joseph, 36
Trélat, Marie, 108, 126–27, 144–45, 275
Trianon, Henri, 85–86, 94
Trochu, General Louis-Jules, 167
Turgenev, Ivan, 57, 213n
Tutin, 240
Trieste, 40
Tübingen, 245
Turin, 45

Universal Edition, 244

Valence, 35
Vasco da Gama, 47, 49
Vauthrot, François-Eugène, 138, 176
Venice, 45, 52–53, 57
Vercingetorix, 156
Verdi, Giuseppe, ix, 4–5, 10, 37, 42, 45, 51, 62, 69, 82, 90, 95, 97, 102, 121–23, 189, 233, 275
  Aida, 156, 182
  Ballo in maschera, Un, 42
  Don Carlos, 94, 121, 156
  Lombardi, I, 36
  Macbeth, 90, 95, 134
  Rigoletto, 26, 51, 81, 83, 86, 88, 98, 154, 159, 164
  Traviata, La, 26, 51, 90, 132, 164
  Trovatore, Il, 25–26, 51
  Vêpres siciliennes, Les, 26, 90
Vernet, Horace, 36
Veroli, 46
Verona, 45
Vésinet, Le, 88–89, 91, 114–16, 142, 155, 165, 173–75, 200, 208, 235
Viardot, Pauline, 17–18, 54, 59, 71, 107, 113, 198
Victor Emmanuel, King, 45, 54
Victoria, Queen, 26
Vidal, François
  Lou Tambourin, 191
Vienna, 236–37, 240, 244
Vienne, 36
Villafranca, 47
Virgil, 232
Viterbo, 52
Voltaire, 41
Voss, Paul, 247
Vuillermoz, Émile, 246

Wagner, Richard, ix, 5, 17, 28, 54, 61–63, 82, 102, 112, 135, 154, 164, 178, 181, 187, 189, 226, 231, 233, 246, 275
  Ange, L', 63, 268
  Faust Overture, 164
  Fliegende Holländer, Der, 154
  Lohengrin, 96, 140, 154, 164

Wagner, Richard (*continued*)
   Meistersinger, Die, 46, 164
   Rienzi, 154
   Tannhäuser, 62, 64, 66, 112, 121, 159
   Tristan und Isolde, 62
Walewski, Count, 73
Warsaw, 242
Wartel, Pierre-François, 9, 135
Wartel, Thérèse, 9
Washington, 165
Weber, Carl Maria von, 19, 27, 36, 72, 93
Weber, Johannès, 135, 192
Weckerlin, Jean-Baptiste-Théodore, 123, 243
Weimar, 240
Weingartner, Felix, 244
Wieniawski, Henryk, 13
Wieniawski, Josef, 13
Wilder, Victor, 11, 126, 148, 158, 246
Wilhelm I, King of Prussia, 121, 165
Williams, Howard, 245
Wright, Lesley A., x, 85, 225, 247–48

Ymbert, Théodore, 59
Yradier, Sebastián
   El Areglito, 215

Zanardini, Angelo, 240
Zaragoza, General, 84
Zeph, 52
Zimmerman, Anna, 18–19
Zimmerman, Pierre, 10, 12–14, 16, 18–19, 29–30, 275

www.ingramcontent.com/pod-product-compliance
Ingram Content Group UK Ltd.
Pitfield, Milton Keynes, MK11 3LW, UK
UKHW041903230426
12049UKWH00002B/28